INSIDE THE CRIMINAL COURTS

INSIDE THE CRIMINAL COURTS

SECOND EDITION

David R. Lynch

Carolina Academic Press

Durham, North Carolina

Library of Congress Cataloging-in-Publication Data

Lynch, David R. (David Richard)
  Inside the criminal courts / David R. Lynch. -- 2nd ed.
      p. cm.
  Includes index.
  ISBN 978-1-59460-744-8 (alk. paper)
  1. Criminal procedure--United States. 2. Criminal courts--United States. 3.
Criminal justice, Administration of--United States. I. Title.

  KF9619.L96 2009
  345.73'01--dc22

                                                        2009029353

Carolina Academic Press
700 Kent Street
Durham, North Carolina 27701
Telephone (919) 489-7486
Fax (919) 493-5668
www.cap-press.com

Printed in the United States of America.

To: My wife Kathy, and children Joseph, Nicole and Ryan

CONTENTS

ACKNOWLEDGMENTS

The author wishes to acknowledge the assistance given by his three excellent research assistants—Brady Fitzpatrick, Jenifer Okey, and Chris Roberts—in the proofreading of this manuscript and in ideas for a teacher's manual and "Questions for Class Discussion."

INSIDE THE CRIMINAL COURTS

CHAPTER ONE

The Legal Education of
Lawyers and Judges

Law school thus far had been exquisitely painful for second year student Wendy Murphy. So harsh that hardly a month ever passed by that she did not give serious thought to dropping out. At the end of her first semester she was determined to do just that but decided to finish out the year just to make sure. Then, having completed an entire year, she did not want to throw it away by dropping out. Now she was well into her second of the three years. She took strength in her fervent desire to be a public defender, an ambition formed during her first year of undergraduate studies at the state university. As far as she could tell, she was the only student in her elite law school that wanted to be a public defender.

Wendy had started college as an art major. She imagined herself one day teaching art in the public schools. But her ambitions changed after the prosecution of her brother Jim for selling drugs.

Jim was a junior in college when Wendy was a freshman. Jim lived with a roommate in a run-down house. His roommate was an addict and a seller of cocaine. Jim knew this but liked him anyway. Jim was neither an addict nor a seller but did buy and use some of his roommate's drugs on occasion.

One day the police came to Jim's residence with a search warrant. They found several small bags of cocaine attached to the inside lid of the toilet. Jim claimed he knew nothing of it. So did his roommate. The police believed neither and charged both with conspiracy to sell cocaine.

Jim's parents believed Jim. They were not against the idea of Jim being punished for possessing drugs but did not believe he had anything to do with planning to sell them. They did not have much money but were adamant that their son would not use a public defender. They managed to hire a private attorney who had a big advertisement in the phone book. The case went to trial. Jim was convicted of conspiracy to sell drugs and was sentenced to eight years in prison.

Financially exhausted, Jim's parents watched with skepticism as the public defenders saw to Jim's appeal. To the amazement of Jim and his parents, the conviction was overturned and a new trial ordered. The public defender then

3

talked the prosecutor into agreeing to a time-served disposition in return for a guilty plea to the lesser charge of possession of drugs for personal use. Jim, his parents, and Wendy were overjoyed. But for Wendy (like Jim) it was completely life-altering. Wendy had found her new career goal.

Getting Admitted to Law School

With law school as her goal, Wendy decided to talk to the university's pre-law adviser, Dr. Goth of the political science department. Goth had never been to law school, so he did not know too much about what day-to-day law school life was like. But he knew more about getting in to law school than anybody else on campus, including staff with law degrees. Wendy had a host of questions for the knowledgeable Dr. Goth.

"Dr. Goth, I'd like to go to law school and wanted to know how hard it is to get in."

"That depends on where you want to go," said Goth. "There are four **strata of law schools**: elite, national, regional, and commuter.[1] To get into the elite schools, you need nearly perfect grades and high scores on the LSAT. To get into a commuter school, you might get by with a 3.0 and much lower LSAT scores."

"What exactly is the LSAT?" asked Wendy, who had heard of the test but wanted to know more about it.

"The **LSAT** is short for the Law School Admissions Test. It is a standardized test that takes a half day to complete (five 35-minute sections). It tries to measure skills believed to be important for law school success. Hence, there is one section on reading comprehension, one section on analytical thinking, and two sections on logical reasoning. There also is a writing component that is not graded but sent to the law schools to which you apply for their own evaluation. The standardized portion of the exam results in a score falling between 120 and 180 points, the higher the better. At one time the test had a math section as well, but no longer.[2] I guess they figured that math has little to do with law school."

"When do people take this test?" asked Wendy.

"Most pre-law students take the test during Fall of their senior year in college. In admission decisions at many law schools it counts a lot, as much as

---

1. Abadinsky, Howard. (1995). "Legal Education and the Practice of Law." Chapter 3 in *Law and Justice: An Introduction to the American Legal System,* (3rd ed.). Chicago: Nelson-Hall Publishers.

2. Law School Admission Council. (2008). *LSAT & LSDAS Information Book, 2008–2009 edition.* Newtown, PA: LSAC, Inc.

your undergraduate GPA Imagine, one test can count as much as four years of grades in college. So this one test is something that can absolutely make or break you. So you'd be crazy not to study for it."

"Well, my GPA is 3.5 and I got in the 95th percentile on the SAT in high school," Wendy explained. "So I'm sure I could get into some law school. Would it even matter what law school I went to?"

"Yes, it matters enormously," Goth insisted. "The legal profession has a hierarchy just like law schools do. Certain legal jobs are closed to those who do not attend elite schools like Stanford or Yale. For example, if you wanted to work in a large city firm representing major corporations instead of doing divorces and personal bankruptcies for individual consumers, you would have no chance if you went to a commuter school, even if you graduated at the top of your class. What kind of lawyer do you want to be?"

"I want to be a public defender," replied Wendy.

"Well, you can be a public defender if you went to almost any law school. Criminal law is not considered a high strata legal specialization. Jobs are found as much through local contacts as anything else. But some public defenders do come out of elite schools, especially federal public defenders or some who work in large defender associations like those in New York City or Washington. But not many graduates of elite law schools choose to be public defenders. Most people who can make a lot of money—and graduates of elite schools can—choose to follow the money."

"What is a good major for law school?" asked Wendy.

"Traditional majors are subjects like English, history, political science and philosophy," replied Goth. "But the major does not matter."

"What if somebody wanted to major in art?" asked Wendy.

"Art is good. So is nursing, chemistry, music, or anything else. What is key is that you do well in something. It does not matter what the subject is."

"But law schools must have some preferences," insisted Wendy, "or at least some required course work. Wouldn't it impress them if I took some undergraduate-level law classes while in college?"

"They really do not have preferred majors. And unlike medical school there are not even any courses one needs to take. As for law classes, law schools prefer that you save your legal study for law school. You just need to take a broad array of liberal arts courses and earn a bachelor's degree in a field that you can excel in."[3]

---

3. Law School Admission Council. (1999). *The Official Guide to U.S. Law Schools, 2000 edition*. New York: Times Books, p. 6.

"That's it?" asked Wendy.

"That and the LSAT score. Of course, law schools also consider other things like letters of recommendation, employment, and life experiences, but the GPA and LSAT score are usually extremely important."

Wendy told Dr. Goth that she wanted to gain acceptance to the best law school possible. He advised her to study hard and do well on the LSAT and be prepared to get good letters of recommendation from professors.

Wendy thanked the professor for his time but before allowing her to leave, Goth wanted to get in a parting shot.

"One more thing," he said. This is very important. Don't go to law school for the wrong reasons."

"Like what?" Wendy inquired.

"Oh, like money, glamor, or because you don't know what else to do with a liberal arts degree."[4]

Goth continued, "The money is not as good as some imagine. Starting salaries for new law grads in small firms (where the bulk of grads find jobs) are not six figures like many think but rather only about $70,000. Even lawyers with tons of experience only have median salaries in the very low $100s.

"As for glamor, don't think its like all those lawyer dramas on television. Think more in terms of conflict and/or paperwork. Lawyers tend to do a lot of one or the other. And, by conflict I'm not talking about college debate-team mental games but real conflict.

"And, as for using law school as something to do with a useless bachelor's degree, forget about it. Law school is three long years of expensive hell on earth. Hardly something to inflict upon yourself just because you don't know what else to do."

Wendy again thanked Dr. Goth and went home, where she promptly started searching the internet on the subject of law school admissions. She soon discovered the U.S. News annual rankings of American law schools, perhaps the best known (though controversial) rankings list. U.S. News attempts to rank schools using criteria such as LSAT scores, undergraduate GPA's, reputation among lawyers and judges, and percentage of graduates employed nine months after graduation. Part of the list that Wendy saw appears in Table 1.

Reading elsewhere, Wendy learned that the very top schools admit students with median LSAT scores of 165 or better coupled with median undergraduate GPA's of 3.6 and better.[5] True, most schools had much lower standards,

---

4. The following brief discussion is based on: Furi-Perry, Ursula. (Spring 2009). "Are You Ready for Law School?" in *Pre-Law Magazine*. San Diego, CA: Cypress Magazines.

5. *Boston College Law School Locator*. (2009).

Table 1   Top 10 Law Schools — U.S. News & World Report Rankings

1. Yale	6. (Tie) Berkeley	10. (Tie) Duke
2. Harvard	Chicago	Northwestern
3. Stanford	8. Pennsylvania	Virginia
4. Columbia	9. Michigan	
5. New York Univ		

Source: America's Best Graduate Schools. (2009). *Best Law Schools.* U.S. News.

Table 2   Law School Admission Difficulty

(By GPA's and LSAT scores — 25th to 75th percentiles)

Very Hard to get in (GPA > 3.60, LSAT > 165): Yale, Harvard, Stanford, etc.

Hard to get in (GPA 3.40–3.60, LSAT 160–165): UCLA, Brigham Young, Notre Dame, etc.

Less Hard to get it (GPA 3.00–3.19, LSAT 150–154): Baltimore, West Virginia, Idaho, etc.

Easier to get it (GPA < 2.80, LSAT 145–149): Faulkner, Appalachian, Thomas Jefferson, etc.

Source: Boston College Law School Locator: 2008–2009.

but Wendy had made it her goal to get into an elite school. (For a rough idea of the wide range of admission standards among law schools, see Table 2.)

Wendy wanted to be accepted into an elite school because she had read that there was a **lawyer glut** (too many lawyers chasing too few jobs and too few clients). In fact, though the United States has only 5 percent of the world's population, it has two-thirds of the world's attorneys.[6] Wendy wanted to maximize her chances of getting a job in a major defender's office. She thought that going to an elite school might help her to get interviews with such offices.

Working hard at her studies, Wendy improved her grades. She went from being a good student to a stellar one. In the fall of her senior year she studied hard for the LSAT. She had read that most students do indeed prepare and practice for the test and that such preparation and practice can make a big difference. In fact, the Law School Admission Council even mentions in its "Official Guide" that "most law school applicants familiarize themselves with test

---

6. Stumpf, Harry P. and John H. Culver. (1992). *The Politics of State Courts.* New York: Longman.

mechanics and questions types, practice on sample tests, and study the information on test-taking techniques and strategies ... Very few people achieve their full potential without some preparation."[7]

In December Wendy took the test and scored at the 90th percentile. This was an adequate score for all but the most elite schools. But Wendy wanted to get into an elite school. She hoped her stellar GPA would boost her chances.

To Wendy's delight, she was accepted to one of the top law schools in the country. She wondered if being a woman helped her to get in. But then she remembered that nearly half of all law students these days are women. Her law school adviser thought that her wanting to be a criminal lawyer probably helped her to get in. Few applicants at such a school had such a goal and in that sense she offered diversity. The well-endowed school even had a **debt forgiveness program** for students who graduate and go into low-paying public interest law. Without such programs, heavily indebted students graduating from high-tuition schools would simply find such jobs unaffordable. Wendy felt lucky to be accepted to such a progressive and well-funded institution.

Law School Curriculum

Wendy reported to law school keen to learn. Her law school basically told her what courses she would take her first year. The second and third year courses were completely up to her (electives). She learned that most courses were three credit hours and she needed ninety credit hours to graduate. This meant that she had to average fifteen credits per semester for all three years. Her **first year courses** (required of all students) are outlined in Table 3.

Wendy's problems began on the first day of classes. She showed up for her morning classes without having read the assignments for the first day that were posted on the bulletin boards throughout the school. Unlike most of her fellow students, she had not seen the postings and had assumed that the first day would involve introductory lectures and orientations by the professors to the various courses. To her surprise, the professors launched into discussions of the cases assigned for the day by calling on students to stand and be interrogated about them. She was lucky not to have been called on but sat on pins and needles throughout the day. She left school in mid-afternoon and spent the next four hours reading the first day's assignments and another five reading the second day's assignments. Her eyes ached under the strain.

---

7. Law School Admission Council, *The Official Guide, supra* note 3 at 7.

Table 3   Typical First Year Law Courses

Torts: Private wrongs such as negligently hurting others, defamation of character, etc.

Contracts: The study of legally enforceable promises and the damages when broken

Civil Procedure: The mechanics of commencing and maintaining law suits, jurisdiction, etc.

Constitutional Law: Legislative powers, executive powers, civil liberties, Bill of Rights, etc.

Criminal Law and Procedure: Wrongs against public order, search and seizure law, etc.

Property: Rights regarding the ownership of land, objects, buildings, and natural resources

Legal Research and Writing: Instruction in use of a law library and in writing legal briefs

Source: Law School Admission Council. (2009). *The Juris Doctor Degree.*

Wendy was being rapidly socialized into the **case method** of instruction, which virtually all American law schools use. The case method shuns textbooks in favor of original appellate court decisions written by judges in legalese. It is an extremely inefficient method to learn the law. For example, instead of reading about abortion rights, a student will read the original opinion written by the Supreme Court in *Roe v. Wade* as well as several other cases. Often students will read a lengthy case only to read another lengthy case that indicates that the former is no longer the law. The objective is not to teach the law but to teach students to think critically—to see all sides of a problem. Law professors like to think of themselves not as teachers of the law but as trainers of the mind—helping students to **think like a lawyer** (that is, critically, analytically, and creatively). Students often get upset with this approach, first implemented by Christopher Columbus Langdell, dean of the Harvard Law School, over a century ago.[8] Frustrated, they often wish that the instructor would just tell them what the law is since they sometimes leave class not knowing what in fact the current state of the law is on a particular point. All of this is of little concern to the professor, who sees his or her role more as an exerciser of the mind than as a conveyer of the black letter of the law.

---

8. Friedrichs, David O. (2001). *Law in our Lives.* Los Angeles: Roxbury Publishing (p. 185).

Wendy found the cases assigned to her almost incomprehensible. The appellate decisions were written by judges for lawyers. These authors never would have guessed that their opinion would be read by novice law students who were unfamiliar with legal vocabulary. Wendy was not familiar with legal terms and found the reading slow-going and difficult. Her anxiety level was high.

Wendy also found the Socratic method of classroom discussion to be intimidating. The Socratic method was also implemented by Dean Langdell at Harvard along with the case method of study.[9] Like the case method, the Socratic method swept the country and became the standard at law schools for student-teacher interaction. In a nutshell, the **Socratic method** (named after Socrates who employed it with his own pupils) involves the constant questioning of students rather than providing them with a lecture. It can be a very anxiety-producing way to learn. In Wendy's law school, professors liked to call upon a student, asking him or her to stand up.

The professor would then begin to grill the student on one of the cases assigned for reading for that day. The professor would probe and probe the depths of the student's understanding of the case. The instructor would then alter the fact patterns of the case again and again to test the student's ability to apply the underlying principles to new situations. May heaven help the student who did not thoroughly prepare the night before or who dreaded the public spotlight.

Wendy did in fact dislike being grilled before her classmates. She believed the Socratic method to be mean-spirited. She is not alone. Some feminist legal scholars have gone so far as to suggest that traditional methods of teaching law are based on male values of aggressiveness and combativeness. They argue that women do not share such values and are victimized by the way law is taught. These scholars believe that women are handicapped in the classroom vis-á-vis males because males are socialized since boyhood into rough and tumble play while females more typically engage in cooperative games as children.[10] Few would argue with their observation that the Socratic method often is a very stressful way to learn, though some would suggest that males probably are every bit as stressed by the method as are females.[11]

---

9. LaPiana, William P. (1995). "Honor Langdell!" *Law & Social Inquiry.* 20: 761–764.

10. Menkel-Meadow, Carrie. (1996). "Women's way of knowing the law." In N. Goldberger, J.M. Tarule, B.M. Clinchy, & M.F. Belenky (Eds.), *Knowledge, Difference and Power: Essays Inspired by Women's Way of Knowing* (pp. 57–84). New York: Basic Books. See also, Harrington, Mona. (1994). *Women Lawyers: Rewriting the Rules.* New York: Alfred A. Knopf.

11. Lynch, David R. (2000). "Heightened sensitivity to conflict on the part of female criminal defenders: Myth, reality or hyperbole?" *Women & Criminal Justice,* 11(1):1–20.

Wendy eventually adjusted to the case method and by her second year could read law cases almost as quickly as she could read a newspaper. But she never did come to appreciate the confrontational approach to learning that some of the professors used in their version of the Socratic method.

What bothered Wendy the most, however, was her feeling that she never seemed to be learning any practical skills that could help her in the real world of legal practice. For example, Wendy took a course on Family Law (which covers divorce law, child custody rules, etc.) during her second year but at the end of the course had no idea how to actually file for a divorce. She took a course on Wills and Estates but was never taught the steps of how to probate a will. She had an entire year of criminal law and criminal procedure (during her first year) but did not know how to get objects admitted into evidence during a trial, how to negotiate a plea bargain, or what to do to try to get someone's bail reduced. All that her professors were interested in was **legal education** (the teaching of theories and philosophies concerning the law). They had little interest in **legal training** (the teaching of practical skills). Wendy felt like she was being taught how to make eggs Benedict but did not know how to boil water. Wendy felt that she would be more comfortable arguing an appeal before the U.S. Supreme Court than she would representing a home buyer at a routine real estate settlement.

Wendy's concerns are shared by most law students and new lawyers. As long ago as 1983, at least one critic of the legal profession suggested that law schools should shift from a near total emphasis on legal doctrine and the Socratic method to a curriculum that would be fifty percent devoted to educating law students and fifty percent devoted to training them.[12] Law schools have yet to adopt such a view, however.

The Dampening of Idealism

Wendy found herself wondering about more than just the way law was being taught in her law school. She found during the course of her studies that her very desire to become a public defender was being eroded. She found herself wondering if she should not join the crowd and go into more lucrative areas of practice. **Diminishing idealism** is not uncommon for law students like Wendy. A socialization away from idealism can take place. Studies show that most students who begin law school with idealistic desires to practice

---

12. Margolick, David. (1983). "The trouble with American Law School." *The New York Times Magazine* (May 22):20–38.

public interest law change their minds during their law school years. These studies suggest that the law school experience, in which professors aggressively question students with regards to all sides of every question, does little to nurture idealistic career ambitions.[13] One law professor some time ago even went so far as to state that the "ordinary religion of the law school classroom" consists of "a moral relativism tending toward nihilism, a pragmatism tending toward an amoral instrumentalism, a realism tending toward cynicism, an individualism tending toward atomism, and a faith in reason and democratic processes tending toward mere credulity and idolatry."[14]

At one weak point in her second year in law school, Wendy even researched salaries she could expect as a public defender versus the salaries she might get if she got a job with a large, prestigious law firm. First, she looked at starting salaries for public defenders. She found that American public defenders in 2008 had an entry-level median salary of just under $50,000. After 5 years this increased to about $60,000. And by 12 years into the job, public defenders were making about $75,000 on average.[15]

Disappointed by such wages, Wendy decided to check and see what some of the graduates from her elite law school who planned to work for large, prestigious firms might expect to earn. She learned that first year associates at large firms of 101–250 lawyers had a median starting salary in 2008 of $110,000 per year. Giant firms of several hundred attorneys offered median starting salaries of $145,00 per year. She realized that graduates of ordinary law schools would not qualify for such jobs and would have to settle for much smaller salaries (median of $70,000 per year) at firms of 50 or fewer attorneys.[16] But she was doing well as a student at a top law school and had a real chance for the highly paid positions.

She agonized not just over the salaries but over the fact that many of the elite law graduates with whom she went to school might look down on her for practicing criminal law. As mentioned earlier, there is a **stratification of the**

13. Erlanger, Howard S., Mia Cahill, Charles R. Epp, and Kathleen M. Haines. (1996). "Law student idealism and job choice: Some data on an old question." *Law & Society Review* 30:851–864. See also, Granfield, Robert. (1992). *Making Elite Lawyers: Visions of Law at Harvard and Beyond.* New York: Routledge, Chapman and Hall. See also, Kahlenberg, Richard D. (1992). *Broken Contract: A Memoir of Harvard Law School.* Boston: Faber & Faber.

14. Cramton, Roger. (1978). "The ordinary religion of the law school classroom." *Journal of Legal Education* 34:155–167.

15. National Association of Law Placement. (2008). *Median Salaries for Lawyers by Type of Organization and Years Experience.*

16. Id.

legal profession. The highest stratum consists of lawyers who are partners in large, national law firms who represent wealthy corporate clients. The second stratum are the associates who work for the large law firms (many of whom hope to make partner some day), as well as certain very elite government lawyers. The "bottom" 90 percent of lawyers fall within the next or third stratum. They typically represent people rather than institutions. Their small firms cannot count on a consistent income from clients who come and go. These lawyers do divorces, handle child custody matters, attend real estate settlements, draft and probate people's wills, sue on behalf of people hurt in automobile accidents, and represent defendants charged with crimes.[17] A few of the lower stratum lawyers are rich. But most have incomes that are a tiny fraction of the elite lawyers whose firms typically bill steady, institutional clients at the rate of hundreds of dollars per hour.

Wendy was almost seduced by the higher salaries and occupational prestige offered by the large firms. But during a conversation with an adjunct professor she recommitted herself to her original goal of becoming a public defender. He pointed out the fact that as a public defender she would only work a forty hour week. Large law firms considered forty hours per week to be part time. He also convinced her that she would not be alone as a public defender who attended an elite law school, especially if she went to work for a public defender's office in a large city like New York or Los Angeles where competition for public defender jobs can be quite keen. Furthermore, career public defenders in such large offices do make respectable salaries eventually as they move up into executive positions. Even more persuasive to Wendy, however, was the part-time professor's reminding her that she came to law school for a purpose and that she should not let money alone sway her from that goal. She decided to stick with her original plan.

Competition for Grades

Wendy was doing well in law school. After a poor first semester, she was able to adapt to the strange way in which grades were earned there. To Wendy's surprise, class attendance and participation seemed to have little effect on her grades. Perhaps this is why many professors in her school required class attendance and even passed a roll around. Professors who did not require attendance often had half the class skipping lectures the last month of class. Stu-

---

17. Abadinsky, *Law and Justice, supra* note 1 at 117.

dents knew that they could do better on their exams by studying commercially produced **Law Outlines** (in-depth summaries of the law on a particular subject) than they could by listening to long and drawn out student-teacher interactions. There was an outline for nearly every subject taught at the law school. Wendy would purchase these detailed outlines at the university bookstore and could learn the nuances of the law of a particular subject better than if she attended class lectures. She saw little correlation between class discussion and what was actually tested on the professor's exams. She actually did better on exams by studying the detailed and lengthy outlines than she did by focusing on her course notes. The outlines not only taught the black letter of the law better than did the professors but also anticipated and prepared students for the sort of doctrinal questions and issues that professors typically love to raise on exams.

Wendy found other preparation short-cuts as well. For the first year she had dutifully read every word of every case assigned by the instructor. This was incredibly time-consuming in that the material was dense and technical. Wendy found that she could only manage about ten pages per hour, because not only did the professor expect students to read each case but also to brief each case for class discussion. These briefs were not collected by the instructor, but students were nevertheless expected to generate them as an aid in understanding what was read. The essential elements of any brief made for class are found in Table 4 below.

Wendy was assigned many, many lengthy cases to read each night. After the first couple of semesters, she felt that she was no longer gaining enough from the case method of study to justify such an inefficient way to learn the law. She already had learned how to read and brief and analyze cases. She did not care if she could perform well in class if called upon—she just wanted to know enough to avoid a tongue lashing by the professor in case she were called upon.

She preferred to use her time studying legal outlines that could better prepare her for the exams. It especially irked her that much of what she read would never wind up on an exam and class participation did not count towards one's grade.

One day she was talking to a student who told her about paper-back books of case summaries that one could order through the mail or even sometimes buy at the university bookstore. These **canned case briefs** would reduce a long and boring case of ten or so pages down to just one page. (Wendy's friend liked to use a series called "Casenote Legal Briefs" produced by a California firm called "Casenotes Publishing Company.") Amazingly, there was a book of case summaries available for purchase that was specifically tailored to each of Wendy's case books. For example, if Wendy's contract law professor used a book entitled, "Contracts: Cases and Materials" by author John Doe, there was

Table 4   Elements of a Case Briefed for Class

FACTS—A paragraph or so summarizing the essential story of the case, e.g., who did what to whom and how a legal controversy ensued. For example, the facts of State vs. Smith might be that twenty-five-year-old Smith had consensual sex with Sally Jones who was sixteen years of age but objectively looked to be twenty-one. Furthermore, Sally lied to Smith when he asked her age by telling him that she was twenty-one. Smith lives in a state in which a person who is over twenty-one has sex with someone who is under seventeen is guilty of statutory rape, even if the minor consented to the sex.

ISSUE—The question on appeal. What is the court struggling to answer? Why is this case in the case book? For example, the issue in State v. Smith might be, "Is it cruel and unusual punishment to punish someone for statutory rape when the defendant made a very reasonable and honest mistake about the victim's age?"

HOLDING—The ruling of the appellate court regarding the issue. For example, in State v. Smith, the holding might be that a good faith and reasonable mistake as to age is constitutionally required to be recognized as a defense to statutory rape.

RATIONALE—The reasoning of the court for why it ruled the way it did. For example, in State v. Smith the court's rationale might be that every crime with a serious penalty requires the defendant to have had a bad mind of some sort (what lawyers call mens rea). When someone makes a reasonable and understandable mistake as to age, he has no bad mind (no mens rea) and it would be cruel and unusual to punish such a person.

a case summary book that was advertised as "adaptable to" or "paralleling" courses using John Doe's casebook on Contracts: Cases and Materials. The case summaries would provide the essentials (facts, issues, holdings, and rationales), which professors expected students to glean from each case the long and hard way. Though Wendy felt guilty using such summaries, she found herself depending on them more and more. Though not considered technically cheating, professors are hostile to student use of such case summaries and Wendy and the other students who used them tried to be discreet about it.

Wendy cared deeply about her grades as did every student. Law schools are notorious for generating competition for grades by actually issuing **student rankings** at the end of each year. For example, Wendy was notified by mail after her first year that she was ranked 65th out of the 201 students in her class.

This was a respectable ranking given the quality of the school. Wendy was disappointed, however, that she was ranked too low to be invited to join the prestigious **law review**, a scholarly club reserved for those students who finish the first year in the top ten percent of the class. Students on the law review are privileged to select, edit, and publish articles submitted by law professors from around the country who are trying to publish in order to achieve tenure. In other words, law professors submit their work to law reviews and hope the students of that law review will select their work for publication. Since Wendy attended a prestigious law school, its law review was considered a prestigious forum for publishing. Wendy had hoped to be able to put "member of the law review" on her resume but had no hope of ever doing so given her class rank.

Despite missing out on the law review, Wendy fought hard to maintain her respectable ranking. Wendy was surprised how hard it was to move up in the rankings and how easy it was to move down. Wendy was very bright and hard working. She always made stellar grades in grade school, high school, and college. For the first time in her life, she had hit her wall. This is an experience that many law students confront. Law students are often bright, ambitious, and hard-working. They are used to making great grades as long as they are willing to work hard for them. They are obsessed about grades, especially since legal employers care so much about them (some employers will only interview students who are in the top 10 percent of their class, the top 20 percent, the top 50 percent, etc.). But for the first time in their lives, many law students (especially at the more selective schools) are confronted with the limits of their abilities. They realize that many people exist who are smarter than they are, and that no amount of hard work can overcome this reality, especially since these smart people are every bit as hard working as they. It is a humbling experience to be smart and hard working and yet get C's and B's in law school (laws schools do not grade inflate like graduate schools notoriously do—in part because there must be enough variation in grades to be able to rank each student). Wendy's law school GPA was a 3.0. (Her brother Jim, who was working much less hard towards his Master's degree in Pennsylvania had a GPA of 3.5, which was barely above the median in his program.)

At times during Wendy's law school career, the competition for grades turned ugly. Wendy could recall with disgust how students in her first year legal research course would hide books so that other students could not complete their library assignments. Students would also become stingy around exam time when a fellow student would seek help in understanding a complex legal principle that they were not mastering (civil procedure especially could be tricky). But most students simply tried to suffer with grace and dignity, something hard to do when test time came around.

Wendy's law school followed the traditional method of testing. In most courses there was only one test (a final exam) and this one test constituted the entire grade for the course. The exams typically last three hours each and were essay-based. At the beginning of the exam, a student would be given a lengthy fact pattern (a lengthy story) and would be asked to spot the legal issues and indicate the proper resolution of them. These fact patterns would be unlike anything that students ever discussed in class. The goal was to see if the student would be able to analyze a fresh set of facts by spotting potential legal issues and properly applying legal principles to them. Typically, the exam was structured in such a way as to place severe time pressures on the student. There would be too much to do given the time available. This was done to test a student's ability to think quickly while under stress, and to test the student's ability to prioritize his or her time by choosing the more important issues over the less weighty ones.

Wendy prepared for these exams the first semester by carefully reviewing her class notes and by memorizing the briefs she had made for the cases from the book. She expected her exams to be like those in college and high school, that is, mostly tests of memory regarding what was specifically covered in class or in the book. Wendy did not sleep the night before for each exam, spending the entire night memorizing the holdings and rationales of all cases that had ever been assigned for reading. She also memorized the points made by the professor as found in the notes she had taken in class. She was distressed to find that her hard studying did not pay off. Despite knowing the law as covered in the book and class, there were large gaps in Wendy's ability to spot issues in exam questions. Rather than being asked, "What is the holding of State v. Smith?" or "is a reasonable mistake about age a defense in statutory rape?" she would be presented with a set of strange facts that seemed to have nothing to do with anything ever covered in class or in the book. She panicked on the exams and sometimes felt as if she were writing "mere streams of consciousness," as she put it.

Wendy was very disappointed with her first semester test scores. She received C's and B's—mostly C's. Rather than giving up, Wendy decided to change her preparation strategies. The next semester she put less effort into preparing for class, though she did try to prepare enough to avoid humiliation if called upon. She took notes in class as before, only she realized that she would have to do more than just rely on assigned reading and class notes to do better on the finals. Wendy spent many hours putting what she learned in class into context by studying the commercially published legal outlines on each subject she was taking. By doing this, she understood the bigger picture of how the materials the professor covered fit into the scheme of things. She learned the law better this way and had a real sense from the legal outlines of the sort of issues she could probably expect on her exams. The week before finals of her second semester was spent not memorizing holdings and rationales but rather producing **exam checklists** (outlines of outlines regarding the law), which she could memorize the night before each of the finals. When confronted with an exam question on test day, she would then mentally review her checklist, systematically asking herself, "Does this checklist item apply? Does this item apply?" as she covered her list from top to bottom. Operating in this fashion, Wendy found herself spotting many obscure but important issues that were embedded in each exam question. Once an issue was spotted, Wendy would not begin to write in her blue book until she first jotted down (on scratch paper) a brief outline of all the nuances of the law regarding the issue that she could remember from her earlier study of cases, class notes, and the commercially produced legal outlines. She did the same scratch paper outlines of all the issues she spotted before writing down a single word in the blue book. Of the three hours she had for the exam, Wendy would spend the first hour writing on scratch paper, and the final two writing furiously in the blue book. Wendy's new strategy paid off. Her scores on the second semester exams improved dramatically—enough to put her solidly into the top half of her class.

Wendy continued to do quite well on her exams the second and third years of school. Being solidly above-average was doing well even though she was never known as a top student. But this was an elite school after all, and the competition was brutal.

Wendy was happy to have survived her first year, especially since the common wisdom is that the first year of law school is the hardest (no electives, having to master legal jargon while one reads, etc.). However, Wendy actually found the second and third years harder still. But this had little to do with the difficulty of the material.

Persevering to the End

Wendy had grown tired of reading long and dry cases. She tired of the professors' aggressive questioning of students. She could barely force herself to pull the "all-nighters" at the end of each semester like she and most students had been doing. She found herself (to her shame) relying more and more on the commercially-prepared, canned summaries of the cases assigned for reading rather than on reading the lengthy original cases herself. When she did read the cases in full by herself, she could barely keep from falling asleep.

Once mastered, the case method of study can seem to many students like unnecessary, time-consuming exercises. "I already know how to analyze cases,"

Wendy would think, "why do they keep making us read them?" Wendy found herself yearning more and more for graduation. She anticipated it the way one anticipates the end to a long and dull cross-country road trip. During her last year, she found herself completely unable to drag herself out of bed one or two mornings per month. But dutifully, she always would somehow wind up in the law library for a long self-study session before too much of the day was over.

Boredom was not the only challenge for Wendy. She also worried about her lack of a social life. In college she had many friends and many hobbies. In law school she did not have time for friends or hobbies. For the first time in her life, she became a loner. "Law is a **jealous mistress**," her class was told by two or three law professors during the first week of school. "You are to have no hobbies, no interests outside of the study of law," one of them actually told them. "What a jerk, I thought he was," said Wendy to herself. "Yet, I have been a slave to my studies the whole time I have been here."

Wendy took Friday nights off each week for "fun" (usually television). She went to class or studied all the rest of the time. She did this for three years. At the end of each semester her eyes would become so strained that she had trouble reading the time on a clock across a room. Her roommates (all undergraduates) never understood how somebody could be so boring and pathologically hard-working as Wendy. But her fellow law students understood. When Wendy would leave the law library each Saturday night at the 10pm closing time, she was in a lot of company.

Wendy's favorite class in all of law school was one she took her third year, entitled "Criminal Trial Practice." This was a **clinical course** (real world-oriented) rather than an **academic course** (theory-oriented). Depending upon the law school one attends, such "hands on" courses may exist in abundance or may be quite rare, depending upon the teaching philosophy of the particular school.[18] At Wendy's school, such courses were rather rare. As for the criminal trial practice course, none of the tenured or tenure-track faculty at Wendy's elite school were interested in teaching it (indeed, none of them probably had ever acquired the practical skills to teach it). It was taught by a part-time instructor whose "day job" was working as a prosecutor in the U.S. Attorney's office. Like Wendy, he had attended an elite law school and was able to secure a job as a federal (rather than as county-level) prosecutor. He was the only "professor" at the school with whom Wendy felt really comfortable, something which surprised her given her desire to one day become a legal ad-

---

18. Law School Admission Council, *The Official Guide, supra* note 3 at 3.

versary of prosecutors like him. The class was tiny: only three students and the instructor. All three students wanted to practice criminal law. "Don't any of you care about making a decent living?" the instructor would say in teasing them. The instructor had each student craft and deliver opening statements to the class, negotiate plea bargains with one another, argue for reductions in bail, present a case to a fictional grand jury, etc. He also took them on field trips to the courthouse to watch real proceedings there.

Finding Employment

This instructor helped Wendy outside of class as well. He gave her advice about something she worried about every week: how to find a criminal defense job without any contacts. Plenty of legal recruiters came to Wendy's law school each spring to recruit. But few criminal law employers bothered showing up. This was due to several reasons.

First, employers realized that few students from schools like Wendy's school had any interest in practicing criminal law. Criminal law as a specialization just did not pay enough.

Second, recruiters realized that the practice of criminal law (the essence of which is negotiating plea bargains and dealing with clients) required a type of intelligence not necessarily found in any more abundance in elite schools than in other schools. Unlike some of the more prestigious areas of legal practice, criminal law demanded "people skills" more than analytical and research skills. Some of the best criminal defense lawyers went to lower-tiered schools, while some of the most "book-smart" defenders made ineffective attorneys.

Third, the lawyer glut in America had become so pronounced that criminal law offices did not have to recruit anybody. People come to them, despite the relatively low pay.

Wendy's favorite instructor (the deputy U.S. Attorney) counseled her to seek employment either with the federal public defenders or with an elite big-city public defenders' office. They tended to attract more graduates of elite schools than do most public defenders' offices, and her degree from an elite school would be more appreciated there. Besides, he knew several people who worked in such offices and could help her to get an interview.

Wendy managed to get an interview with the New York City Legal Aid Society (the primary public defenders' office of that city) and was offered a job contingent upon her first passing the New York State Bar Exam the summer following graduation. As soon as she graduated in early May, Wendy turned her full attention to passing the exam.

Preparing for the Bar Exam

Wendy graduated with a **Juris Doctor** (or **J.D.**) degree. If she had wanted to do work beyond the normal three years of school, she could have earned the L.L.M. degree (master of law) in a specialized subject. At one time law schools granted (and a few still do) the L.L.B. degree (bachelor of laws). But since modern law schools require a bachelor's degree just for admission, the J.D. degree became the new credential starting in the 1960s. (Ironically, the higher law degree, the L.L.M. or master of law, still retains its old designation despite the abolition of the bachelor of laws degree. Hence, the strange situation exists in which the juris doctorate is lower than the master's degree.)

Though her degree from a school with **A.B.A. accreditation** (accreditation granted by the American Bar Association) qualified Wendy to sit for the bar exam of any of the fifty states, Wendy could not practice law in any state until she passed a state bar exam. Wendy realized that she had to study for the bar exam in order to have any hope of passing it. Three years of law school does not usually prepare one to pass the bar exam, especially if one had attended an elite or national law school. (Amazingly, some of the schools with the highest pass rates on state bar exams are commuter law schools, which "**teach to the bar exam.**" The more selective law schools send their graduates to firms all over the country, and, hence, there is no one state bar exam for which to prepare their students.)

To get ready for the New York State Bar Exam, Wendy payed hundreds of dollars to take a bar-review course offered by for-profit outfits at various locations around New York State. She spent most of her summer learning the specific points of New York law (never taught in her elite law school even though it was located in New York). Wendy knew that the New York Bar exam was a difficult one. Not all state bar exams are of equal difficulty. Some (e.g., Pennsylvania) have reputations of being much easier to pass than others (e.g., New York or California). The New York exam had a couple of dozen different subjects on it, only one of which was the criminal law in which Wendy was interested in specializing. In addition to studying the New York details of subjects with which she had some familiarity from law school (like Torts and Contracts), Wendy found herself studying subjects which she had never taken in law school (like the Law of Common Carriers).

The bar exam took two full days for Wendy to complete. The first day she took what was called the "**multi-state bar exam.**" This is a multiple-choice, standardized exam given by most state bar examiners throughout the country. It covers generic legal principles that do not really change much from state to state. The morning session of the multi-state exam was so difficult that

Wendy felt certain that she was failing. The afternoon segment seemed to go much better, however, for Wendy.

The second day Wendy took a full-day essay exam which covered matters unique or peculiar to New York State. States typically administer the multistate exam on one day and then give the essay exam unique to their state on the other day. Wendy felt like she did alright on the essay test but was not absolutely certain that she passed.

Luckily for Wendy, she passed the bar exam on the first try. Not everybody does so. In fact, some people are never able to pass their state's bar exam no matter how many times they take it and no matter how much they study for it. (Wendy's cousin took his state's bar exam six times before finally giving up. He had to wait half a year between each try. He said he could tell that he failed the test merely by the thinness of the envelope in the mailbox. After three painful and expensive years of law school, he wound up becoming a loan officer at a bank.)

Would Wendy do it all over again if she were back in college? "No," she told herself. She could never go through law school again knowing what she knew now. She was glad to have her new job as a public defender waiting for her but she felt the younger version of herself paid a terrible price for where the well-situated, older version of herself found herself to be.

A year or so after graduation, Wendy took an afternoon off from her public defending duties to sit on a panel at a luncheon put on by the pre-law club at her old undergraduate university. She was one of five invited panelists who had recently graduated from law school. After the panelists spoke in general terms of the value of a legal education, one of the students in the audience raised her hand and asked Wendy point-blank if she had liked law school. Caught off guard, Wendy confessed that her law school years were "far and away the most miserable three years" of her life. Embarrassed by her own honesty and feeling like a malcontent, Wendy felt better when all of the other panelists agreed enthusiastically with her assessment.

*****

Questions for Class Discussion

1. How can one best prepare for law school during college?
2. It is said that any course of undergraduate study is suitable for a prospective law student. Why is there no specific "pre-law" major? If you were forced to single out one college major as a preferred one, which would you pick?

3. What difference, if any, does it make what law school you graduate from? What are the different strata of law schools? How do law schools in your state fit into all of this?

4. Why would elite law schools offer debt-forgiveness programs to students entering certain fields of law? Should wealthy schools expand such programs to non-law school students who are willing to enter low paying, public-service jobs?

5. Would you like it if most of your current classes were taught like law school classes, that is, by making use of rigorous questioning as opposed to more traditional lectures? Would it work better for some types of classes you have taken than others?

6. What specifically are some of the benefits and liabilities associated with the Socratic Method of instruction?

7. Do you think that the Socratic Method is unfair to certain types of students? Why? Should law schools abandon this very old tradition in favor of more modern methods of instruction? Like what?

8. What would you think of a law school switching completely to offering only online degrees? Should such a law school be accredited? What would be the advantages and disadvantages of delivering instruction completely online?

9. Is getting a law degree worth three years of sacrificing a social life? Should law professors cut back on the amount of work they require for the degree?

10. Why would "people skills" be so important in the practice of law? What aspects of criminal law require people to be socially skilled? Should law schools seek to admit people who can offer evidence of such skills? If so, what type of evidence could schools expect to be offered?

11. Would a law career be something you would seriously entertain even knowing that the field may be glutted and competition for good jobs keen? Are there other fields that pay well that are better guarantees for a lucrative income?

12. What is the "LSAT?" What specific abilities does it attempt to measure? Other than social skills, are there other traits that successful lawyers should have that are not measured by the LSAT?

13. Why do you think that law schools place so much importance on the LSAT? Is it fair to rely so much on one test? Do you think that standardized tests do a good job at predicting how well someone will do in an academic program? At how well someone will do in a career?

14. Would law schools be justified in using racial, gender, class, geographic or other preferences if that is what it takes to achieve a diverse class? If

you believe preferences might be OK, are there any groups of people currently being overlooked in achieving balanced student bodies?

15. Should law schools seek to higher professors with diverse political views and/or values systems? Do all such backgrounds seem adequately represented in your undergraduate institution?

16. What is a Law Review? Who gets to serve on it? Do you think it would be fun or boring to work for one?

17. How can students cut down on the time-consuming cases they are assigned to read? Are such short-cuts ethical? Would you take advantage of them if given the chance?

18. What is the difference between legal "education" and legal "training?" What does law school emphasize? Why? Do you agree with this emphasis? Do law schools go too far in their emphasis?

19. What does it mean to teach students to "think like a lawyer?" What might be the dark side of such an undertaking? How might idealism be lost in the process?

20. What are some of the reasons that a country with just five percent of the world's population has two-thirds of the world's lawyers? Which countries would you expect to have the fewest lawyers? Why?

21. The following passage from the text is quite powerful, but sounds like something only a law professor would understand. Discuss, as best you can, the various points attempting to be made:

> "One law professor some time ago even went so far as to state that the 'ordinary religion of the law school classroom' consists of 'a moral relativism tending toward nihilism, a pragmatism tending toward an amoral instrumentalism, a realism tending toward cynicism, an individualism tending toward atomism, and a faith in reason and democratic processes tending toward credulity and idolatry.'" [citing, Roger Cranton, "The Ordinary Religion of the Law School Classroom."]

*****

Key Terms: strata of law schools, LSAT, lawyer glut, debt forgiveness program, first year courses, case method, think like a lawyer, Socratic method, legal education, legal training, diminishing idealism, stratification of the legal profession, law outlines, canned case briefs, student rankings, law review, exam checklists, jealous mistress, clinical course, academic course, Juris Doctor (J.D.), A.B.A. accreditation, teach to the bar exam, multi-state bar exam

Additional Concepts: Motivation for law school, getting into law school, pre-law advisors, importance of undergraduate GPA, pre-law majors, top 10 law schools, first day of class, law school electives, feminist critiques of legal education, starting salaries, competition for grades, elements of cases briefed for class, law school exams, lack of grade inflation, persevering, boredom, finding employment, preparing for the bar exam

CHAPTER TWO

A DAY IN JUVENILE COURT

Assistant District Attorney Ryan Larsen was angry that he was the one asked to cover "kiddie court," a term of his which both proved his contempt for and ignorance of what took place in juvenile court. Larsen, who was regularly assigned to adult court, was given the temporary assignment due to an unexpected staff illness. But being given the chore was also due to his relative newness in the office. He was only in his sixth month with the district attorney's office, and often was asked to do the things others more senior found inconvenient.

Larsen, despite being a criminal lawyer, knew virtually nothing about juvenile court. His law professors had barely discussed the topic. If they had, he might have appreciated all that the **child savers**, 19th Century social activists, had done in shifting the focus of processing and punishing juvenile offenders like adults to treating them as children in need of help. Prior to 1900, at least ten children under the age of fourteen had been executed in the United States (including an eight year old hung in colonial Pennsylvania for burning down a barn). Many more children languished and died in adult prisons. Such incidents motivated reformers to push for changes, and in 1899 the first separate juvenile court was established in Illinois.[1]

If Larsen had possessed a more enlightened attitude, he might have realized that as an officer of the court, he could help buttress the doctrine of **parens patriae** which holds that government, acting as a sort of default parent, has an obligation to help those children who need supervision and guidance when parents or natural guardians cannot or will not give it. Instead, he saw juvenile court as work with no glory: nobody except the mysterious and secretive juvenile court regulars seemed to know or care what took place there.

Larsen took some consolation in the fact that only one juvenile matter was scheduled for that day: the case of a thirteen-year-old burglar named Charles

---

1. Shepherd, Robert E. (1999). "The juvenile court at 100 years: A look back." In, *Juvenile Justice, 6(2)*:13–21.

Baker, or "C.B." as he was known on the official docket. Apparently Charles had burglarized a neighbor's home while its occupants were at work and while Charles was skipping school (again).

Resigned to his fate, Larsen pulled himself away from his normal routines and took the courthouse elevator upstairs to the juvenile courtroom. The first thing he saw upon exiting the elevator was a sight that would alter his perception of juvenile court forever: a short, skinny, scared Charles being escorted in leg irons down the hallway toward the courtroom. The boy, who looked even younger than he was, was taking baby steps to avoid tripping over his own shackled feet. It actually pained Larsen, a parent himself, to see a child being treated in such a fashion. Larsen realized he had entered a new professional world. His thoughts were soon interrupted, however, by the voice of Amy Hoda, the public defender permanently assigned (by choice) to juvenile court.

"Hi Ryan, what are you doing here?" inquired Hoda.

"I've been told to handle the Charles Baker case," responded the suddenly nervous prosecutor. "Can we cut a deal or something with this kid?" Larsen liked deals.

"Well, we would have to clear any suggestion with the judge before even approaching my client. Up here in juvenile court, the judges like to be involved in any negotiations."

That was strange to Larsen. In adult court, judges were forbidden by state law to involve themselves in plea bargain negotiations for fear that they would lose their neutrality. Some judges ignored the law but did so quietly. Could things be so different up here?

"In any event," continued defense counsel, "I think the judge would want a full blown **social investigation** by the juvenile probation office before deciding what to do with this particular case. This case is a tricky one, given the kid's priors. I suspect that the judge will want the kid to admit to the allegations—in which case he will order the social investigation—or else will want the kid to have a full-blown hearing, in which case he'll order the S. I. once a determination of delinquency is found, if it is found. The bottom line is that I doubt an agreement can be made here without input from the juvenile probation office."

"What is she talking about?" wondered Larsen. It began to dawn on Larsen that plea bargaining was not as free and open in juvenile court as he was used to in adult court. He also guessed (correctly) that a social investigation was the juvenile court equivalent of a pre-sentence investigation (a report prepared by the probation office at the request of a sentencing judge, which provides background information on an offender and recommendations for treatment or placement).

Larsen thought he had better start looking at the file a little more closely. The truth be told, Larsen had barely reviewed the file before coming to court. He was busy with adult cases and was probably manifesting some passive aggressiveness in not preparing the Baker case. Besides, it was just a residential burglary, and even though he was new as a prosecutor he had already handled four or five of those. But this was juvenile court with its own culture. And to complicate matters, Larsen began to notice in the file that Baker had a long history of juvenile offenses, including several residential burglaries. " 'C.B.' must stand for 'Crime Boy,' " thought Larsen.

In seeing Charles' prior record, Larsen began to understand why the juvenile probation office exercised its discretion in bringing this matter to court rather than handling it internally and less formally. Larsen had enough friends in the probation office to have at least learned that a juvenile **intake worker** (a juvenile probation officer trained to screen incoming cases) tried his or her best to avoid formal hearings whenever possible. Oftentimes the intake worker would merely reprimand an errant child or perhaps impose a curfew and some community service. Even for serious offenses, juvenile probation officers preferred to draw up a treatment contract (perhaps providing for professional counseling) rather than to take the drastic act of filing a **petition** (the juvenile court equivalent of an indictment or criminal information). Once a petition was filed, Larsen knew that unless a "guilty plea"(called an **admission** in juvenile court) was voluntarily entered, a bench "trial" (called an **adjudicatory hearing** in juvenile court) would ensue. If Baker was not always getting into trouble, his burglary quite possibly would have been dealt with informally, even though the charge was not a minor one. But C.B. had bit at the juvenile court apple many times. Larsen was not sure what he was supposed to do next.

"Where do we go from here?" Larsen asked the public defender.

"Well, I'll go and ask Baker if he is willing to admit the offense. If he will admit it in court, the judge will just order the social investigation. If not, I guess you'll just have to put on your witnesses and try to prove the burglary. If the judge finds Charles delinquent, he'll order the S. I. If the petition is unproven, Charles goes free. I hope that Charles admits the burglary because the kid really needs help. This judge is really good at helping kids get back on the right track."

This was weird. Larsen thought that the public defender seemed more interested in getting the kid to admit the charge than in getting the kid off. Even though her client was a child, Larsen wondered if the defense attorney was inappropriately mixing social work with legal representation. "Shouldn't she do what is in the best interests of her client as her client perceives those best interests to be?" thought Larsen. "On the other hand, the client is just a boy. Can he really understand what is in his best interests? Would Hoda be effectively representing him by getting him off like he probably would want, knowing that he would not get the help he probably needs from this judge? But if she did not try her best to get him off, can she call herself a lawyer?"

"Why is Charles so troubled?" asked Larsen of Hoda. Larsen did not realize that he had begun to refer to C.B. as Charles rather than Baker, like the public defender had been doing all along.

"His mother is in prison for selling drugs and for burglaries. His father's whereabouts are unknown. Charles lives with his grandmother, who rarely is at home. The grandmother provides him with food and that is about it. Charles has basically been raising himself since he was five or six years old. Even when he was in kindergarten, Charles would get himself ready and put himself on the bus while grandma slept, and let himself into an empty house when he got home. When he lived with his mother before she went to prison, he was even more neglected. They say neglect can be worse than abuse and I have come to believe that."

"What's with the leg irons? Is that normal?" asked Larsen.

"Every time Charles gets caught doing an offense he tries to run. That is why they put him in leg irons as they marched him down the hall to court. His habit of running is also why the judge did not let him go free at the **detention hearing**" (juvenile equivalent of a bail hearing, only no bond is set—you either are released without posting money or **detained** until court).

Assistant District Attorney Larsen was quickly learning the degree to which he had truly entered a new world. In fact, in some states he could not have even entered it without going to a completely different courthouse with its own set of specialized judges. But even in this mini-world within his old familiar courthouse, the language was different. The culture was also.

In fact, juvenile courts are not merely junior versions of adult court. Since the founding of the first juvenile court devoted to parens patriae in Illinois in 1899, these courts have strived towards a **rehabilitation focus** rather than one of adult-court-style punishment. These courts have their own procedures (as will be shown shortly). They also have their own agenda. Juvenile courts traditionally are charged with doing what is in the best interests of the child. Hence, a whole lexicon has developed in order to facilitate the goal of avoiding the labels which can stigmatize a child, prejudice courthouse actors against the child, or hinder his or her rehabilitation (see Table 1).

While the public defender went to talk to her client, the prosecutor decided he better interview his own witnesses in case Charles refused to admit the offense. The witnesses were standing patiently just a few yards down the hall, outside the courtroom door to which they had been ordered to report in their

Table 1   Legal Terms of Adult v. Juvenile Court

Adult Court Term	Juvenile Court Term
State v. Charles Baker	In re C.B.
Indictment/Information	Petition
Trial	Adjudicatory hearing
Convicted	Adjudicated delinquent
Sentence	Disposition
Pre-Sentence Investigation	Social Investigation
Incarcerated	Placed in a secure facility

subpoenas. Larsen introduced himself and began to quickly go over the substance and style of their testimony. This quick preparation for the potential hearing relaxed Larsen. Even though this was in a sense a "trial," the fact that a judge rather than a jury would be used reminded him of preparing for an adult preliminary hearing, something he was quite used to doing in his felony adult cases.

The Hearing

Upon finishing with his witnesses, Larsen felt confident that he could prove the burglary. But he hoped that Hoda could convince Charles to admit the offense. In part, he hoped this for Charles' sake. The boy needed help. But mostly, he hoped Charles would admit the burglary so that he could get back to adult court work. It was not that he was feeling lazy or even busy anymore. He was simply nervous. He never had prosecuted a juvenile and was afraid of being embarrassed in front of the judge, his witnesses, Hoda and even Charles. Perhaps some day he would have to prosecute a juvenile in court, but it did not have to be this day. Maybe he never would have to do it if he got more seniority in the office before the regular juvenile prosecutor unexpectedly got sick again.

Larsen saw Hoda coming his way. She looked frustrated and was not making eye contact with him, a bad sign. Larsen braced himself for the inevitable bad news. "It's a hearing Ryan, the kid refuses to admit the burglary. He says he did not do it and won't admit to it. He is mad at me for trying to talk him into admitting it so I'm not going to push him any more on it. Are you done talking to your witnesses? Shall we tell the judge we are ready to start?"

"Yes, I'm ready. Let's go tell the judge."

Larsen followed Hoda over to the judge's chambers and stood silently while Hoda announced their business to the judge's secretary. The secretary escorted them back to the judge's office. Upon seeing them and their expressions, Judge Wood intuitively realized that a hearing was in the works. The judge was almost as disappointed as Larsen was that Charles would not admit the burglary. But, not because the judge was nervous. Rather, he thought that admitting the offense was a great aid in rehabilitation. Besides, hearings took a lot longer than a simple admission in court.

"The kid is only thirteen," the judge pointed out to Larsen upon being told there would be a hearing. "You aren't going to try to ask me to waive this to adult court are you?" The judge was afraid that given the juvenile's priors, Larsen might be tempted to make such an unusual request.

"I don't think so," responded Larsen, not quite sure what the judge was talking about.

"Well, make a decision," said the judge. "Personally, I would frown upon a waiver request and you should know that up front."

"Judge, I'm new in juvenile court. What exactly are we talking about?"

The judge was surprised that Larsen did not understand the concept of **waiver**. He knew Larsen had only been practicing law for six months and that he was unfamiliar with juvenile court ways. But he thought that Larsen would at least know what "waiver" was. "Wasn't that on the bar exam?" he wondered. The judge was not sure. Suddenly remembering his first juvenile hearing as a young lawyer and how a patient judge helped him get through it, he decided to be charitable.

The judge explained that in their state an offender under the age of sixteen was presumed to be incapable of fully appreciating the wrongfulness of his offense and ordinarily should be processed in the juvenile justice system with its emphasis on rehabilitation rather than punishment. (This age varies from state to state—age eighteen is the most common upper cut-off point for juvenile court jurisdiction, but some states use age seventeen and a few use age sixteen—see Table 2.) But, there were exceptions to this presumption. A juvenile judge, at the request of a prosecutor or on the judge's own motion, could "waive" jurisdiction to adult court, in which case the offender would be tried and punished as an adult. The closer the offender was to the cut-off age, the more serious the offense, and the more serious the prior juvenile record, the more likely a request for a waiver to adult court would be granted. For example, a juvenile who raped someone after having been "treated" by the juvenile justice system before for rape, and who committed this new rape just prior to turning sixteen, stood a very high chance of being tried as an adult. But a twelve-year-old who committed theft and who had a scanty juvenile record would risk no chance of being waived to adult court. The judge explained that Charles had a bad record and a serious new charge. But he was only thirteen and the new charge was not horrific. Larsen got the point.

"I'm not seeking a waiver your honor," announced Larsen.

Table 2   Age Cut-Off Points for Juvenile Court Jurisdiction by State

Age 16	Age 17	Age 18	
New York	Texas	California	Oregon
Connecticut	Missouri	Washington	Idaho
North Carolina	Illinois	Nevada	Arizona
Michigan	Montana	Wyoming	Nebraska
Massachusetts	New Mexico	Colorado	Oklahoma
South Carolina	Georgia	North Dakota	Mississippi
	Louisiana	South Dakota	Florida
		Kansas	Kentucky
		Arkansas	Minnesota
		Alabama	Indiana
		Tennessee	Pennsylvania
		Iowa	West Virginia
		Wisconsin	Delaware
		Ohio	Rhode Island
		Virginia	New Hampshire
		Maryland	Alaska
		New Jersey	Utah
		Vermont	D.C.
		Maine	
		Hawaii	

Source: Puzzanchera, Charles, M. 2001. "Delinquency cases waived to criminal court, 1989–1998." Washington, D.C.: Office of Juvenile Justice and Delinquency Prevention, 2001.

The judge was pleased that Larsen was not inclined to waste court time in hopelessly seeking a waiver to adult court. It was the judge's experience that attorneys new to juvenile court were always the most at risk of wasting court time through misplaced aggressiveness. "Are you ready to call your witnesses and present your evidence, Mr. Larsen?" queried the judge. "If so, let us assemble in the courtroom."

A few minutes later, Assistant District Attorney Larsen found himself seated in the juvenile courtroom at a table a few feet away from his "adversary," Assistant Public Defender Hoda. Seated just behind Larsen were his witnesses: a neighbor of the burglary victim who saw young Charles enter the victim's house, the police officer who apprehended Charles at the scene in response to the neighbor's "911" call, and the home owner who would testify that she never gave permission for Charles to enter her home and take her DVD player and beer.

Larsen glanced at Charles to see how he was holding up. Larsen was not used to "beating up" little kids like Charles, even if they were offenders. Charles was sitting at the defense table in between Hoda and his grandmother. Larsen wondered if he (the attorney) or Charles (the young offender) knew better as to how such hearings proceeded. Larsen decided he would just get his cues from the judge and Hoda. His main job was simply to get his witnesses on the stand to tell what they knew. That should not be too difficult. He was grateful that there was no jury present in case he made a fool of himself in the first juvenile "trial" of his life.

If Larsen had been practicing law in the early 1900s rather than a century later, he could have sat back and let the judge run the entire show. Though Larsen did not know it (nor Hoda for that matter), juvenile proceedings were essentially ruleless back then. Since the court was supposedly trying to do what was in the best interests of the juvenile, it was believed that procedural rights would do more harm than good. After all, the whole focus of juvenile court was on rehabilitation, and key to rehabilitation was confession. Procedural rights would only get in the way of that. In short, it was felt that formal process belonged in adult court where punishment was being sought, but had no more place in juvenile court than it would at home (no sane parent would give a disobedient child the right to remain silent or trial by peers).

Juvenile adjudicatory hearings in the early 20th Century resembled intimate conferences more than hearings. Juvenile cases were frequently heard in judges' chambers rather than in courtrooms. Often the judge would chat with the offender, call him or her by the first name, and encourage a confession. Neither stenographers nor clerks would be present. Defense counsel did not adopt the role of a true advocate but rather attempted to help the parents and the offender understand that the court was there to help. Courts relied on politically appointed juvenile probation officers to investigate cases and trusted them to do so with accuracy and fairness. Evidence was not tested through cross-examination, and, in fact, the accused had no legal right to even confront his or her accusers.[2]

By the mid-twentieth century, the Supreme Court began to question this setup. Though juvenile court judges liked to think of themselves as physicians attempting to heal the children coming into their courts, this **medical model** had some serious shortcomings. First of all, unlike true medical treatment, treatment ordered by the juvenile judge was not voluntary. Additionally, unlike physicians, juvenile judges would intentionally inflict pain as a form of treatment.[3]

---

2. Faust, Frederick L. and Paul J. Brantingham. (1974). *Juvenile Justice Philosophy*. St. Paul, Minn.: West Publishing Co., pp. 146–162.

3. Ibid.

Eventually, the U.S. Supreme Court became convinced that many juveniles were being treated in an arbitrary manner and that something had to be done. The Court started to doubt the rationale of very early twentieth century decisions like *Commonwealth v. Fisher*,[4] which held that since parents need not use any particular procedures, then neither does the salvation-seeking state. But, beginning in the 1960s, the Supreme Court began to require basic due process rights such as: advance notice of charges, right to counsel, right against self-incrimination, right to confront and cross-examine accusers, and proof beyond a reasonable doubt. The 1967 Supreme Court case of *In re Gault*[5] was the single most important case of that era, and would cause Prosecutor Larsen to do more than just sit back like in the good old days.

Back in 1964, fifteen year old Gerald Gault, who was already on probation for being in the company of a thief, was accused by a neighbor of making a lewd phone call to her. Gerald was picked up by the police while his parents were at work. The probation office filed a petition against him but no facts were alleged—just that he was "delinquent." The petition, as poor as it was, was never served on his parents—they had to make inquiries to even know where the boy was. The adjudicatory hearing took place the very next day. Mrs. Cook (the alleged victim) was not even there. Nobody was sworn in and no transcript was made. Gerald was adjudicated delinquent and was placed in the Arizona Industrial School until he reached the age of twenty-one. (If Gerald had been an adult, the maximum penalty for a lewd phone call would have been two months in jail.)

In overturning the findings, the Supreme Court ended the era of parens patriae being used as an excuse to deny all due process rights. First, it held that notice of the specific allegations must be given and sufficiently in advance of the hearing to allow a defense to be prepared. The phony argument that keeping the allegations secret helped the child's privacy was rejected.

Second, the court held that any juvenile who may be committed to an institution has the right to an attorney, including a free one if too poor. The argument that the probation officer could protect the rights of the juvenile was found unacceptable since a probation officer in this context is akin to an arresting officer. An attorney rather than a probation officer is needed to make skilled inquiry into the facts and to insist on regularity of proceedings.

Next, the court held that juveniles have the same right as adults to not incriminate themselves. It reasoned that a child who is persuaded to confess for

---

4. *Commonwealth v. Fisher*, 213 Pa. 48, 62 A. 198 (1905).

5. *In re Gault*, 387 U.S. 1 (1967).

Table 3   Summary of Due Process Rights of Juveniles

Case	Due Process Rights Given
Kent v. U.S. (1966)[1]	Right to a hearing before transfer to adult court
In re Gault (1967)[2]	Notice of precise charges, right to legal counsel, privilege against self-incrimination, right to confront and cross-examine witnesses
In re Winship (1970)[3]	Right to proof beyond reasonable doubt at adjudicatory hearings
Schall v. Martin (1984)[4]	Preventive detention (being held until the hearing) cannot be imposed without prior notice, a fair detention hearing, and a statement by the judge as to why preventive detention is necessary
Illinois v. Montanez (1996)[5]	A concerned adult must be present at a juvenile's interrogation; otherwise any confession obtained must be suppressed

1. *Kent v. United States,* 383 U.S. 541 (1966).
2. *In re Gault,* 387 U.S. 1 (1967).
3. *In re Winship,* 397 U.S. 358 (1970).
4. *Schall v. Martin,* 467 U.S. 253 (1984).
5. *Illinois v. Montanez,* No. 95-1429 (1996), certiorari denied.

his or her own therapeutic good and then is punished severely feels tricked and bitter rather than helped. Furthermore, confessions by children are notoriously unreliable. And, the argument that the 5th Amendment does not apply to juvenile hearings since they are civil rather than criminal proceedings is form over substance. This is especially true in a case like this one where a youth is to have his liberty taken away for many years.

Finally, the court held that juveniles have the right to confront and cross-examine the witnesses against them. The stakes were just too high to not test the evidence in this manner.

No doubt, the court ruled the way it did on these issues because it was shocked by the amount of liberty that could be taken away with so little formality. Later cases expanded the due process rights of juveniles even further and totally changed the face of juvenile court for future prosecutors like Larsen. A summary of the various cases and the legal principles they articulated can be found in Table 3.

With all these due process rights, one might wonder what if any differences remain in the judicial processing of juveniles versus adults. One huge right still not afforded juveniles is the right to a jury trial. In the 1971 case of *McKeiver v. Pennsylvania*,[6] the Supreme Court ruled that juvenile court jury trials would do little to bolster fact finding ability while bringing about the traditional delay, formality and adversarial ways of adult courts. Fearing the collapse of the juvenile court system if it were to rule otherwise, the court would not expand juvenile due process rights to include jury trials.

Though initially comforting to Assistant District Attorney Larsen, this last point (the lack of a jury)—when coupled with juvenile court judges' desire to create a therapeutic environment in court—was now worrying him. He knew how to conduct himself before juries. He knew how to conduct himself in an adult bench trial. But, he was not sure of how to conduct himself in the juvenile arena. He would have to learn through trial and error, the same way he did a half year previously in adult court. He just did not want to go through the indignity of such a schooling once again.

The time for the hearing to start was signaled by the entrance of the judge into the courtroom. Assistant District Attorney Larsen reflexively rose to attention but quickly sat down again when he noticed that nobody else had risen. "What ever happened to 'all rise'?" wondered Larsen. He would be told afterwards by Hoda that the judge wanted to mitigate the intimidating atmosphere of juvenile court as much as he could. The judge chose purple robes for that same purpose—black "witch-like" robes were much too severe in this forum.

"You may call your first witness, Mr. Larsen," suggested the judge. "That is unless you have an opening statement."

Larsen had in fact prepared a rather dramatic and lengthy opening statement, at least relative to the amount of time he had to prepare. But he sensed that brevity would serve the state's interests better in this type of proceeding.

"Your Honor, I just have a couple of things to say," began Larsen. "This is a burglary case. There will be just three witnesses. First, Jane Ellsworth, the neighbor of the alleged burglary victim, will tell the court how she observed Charles Baker enter the alleged victim's house through an unlocked side window and how she called "911" immediately. Officer Keltner will tell the court how he responded promptly to the scene only to find Charles bolt out the back door carrying a DVD player and a six pack of beer. He chased Charles but Charles got away after dumping the stuff and jumping the back yard fence. He

---

6. *McKeiver v. Pennsylvania*, 403 U.S. 528 (1971).

clearly recognized Charles from past encounters. Finally, Ms. Gibbons, the homeowner, will testify that the taken items belonged to her and that Charles had no permission to enter her home nor take those things. I suggest that after I present my case, the court will feel comfortable in finding Charles guilty of the theft and the burglary. Thank you."

"Thank you, Mr. Larsen," replied the judge. "Please remember though that nobody is trying to find Mr. Baker 'guilty' of anything. He may or may not be adjudicated delinquent."

"Yes, of course your Honor," replied Larsen. Larsen realized the judge was teaching him some important vocabulary. He also promised himself to refer to "Charles" as "Mr. Baker" from now on, though that particular custom did not seem to make much sense to him.

"Ms. Hoda, do you wish to make an opening statement?" queried the judge.

"I just want to say that the whole case will depend upon the officer's ability to identify Mr. Baker as the young man fleeing the scene, and would ask the court to focus primarily on that aspect of the state's case. I do not believe they will prove such identity beyond a reasonable doubt."

"Very well," responded the judge. "Mr. Larsen, you may call your first witness."

The prosecutor proceeded to call his first witness, the neighbor who, in matter of fact fashion, relayed facts just as Larsen had summarized them. The only cross-examination by Hoda involved the degree to which the neighbor could recognize the perpetrator of the burglary. She was too far away to identify him beyond the fact that he was definitely male, thin, and very young. His race matched that of C.B. as well.

The second witness, the police officer, testified that he responded to the scene within four minutes of the neighbor's call. As he started checking the side window, he saw Charles Baker flee out the back door with a DVD player and a six pack of beer in hand. The officer yelled for Baker to halt, but was ignored. The officer gave pursuit and was making some headway until Baker threw down the objects in his hands and rapidly scaled a high fence to freedom. The officer had trouble scaling the fence and the youth got away. He was sure that the youth was Charles Baker. He told the court how five or six times he had either arrested Charles Baker himself in the past or had been present at the station when he was brought in by others. He testified that there was no doubt in his mind that the sneak thief was Charles Baker.

On cross-examination, Ms. Hoda went through the usual eye-witness impeachment questions, such as distance between the officer and the suspect, length of time in sight, the fact that the officer was under stress, the fact that Charles looked like many other youth his age, the fact that the officer did not like Charles, the fact that in the past he had mistaken people's identity from time to time, etc.

Ms. Hoda's cross-examination of the officer now completed, Ryan Larsen called his last witness, the home owner Ms. Gibbons. Ms. Gibbons testified briefly about her being at work during the incident. She had locked the doors before going to work, but had forgotten that the side window was unlocked. She had not given anyone permission to enter her home that day—certainly not Charles Baker or any other youth. She identified the DVD player and beer found in the yard as belonging to her and to her home.

Defense Attorney Hoda asked no questions on cross, other than to establish that this victim never saw her client that day nor had any relationship with him of any kind. With Hoda's brief cross-examination completed, Larsen informed the court that the prosecution rested its case.

"Very well, does the defense wish to put on any witnesses?" asked the judge.

"We have just one witness, your Honor," responded Hoda. "The defense would like to call Charles Baker to the stand."

"Very well, Ms. Hoda," stated the judge. "However, before Mr. Baker takes the stand I want to make sure that he understands his Fifth Amendment rights. Mr. Baker, do you understand that you have no obligation to take the stand and that I will not use your decision to avoid testifying in any way against you?"

"What?" asked Charles.

"Ms. Hoda, your attorney, wants you to come up here and tell the court your side of things. You do not have to do that unless you want to. If you don't want to, I won't take that to mean that you did the burglary or didn't do the burglary. You don't have to take the stand and that will be alright. But you can if you want to. It is completely up to you."

"I want to tell my side of it," replied Charles.

"Before you decide, I want to make sure that you understand that you will be put under oath and that the prosecutor will be able to ask all the tough questions he wants. If you don't take the stand, the prosecutor cannot ask you any questions. Do you wish to back out of taking the stand?"

"No, I'll take the stand, sir," replied Charles.

"Ma'am," the judge said, directing his words to the elderly lady seated next to Charles at the defense table, "are you Mr. Baker's grandmother?"

"Yes, I am his grandmother. The boy lives with me. His mother can't take care of him right now."

"As an adult who is concerned about the boy's welfare, do you also agree that he should give up his right to remain silent and take the stand. Again, he has the absolute right not to take the stand and his not taking the stand cannot be used against him. It would also spare him from being asked any questions by the other side."

"He can take the stand if he wants to, your Honor," responded the grandmother.

"Very well, Mr. Baker, you may take the stand," directed the judge.

As Charles was walking up to the stand, Larsen reflected upon the strange dialogue that just took place. He now realized that juveniles not only have an attorney to look out for them but apparently are required to have an **interested adult** weigh in on any big decisions as well. He realized that even if he and Hoda had made a deal, this old grandmother would probably have been required to give her consent as well Charles.

Larsen watched as Charles was sworn in. Responding to Hoda's gentle probes, Charles testified that he was at home on the day in question as he was tired and needed a break from school. He spent the entire day watching television and playing video games. He never left home because he was afraid someone from school might see him. He said he was not too surprised that the officer claimed to recognize him at the crime scene since the officer did not like him and probably assumed it was him. Charles adamantly denied he was ever there, and said he would not even know how to get to the place described in court. Charles admitted that he did do "bad things sometimes," but with moral indignation in his voice asserted that "I don't break into ladies' homes."

On cross-examination, the prosecutor aggressively led Charles through a series of questions. He was able to get Charles to admit that he liked to watch DVD movies but did not own a DVD player. He got Charles to admit that he drank beer at times. The most damaging admission occurred when Charles verified that the officer who claimed to spot him running from the home with the DVD player and beer knew him "really well" and had seen him "many times" in the past.

With the evidence now complete, the attorneys made brief closing remarks. Hoda spoke first and pointed out that the officer may have made a mistaken identification. She noted that everybody was in agreement that Ms. Gibbons' house was burglarized. Her client was simply saying that he was not the burglar. She reminded the judge that eyewitnesses are notorious for making honest mistakes and this was just one more example of that. She suggested that there was plenty of reasonable doubt and that the court should err on the side of Baker.

Larsen in his brief closing agreed that the case hinged on Officer Keltner's identification. He pointed out that by Baker's own admission, both he and the officer knew each other quite well and were easily recognizable to one another.

He suggested that Keltner showed no hesitation whatsoever in identifying Baker as the burglar at the scene. Furthermore, Baker was not at school that day (that was no coincidence) and had the opportunity and motive (he likes beer and DVDs) to commit this act. He asked the court to adjudicate him delinquent for the burglary and theft.

The judge took a minute or two to reflect upon what had been said by both Hoda and Larsen. He then told all present he had come to a decision. While Charles remained seated (again an informality that the prosecutor found strange), the judge announce to Charles that he was adjudicated delinquent for both the burglary and the theft. He entered an order on the record for the juvenile probation office to promptly conduct a social investigation of Charles in order to help the court decide what course of action would be best for Charles' rehabilitation. He told Ms. Hoda that the **disposition hearing** (the juvenile version of a sentencing hearing) would take place in two weeks at 10 a.m. in the very same courtroom. When the judge noticed the prosecutor writing the date in his own calendar book, he called him aside and gently told him that his presence would not be necessary—unlike adult court, only the defense attorney was invited to the disposition hearing. That was fine with Larsen. He was busy enough as it was.

Larsen returned to his offices grateful that he had survived his first day in juvenile court. He was proud of the outcome and tried to brag to his fellow prosecutors about his victory in court. He called it a "trial win." Nobody cared. To them it was still "kiddie court."

The judge cared about the outcome. For him, the hardest part of the case was yet to come: what to do with delinquent Charles Baker.

The Judge's Disposition

Judge Wood sighed when he first saw the social investigation report on Charles Baker sitting in his in-basket. It had been ten days since the hearing and the judge had put it mostly out of his mind. But now he had to deal with it once more. This was the hardest part of his job. He did not order social investigations on the easy cases—he just ordered probation with various conditions and let that be the end of it. But Charles was a tough case. He did not seem to respond favorably to former juvenile probation officers' attempts to rehabilitate him. He read in the report that Charles had been on probation twice before, and that the second time had gone to court-ordered counseling at county expense. The older offenses involved shoplifting offenses and residential burglary. (There were even older offenses which never resulted in formal court proceedings.) But now Charles had committed yet another residential burglary. Something had to be done. The boy was not improving. His grandmother was of little help.

The judge felt genuine empathy for Charles. He knew that his problems involved just not delinquent acts but also some rather serious **status offenses** (acts that are only illegal due to one's status as a minor). Charles obviously liked to drink beer and might even be a budding alcoholic. The probation office's report indicated that Charles was much more than an occasional drinker. Charles also liked to skip school (the report indicates that it was a weekly occurrence and the school counselor was fed up working with him). The judge noted that the author of the social investigation report recommended **placement** in a **secure facility**, a juvenile "jail" called Lake Meadows, for a term of six months. There Charles would be forced to attend academic classes as well as "theft class" (which tried to teach empathy for victims) and substance abuse counseling. The judge was loathe to place any child in a secure facility but thought in this case there might be no alternative. To ease his conscience, he made a quick mental review of the various programs and options that were at his disposal. He thought about **regular probation** (with conditions like curfews and counseling and monthly meetings with the probation officer), but that road had led to nowhere in the past. He considered **intensive probation** in which Charles could have the close and almost daily attention of a probation officer assigned to Charles and only a handful of other clients. But, he thought even that would not suffice. He wondered momentarily if Charles might not benefit from some of the more creative treatments out there like working on a **youth ranch** for troubled children or attending a **wilderness experience** for offenders. Maybe counselors there could "unfreeze" Charles, get him pointed towards the right destination, and "freeze" him up again once he got there. But given Charles' history of dodging school and trying to run away each time he was arrested, Judge Wood did not want to risk sending Charles to any such non-secure settings. In the end, the judge concluded that the only realistic option was to send him to the secure-detention **training school** at Meadow Lake, complete with lock down, slit windows, and barbed wired exercise yards.

Judge Wood did not look forward to sending Charles off to Lake Meadows. He did not want to turn Charles into one of those **state-raised youth**. He realized that "training schools" (he remembered when they used to be called "reform schools") were little more than glorified jails with some academic classes thrown in as part of the mix. But Charles was becoming dangerous. For his own good, he needed to be taught a lesson. But the real offenders in Judge Wood's views were Charles' parents and even his neglectful current guardian.

The judge realized that much of delinquency can be explained by one of two things: dysfunctional families and/or bad peers.

The judge knew that family **child abuse** (which might include physical, emotional or sexual mistreatment) was one of the biggest explanations of juvenile delinquency. In fact, two of the largest predictors of juvenile delinquency are past delinquent acts on the one hand and child abuse and neglect on the other.[7] But Charles had never been abused. Instead, he suffered what might be even worse: severe **child neglect** (the failure to provide supervision, love, help, security or sometimes even life's physical necessities). Charles was given food and shelter but little more since he was a little boy. His grandmother was kind enough to house and feed him, but was unable or unwilling to do anything else. The judge realized it was better for Charles to be a state-raised youth at the training school than to be a self-raised youth heading for a life of adult crime.

The judge knew that involvement with wayward peers, especially in the form of **youth gangs**, was also a major cause of delinquency (as well an effect of it). This has been known for a very long time. For example, as far back as 1927 Frederick Thrasher wrote in his classic book, *The Gang*, that "the spontaneous efforts of boys to create a society for themselves where none adequate to their needs exists" is the fundamental explanation for the origin of youth gangs. Thrasher went on to note that "what boys get out of such associations is the thrill and zest of participation in common interests, more especially in corporate action, in hunting, capture, conflict, flight, and escape."[8] Many poorly supervised youth turn to gangs for love and support when little exists at home. Having joined the gang, they often are socialized into heavy deviance. But, Charles was a loner. He had few friends (let alone wayward ones) and no gang affiliation. His delinquency appeared to the judge to be almost entirely a product of his neglect at home. The secure-detention school would solve part of the neglect problem—at least Charles would have structure in his life and the attention of staff counselors. But, the judge knew that exposing Charles to cliques in the secure facility might expose him to even more unconventional values. This was the major reason that Judge Wood felt strongly hesitant about sending young Charles to Lake Meadows. Would he

---

7. 12. Child Welfare League of America. (1997). *Sacramento County Community Intervention Program: Findings from a Comprehensive Study of Community Partners in Child Welfare, Law Enforcement, Juvenile Justice, and the Child Welfare League of America*. Washington, D.C.: C.W.L.A.).

8. Thrasher, Frederick. (1927). *The Gang*. Chicago: University of Chicago Press, pp. 32–33.

be sending him from the pan into the fire? Would he be exacerbating the effects of his neglect by forcing him to associate for the first time with bad peers? But, if he did nothing the boy would surely fail.

In the end, the judge, at the disposition hearing, announced to Charles, his attorney, and the grandmother that Charles would have to go to Lake Meadows for four months (reduced from the six months recommended by the juvenile probation office). Charles took it well. He knew that this juvenile adjudication was not a criminal conviction and would result in no public labeling of him as a law violator. As with all juvenile cases which have rehabilitation as their official goal, his case would result in a **sealed record** to which nobody outside the court community (including future potential employers) would ever have access. Ms. Hoda, his attorney, took it well also. She was privately glad that something was being done to at least try to help her young client. To everyone's amazement, it was Charles' grandmother that became emotional. She angrily told the judge that she now knew what it was like to have someone's loved one kidnaped by strangers.

The Extent and Future of Delinquency

Returning to his chambers, Judge Wood took a few minutes to reflect upon Charles as well as many of the other young people he had to regularly deal with in juvenile court. He knew that juvenile offenses were a serious problem in his community and throughout the nation. Judge Wood knew from personal experience what criminologists have known for a long time: age is more strongly correlated with criminal activity than social class, intelligence, race, or just about anything else.[9] The simple truth is that as people leave their younger years, they tend to **age out** of crimes.[10]

Currently, about two million people under the age of eighteen are arrested each year.[11] Of course, the problem is much worse than that. Nearly every teenager probably commits an offense for which he or she could be arrested. Most simply do not get caught. Of those that do get caught and arrested, minorities (who are much more likely to live in family poverty and broken neighborhoods than whites) are disproportionately represented. For example,

---

9. Hirshi, Travis and Michael Gottfredson. (1982). "Age and the explanation of crime." *American Journal of Sociology*, 89:552–584.

10. Id.

11. Federal Bureau of Investigation. (1999). *Crime in the United States, 1998*. Washington, D.C.: U.S. Government Printing Office, p. 220.

though African Americans make up only 12 percent of the population, they represent 30 percent of those arrested for serious crimes like burglary and motor vehicle theft and 50 percent of arrests for violent crimes.[12]

Though crimes of violence reach their highest peak in the teenage years, property crimes like the burglary and theft committed by Charles Baker are even more strongly associated with youth than are violent crimes. Property crimes start to rapidly take off at about age twelve, reach their peak at about age sixteen, then show a dramatic drop until returning to relatively low levels by age twenty.[13]

This strong correlation between youth and crime suggests why the topic of juvenile justice is so important and why jobs like that of Judge Wood are so critical. First, society needs protection from these young perpetrators. Second, the youthful offenders need to receive correctional intervention before it is too late. True, most offenders naturally will diminish their criminal activities as they approach adulthood with or without court assistance. But, a small but important minority will not. Judge Wood's struggle to find a way to reduce the likelihood that Charles Baker would become an adult offender is a noble attempt to be a 21st Century child saver.

What does the future hold for the Charles Bakers and the Judge Woods of this world? What is the future of juvenile justice in America? Nobody knows. However, certain trends seem to be taking shape.

First of all, the series of judicial decisions handed down over the past few decades that greatly expanded the due process rights of accused juveniles ironically indicates a possible weakening of parens patriae and the rehabilitative ideal. The more due process rights are given to youthful offenders, the more difficulty juvenile courthouse actors will face in delivering rehabilitative services to the offender. Legislatures also seem to be moving away from rehabilitation and more towards a punitive orientation. Since the early 1990s, forty states have made it much easier to try juveniles as adults.[14] In fact, some scholars suggest that our juvenile justice system may be more oriented toward punishment than at any time since the juvenile court system was first begun.[15]

In the future, will we see younger and younger offenders tried and punished as adults? Will judges worry more and more about protecting society and less about rehabilitation? Will juveniles one day have the right to a jury

---

12. Bartol, Curt R. (1998). *Delinquency and Justice: A Psychosocial Approach.* Upper Saddle River, N.J.: Prentice-Hall, p. 40.

13. Id. at 43.

14. Baron, Stephen W. and Timothy F. Hartnagel. (1996). "Lock 'em up: Attitudes toward punishing juvenile offenders." *Canadian Journal of Criminology, 38(April),* 191–212.

15. Id.

trial, thus completing the evolution of due process rights begun decades ago? Or will the pendulum begin to swing back towards informality and what needs to be done for the young offender's own good? Only time will tell.

Most likely, the juvenile justice system will continue to be there in some distinct form for people like Charles Baker. Some things probably will not change much. Most juvenile offenders who are arrested will continue to undergo **diversion** (having their cases handled informally by the intake officer) rather than having their cases resolved through formal court hearings. Limited resources, if nothing else, will probably see to that. Furthermore, though the age may go up or down, immaturity will probably always be recognized by society as a legitimate defense to a full-blown crime. Society will probably continue to hold out more hope in rehabilitation for young people than for older people set in their ways. The due process rights that courts have thus far articulated on behalf of juveniles will almost certainly continue to be provided (precedent is a strong legal tradition), but it is unlikely courts will ever allow the distinction between adult and juvenile court to completely disappear. Society and its juvenile justice system will likely always have a soft spot in its heart for its troubled children like Charles Baker.

*****

Questions for Class Discussion

1. Should we even bother having a separate court system for juveniles? Why or why not? Does your answer depend on the type of injury the juvenile has committed?
2. Why are juveniles referred to only by their initials on the docket? Why are proceedings closed to the public? Do you agree with these policies?
3. At what ages do states draw the line between presumptively trying someone as an adult vs. processing them as a juvenile? What age does your state use? What age would you pick if it were completely up to you? Can anyone make an argument for an age older than 18?
4. In a juvenile court, the idea of an adversarial system is often thrown out the window. Many times it appears that the defense attorney is working as hard as the prosecutor to get the juvenile adjudicated delinquent in order to get the youth the help that is needed. Is this notion of everyone working together really beneficial to the juvenile or should juvenile court be conducted in a more adversarial manner?
5. Is a juvenile defense attorney who is more interested in getting his or her client help than in getting the client "off" acting ethically or unethically

as an attorney? Would your answer be the same with regards to an adult client who had some serious, treatable problem?

6. Should juveniles be allowed to make bail and/or have a jury trial like adults? Is it fair for one person (a single judge) to decide "guilt" or "innocence," especially in a case that may result in years of confinement?

7. What is "waiver?" What are some of the factors that make a juvenile case at risk for being "waived" to adult court? Do you think that if you were a juvenile court judge, you would be somewhat reluctant or somewhat eager to waive juveniles to adult court?

8. What does the "medical model" of the early 20th century refer to? Do juveniles typically suffer from social handicaps not of their making? Do adult criminals?

9. Is it appropriate to continue to have a juvenile system that focuses more on rehabilitation than on retribution? Are children more likely candidates for rehabilitation than adults? How robust or malleable is personality in young people? In adults? Is trying to rehabilitate juveniles mostly a waste of time? Do we have an ethical duty to at least try?

10. How was juvenile court conducted prior to the mid-20th century? How are things quite different today?

11. Rights given to young people being processed in juvenile court greatly expanded after the mid-20th century. What were some of the landmark legal cases and the specific rights associated with each landmark case?

12. What are some of the factors that lead to (cause) juvenile delinquency?

13. Do you think that bad peers cause delinquency or do you think it is more likely that bad kids seek out others like them to hang out with? Have any of you ever lived in a "bad neighborhood?"

14. How can delinquency be explained by dysfunctional families? Do most children who are raised in bad homes wind up delinquent? Why not? Do children raised in great homes ever wind up delinquent? Why?

15. Why might "child neglect" be even worse than "child abuse?" What are some examples of child neglect you have witnessed in families other than your own? What are some examples of child abuse you have witnessed in families other than your own? How common is neglect and abuse in our society?

16. Should adult offenders who, as children, were raised in very neglectful or abusive homes be treated less severely than those who had the fortune of growing up in functional and healthy homes?

17. What are some things, if any, that government should do to strengthen dysfunctional families and, hence, cut down on some of the root causes of delinquency?

18. Discuss the legal terminology used in adult court and how these terms differ from expressions used in juvenile court.
19. What are some of the advantages in using informality rather than formality in conducting juvenile court? What are some examples of this informality?
20. Who were the child savers? Are there any modern versions of them in today's society? Have you ever known any teachers or other adults you would describe as a modern-day "child saver" of sorts? Which celebrities, if any, would you tend to label as "child-harmers?"
21. Many programs have been set up to keep juveniles out of detention facilities. These include youth ranches, wilderness experiences, and boot camps. Are these programs beneficial, harmful, or a waste of time? Would you be willing to work in any of these types of programs? As a child offender, would you prefer one of these programs over the others?

*****

Key Terms: child savers, parens patriae, social investigation, intake worker, petition, admission, adjudicatory hearing, detention hearing, detained, rehabilitation focus, waiver, medical model, interested adult, disposition hearing, status offenses, placement, secure facility, regular probation, intensive probation, youth ranch, wilderness experience, training school, state-raised youth, child abuse, child neglect, youth gangs, sealed record, aging out of crimes, diversion

Additional Concepts: relative status of juvenile vs. adult court, secretive nature of juvenile court, role of defense attorney, role of prosecutor, role of judge, interaction of juvenile courthouse actors, plea bargaining in juvenile court, historical legal abuses, modern due process rights, famous constitutional cases, informal atmosphere of juvenile court, unique legal vocabulary of juvenile court, age cut-off points for juvenile court jurisdiction, extent of delinquency, future of juvenile court

CHAPTER THREE

JUSTICE DELAYED

Delayed justice may be watered-down justice but courthouse delay seems as inevitable in 21st Century America as death and taxes. Two courthouse regulars who owe their professional existence to court delay are the court administrator and the bail bondsman. The former has the never-ending task of reducing delay; the latter earns a living by easing delay's harmful effects. Their stories follow.

The Court Administrator: Life in the Slow Lane

Tim Moss regretted the day he ever left his relatively cushy job as an adult probation officer to accept the awful job as executive administrator in the local district attorney's office. When he read the announcement of the opening on the courthouse bulletin board, he thought it would be a step up for him: more money and more prestige. After all, the announcement said that a law degree was preferred (though not required). Moss did not have a law degree, but he thought that given the high educational preference associated with the position, there must be a fair amount of prestige and money attached to it. Moss was right. The money represented a ten thousand dollar raise for him. And his name was to become well-known to judges and lawyers alike. But what Moss did not adequately appreciate was the gut-wrenching stress associated with what was to be his new position.

Moss's predecessor was so stressed out by the job that she found herself unable to get pregnant. Her fertility doctor told her she had to quit. (Four weeks after leaving the position she became an expectant mother.) What was so bad about this job that it caused Moss's predecessor health problems and drove Moss himself to take up his old smoking habit two weeks into the job? The answer lay in the principle duty of the position: scheduling cases for court.

Air traffic controllers are said to have high-stress jobs, especially at busy airports. They must see that endless numbers of airplanes take off and land safely. Much is riding on their shoulders. In addition to safety, they have to deal with frustrated pilots who become angry if placed in line for too long.

Criminal courthouses are much like busy airports, only much busier. Somebody has to schedule cases for court. This person can be a judge scheduling his or her own caseload, a professional **court administrator** (a person trained to manage busy courthouse dockets), or (as in the case with Tim Moss) a member of the district attorney's office.[1] Each person has distinct disadvantages.

Judges who schedule their own cases for court often lack expertise and interest in caseload management. They also have a conflict of interest in that the more efficient they are at scheduling and processing cases, the more replacement cases they often wind up having assigned to them by the presiding judge.

Court Administrators are probably the best at managing courthouse dockets. They often have master's degrees in public administration or similar degrees and can focus their full attention to docket management. One disadvantage is that they are not in the trenches like judges and lawyers and may be out of the loop at times when it comes to understanding what is taking place in courts.

Perhaps the worse system for case scheduling is making use of a member of the prosecutor's office to take care of the chore. People who work for the prosecutor are down in the trenches and have a good feel for what is going on in their criminal courts. They receive constant feedback from prosecutors whose office area they share. However, like judges they have a conflict of interest: the person who gets to decide when and before which judge a case will wind up is working for the very office that is prosecuting the accused. Nevertheless, many courthouses around the country allow prosecutors or members of their offices to make such decisions under the theory that the prosecutor knows best when a case is ready to proceed.

The Right to a Speedy Trial

One thing that Tim Moss had to constantly worry about was the **Sixth Amendment** to the Constitution. This provides that a criminal defendant not only has the right to a trial but to a "speedy" trial.[2] When one is charged with

---

1. Luskin, Mary. (1987). "Social Loafing on the Bench: The Case of Calendars and Caseloads." *Justice System Journal* 12:177–195.

2. The Sixth Amendment provides that "in all criminal prosecutions, the accused shall enjoy the right to a speedy and public trial." U.S. Constitution, amendment VI.

processing thousands of cases per year, guaranteeing that every defendant receives his or her right to swift disposition of a case is nearly impossible. Yet, failure to achieve such a goal can be catastrophic. After beating around the bush for decades, the U.S. Supreme Court finally ruled that the remedy for being denied speed in the processing of one's criminal case is complete and final dismissal of that case. No watered-down remedy (e.g., reduction in sentence) would be allowed to substitute for the dismissal.[3]

Fortunately for Tim Moss, appellate courts have given a lot of leeway when it comes to defining "speedy." Though lay people (and constitution drafters) might think of "speedy" in terms of weeks or perhaps a couple of months or so, modern jurists refuse to put a number on it. They believe that what is speedy or slow depends on many factors, including such squishy things as length of the delay, reasons for it, harm to the defendant by it, and whether the defendant has made any complaints about it (though the latter is not strictly necessary).[4]

People like Tim Moss for awhile could take comfort in the breathing room given by such vague appellate court guidance. However, they now have to worry about pesky legislators who in more and more states have passed **speedy trial statutes**. Under such statutes, cases are mandated to be processed within so many months, despite the traditional willingness of appellate courts to be less time-sensitive.

Congress helped to get the ball rolling by passing the **Federal Speedy Trial Act**, which requires that defendants charged with federal crimes be indicted within thirty days of arrest and brought to trial within another seventy days thereafter. (Cases can sometimes exceed these deadlines if a judge determines the case to be unusually complex or if the "ends of justice" otherwise demands an extension. Also, the clock stops running whenever the defense—rather than the prosecution—causes or requests the delay.)[5]

Since the passage of the first version of the Federal Speedy Trial Act in 1974, many states have followed suit by passing similar speedy trial statutes for crimes tried in their state courts. Before the state legislature in Moss's state passed its own speedy trial statute in the 1980s, cases often took twelve, sixteen, or even eighteen months to come to trial. Now, the speedy trial statute required that criminal cases in Moss's state come to trial within six months of arrest if the defendant was waiting for trial in jail and within twelve months if the person was out on bail.

---

3. *Strunk v. United States,* 412 U.S. 434 (1973).

4. *Barker v. Wingo,* 407 U.S. 514, 531 (1972).

5. *Speedy Trial Act,* 18 U.S.C. sections 3161–3174 (2000).

Even though Moss's state statute was much more generous time-wise than its federal counterpart, Moss hated it because of the stress it caused him. Getting cases tried on time meant obsessively tracking every hearing, motion, and pre-trial ruling so as not to forget where a case stood at any one particular moment. It also meant predicting which cases would go to trial rather than be plea bargained so that precious court time could be rationed for those time-consuming cases.

One day, a month or so after he started work, Moss found to his horror that his predecessor had, through mismanagement, allowed over six hundred criminal cases involving bailed defendants to surpass the twelve month outer limit imposed by their state's speedy trial statute! This meant that all of these cases would eventually be dismissed by judges merely at defense attorney request. Most of these involved minor crimes but there were a few felonies as well. They were all assigned to overwhelmed public defenders whose "just in time" style of lawyering had contributed to the non-discovery of the mistake—less busy private lawyers would have spotted the fatal error long before the prosecutor called the case for court and have already asked for a dismissal.

Moss worried about the potential public relations disaster for his new office should the press ever find out about this situation. Moss came up with a bold solution borne of desperation. He told each assistant district attorney that he would "slip" these stale cases into the court docket for processing—a few each month per judge until all were taken care of. When the stale case came up for court, the prosecutor was instructed to casually **nolle prosequi** the case (inform the court that the prosecutor was declining prosecution in the interests of justice) just like they do every month for legitimate reasons. By doing this over time, it was hoped that judges would grant the nolle prosequi requests without inquiring into any specifics (as was common practice).

Amazingly, the strategy worked. The judges liked it when prosecutors declined prosecution and did not ask many questions, especially since nearly every case was relatively minor. Once in a while when pressed, a prosecutor would state that the reason for the nolle prosequi was that a case's speedy trial deadline had passed. This was revealed so infrequently though that judges never caught on to any pattern.

The Human Desire for Delay

Moss felt very guilty for having to cover up for the office because of what his predecessor had done. He was determined that no case would be dismissed pursuant to a speedy trial statute due to his own mistakes in office. Towards this end Moss painstakingly kept a log of each case assigned to each prosecutor and developed a computer system which would consistently "red flag" cases approaching an automatic dismissal deadline. (He also instructed prosecutors to keep track of their own caseloads but knew he could not entirely rely upon them—that is what his predecessor had done unsuccessfully.) Moss felt confident that his obsessive-compulsiveness in tracking cases would prevent future dismissals based on forgotten files. But tracking files and their "drop dead" dates alone was not enough to get a case processed. Moss learned that there was a human dimension to delay that had to be dealt with.

The conventional wisdom about case delay is that it is caused by too much volume and too few resources.[6] But Moss noticed an even more significant cause. All of the important actors in the courtroom seemed to like delays. Victims, of course, did not like them. However, the opposite was true of defense attorneys, prosecutors, and judges. Defense attorneys liked delay in the hopes that prosecution witnesses might forget or move away, that victims might become less angry with the passage of time and agree to better plea bargains, and that they might have more time to collect fees owed them. Prosecutors liked delay in order to postpone weak cases that they did not want to have to deal with. They also liked delay when a defendant sat in jail unable to make bail since the delay might soften the accused up to an eventual "time served" guilty plea. Judges liked delay in the hopes that a yet-unresolved case might in the interim be resolved by a plea bargain instead of a time-consuming trial.

In order to get a postponement for a case docketed for trial, either the defense attorney or the prosecutor had to ask the judge for a **continuance**. Judges are very prone to grant such requests, especially if opposing counsel does not object. Prosecutors might ask for a continuance in order to have more time to prepare for trial or in order to locate a missing witness. Defense attorneys often ask for continuances for similar reasons. Both defense lawyers and prosecutors sometimes ask for continuances due to conflicts with their schedules (they cannot be in two courtrooms at once).

Prosecutors have to be careful in requesting continuances since such continuances might run up against dates imposed by a speedy trial statute. On the other hand, a defense continuance will always **stop the clock** for the duration of the postponement. For this reason, cases that drag on for long periods are almost always being delayed at the request of defense counsel.

---

6. Flemming, Roy, Peter Nardulli, and James Eisenstein. (1987). "The Timing of Justice in Felony Trial Courts." *Law and Policy* 9:179–206.

Moss learned that an unspoken code existed among lawyers in his court-house in which opposing counsel were expected to refrain from objecting to "reasonable" requests for continuances. After all, an objector will inevitably need a continuance soon in one of his or her other cases. (A lawyer who objects to the other side's continuances might find herself unable to attend her daughter's college graduation when she needs a continuance.) In Moss's court-house, such a tradition of relatively unopposed continuances was so entrenched that defense attorneys often asked for and were granted **Rule One Continuances** (code for "I need a continuance because I have not been paid yet"). In return for such professional courtesy, prosecutors needing a continuance for personal reasons (vacation, etc.) would expect defense attorneys, when asked, to put the continuance on the defense so as to stop the clock. Defense attorneys owing favors would usually comply.

Harms of Delay

As a member of the prosecutor's office, Moss sometimes worried about how continuances and other delays hurt the victims his office was there to help. He would sometimes get a call from a victim asking when he or she would ever be able to achieve closure. Moss came to realize that from a victim's perspective, the only complete justice was swift justice.

Society also was harmed by slow justice. People out on bail were free to commit new crimes. People in jail waiting for trial used scarce local jail space rather than being transferred to larger, better-equipped state prisons. Most frustrating of all, cases sometimes had to be dismissed because key prosecution witnesses moved out of the area, simply disappeared, or forgot critical details of the case before it was called to court.

What did not concern Moss (but should concern him) was the harm done to defendants by delay. In addition to having been handicapped in preparing a defense, someone sitting in jail lucky enough to be eventually acquitted was released without even so much as an apology. Defendants on bail had to put their futures on hold. Some no doubt worried incessantly about their cases and what their eventual fates might be. Would they be acquitted, given probation, or incarcerated? Should they start school, get married, avoid pregnancy, look for a better job? Defendants, like victims, need closure. Waiting can be much more taxing than the eventual sentence.

Moss realized that justice delayed is indeed justice denied. He just did not know what he could do about it. Spending more money to hire more judges, prosecutors, and public defenders would help. De-criminalizing some offenses that contribute greatly to the backlog (drugs for example) would help as well.

But, society seems unwilling to do either. Instead, the system grinds on year after year in its slow paces.

The Sixth Amendment right to a speedy trial has a lot in common with the Fourth Amendment. For a long time, the Fourth Amendment prohibition against unreasonable searches and seizures was merely a form of words that was not actually enforced by the courts. *Mapp v. Ohio* put real teeth into it for the first time in state courts by requiring that evidence obtained pursuant to illegal searches or seizures be suppressed.[7] But it took all the way from the drafting of the Constitution until 1961 for the promise of the Fourth Amendment to be put into effect in state courts. Has the Sixth Amendment promise of speedy trials yet to be achieved by the states? It seems highly unlikely that what most people would consider "speedy" is taking place with regards to the processing of criminal cases. Moss knew enough to know that illegally obtained evidence would often cause a case to be dismissed. He figured it would probably be left to a future generation to salvage the Sixth Amendment the way an earlier one did the Fourth.

Scheduling Trials

Even when Moss was not pulling out his hair due to the constant ebb and flow of endless continuances, he still had to face the Herculean task of actually finding enough trial slots for all the cases heading for trial. In order to do this, he invented what came to be known as the "war board."

Assistant District Attorneys first saw the war board when they reported to work on a Monday a few weeks after Moss had started with the office. This was the first day of what would be two weeks of criminal court being in session. (In Moss's courthouse only two weeks per month were devoted to the processing of criminal cases. The other two weeks were reserved for civil court and other matters.)

The war board was a huge chalk board with the name of each judge available to hear trials that day arranged in individual columns followed by the trial-bound cases Moss wanted tried before that particular judge that day. Of course, most cases in the office were not trial-bound but were destined for guilty pleas, since plea bargains had been offered by prosecutors and accepted by defense counsel. All such cases were assigned by Moss on his war board to "guilty plea court" where one judge and one prosecutor would do nothing but process guilty pleas all day. (Moss knew which cases were trial-bound or not

---

7. *Mapp v. Ohio,* 367 U.S. 643 (1961).

trial-bound based on last week's interview of each prosecutor about his/her caseload.)

Prosecutors were expected to start the trial of all cases listed on the war board that were not destined for "guilty plea court." Moss made it clear that any prosecution continuances or lack of objections to defense request for continuances would have to be cleared by him in advance.

For each trial-bound case he wanted disposed of, Moss listed the name of the prosecutor and the defense lawyers assigned to the case, as well as the judge who would preside at the trial. Moss realized that most of these cases that seemed headed for trial would wind up somehow being negotiated in a last minute plea bargain. To assure that judges and courtrooms slated for trials would not be wastefully idled, he would have back-ups, and back-ups to the back-ups, assigned to each judge ready to do trials. A replica of Moss's war board is reproduced in Figure 1.

When the assistant district attorneys saw Moss's war board upon reporting to work they also saw him pacing in front of it over and over again like a wolf eyeing a kill. The attorneys did not know what to think of this. Should they get mad at Moss, the non-lawyer, for trying to tell them what to do? Does the district attorney know what Moss is up to? They decided to get angry at Moss.

Just as the assistant district attorneys started to balk and contemptuously defy Moss, the district attorney walked up to Moss, put his arm around him, and announced that "When Tim Moss says 'jump' you are to ask 'how high?' Anybody who has a problem with that will have to deal with me!" The district attorney liked what Moss had done. He thought that the old system, which his assistants liked, was an undiscovered scandal. He hoped Moss's system would unclog the backlog that had built up under Moss's predecessor's tenure.

The district attorney's faith in Moss was validated by the end of the first two-week criminal court session. The number of cases that were continued to a future session dropped to a fraction of what had been the norm in past criminal court sessions. Office productivity soared. Judges stopped complaining about how their courtrooms sat empty while lawyers haggled all day over deals. Best of all, the district attorney could sense that Moss had a handle on not allowing any more cases to be dismissed due to the speedy trial statute. Moss and his computer knew when each case's speedy trial statute date would expire, and the older the case, the more priority it was given on the war board. Moss was an ill-tempered neurotic who would flare up at each prosecutor or defense attorney who he had heard asked for a non-legitimate continuance. The attorneys in the office came to think of Moss as their boss, which in a sense he now was.

Figure 1   Moss's War Board

Monday

Judge Davis: Courtroom #2—9:30 a.m. sharp

    Trial of Bill Zaug/ D.A.=Wilson; Defense Atty=Green

    Backup #1: Trial of James Mann/ D.A.=Mahan/ Defense Atty=O'Neil

    Backup #2: Trial of Carol Martin/ D.A.=Cheney/ Defense Atty=Burton

    Backup #3: Trial of Burt Innis/ D.A.=Gladstone/ Defense Atty=Shinner

[All Prosecutors and Defense Attys listed above must be ready for trial at 9:30. Backups will be telephoned if needed and must be on standby. Their case could go at any time. Let Tim Moss know where you are. Any back-ups that don't go today will go tomorrow. NO CONTINUANCES WITHOUT MOSS'S APPROVAL. Any last minute plea bargains are to be sent to Judge Cook's guilty plea court for processing immediately.]

Judge Ott (similar listing as above)

Judge Burns (similar listing as above)

Judge Belnap (similar listing as above)

Judge McKay (similar listing as above)

Judge Litman (similar listing as above)

Judge Cook: GUILTY PLEA COURT/Asst. D.A. Watkins

9:00 Guilty Pleas of:	Case 1121/ Public Defender	Case 0898/Atty. Lee
	Case 2212/Atty. King	Case 1787/Public Def.
	Case 1145/ Public Def.	Case 1654/Public Def.
	Case 2312/Public Def.	Case 1998/Public Def.
	Case 1108/ Atty. King	Case 1565/Atty. Tores
	Case 0098/ Public Def.	Case 1818/Public Def.
	Case 1888/Public Def.	Case 2072/Atty Knight
	Case 1934/ Atty. Knight	Case 1110/ Public Def.
	Case 1515/ Atty. Tores	Case 1833/Public Def.
	Case 1475/ Public Def.	Case 2221/Atty. Wood

10:00 [list of 20 defendants and their attorneys]

11:00 [list of 20 defendants and their attorneys]

12:00 LUNCH

1:00 [list of 20 defendants and their attorneys]

2:00 [list of 20 defendants and their attorneys]

3:00 [list of 20 defendants and their attorneys]

ANY DEFENDANTS ABOVE WHO REFUSE TO PLEA GUILTY TODAY WILL HAVE THEIR CASE ASSIGNED FOR TRIAL IN THE NEXT AVAILABLE COURTROOM

Moss's Pathologies

As Moss settled down in his job, confident that the district attorney was pleased with his ability to get cases processed on time, he became more and more powerful in the courthouse. Little by little, Moss started to take upon himself duties that could only be described as practicing law without a license. When prosecutors could not broker a deal with a defense attorney, Moss would personally contact the attorney and try to get him or her to see the light. He felt he could not allow a case to use up precious trial-time without at least trying his personal best to avoid it. Prosecutors could sometimes hear Moss and a defense attorney yelling at one another in his office a few days before each two-week criminal court session. When the defense attorney would question Moss's right to engage in plea bargaining, Moss would reply that even a lay person could see that their client's case was a dead bang loser and that he had reviewed enough files to know what the "going rates" were.

As time passed Moss became more and more bold, and what was once a hopeless docket backlog kept shrinking. One thing that Moss liked to do was offer what he called his "blue light specials." Moss got the idea of a "blue light special" from a discount department store he and his wife were patronizing one day when the store manager announce that "all shoes would be 30 percent off" but only while the imaginary blue light was on for the next twenty minutes. Moss observed with keen interest as his wife (who had come to the store to buy a shirt, not shoes) rushed to the shoe department to select some shoes before it was too late. Taking this idea to his job, Moss started calling defense attorneys during periods in which too many cases seemed stalemated and would tell them (sometimes without even the consent of the prosecutor assigned the case) that if they could get their client to come to court and enter a guilty plea within the next ninety minutes, the jail time previously negotiated would be cut by a full 30 percent. Like most other of Moss's "reforms," this worked like a charm in moving cases along.

One thing that defense attorneys really resented for awhile was the fact that Moss had power not only to decide when a case would be listed for court but also which judge it would be assigned in front of for trial. Moss saw nothing wrong with this but prosecutors would sometimes be embarrassed when they would be asked by Moss right in front of defense counsel, "which judge would you like to preside at the trial of such and such case?" Prosecutors enlightened Moss as to the potential constitutional problem of the prosecutor's getting to pick not only the time of a competition but the referee of the match as well. Moss learned to be more discreet—he soon started asking prosecutors about their judicial preferences outside the hearing of defense attorneys.

The darkest side to Moss came out when he started refusing to schedule defendants for court who never made bail but who eventually clearly qualified for a time-served sentence. Moss found out that prosecutors would often offer time-served plea bargains to defendants in relatively minor cases in exchange for their guilty pleas. Often, these defendants could get a time-served sentence even without a plea bargain merely by appearing before a judge and just admitting guilt. But a defendant did not appear before a judge until Moss scheduled the matter for court. Moss developed a policy of refusing to schedule such cases for court until either the statutory speedy-trial clock was about to expire or until the defendant would agree to enter a guilty plea. Defendants who refused to accept a time-served disposition because they wanted a trial that might exonerate them would be told that their case would not be called for court. Moss did not want to waste precious trials on such minor offenses but neither did he feel right about seeing the charges dropped. Instead, he would tell the defense attorney that if the client would accept a time-served guilty plea, the case would be immediately listed for court. But, if the client "arrogantly" insisted on having a trial he or she would have to wait in jail for a couple more months. Defense attorney's invented a name for this: "doing Moss time." Little did the local courthouse actors know that their jurisdiction was hardly alone in having a version of "Moss time." In South Carolina, for example, where county prosecutors—called "solicitors"—have the responsibility of scheduling criminal cases for court, the phenomenon is known as having to do "**solicitor's time.**" Defense lawyers there are upset with the practice but apparently are unwilling or unable to effectively challenge it. As one South Carolina public defender put it, "This guy's asking why he can't have a speedy trial … Even if he was the only person I had I can't make the solicitor call the case."[8]

Post-Script on Moss, Executive Administrator

When Moss was first hired by the district attorney he took a job that no lawyer was willing to take. He found gross inefficiency and through hardwork, courage, neuroticism, and even some questionable practices was able to "make the trains run on time." People like Moss, with the help of prosecutors, defense attorneys and judges who are willing to act more like professional plea bargainers than trial attorneys, are able to keep the system afloat. Whether

---

8. See, Lynch, David R. (1998). "In Their Own Words: Occupational Stress Among Public Defenders." *Criminal Law Bulletin* 34(6):473–496 (at 483–484).

the Sixth Amendment promise of a speedy trial is actually being fulfilled is another question. Even with speedy trial statutes, most defendants wait months for their day in court only in the end to be tempted or counseled vigorously to plea guilty.

Bail: Solution to Delay or Modern Form of Ransom?

One of the most serious risks of delayed justice is the chance that potentially innocent people might lose their freedom while waiting for a chance to exonerate themselves in court. The drafters of the Constitution worried enough about this to not only require that trials be speedily offered but to back up this safeguard by providing for a right to bail prior to trial. The **Eighth Amendment** to the Constitution, reflecting old English law dating back many centuries,[9] states that "excessive bail shall not be required."[10] The wording of the Eighth Amendment is completely ambiguous regarding one critical point: do dangerous criminals have to be released on bail if they are likely to appear for trial? If people are extremely dangerous, do they even have the right to bail in any amount?

For a long time nobody knew the answer to this question. Many magistrates who simply wanted to protect society from dangerous people often would justify setting extremely high bail by exaggerating their concerns about risk of flight. Then finally, in 1984, the U.S. Supreme Court ruled that magistrates could stop pretending: the Eighth Amendment does not mean that everyone who is likely to come back for court is entitled to bail. Rather, when bail is appropriate it should not be any higher than is necessary to prevent the perceived risk of flight. But bail is not always appropriate. If a person is extremely dangerous, bail need not be set at all. This is deemed constitutional since the purpose in denying dangerous people bail is something other than punishment.[11]

In ordinary cases involving non-dangerous people, the setting of bail is critical because of the terrible harms one can suffer while waiting in jail before one is convicted of anything. A person could lose a job and even a career. A college student could miss all of his or her classes. Jail can cause one to become socially stigmatized. Jail to some can present a frightening, violence-prone atmosphere. Being incarcerated prior to trial severely handicaps one in

---

9. Goldfarb, Ronald L. (1965). *Ransom: A Critique of the American Bail System.* New York: Harper & Row.

10. U.S. Constitution, amendment VIII.

11. *Schall v. Martin*, 467 U.S. 253 (1984). See also, *U.S. v. Salerno*, 481 U.S. 739 (1987).

preparing a defense. A defendant's family can suffer as well while he or she is in jail.

Capitalism is creative. An entrepreneur has emerged which the system can now rely upon to help solve the problem of too much pre-trial detention. This person is known as the bail bondsman.

The Bail Bondsman

Bob Wright, Juris Doctor, was owner of "Bob's Bail Bonds." Bob had a J.D. but could not practice law: he failed the state bar exam four times before finally giving up. For awhile he worked as a mortgage loan officer in a local branch of a big bank. But if he could not be a lawyer, Bob decided he would rather be a **bail bondsman** than a bank bureaucrat: being a bail bondsman at least had some pizzazz to it. Furthermore, it was a law-related occupation that made him feel like his legal education was not going to complete waste. Best of all, he was making money—his annual income was twice what many of his local criminal lawyer friends were making.

The only hard part was getting started. The licensing process was a nightmare (more in terms of paperwork than anything else). But Bob could handle paperwork (he chased paper for three years of law school). What really was difficult was begging his parents to help him financially. Feeling sorry for him, they loaned the money needed to seed his new venture.

Bob obtained most of his clients through word of mouth. He was on good terms with many local police officers, defense attorneys, jail guards and magistrates who would often mention his name to potential clients. Bob made sure to befriend his benefactors whenever he could. In the case of defense attorneys, he had his list of buddies owed referral favors whom he would recommend to his own clients. Bob also took out a big advertisement in the yellow pages. His advertisement noted his service was "fast, confidential, and available seven days a week, twenty-four hours a day." In addition to mentioning that someone in the office spoke Spanish, the advertisement promised a free "Jail Sucks" t-shirt to anyone who used his service.

Bob's interest in bail bonding was primarily mercenary. However, Bob also was unwittingly helping to ensure that the innocent (everyone is innocent until convicted) are not punished without first being given their due process. Bob in a sense was acting as a government sub-contractor whose job was to do the flight risk analysis that courts are too busy to do themselves. If someone represented a huge flight risk, Bob would have little interest in bailing the person out. If the flight risk was small, Bob would more likely take a chance on the person. Without Bob, many people would unnecessarily languish in jail waiting for trial. In fact, studies show that most people who remain in jail do so not because they are unlikely to appear for court (or even because they are dangerous) but rather because they are simply too poor to post the full bond.[12]

Factors in Setting Bail and Types of Bail

When a person is arrested, he or she is promptly taken before a judge or magistrate (low-level judicial officer) for a brief encounter known as the **first appearance** (sometimes called a preliminary arraignment or magistrate's review). Local rules vary as to how soon such an appearance must occur but the U.S. Supreme Court has ruled that in order to be "prompt," the judicial encounter must occur at least within 48 hours.[13] At this initial appearance, the judicial officer advises the defendant as to why he or she was arrested, how the defendant may apply for a free lawyer if the defendant so desires, and how much bail must be posted in order to be released pending further court proceedings.

From the point of view of frightened people just arrested, the setting of the bail amount is of extreme importance. Getting released is of utmost concern and occupies all of their thoughts. For relatively minor crimes, magistrates in many jurisdictions simply set bail according to a **bail schedule** (a standardized guideline used throughout their jurisdiction). But for more serious crimes or otherwise non-routine cases, setting bail requires use of discretion. In exercising such discretion, magistrates often consider both legal factors and extralegal factors.

Basically there are just two broad **legal factors in setting bail** that courts may properly use. These are a defendant's **risk of flight** and his or her **danger to the community**.[14]

In considering risk of flight, courts may legally take into account such things as seriousness of the current offense, prior record, the strength of evidence against the defendant, and the defendant's community ties (length of residence in the jurisdiction, employment history, family ties, fact of home ownership, whether the defendant has shown up in the past for court dates, etc.).[15] In considering dangerousness to the community, courts may consider

---

12. Patterson, E. Britt and Michael J. Lynch. (1991). "Biases in Formalized Bail Procedures." In Michael J. Lynch and E. Britt Patterson (eds.), *Race and Criminal Justice*. New York: Harrow and Heston.

13. *McNabb v. United States*, 318 U.S. 332 (1943).

14. *United States v. Ramirez*, 843 F.2nd 256, 257 (7th Cir. 1988).

15. *United States v. Torres*, 929 F.2d. 291, 292 (7th Cir. 1991).

the likelihood that the defendant, if released, might commit certain designated offenses considered especially dangerous to the community, including such things as rape, assault, and even economic harms.[16]

In addition to the legal factors mentioned above, magistrates sometimes use **extralegal factors in setting bail** (criteria that they should not properly use but do anyway). For example, an outraged magistrate may post bail higher than it should be in order to start punishing the defendant in advance of a determination of guilt. A magistrate may raise or lower bail in an arbitrary manner according to the amount of space available in the local jail: the more space the higher the bail. A magistrate might improperly set high bail to help "soften up" a defendant for an eventual time-served guilty plea. Finally, a magistrate might allow himself or herself to be influenced by such irrelevant criteria as race (magistrates tend to give lower bail to whites than to minorities—all other things equal) and gender (magistrates tend to give lower bail to women than to men—all other things equal).[17]

In doing his flight risk analysis, Bob Wright the private bail bondsman used the same criteria that courts are supposed to use themselves in determining the amount of bail. Bob was better at it though since, unlike the magistrates, he actually had the time to check out the truthfulness of what defendants would tell him. Bob had the time to make phone calls to confirm that a defendant's community ties really existed. He could call an employer to confirm employment or verify in the courthouse deeds office that a defendant owned a home like he or she claimed.

At one time bail was not just the posting of hostage money but involved an actual hostage. For example, if I wanted to post bail for my cousin, I would have to post myself as the surety. In the event my cousin did not show up for court, the court would seize me and do to me whatever punishment would have befallen my cousin (including execution)!

Bail today has exchanged hostage money for human hostages. Nevertheless, it arguably remains a primitive way of providing for pre-trial release. As crass as the use of private bail bondsmen like Bob Wright might seem to some, the use of private bail bondsmen in some way helps assure that extralegal factors will not be used in deciding who gets pre-trial release and who does not. People like Bob typically only care about one thing in determining whether to post surety for someone: will this person show up for court as ordered? If Bob

---

16. *United States v. Himler,* 797 F.2d 156, 160 (3rd Cir. 1986); *United States v. Reynolds,* 956 F.2d 192 (9th Cir. 1992).

17. Patterson and Lynch, supra note 12.

is convinced that the defendant will appear for court, he will post the surety and the defendant will be freed. Unlike judicial officers, Bob as a businessman really does not care about anything else. Though Bob does not really care about a defendant's danger to the community like a magistrate would, neither does Bob care about many of the extralegal factors that magistrates often improperly consider.

Private bail bondsmen work purely on a cash basis. But, people who wish to post bail have several ways of doing so: they can post **100 percent cash bail** with the court. But cash (or even credit cards as more and more jurisdictions are now accepting) is usually not much of an option to many defendants charged with serious felonies requiring the posting of huge amounts of surety. Another alternative is to post **property bail**, usually in the form of real estate. Under this option, the defendant or a relative pays to have the property's value attested to by a certified assessor. In the case of real estate, a lien is then placed on the property by the court which will not be removed until the defendant shows up for court. Yet another option (quite common) is for the magistrate to allow **R.O.R. bail (release on recognizance)** in which the defendant's promise to return is the bail (his word is his bond). Finally, defendants can seek out a **bail bondsman** like Bob who will post the full amount of the bail for them in return for a **10 to 15 percent fee**, which they will keep as their profit even if the defendant shows up for court (if the defendant jumps bail the bail bondsman loses the full amount he or she has posted).

Bounty Hunters

Bail bondsmen hate it when someone jumps bail. Usually it is easiest to just write the loss off as an on-going business expense. However, when a bail bondsman is out a lot of money, he or she has the option of hiring a bounty hunter to bring the **absconder** back.

Bounty Hunters work for bail bondsmen and are paid a percentage of the forfeited bail if they are able to produce the defendant for court. If the defendant is brought to the authorities, the forfeited bail will be returned to the bail bondsman who posted it. Bounty hunters do not always like to be referred to as such. Many prefer other terms such as **bail enforcement agent**, which they believe more accurately reflects their law enforcement function.

Bounty hunters can often make a lot of money for a little work. Oftentimes, people who fail to show up for court have not fled the jurisdiction but are very close by. A few simple inquiries can often help determine their current location (amazingly, they often are at the very address they provided the court when bailed out—they simply were too lazy to come to court).[18]

When a person initially fails to appear for court, the judge issues a **bench warrant** for his or her arrest. This warrant does not necessarily produce any results. Police may or may not go out looking for the absconder. Sometimes, law enforcement officials do nothing more than enter the warrant into the computer network and hope that some day the absconder will be pulled over for a traffic violation and arrested for jumping bail. But private bail bondsman have the option of going after absconding clients themselves or (much more likely) hiring a bounty hunter to do the work for them.

Unlike police officers and other public officials, private bounty hunters are given extraordinary powers in returning bail jumpers to court. Since they are not government officials or government agents, the constitution does not apply to them. Hence, bounty hunters do not have to concern themselves with such things as search warrants, arrest warrants, or formal extradition procedures.[19] This incredible state of the law dates back a long time. In most states little has changed since the United States Supreme Court noted in the 1872 case of *Taylor v. Taintor*[20] that:

> Whenever they [bounty hunters] choose to do so, they may seize him and deliver him up in their discharge; and if that cannot be done at once, they may imprison him until it can be done ... They may pursue him into another State; may arrest him ... and if necessary, may break and enter his house for that purpose ... The bail have their principal on a string, and may pull the string whenever they please, and render him in their discharge.[21]

Since the Fourth Amendment prohibition against unreasonable searches does not apply to them, bounty hunters sometimes even force their way into homes belonging to people other than the absconder in their apprehension efforts. When Arizona passed a law (the only state yet to do so) forbidding

---

18. Lynch, David R. (2001). Interview with a licensed Utah Bail Enforcement Agent—Nov. 2001.

19. See, Drimmer, Jonathan. (1997). "America's Least Wanted: We Need New Rules to Stop Abuses." *Washington Post, September 21, 1997,* at C6(in which the author notes that constitutional restrictions governing the actions of public law enforcement officials do not generally apply to private bounty hunters since the constitution is designed to protect us from government actors not private ones).

20. *Taylor v. Taintor,* 83 U.S. 366 (1872).

21. Id. at 371–72.

bounty hunters from entering homes without permission,[22] bounty hunters in that state complained that Arizona legislators were helping fugitives because now "they'll be hiding out at Mom's house and not answering the door."[23]

Some enterprising student might wonder how he or she could become a bounty hunter. Unless one resides in a couple of states, it does not take very much effort. Nevada and Utah are the most demanding. Nevada requires those wishing to become bounty hunters to first complete eighty hours of training. Utah requires 1,000 hours of prior work either as a law enforcement officer or as an "apprentice" to a bounty hunter before the state will grant a license. But most states only require that new bounty hunters seeking licenses have no prior felony or violent records and a licensed bail bondsman willing to supervise them.[24]

Post-Script on Bail Bondsmen and Bounty Hunters

One might wonder what future generations will think of our era with its continued reliance on hostage money and private bounty hunters to help ensure someone's appearance at trial. Perhaps someday these rather primitive practices will come to an end. In the meantime, some slow progress has been made. A few states are beginning to require at least some rudimentary training for bounty hunters. As for bail bondsmen, some jurisdictions have been trying to put them out of business entirely. For example, some counties in Pennsylvania have created a **government bail agency** in which county-paid agents interview pre-trial detainees and decide whether or not they should qualify for 10 percent bail. Unlike local magistrates, these agents have the time to carefully interview each applicant and verify what they have been told. If an applicant is a good risk, they are granted 10 percent bail by the government bail agent. If the applicant does not abscond, most of the 10 percent posted is returned to the defendant (only a small fee is held back). Thus, the defendant has more of an incentive to return to court than is the case with private bail bonding in which the defendant loses the ten percent even if he or she shows up for court. Counties that have implemented such programs have ef-

---

22. Merry, Ann L. (1999). "Comment: S.B. 1257: Arizona Regulates Bounty Hunters." *Arizona State Law Journal* 31: 229–257, footnote 53.

23. Id., citing McCloy, Mike. (1998). "Bounty Hunter Bill Advances: Kin of slain Pair Testify to Panel." *Arizona Republic, February 26, 1998*, at B1.

24. Id. at 240. See also article's Appendix for a state by state summary of licensing requirements for bounty hunters.

fectively driven private bail bondsmen (with their arguably exorbitant fees) out of business.[25]

Perhaps someday American taxpayers will be able to afford (or cease refusing to afford) a system in which speedy trials actually occur. In that event, those who are unable to make bail will at least have their pre-conviction detention greatly shortened. Perhaps police officers will take it upon themselves to more actively pursue absconders rather than relying upon the private sector to do so. Private enterprise is a great thing but when it comes to the criminal justice system, some things are perhaps better left to public officials.

*****

Questions for Class Discussion

1. Sometimes a "speedy" trial apparently can mean many months, or even up until a year, of waiting. Is this what the Founders would have tolerated? What would be their definition (time-wise) of "speedy?" What would be your definition (time-wise) of "speedy?" Does your definition of speedy depend on certain factors? Should the notion of what is "speedy" change depending upon whether or not the person can post bail?
2. In practice, is there really a right to a speedy trial in the U.S.A.? Or, is this aspect of the Sixth Amendment currently a promise not being fulfilled? What would it take to fulfill it?
3. Would you favor the legalization of certain practices now made criminal (e.g., possession of illegal drugs for personal use) if that is what it took to give a speedy trial to all people charged with crimes?
4. What are some of the causes of all of the court delay that is going on?
5. What are some of the specific harms done to defendants when speedy trials are not given? What about harm to victims caused by slow justice? Harms to society as a whole?
6. Why do certain judges, defense attorneys, and prosecutors seem to actually like court delay?
7. What do you think of a "Rule One" continuance mentioned in the book? If you were a judge, and a defense attorney asked for one, would you probably play along? Why or why not?

---

25. Information known to author who practiced as a public defender in a Pennsylvania county making use of a government bail agency.

8. What is meant by doing "solicitor's time?" What would the drafters of the 6th Amendment think of it? What do you think of it? Why don't judges put an end to it? Why doesn't the public seem to know about such practices? Would the public care if it did know?

9. What are some of the things that make the person who schedules cases for court have a stressful job?

10. What sort of personality characteristics would be needed to make someone a good court administrator? A poor one?

11. What sort of degree or training or background should we expect of people who want to become a court administrator? Should a law degree be required?

12. Why do you suppose the drafters of the Constitution provided for the right to bail in most cases? Would you be ok with eliminating the right to bail? Does bail unfairly advantage people of means over the destitute?

13. What are some of the harms done to people who cannot post bail, even though they are later acquitted of all charges?

14. Should "ability to pay" be something a judge considers in setting the bail amount? What other factors should judges consider in deciding the appropriate amount for bail?

15. What are some examples of "ties to the community" that are considered in the bail decision? Do you have sufficient community ties to justify a very low bail in most cases? If you are single and don't have a good job yet or own a home, should these facts be used against you in setting higher bail?

16. Suppose you were charged with a serious crime and made bail. Suppose further that you were sure you would be convicted if you show up for court. Would you consider jumping bail and living your life as a fugitive if you were looking at two years in prison? Ten years in prison? Twenty years? Life? What would you do to start a new life on the run?

17. What are some "extralegal" factors judges use sometimes in setting bail?

18. Should "danger to the community" be a legal factor for judges to consider in setting or denying bail? Or, should judges be limited to ascertaining the likelihood of returning for court and nothing else? How accurately can judges predict someone's future dangerousness? How might unfair prejudice play a roll in predicting future dangerousness?

19. Are bail bondsmen a good thing or a bad thing for our society? Are they necessary? Do they provide an honest service or do they take too much advantage of people in a jam?

20. Is bounty hunting a noble profession? Should we ban them and leave their functions to publicly paid people like the police? Are bounty hunters afforded too much power?

21. Would any of you consider a career as a bail bondsman? As a bounty
hunter?

*****

Key Terms: court administrator, Sixth Amendment, speedy trial statutes,
Federal Speedy Trial Act, nolle prosequi, continuance, stop the clock, Rule
One Continuances, solicitor's time, Eighth Amendment, bail bondsman, first
appearance, bail schedule, legal factors in setting bail, risk of flight, danger to
the community, extralegal factors in setting bail, 100 percent cash bail, property bail, R.O.R. bail, bail bondsman, 10 to 15 percent fee, absconder, bounty
hunters, bail enforcement agent, bench warrant, government bail agency

Additional Concepts: congested courthouse, who should schedule cases,
caseload mismanagement, human desire for delay, harms of delay, war board,
blue light specials, prosecutor input into trial judge selection, denial of bail,
powers and training of bounty hunters

CHAPTER FOUR

THE CRIMINAL DEFENSE ATTORNEY

After four long years with the Lincoln County Public Defender's Office, Jill Lane realized that it was time to leave. She was sick and tired of her clients, the judges, her boss, her colleagues, her over-stuffed filing cabinet, and anything and everyone connected with public defending. Her desire to leave had been building up for some time. But she absolutely knew she had stayed too long when, to her horror, she read in the newspaper her description of her job given during an interview with a local crime-beat reporter:

Reporter: "What is it really like being a public defender? Is it intrinsically rewarding?"

Jill Lane: "Intrinsically rewarding? Let's see. I've been blamed for families breaking up. I've been blamed for people in jail, for people losing their liberties. Most of the people you represent, based on their socioeconomic status or whatever, have never taken any responsibility for anything in their life, including their constant criminal wrongdoings. So what happens is that you become the focal point of blame. I have to walk them through the system and it's not my fault that they got into the damn system!"

Jill Lane's face turned bright red as she read what she had said to the reporter for all to read. What really scared her was that the bitterness expressed in her comments was not fleeting. It had become a part of her. Not liking what she had become, she decided she had to leave the only legal job she had ever known.

Jill wanted to try to figure out how she had become so burned out. She had originally become a public defender with the best of intentions: to defend the poor and downtrodden. Now she had learned to hate the poor and the downtrodden and think of them as creepy, self-absorbed losers.

Despite the embarrassment Jill had brought to the office by her public diatribe, Jill's boss did not want her to quit. She had always been able to outwork anyone else in the office, and he was not sure that his bright, office warhorse was replaceable. He told her to take two weeks of paid vacation and if she still insisted upon leaving, he would understand. Jill took him up on the offer and flew down to her parent's retirement home in coastal Florida to spend time walking the beaches and thinking.

After resting for a couple of days, task-oriented Jill decided to sketch out all of the things she hated about her job. She did this for the therapeutic value it might have but also as a rational way to analyze what, if anything, she could do to make her job more tolerable. Since graduating from law school Jill had never done anything but public defending. She was not even sure how to go about looking for any other kind of a legal job (except maybe one prosecuting). "Maybe if I identify what is wrong with public defending, I can mitigate the hardships and still keep my job," Jill reasoned to herself.

Jill's mother counseled her to start her review by first focusing on the positives of her job and afterwards on the negatives. Jill was able to come up with several things that she liked about her job and several important things that potentially could bother her but did not.

Role of the Defense Attorney

One thing that Jill liked was the official role of the criminal defense lawyer. Jill was and always had been in love with that role as taught to her in law school. She had been taught that the **role of the criminal defender** is to protect the constitution by forcing the state to prove its case against a citizen beyond a reasonable doubt. An attorney best protects the constitution by zealously representing the interests of the client. The job of the defense attorney is to be a cog in the well-oiled machinery of the state as it seeks to take away an individual's liberty, property, or life. According to what she had been taught, a person may be **factually guilty** but is not **legally guilty** unless the government can prove its case. Her job was to put the government to its very high burden of proof.

Jill had been privately indoctrinated by her criminal law professor that a public defender is the ultimate criminal attorney. He had told her that "private criminal defense attorneys were merely in it for the money and prosecutors were merely a bunch of Joe Six Packs with law diplomas." Jill thought that her professor was a bit snobbish but being a devout liberal herself found his prejudices rather charming. (This elitist attitude apparently really does exist in some law school quarters. A professor at Stanford Law School has noted that at "high-ranking law schools" the "overwhelming majority" of students seeking careers as criminal lawyers choose public defending over prosecution, with the possible exception of those seeking federal prosecutor positions.)[1]

In addition to her official role, Jill also liked the comradery that she usually felt in criminal court. Criminal lawyers constitute a **bar within a bar** and all tend to know each other quite well. In any particular county, there usually are not very many public defenders or prosecutors and typically just a few private criminal defense attorneys represent the big majority of paying clients.[2] Prosecutors in Jill's courthouse even went so far as to nickname each of the public defenders. Jill's nickname was "the iron maiden," which the prosecutors actually meant as a compliment.

Jill also liked the security that the job offered her. She never had to worry about **rainmaking** (securing clients), billable hours, office overhead, meeting a payroll, or being laid off due to lack of work. The starting salary was not good, but if one stuck around one could expect to eventually be paid a living wage. Jill fortunately worked in a county where public defenders were paid the same as prosecutors (some long-term public defenders in her office were making over $80,000).

Jill also liked the fact that she was rarely bored. She always had weird clients to counsel, strange cases with which to deal, and quirky judges and juries to bedazzle. Jill's job was so action-packed that she actually looked forward to days when she could get bored.

In addition to the things that Jill liked, there were other things that she knew she did not like but could easily tolerate. For example, she had no problems in representing defendants charged with serious crimes, even clients whom she knew to be guilty. She had no problems in arguing positions in which she did not personally believe. She justified this (as most criminal lawyers apparently do) by reasoning that she was just doing her job—the job that the constitution asks her to perform. During her interview with the newspaper reporter, she was asked about this very issue:

Reporter: "What percentage of your clients do you believe are guilty?"

Jill Lane: "Oh, I'd say about 95 percent."

Reporter: "Wow. Lawyers in television shows mostly seem to represent people whom they somehow personally believe to be innocent. Do you really believe that almost everyone you represent is guilty?"

---

1. Weisberg, Robert. (1994). "The Impropriety of Plea Agreements: An 'Anthropological' View." *Law & Social Inquiry* 19(1):145–148, at 146.

2. Nardulli, Peter. (1986). "'Insider' Justice: Defense Attorneys and the Handling of Felony Cases." *Journal of Criminal Law and Criminology* 77:379–417.

Jill Lane: "Real lawyers for the most part represent people they believe are guilty. If a public defender refused to do otherwise, he or she would be fired. If a private lawyer only accepted clients the lawyer thought were innocent, that lawyer would go bankrupt."

Reporter: "How do you feel about defending so many guilty people? Do you have any ethical qualms at all about it?"

Jill Lane: "No, not really. It has never bothered me, except maybe representing child molesters. Look, I've gone to trial with people I've personally, literally hated but damn it you do what you have to do. You test the evidence."

Reporter: "How do you find the strength to do that? I mean, some of these guys are serious offenders, real S.O.B.s."

Jill Lane: "I don't need to find the strength. It's just there. That's my job. That's my constitutional responsibility. That's what I've been hired to do. Do Air Force pilots feel guilty when they are ordered by their government to bomb a target? No, that's their job. That's their professional responsibility. I've never felt guilty representing someone who is guilty. I've only felt guilty when I've done a crappy job."

Jill's lack of remorse about representing the guilty is not uncommon. In fact, very few criminal lawyers are bothered much by their constitutional role.[3]

So, if Jill liked defending the constitution, enjoyed the comradery of the courthouse, could live with the pay, and was not bothered by having to represent guilty offenders, what did she hate about the job? Plenty.

Stressors of Criminal Defense Work

Criminal defense attorneys report a number of things that really bother them about their jobs. These **stressors of criminal defense work** are: having too much work to do; being unable to always predict which cases might go to trial; having a "dead bang loser" headed for trial; dealing with angry clients; arguing with unreasonable prosecutors; putting up with judicial pressures to avoid trials; and having to do death penalty cases.[4]

---

3. Lynch, David R. (1997). "The Nature of Occupational Stress Among Public Defenders." *The Justice System Journal* 19(1):17–34. Lawyers report that the frequency of representing serious offenders and advocating positions they do not believe in is very high but the guilt they feel from doing so is very low.

4. Id. at 26–27.

Not all criminal defense attorneys have too much work to do. Private lawyers certainly prefer to keep busy with fee-generating cases. But there are very few private criminal lawyers. First, of all, of the million or so Americans with law degrees, only 10,000 to 20,000 of them accept criminal cases on anything more than an occasional basis, including the 5,000 or so who are public defenders.[5] Secondly, the public defenders are doing the bulk of the defending; a strong majority of criminal defendants in this country require the services of free lawyers.[6]

In his interview with Jill Lane, the crime-beat reporter asked her about the size of her caseload:

Reporter: "Are your caseloads manageable?"[7]

Jill Lane: "Are you kidding me? The caseload is unbelievable. There are other things but caseload is the mother of all stress. The ABA says you should only close fifty felony cases a year—I think it's fifty. Or maybe it's 150. What does it matter? One day last week I was expected to close eleven felonies in one afternoon alone."

Reporter: "How many clients do you have right now?

Jill Lane: "Oh, shoot, right now I've got 220 active files. I probably do about a 1,000 per year. We don't count those per charge."

Reporter: "Per human?"

Jill Lane: "Yeah, per human. What we have here on any one criminal court day is a roll call system. I might have fifty or sixty people sitting out there answering "not guilty" and then immediately clamoring to see their lawyer. It's really difficult trying to keep the facts straight, trying to keep the defendant's personal profile in our mind, which prosecutor has the case, what they talked to you about, where in the process the case is really. You've got bail bonds; you got prelims; you've got court; plus, how are you going to prepare for trial, go to the jail, meet with the cop, and have their mothers call you all day long (which they do)? I think most of the

---

5. Cole, George F. (1992). *The American System of Criminal Justice,* 6th ed. Belmont, CA: Brooks/Cole.

6. Wice, Paul B. (1985). *Chaos in the Courthouse: The Inner Workings of the Urban Criminal Court.* New York: Praeger.

7. Much of the fictional interview comments that follow are composites taken from real life interviews conducted by the author with public defenders in New York, North Carolina, and South Carolina. See, Lynch, David R. (1998). "In Their Own Words: Occupational Stress Among Public Defenders." *Criminal Law Bulletin* 34(6): 473–496.

stress comes from not being able to manage your time because it gets overwhelming. I went to the doctor complaining of extreme migraine headaches. He said it was just from all the stress."

Another thing that greatly bothers criminal defense attorneys is never being sure which cases will go to trial on any particular day. The courts are so over-loaded that they can only be described at times as chaotic. This makes trial preparation very difficult. As Jill Lane complained to her boss just before leav-ing for vacation, "Last Monday morning on the first day of the criminal court session, they had a trial calendar with fifty cases set for trial. You would have no idea who's really for trial, okay. You didn't know if you were first, last, in between, and the D.A. didn't really know because he didn't know who was going to show up, who was going to jump bail, who was going to change their mind and take a last minute plea bargain. How am I supposed to know which case to prep for trial?"

Something else that greatly bothers criminal defenders is having an indefen-sible case that somehow goes to trial. These **dead bang losers** cause defense at-torneys considerable stress. Imagine having to argue a burglary case to a jury in which several reliable eyewitnesses will testify that the defendant was the per-petrator, the stolen goods were found in the defendant's car, and the defendant's fingerprints were found at the crime scene. Or, imagine having to defend a drunk driver in a jury trial who crashed his car on the way home from a bar, failed all the field sobriety tests, and had a blood alcohol content three times the legal limit. Cases such as these cause stress for two reasons. First, such cases make the attorney appear to the judge that he or she has no **client control** (the ability to talk a client into accepting a plea bargain when it is in the client's clear best interest to do so). Second, they tend to bring humiliation to defenders who have little choice but to make ridiculous arguments to a jury. As a commiserat-ing public defender told Jill Lane upon hearing that she might quit:

"Don't look to me to tell you why you shouldn't quit—at least not today anyway. I've just come from court where I've never been so humiliated in my whole life. The D.A. had offered my client a great deal which he refused. I couldn't get him to change his mind even after yelling at him for thirty min-utes down in lock-up. So we went to trial and lost. In making my closing ar-gument I kept thinking, 'I hope the jury's not thinking I really believe this.' Then after my client was found guilty, the judge railed on me. He said, 'Mr. Hammond, I told you that you'd lose this case. That was a dog case. You've got to have some client control; let your clients know when they should plea.'"

Dealing with angry clients and arguing with unreasonable prosecutors are also big sources of stress in the lives of defenders. Lawyers are taught to debate and to intellectually argue but are never trained in their legal education to deal with the sort of personal conflict and acrimony that can occur in practicing criminal law.

Conflict with clients can be especially painful. Attorneys must be the bearers of bad news. In exercising "client control" they are expected to sell deals to reluctant defendants. Nobody wants to go to prison. People often become emotional when told they probably have no choice but to agree to incarceration. The problem can be exacerbated if (as is the case with most felony cases) the defender is a free lawyer rather than a privately retained one. Public defender clients are convinced that public defenders are not **real lawyers** (like privately-retained attorneys). They perceive their attorneys to be incompetent and call them names like "public offenders," "pubic defenders," or "public pretenders." Some clients even become convinced that their public defender must be corrupt as well as incompetent: after all, they are ultimately on the payroll of the government that is trying to punish them. Though public defenders learn to have a thick skin, such abuse does come with a toll. It is especially handicapping since public defenders are expected to "sell deals" to clients who have little trust or confidence in their abilities or motivation.

The irony here is that studies consistently show that public defenders (as a group) do as well as, if not better than, private defense attorneys in terms of actual results for clients. Specifically, public defenders do just as well as private attorneys overall when it comes to achieving acquittals and attractive plea bargains,[8] as well as achieving successful appeals.[9]

In addition to confronting conflict with clients, defenders also face conflict with prosecutors. Prosecutors sometimes have immense pressure from victims or police or (perhaps most often) their own conscience not to go lightly on a defendant. Defense attorneys, of course, face pressure from clients who wish to avoid excessive punishment (or sometimes even any punishment). When prosecutors offer what defense counsel considers to be unreasonable plea agreements, tempers can flare. Most prosecutors are reasonable most of the time and their plea offers are "relatively open for discussion."[10] A few though are unreasonable and refuse to negotiate, giving defense counsel "take it or leave it" ultimatums.[11]

---

8. Hanson, Roger, William Hewitt, and Brian Ostrom. (1992). "Are the Critics of Indigent Defense Counsel Correct?" *State Court Journal* (Summer):20–29.

9. Williams, Jimmy. (1995). "Type of Counsel and the Outcome of Criminal Appeals: A Research Note." *American Journal of Criminal Justice* 19:275–285.

10. Lynch, supra note 3 at 30.

11. Id.

Jill Lane would be the first to admit that though there are "one or two pros-ecutors that are difficult to work with, overall they're pretty reasonable." One prosecutor in her courthouse though was horrible to work with. She once tried to complain to the head prosecutor about him:

"You have to understand, Steve, what is happening with your assistant. He is very, very self-righteous, too self-righteous. He thinks he controls the game and he alone has all the power. He dictates what is to him a reasonable offer, which is what he thinks he can get away with. That's why there are so many backlogged cases on his calendar, because his deals are so unreasonable."

As stressful as all of the above are for defenders, the greatest stressor of all (apart from having to litigate death penalty cases) is, according to at least one study, a feeling among many defenders of having no realistic trial options due to judicial policies of excessively punishing those who exercise their right to trial.[12] Certainly not all judges engage in such policies. But enough do to cause some attorneys a lot of stress. (Attorneys interviewed by the author in three different states all consistently reported this as a rather common phenome-non.)[13] In Jill Lane's jurisdiction the common wisdom among defense attor-neys was that "if you want to go to trial, go to trial. But if you lose the trial your client will automatically get the maximum for forcing the judge to put the system through all its steps."

Such policies when they exist cause defenders like Jill a lot of hardship. De-spite the wish of judges for attorneys to exercise consistent "client control," a small minority of defendants simply cannot be talked out of a trial no matter what is offered them. Others really do have a shot at an acquittal and cannot understand why their lawyer is insisting that they take a plea bargain. Lawyers do not mind taking a risk by refusing a plea bargain and going to trial. But the risk has to be a reasonable one. Giving every defendant who goes to trial a draconian penalty takes away from defense attorneys' permission to fail in achieving a plea bargain. Apparently, attorneys need permission to fail some-times in achieving the elusive "client control."

This brings us to the last high stressor: litigating death penalty cases. As bad as this stressor can be, many lawyers never have to deal with it. Perhaps they live in a state that does not have the death penalty or in a county with a low homicide rate where it is rarely sought. Jill Lane never had to deal with this stressor. In her jurisdiction, in order to defend a capital case, an attorney needed to be **death penalty qualified**. This meant that an attorney had to have

---

12. Id., at 27–28.
13. See Lynch, supra note 7 at 482–484.

five years experience as a criminal attorney, including at least three years devoted to felony trials. The attorney also must have sat as "second chair" to a lead attorney in at least one death penalty case.

Jill's boss had asked her numerous times to seek certification as a death penalty qualified attorney. He even sent her to seminars for training, but she always refused to apply for certification. She just had no interest in handling such cases. It was his own fault. The first time he asked her to become certified, he had made the mistake of honestly answering her question concerning how hard it was to take on such cases. He told her that:

"Such cases are in a category by themselves. You will probably do somewhere between five and ten times the work you do on a regular felony case. You have to know everything about this guy. You have to know everything from his blood type to his shirt size basically. You have to assume you're going to lose the guilt or innocence phase of the trial, and then it's going to be about whether this guy lives or dies. And you know everything you can. The files are expansive. I met with somebody today on a homicide case. The file must weigh twenty-five pounds.

"I can still remember the first time I waited for a jury to come back and my blood pressure was literally so high I could see the blood coursing through my little capillaries. I didn't realize what it was at first but it was rhythmically pulsating. It's very stressful."

Jill Lane might not be able to dodge handling death penalty cases forever. She realized more and more that it was probably unfair to others not to shoulder her share of the load. But, she might be quitting anyway. She would worry about her duties to her colleagues only if she decided to keep her job.

The Right to Counsel

One might wonder how public defenders like Jill Lane came to be in the first place. After all, there is no constitutional right to free medicine, free dental care, or even a free public education. There is no right to free food even if one is starving, or free shelter even if one is freezing. Government provides many of these things voluntarily but there certainly is no constitutional mandate that it do so. If a state wanted to, it could abolish all public schools and require any child wishing to be educated to come up with the tuition for a private school. How then, can the constitution be construed to require free attorneys to those charged with crimes?

For a long time, the **right to counsel** as mentioned in the Sixth Amendment was believed to mean that if a person could afford to hire an attorney, that person had the right to have the attorney help defend him. If a person was too poor to hire an attorney, the individual would simply have to represent himself. The idea that there was a constitutional right to a free lawyer was preposterous in light of the fact that there was no right to free food, shelter, education, or medical care. Government could give charity if it so chose but the constitution was not a guarantor of it.

Such was the state of affairs in state courts until a man named Clarence Gideon allegedly burglarized a poolroom in Florida and requested the court to appoint a free attorney to help him at trial. The trial judge informed Mr. Gideon that he had no such right and would have to defend himself as best he could. Mr. Gideon told the court that the U.S. Supreme Court said he had the right to a government paid lawyer. Mr. Gideon was wrong and the Florida court was right—but not for long.

In the famous case of **Gideon v. Wainwright**,[14] the U.S. Supreme Court ruled that criminal defendants charged with serious crimes had the right to counsel, including the right to free counsel if they were too poor to hire an attorney on their own. The court reasoned that this was not merely the granting of charity like food or medicine because the government (not nature or happenstance) was the entity acting upon Gideon. Since the government was the aggressor, it had a duty to see that fair procedures were followed. The court noted that lawyers were not luxuries but essential to a fair trial. Without legal representation, the state could not fairly take away someone's liberty.

Types of Free Lawyers

In *Gideon*, the Court ruled that states had to provide lawyers free of charge to anyone charged with a felony in state court. A later case expanded this to even a petty crime as long as it results in jail time.[15] But, the Court did not tell states how they had to go about providing such lawyers. States are free to provide free lawyers any way they want to.

States follow three main methods for providing **indigent defense** (legal counsel for people without any means). The first system is that of the **public defender**. Public defenders, like Jill Lane, are salaried government officials just like prosecutors. They may work full-time or part-time but are not paid per case but rather by way of a full-time or part-time salary. If full-time, they usually receive paid vacation days, medical insurance, and a government pension plan. Public defender systems only exist in slightly more than a third of coun-

---

14. *Gideon v. Wainwright*, 372 U.S. 335 (1963).
15. *Argersinger v. Hamlin*, 407 U.S. 25 (1972).

ties nationwide, yet more than 70 percent of the American population lives in these counties.[16]

The second method of providing indigent defense is that of **assigned counsel** programs. It is the second most popular method (in terms of number of clients served), used in about half of all American counties (many of which though have small populations).[17] In jurisdictions using assigned counsel programs, privately practicing attorneys wishing to make some extra money may have their names placed on a list kept at the courthouse by a clerk or some other official. When it is their turn to receive a case, the courthouse official contacts them and offers them the case. Typically they are paid an hourly fee, e.g., sixty dollars per hour. But these attorneys are not salaried government employees like public defenders with a caseload. They work for themselves and merely are appointed cases from time to time with a fee paid for each individual case (they submit a bill when the case is finally disposed of).

The last method for providing indigent defense is that of **contract systems.** This is the least common method used in the United States. Under this system, private law firms act as sub-contractors for the government and provide all of the indigent defense for a county for a specified period of time (e.g., a one year contract). Often, the law firm willing to put in the lowest bid will be awarded the contract. If the law firm of Smith and Jones were to win this year's contract, then all poor criminal defendants would be referred to the law firm of Smith and Jones for legal representation.

Which system a particular area uses depends upon the county in which one lives but states do tend to follow patterns. Table 1 is a listing of the methods most often used in the various states. Remember, a particular county may or may not use the system that most counties in the same state use.

The question arises regarding which system—assigned counsel, public defender, or contracts with firms—provides the best quality of representation. It appears that public defenders provide the best representation and contracts with law firms the worst.

Law firms contracting with counties have a financial disincentive to spend much time on any one case. As private businesses, they are usually more motivated by money than are public defender offices. The more time they devote to indigent defendants, the less time they have to develop other areas of their firm's practice. Unlike contracting firms, public defenders often do nothing but criminal defense of the poor.

---

16. U.S. Department of Justice. (1988). "Criminal Defense for the Poor, 1986." *Bureau of Justice Bulletin,* September.

17. Id.

Table 1   Indigent Defense Systems used in the Majority of Counties per State

Assigned Counsel Programs	Public Defender	Contract Systems
Maine	Massachusetts	Idaho
Michigan	Rhode Island	New Mexico
Ohio	Vermont	Arizona
W. Virginia	New Hampshire	Washington
Virginia	Connecticut	Oregon
North Carolina	New York	Hawaii
Georgia	Pennsylvania	
Alabama	New Jersey	
Mississippi	Delaware	
Tennessee	Maryland	
Kentucky	South Carolina	
Arkansas	Florida	
Texas	Louisiana	
Oklahoma	Indiana	
Kansas	Illinois	
Nebraska	Wisconsin	
South Dakota	Minnesota	
North Dakota	Missouri	
Montana	Colorado	
Iowa	Wyoming	
Utah		
Nevada		
California		
Alaska		

Source: Bureau of Justice Statistics, *Criminal Defense for the Poor, 1986* (Washington, D.C.: U.S. Department of Justice, 1988).

Public defenders also have an advantage over assigned counsel. Devoting much if not of all of their time to criminal defense, they often forge stronger relationships with prosecutors and judges than do assigned counsel. They also can keep abreast of the nuances of the criminal law and of courthouse norms.[18]

---

18. See, Worden, Alissa Pollitz. (1993). "Counsel for the Poor: An Evaluation of Contracting for Indigent Criminal Defense." *Justice Quarterly* 10:613–637.

In addition to not telling states which system they must use to provide poor people free lawyers, the Supreme Court in *Gideon* also neglected to identify how poor is poor enough to qualify for a government-paid criminal lawyer. Counties can differ widely as to this issue. For example, in the county next to Jill Lane's, the public defender's office routinely rejects anybody who works full-time no matter how little they earn per hour. Obviously, few minimum wage earners can afford a private attorney. (In fact, even most middle class people would have difficulty affording one to defend them in a complex felony case.) Stingy counties realize that many of those whom they reject for public defending services will just show up for court unrepresented. At that point, the judge will order the public defender's office to represent them **pro bono** (for free). Technically, the judge is simply engaging in an unpaid court appointment. Any lawyer can be ordered to represent a criminal defendant pro bono (literally for the public "good") by a judge and the lawyer may not lawfully refuse. In the case of stingy counties that make it difficult for defendants to financially qualify, judges simply appoint the public defender (rather than some other lawyer) to represent them. Stingy public defender offices realize that this will inevitably happen but hope that at least some of the initial applicants will somehow show up for court with private attorneys (in fact many do).

Jill Lane's public defender's office goes to the opposite extreme. The attitude of her boss is that anybody who wants a public defender gets one. He figures that if someone is willing to accept a public defender as his or her lawyer, then he or she probably is too poor to retain a private one. (This attitude of accepting nearly all who apply is especially prevalent in urban areas.)[19]

Jill remembers once getting angry about this policy when she had to represent a unionized automobile factory worker on a drunk driving charge even though the client made 150 percent of her salary. When she complained to her boss, he told her that given her salary she too would financially qualify for the public defender if she were ever arrested. After that she stopped complaining.

The Private Criminal Defense Attorney

So far, little has been said about private criminal defense attorneys. Though it is true that most defendants charged with crimes are represented by public

---

19. Wice, supra note 6.

defenders (as high as 80 percent of felony defendants in urban areas),[20] private criminal defense counsel also play a role that must be considered.

Even though public defenders overall, as mentioned earlier, are every bit as competent as private criminal attorneys, just about anyone charged with a crime would prefer a privately retained lawyer. People tend to believe that you get what you pay for and if something is free it must not be very good. Many defendants also do not trust someone who is being paid by the government. They are convinced that this presents an insurmountable conflict of interest. It is not unheard of for public defender clients to try to "bribe" their public defender with a little of their own money in the belief that he or she will then be more loyal to them.

Though most defendants are probably no better off with a private attorney than with a public defender, it still makes sense for a person with a lot of money to hire a private attorney. The average private attorney may be no better than the average public defender but the best private attorneys will be better than average public defenders. One has no choice in which public defender is assigned to his or her case. You may get a mediocre lawyer or a gifted one. But people of means can shop around and ensure that they are hiring someone stellar.

Stellar private criminal defense attorneys like stellar performers in any occupation can get very rich. But such lawyers do not come cheap. Most middle class people could never afford them.

Most private criminal defense attorneys do not represent rich people. Nor are they held in high esteem by fellow attorneys. Criminal lawyers are not considered among the elite of the bar the way a corporate lawyer would be.[21] Like government paid lawyers, private criminal attorneys mostly represent poor people since poverty is so highly correlated with criminality. In fact, many private criminal lawyers see public defenders as competition.

Working class and middle class people commit crimes as well. These people generally have more money or better access to relatives who do, and private attorneys court them vigorously. (For example, drunk driving is one of the crimes middle class people are just as likely to commit as poor people. Hence many efforts are made by attorneys to attract them—as lawyers' yellow page advertisements in a phone book will attest.)

---

20. Smith, Steven and Carol DeFrances. (1996). "Indigent Defense." Washington, D.C.: Bureau of Justice Statistics.

21. Heinz, John, and Edward Laumann. (1982). *Chicago Lawyers: The Social Structure of the Bar.* New York: Russell Sage Foundation.

The amount of financial resources a person has matters a lot to a private criminal defense attorney. People charged with serious crimes will not hesitate to sacrifice money for potential freedom. Hence, in setting a fee, an attorney will take into account not only the seriousness of a charge and the amount of work a case will require but also a potential client's ability to pay. A lawyer may feel that his or her services in a particular case deserve more than the 1,000 dollars or so a potential client can come up with, but may take the case anyway since a 1,000 dollars is better than nothing. On the other hand, if another potential client with similar charges can afford more, the private criminal attorney will likely set a higher fee even though the same amount of work is involved.

Getting paid is always a concern for private criminal defense lawyers. Many people who want to hire them are so poor that even the most flexible attorneys will send them away. Part of the problem is that criminal defense attorneys must be paid out of the small pockets of individual clients rather than out of the deep pockets of an insurance company (as is the case in civil lawsuits stemming from automobile accidents, dangerous products, or medical malpractice).

Another problem is that unlike a lot of businesses, criminal defense attorneys must insist on full payment up front. They know that if they wait to get paid until after the case is disposed of, they will never get paid. As one private criminal lawyer once said, "If I win the case I don't get paid because the client will say 'why should I have to pay someone when I never broke the law.' If I lose the case I don't get paid because the client says will say, 'why should I pay you when you lost the case?'"[22] Criminal defense attorneys know that the best time to get paid is "while the tears are still flowing."

There is yet another reason why private defense lawyers must insist on early and full payment. Once an attorney **enters an appearance** on behalf of a client (notifies the court at the arraignment or some later date that he or she will be representing the defendant), the attorney cannot quit the case for any reason without the consent of the judge assigned to the case. This rule exists so as to expedite the processing of cases. Judges do not want lawyers to be able to back out of cases at the last minute merely because they have not yet been paid. If the lawyer's quitting will slow down the progress of a case, a judge may refuse to allow an attorney to abandon the case mid-stream. A lawyer in a sense is "married" to a client for the duration of a case. The client may "divorce" the

---

22. Remarks made to author by a private criminal defense attorney in the early 1990s in York, Pennsylvania during a court recess.

lawyer but the lawyer (without court approval which is not always given) may not "divorce" the client.

Though most private criminal defense attorneys are not gifted at what they do, most are adequate. One type of dangerous criminal defense attorney is the lawyer who rarely if ever handles criminal work but who decides to take a case. Perhaps this attorney is a tax lawyer whose client requests him to represent her son on an aggravated assault charge. Perhaps it is patent attorney who is asked by the family to represent a poor cousin in a sexual assault case. Most non-criminal lawyers have the sense to refuse to take on something with which they have no familiarity. However, there is no legal impediment for any licensed member of the bar to take a criminal case. Such is not the case in some countries. For example, in Great Britain there are two classes of lawyers: barristers and solicitors. A **barrister** is an attorney who specializes in litigation and very frequently appears in court. A **solicitor** is an attorney who never (or rarely) appears in court but rather drafts legal documents, advises on tax matters, attends real estate settlements, applies for patents, drafts divorce agreements, etc. (When a matter must go to court a solicitor will normally hire a barrister.)

Criminal defense attorneys in the U.S.A. would be considered barristers in the U.K. The strange thing about American law is that with only a couple of exceptions (admiralty law and patent law), the only thing stopping a lawyer from taking on any type of legal case whatsoever is his or her good judgment. Non-litigators (most U.S. attorneys are paper-pushing "solicitors") who attempt to do criminal work thinking it cannot be all that complicated are sorely lacking in good judgment. As will be seen in the chapter on plea bargaining, the practice of criminal law is not for novices.

Nearly all private criminal defense attorneys practice either as solo practitioners or else in very small law firms. When someone wants to hire a criminal defense attorney, he or she usually wants to hire a specific person rather than a firm. Perhaps the reason for this is that people intuitively sense that criminal defense work requires enormous "people skills" that cannot be reflected in one's law school rank or what law school one attended (the criteria big, prestigious firms prefer in hiring decisions). For this reason, many of the best private criminal defense attorneys attended non-prestigious, local law schools and are not necessarily known for their legal scholarship. Negotiating skills and the ability to develop rapport with judges or juries are more important traits for the day-to-day practice of criminal law. These skills are not typically measured by law school admission tests, law school exams, or bar exams, nor taught any better in elite schools than in non-elite ones. (In fact, some of the better clinical programs in the country are found in non-elite law schools which sometimes feel more of a mandate to expose students to practical skills in addition to intellectual discussions of doctrine and theory.)

Ineffective Assistance of Counsel

We now return to Jill Lane and her pondering over whether or not she should remain a public defender. After extensive soul-searching, she decided it would be for the best for her to leave the public defender's office. She decided she would seek a job as a prosecutor or some different position related to criminal law but not to criminal defense. That way she would not have to deal with angry clients. It would also give her a change of pace without requiring her to loose all of the professional knowledge she had gained. She realized that in order to get a job as a prosecutor or some similar job, she would have to be open to moving to a new county if necessary, but she was willing to do that.

In thinking things over, Jill also conjured up an ethical demon that was now haunting her. She had come to the conclusion that criminal defendants (as much as they were now getting on her nerves) were not being adequately represented by her public defender's office. This was not due in any way to the quality of the attorneys in the office, but rather to the massive caseloads which they all had to bear. Most public defender offices around the country are bogged down with massive caseloads, but her county's office was notoriously overloaded.

Jill realized that she could just walk away and wash her hands of the whole ugly issue. However, she was not sure she could leave in good conscience without doing something first. She had a golden opportunity before she left to try to help the over-worked colleagues she was leaving behind and the future clients that would be depending upon them. Jill and others in her office had thought numerous times about mounting a legal challenge over the paucity of resources given to their office. Yet, none of them ever had the courage to advance a challenge due to the political firestorm that might erupt around him or her as a lightening rod. Jill's own boss, the chief public defender, worked at the pleasure of the county commissioners who were responsible for funding the office and who would not appreciate a law suit. Each assistant public defender worked at the pleasure of the chief public defender. (In counties where chief public defenders are not appointed they are elected. In such counties their ability to press for more funds may be even more precarious.)

Jill knew that the best way to coerce more funding for her office from the county was to have a court declare the entire public defender's office ineffective and unable to provide a level of legal representation consistent with the mandates of the constitution. Were a court to do so, the county would have no choice but to fix the problem, the same way states have been ordered by courts to spend more money to reduce overcrowding in prisons.

Upon returning to work, Jill drafted a petition to have her office declared ineffective. In the petition, Jill asked the court to order the county to either provide funding for more attorneys or else to order a reduction in the case-loads of the attorneys in the office (the latter would mean fewer people being prosecuted for their crimes). In the petition, Jill cited the U.S. Supreme Court case of *Strickland v. Washington*[23] which held that indigent criminal defendants not only have the right to free legal counsel but to **effective assistance of counsel** (representation that does not fall below an objective standard of reasonableness). As the court in *Strickland* explained, criminal defendants do not have the right to a great attorney or to one that does not make some mistakes, but they do have the right to an attorney that is at least able to ensure reasonably fair proceedings. Kangaroo courts are not acceptable.

In writing the petition, Jill realized that her work was cut out for her. The burden of proof was on her to prove that her office was ineffective, not on the state to prove effectiveness. The fact that her office mates were bright and hard-working did not help her case. Also, she realized that it was not enough to prove that public defender clients were getting mediocre representation. There are plenty of attorneys (public and private) who are mediocre and courts are hardly likely to declare all of them ineffective. Jill had to prove that attorneys in her office were completely unable to offer even a minimally acceptable defense. In other words, she had to prove that they were not just below generally acceptable standards but outrageously so.

Towards that end, Jill alleged several damning things in the petition.[24] First, she noted that the typical attorney in her office was handling 70 active felony cases at any one time. Clients routinely had to wait 30 to 70 days in jail before an attorney could even first meet with them. In the last seven months, the average attorney in the office represented 418 clients. Attorneys in the office were expected to render assistance in felony trial court, misdemeanor court, juvenile court, traffic court, and magistrate's court. There were almost no funds

---

23. *Strickland v. Washington*, 466 U.S. 668 (1984).

24. The allegations listed in the fictitious petition are based on facts actually alleged in the Louisiana Supreme Court case of *State v. Peart*, 621 So.2d 780 (La. 1993). In that case, the Louisiana Supreme Court declared the New Orleans Public Defender's office was offering ineffective assistance of counsel due to its massive caseloads.

made available for the hiring of expert witnesses nor for the employment of a full-time investigator (the prosecutor's office had two full-time investigators in addition to the investigative aid of police departments). Office turnover was triple that of the prosecutor's office despite similar salary levels.

What Jill did not include in the petition was the fact that one member of her office was driven by job stress to excessive drinking, two more were taking anti-depressants, and one was seeing a therapist due to sleeping disorders. She thought it too indiscrete to reveal such matters.

Jill decided to wait to file the petition until she was sure that she had a new job lined up. When she finally did receive a job offer, the exhausted woman wound up simply tearing up the petition. She quietly moved on to her new job with the state department of corrections defending law suits filed by inmates challenging their conditions of confinement.

*****

Questions for Class Discussion

1. What duty does a criminal defense attorney have with regards to clients they believe or even know to be guilty? Is this duty an unethical one? Do prosecutors wear white hats and defense attorneys grey ones? Could you defend people you know for a fact to be guilty? Is it merely alright to plea bargain in such a situation but not go for a complete acquittal?

2. What is the difference between "factual guilt" and "legal guilt?" Do you like this way of conceptualizing the matter in this way? Is being found "not guilty" really the same thing as being found "innocent?"

3. Why should the state bear the burden of proving someone's guilt without having the right to call a defendant involuntarily to the stand to tell his or her side of things? Wouldn't that help the cause of truth? Does the right against self-incrimination do more harm than good in some situations?

4. Why do criminal defendants not think of public defenders as "real lawyers?" Why are they so suspicious of their motives and capabilities? Is this distrust warranted or unwarranted?

5. The chapter mentions numerous "high stressors of criminal defense work." In what way is each of the following situations highly stressful: too much work to do; being unable to predict which specific cases might go to trial; having a "dead bang loser" case heading for trial; dealing with angry clients; arguing with unreasonable prosecutors; putting up with judicial pressures to avoid trials; having to do death penalty cases.

6. Given the stress and the poor image that comes along with the job, why would anybody want to be a public defender?; what are some of the rewards of the job?

7. Is it OK with you that some judges (especially in states without parole) habitually give the maximum sentence to defendants who take cases to trial and lose? Do you agree with the statement, "You take some of my time, I'll take some of yours?"

8. Our Constitution has been interpreted to require that "indigent" people be provided with free criminal lawyers. Should working people who are not "indigent" but struggling to make ends meet also be provided with the same benefit? What should be the economic definition of "indigent?" If a person who can afford a private attorney does indeed hire one but is later acquitted, should the state be required to reimburse that citizen for out-of-pocket attorney fees?

9. Why do some public defender offices initially reject the applications of the working poor for free legal representation when it is obvious that they cannot afford a private attorney? Do you agree with their strategy behind this policy?

10. Do you ever agree with the Constitutional interpretation set down in *Gideon v. Wainwright*? Why would the Constitution require that poor people be given free criminal lawyers when there is no constitutional right to a free doctor, dentist, public education, or even food? In what ways would not having a defense lawyer make the right to a trial meaningless? What "value" do defense attorneys add to the process?

11. Even though the Supreme Court requires states to provide poor people with free criminal defense lawyers, it did not specify how this had to be done. What are the three systems that states use to accomplish this requirement? Which system provides the best quality of representation? Why? Which provides the worse? Why?

12. What is meat by the term "client control?" How does the expectation of this cause stress for criminal defense attorneys? Do public defenders have a harder time in achieving client control than private attorneys? Why?

13. Does the fact that public defenders tend to have close working relationships with prosecutors and judges create an inherent conflict of interest? If the lawyer representing you did not have such a relationship, would that be a good thing or a bad thing?

14. What does it mean for an attorney to enter his or her "appearance?" Why do some lawyers put this step off for as long as possible? If you were a private attorney who had entered his or her appearance and was not getting

paid as promised by the client, would you strive to do a good job or put in minimal effort? What would ethics require in such a situation?

15. A judge in theory can order any attorney to represent a poor person for free as a condition of bar membership. Is this fair or is it a form of slavery? Should doctors and dentists be under the same requirement? Why would it be unwise for judges to frequently exercise this power to draft attorneys without also voluntarily agreeing to pay the attorney?

16. How is it possible that private attorneys on the whole do not get any better results than public defenders as a whole? Is this a compliment to public defenders or does it suggest something scary about the typical private defense attorney? Despite this reality, why should a person with a lot of money probably want to hire a private attorney of their own choosing?

17. What does it mean to be "death penalty qualified?" Do you think that poor, accused murderers should have the right not just to any publicly paid lawyer but also to one who has been certified as "death penalty qualified?

18. If you lived in Great Britain and had to practice law, would you rather be a solicitor or a barrister? What sort of personality skills should barristers have that are not so important for a solicitor to have?

19. What is the standard for finding "ineffective assistance of counsel?" Do you agree with this standard? Why do the defense attorney, prosecutor, and judge all "circle the wagons" whenever a criminal defendant asserts this against his or her criminal defense attorney?

20. Do you personally have a thick enough skin to be a criminal defense attorney? What parts of the job would stress you out the most? What parts of the job would you like? If the pay were the same, would anyone prefer being a criminal defense attorney to a prosecuting attorney?

*****

Key Terms: role of the criminal defender, factually guilty, legally guilty, bar within a bar, rainmaking, stressors of criminal defense work, dead bang losers, client control, real lawyers, death penalty qualified, right to counsel, *Gideon v. Wainwright*, indigent defense, public defender, assigned counsel, contract systems, pro bono, enters an appearance, barrister, solicitor, effective assistance of counsel

Additional Concepts: attorney burnout, positive aspects of criminal defense, defending the guilty, attorney-client relations, indigent defense systems by state, comparison of indigent defense systems, financial qualification for free lawyers, defendant preference for private lawyers, status of private criminal defense attorneys, lawyers setting fees, lawyers getting paid, inexperienced lawyers taking criminal cases, need for "people skills" on part of defense attorneys

CHAPTER FIVE

The Prosecuting Attorney

Bill Miller's self-esteem was beginning to recover nicely since only graduating in the middle of his class from an average law school. Prior to law school, Bill had always thought of himself as more competent and intelligent than most people. Then law school sent his self-esteem plummeting. But, since joining the Lancaster County District Attorney's office a year ago, he felt he was once again on top of life's game.

Like most prosecuting attorneys in the United States, Bill came from a middle-class rather than an elite background, attended an ordinary university, went on to a non-prestigious law school, and neither excelled nor did poorly in his legal studies.[1] But Bill really knew how to read people and had great control over his emotions, and this is the sort of "intelligence" that really counted in his legal specialty.

Bill was just one of about 25,000 prosecutors in the United States, including both **U.S. Attorneys** (prosecutors serving at the federal level) and **local prosecutors** (serving at the county, district, or state-level). Bill was a local prosecutor, as are the bulk of prosecutors. (Crime control has always been primarily a state and local function, not a federal one.) Bill's title was assistant district attorney, but in other states his counterpart may be called something else: assistant county attorney, assistant state's attorney, deputy prosecutor, etc.

Prosecutorial Discretion

Sometimes, Bill could not believe the amount of raw power that he, at the age of twenty-eight, exercised over his fellow human beings. As a prosecutor, Bill technically worked for the **executive branch** of government. In fact, his

---

1. For a list of several studies that document the ordinary background of most prosecutors, see, Shelden, Randall G. and William B. Brown. (2003). *Criminal Justice in America: A Critical View*. Boston: Allyn and Bacon, p. 200.

boss (the district attorney) was considered to be the **chief law enforcement officer** of the jurisdiction. That meant that Bill—like his boss—was officially a member of the executive branch, nothing more. He was not a legislator and certainly not a judge. But Bill realized that an act was not a crime unless he and his office colleagues chose to enforce it as such. In that sense, prosecutors do indeed act like legislators. They decide what will be and will not be punishable acts in their jurisdictions. They also act like judges. They decide (through plea bargains) what sentences most criminals will receive. In short, they are about the only government officials known to carry out executive, legislative, and judicial responsibilities. As a justice of the U.S. Supreme Court once said, "The prosecutor has more control over life, liberty and reputation than any other person in America."[2] The courtroom judge may have more prestige, but it is the prosecutor (who decides who will be charged, what the charges will be, and usually what the sentence will be) who actually has the most power.[3]

Bill and his fellow local prosecutors have much more power than do many of their counterparts in other countries of the world. They have the power of three foreign office-holders in one: that of the French "procureur publique" to file charges, the English attorney-general to drop charges, and the Dutch "schout" to act with impressive local autonomy.[4]

Bill, an assistant district attorney, got his job by being appointed by the district attorney. He served at his pleasure. He could be fired at will. He could also lose his job if his boss were to lose the next election. In fact, upon assuming office, Bill's boss (a partisan Republican) not only fired all of the former assistant district attorneys (partisan Democrats), but even had considered firing the secretarial staff as well (he wisely decided to draw the line there).

District attorneys (or county attorneys or whatever a state calls them) are elected in all states but Connecticut and New Jersey.[5] Unlike elected judges, their terms are relatively short: typically just four years long.[6] Because they are

---

2. Davis, Kenneth Culp. (1969). *Discretionary Justice.* Baton Rouge: Louisiana State University Press, p. 190. (Citing remarks made by Justice Robert Jackson.)

3. For an excellent discussion on the amount of power concentrated in the hands of prosecutors, see Misner, Robert. (1996). "Recasting Prosecutorial Discretion." *Journal of Criminal Law and Criminology* 86:717–758.

4. Jacoby, Joan E. (1980). *The American Prosecutor: A Search for Identity.* Lexington, Mass: D.C. Heath, p. 3.

5. Cole, George F. and Christopher E. Smith. (2004). *The American System of Criminal Justice.* Belmont, CA: Thomson Learning, Inc., p. 303.

6. Id.

elected for relatively short terms, they constantly have to worry about keeping their jobs. This means that politics can influence their decision-making. They must appear tough and hard on crime.

Ironically though, the fact that chief local prosecutors are elected increases their power more than it limits it. Nobody but the electorate can tell them what to do. A judge can not order a prosecutor to file criminal charges against someone or order a prosecutor to refrain to **nolle prosequi** a case (drop charges). A state attorney general in most states has no power over a locally elected prosecutor—he or she can do little more than offer advice. Not even the governor, the chief executive of the state, can tell a local prosecutor how to act. The chief local prosecutor as an elected official only has to worry about what the electorate might think about a particular decision. This makes the prosecutor very powerful since the only cases the public ever hears or cares about are those that are newsworthy. Since few cases make it into the news, most prosecutorial decisions are invisible to the electorate. (Bill remembers the first time he told the court he was going to "nolle pros" a serious case. He expected the judge to grill him about his decision to drop charges, and for a member of the press to hear about it and expose the "scandal" in the newspaper. None of that ever happened.)

Local autonomy would be scary to continental Europeans like the French who cannot understand the American tolerance—even preference—for local control. In France, all roads lead to civilized Paris. But to Americans accustomed to even the smallest of towns having their own independent police department, the notion of a **decentralized system of prosecution** is not strange at all. (Most prosecutors in America work way down at the county level.)[7]

There are some limits to the power and autonomy of local prosecutors. They may face pressure from voters or police departments to pursue a course of conduct. Judges can limit their charging power by "quashing" grand jury indictments secured by a prosecutor despite a clear lack of evidence. But judicial power to *undo* a prosecutorial decision *not* to prosecute simply does not exist. In the classic 1970 case of *Peek v. Mitchell*, a federal appeals court ruled that because of **separation of powers**, a court simply could not compel a prosecutor to file charges, even against known civil rights violators.[8]

It is not just the chief local prosecutor who wields great **discretionary power**. His or her assistants typically have huge amounts of discretion as well.

---

7. DeFrances, Carol J. (2002). "Prosecutors in State Courts, 2001." *Bulletin(May)*. Washington, D.C.: Bureau of Justice Statistics.

8. *Peek v. Mitchell*, 419 F.2d 575 (6th Cir. 1970).

This is necessarily so. Like police work, prosecution work cannot be effectively done if supervisors attempt to completely bridle discretion. Chief prosecutors who try to take away too much discretion from their assistants run the risk of being ignored.

Chief prosecutors sometimes have very good reasons for wanting to limit the discretion of their assistants. They know that personal values can sometimes thwart what the office as a whole is trying to do. For example, an assistant who personally believes that pornography laws are silly may start dropping cases that involve pornography. An assistant who believes that drug laws have gone too far may adopt a policy of generous plea bargains, despite an office philosophy that a "war on drugs" is necessary. An assistant who personally believes that abortion is murder may be easily persuaded by defense counsel to drop or reduce charges on abortion protestors charged with trespassing.

In Bill Miller's office, the district attorney once tried to pass a rule that all plea bargains would be off the table if not accepted at least 24 hours prior to the time a case was scheduled for trial. He did this out of a concern that witnesses would be dragged down to court only to find out that the case had been settled at the last minute. His rule sounded sensible but had unexpected consequences which his assistants did not like. Chief among them was the anger on the part of busy judges when told that a defendant who was willing to plead guilty would have a lengthy trial due to the district attorney's policy of no last-minute acceptance of bargains. (Many deals are necessarily accepted in the last minute when a defendant, frightened at the prospect of his immediate demise before a jury, finally sees the light.) Judges just could not tolerate being told by an assistant district attorney that sensitivity to witnesses not wanting to be inconvenienced would take precedence over judicial time being wasted. The district attorney's policy was soon ignored by his own assistants. The defiance on the part of his assistants was covered up by prosecutors and judges alike.

Court observers have found that when assistant prosecutors are tightly supervised, morale plummets. Resentment rises and tensions in the office greatly increase. Assistant district attorneys feel that they are professionals who should be trusted to handle their caseloads as they seem fit. They feel uncomfortable with attempts to greatly undermine their **professional autonomy**, even if such attempts are coming from the very person who hired them.[9]

---

9. See, e.g., Eisenstein, James, Roy Flemming, and Peter Nardulli. (1988). *The Contours of Justice: Communities and their Courts*. Boston: Little, Brown.

The Prosecutorial Personality

Bill took his job with the Lancaster County District Attorney's office for several reasons. First, since he did not attend an elite law school, he realized he had little chance to secure a position with a major, big-city law firm representing wealthy institutional clients or to be brought on as part of the in-house counsel of a large corporation. Second, he wanted to do trials. There is no better place to get trial experience faster than at a prosecutor's office. Third, he thought that some day he might want to launch a political career. He knew that many politicians used their time as prosecutors to gain public exposure before running for office. (Bob Dole, former Senate majority leader who ran against Bill Clinton for the presidency, and Rudolph Gulliani, mayor of New York City during the terrorist attack of 2001, both started out as prosecutors.)

Some people assume that all prosecutors are alike. They are sometimes stereotyped as extreme "law and order" types. Bill Miller himself had been called a "Nazi" on several occasions by upset defendants. He and his office mates were once referred to as nothing more than a local branch of "Hitler Youth" by a temporarily upset, older defense attorney.

The truth is that prosecutors, like people in general, cannot be simplistically categorized. Some are extreme "law and order" types. Others hold more libertarian views. Some are extroverts. Others prefer the quiet of their office. Some are legal intellectuals. Others cannot stand the inside of a law library. Some are aggressive. Some are relatively passive. Some are politically ambitious. Others just are there because they need a job. In fact, several of the prosecutors Bill Miller worked with had applied for jobs both at the public defender's office as well as at the district attorney's office. They worked for the district attorney merely because he was the one who had offered them a job first.

Even though prosecutors differ one from another in many ways, they also tend to share similar attitudes on a host of issues in ways that might surprise many lay people. The attitudes of prosecutors, as contrasted with the beliefs of ordinary Americans, are outlined in Table 1.

Bill was glad that he was a prosecutor instead of some other kind of lawyer—criminal or otherwise. He preferred working with people over generating paper in "high brow" corporate legal work. He liked speaking before juries, as long as it was not too frequently required. He liked wearing a "white hat" (he thought criminal defense attorneys wore "gray" ones). He liked winning three-fourths of his trials (defense attorneys lose most of their trials). He liked how "assistant district attorney" would look on his future political resume. He enjoyed being a "crime fighter" and felt like he made a difference in

Table 1   Lay Beliefs vs. Prosecutorial Attitudes

Lay Belief	Prosecutorial Attitude
Adversarial system is best	Cooperative system is best
Speedy trial means speedy	Speedy trial depends on court resources
Jury trials are virtuous	Jury trials are time wasters
Plea bargains benefit bad guys	Plea bargains benefit everybody
Proof should be beyond a reasonable doubt	Proof is met by a "factual basis" (what a judge needs to accept a guilty plea)
Defense lawyers should be thorough	Defense lawyers should be efficient
Judges should sentence people	Prosecutors should sentence (plea bargains)
Judge is most powerful courtroom figure	Prosecutor has the most real power
Factual guilt matters (what really happened)	Legal guilt matters (what can be proven)

Source: Author's observations while serving as a prosecutor and as a public defender.

the quality of life of his community. Some day he would become a judge, or the district attorney, or the mayor, or the state attorney general. But for now he was happy.

Duties of the Prosecutor

Luckily for Bill Miller, he lived in an era in which becoming a public prosecutor was an option. It may seem strange, but America did not always have public prosecutors. In colonial times, crime victims were expected to hire a private attorney to prosecute a criminal case on their behalf. By the late 1700s, states by and large had taken it upon themselves to transfer the prosecution of criminals from the domain of the victim to the domain of the state. The **public prosecutor,** paid by the state and having the people as a client rather than the individual victim (who now became little more than a witness), came into being.[10]

---

10. McDonald, William F. (ed.) (1979). *The Prosecutor.* Beverly Hills, CA: Sage, pp. 22–24.

Today, prosecutors perform many functions. They review criminal complaints and decide whether or not to prosecute people. They make arguments regarding bail. They act as legal advisers to police telephoning them questions from the field. They draft memorandums of law for court. They handle traffic appeals. They attend preliminary hearings, grand jury proceedings, arraignments, and suppression hearings. They conduct trials, make sentencing arguments, and argue appeals. But by far, the role that calls for the most discretion and the greatest exercise of their power (at least in non-routine cases) is that of negotiating plea bargains. As shall be seen in the chapter on plea bargaining, the American system is not a trial-based system but rather one based on negotiated justice. The prosecutor is the central figure in this system.

Oddly enough, law school does very little in preparing future attorneys to do any of the above duties. Mostly they just learn on the job—a process known as **socialization**. Researching and writing briefs and memorandums of law are about the only parts of his job that Bill learned to do as a law student. When Bill received his first cases, he had to ask others what they thought an acceptable plea bargain offer was. He usually was told, "whatever you think is best." After some trial and error with defense counsel, he got the hang of it pretty quickly.

One of the mistakes that Bill made early on was to be unnecessarily **adversarial** with defense attorneys, as brand new prosecutors tend to be. It took Bill a couple of months to become socialized into what was and what was not appropriate opposition. For example, at the conclusion of one of the very first preliminary hearings Bill ever did (an aggravated assault case), the defendant's attorney asked Bill if he could take a quick look at the photos of the beaten victim which he knew to be in Bill's file. Bill refused to show him the photos. Annoyed, the defense attorney told Bill that he had the right according to the local rules of discovery to eventually see the photos anyway merely upon written request. Bill told the attorney that he would let him see the evidence upon the attorney's filing a written request for discovery. Angered, the attorney walked away and later served Bill with a written request to see the photos. Bill wound up showing him the photos as he had the legal duty to do. A few months later, a much less adversarial Bill apologized to the attorney about this incident telling him, "I guess I was still young and foolish." The attorney confirmed that Bill had indeed irritated him, but told Bill that he had been even more obnoxious when he himself first started practicing law.

Not too much time passed before Bill had to do his first jury trial. He was so nervous that he vomited his breakfast before leaving the apartment. He was so unschooled in the art of trials that he did not even know which table to sit at (or if it mattered), or whether he was supposed to ask the judge's permission before approaching the witness. Fortunately for Bill, he had followed the suggestion of an office mentor and told the trial judge privately that since this was his first trial, he would appreciate the court's patience with him. The judge was kind enough to oblige and helped him in the trial as much as was appropriate.

One thing that Bill Miller was grateful for was the decision on the part of the district attorney that his office would make use of **vertical prosecution** (same prosecutor handles a case from start to finish) rather than **horizontal prosecution** (a different prosecutor handles the case at each different stage). Bill well understood that horizontal prosecution had the virtue of efficiency. A prosecutor could become expert at doing nothing but preliminary hearings or negotiating deals or doing trials or writing appellate briefs. But, efficiency came with a price.

First of all, a case could get more easily lost in the system using horizontal rather than vertical prosecution. (Bill never lost track of a case—his desk was full of yellow "post-it notes" which he used as reminders to himself not to miss any critical hearings or filing dates.) Second, victims and police officers do not like horizontal prosecution (they don't like having to deal with a new person every time they turn around). Third, horizontal prosecution made it more difficult for any one prosecutor to take "ownership" of a case. People like Bill took satisfaction in personally seeing a case from beginning to end. Lastly, there was the question of fun. Bill did not want to become expert at one function if it meant having to do the same sort of tasks day after day.

Duty to Do Justice

In carrying out his duties, Bill had a burden that criminal defense attorneys do not have. Defense attorneys only need worry about zealously representing the interest of their clients (within the bounds of the law). Prosecutors, on the other hand, have not just the duty to zealously advocate for their client (the people), but also have a **duty to do justice**. The U.S. Supreme Court has stated:

> The [prosecutor] is the representative not of an ordinary party to a controversy, but of a sovereignty whose obligation to govern impartially is as compelling as its obligation to govern at all; and whose interest, therefore, in a criminal prosecution is not that it shall win a case, but that justice shall be done.... He may prosecute with earnestness and vigor—indeed, he should do so. But while he may strike

hard blows, he is not at liberty to strike foul ones. It is as much his duty to refrain from improper methods calculated to produce a wrongful conviction as it is to use every legitimate means to bring about a just one.[11]

Hence, unlike a defense attorney who may champion a cause or a client which he or she does not personally believe in, a prosecutor may not seek a conviction against someone whom the prosecutor believes to be innocent or to allow a material false impression to go uncorrected. Prosecutors must play fair even when they believe a defendant to be guilty. In a sense, unlike defense attorneys, they have a quasi-judicial role as well as an advocacy one.

Part of being fair is to permit a defense attorney to have access to most of the information in the prosecutor's file so that the defense can better prepare its case. This is known as **discovery** and it is mainly a one-way street. With very few exceptions (like names of alibi witnesses or intention to mount an insanity defense), defense attorneys do not have to divulge anything that they know about the case. Prosecutors have to divulge what they know because part of their job is not just to get a conviction but to get one fairly. Defense attorneys have to follow the law (e.g., they cannot knowingly allow perjury), but they do not have to worry about just results. Their role is to protect their client from the state. It is up to the prosecutor to see to justice.

Different states require different levels of material to be provided defense attorneys by the prosecutor. Typically, defense attorneys upon request, must be given photocopies of such things as police reports, statements of witnesses, and confessions or other harmful statements made by the defendant. They must also be permitted to inspect physical evidence in the possession of authorities, be furnished a copy of the defendant's criminal record, be given the results of any tests, and provided a summary of opinions expressed by government expert witnesses.[12] Prosecutors do not have to provide defense attorneys however with their **work product** (recordings containing their opinions, thoughts, conclusions, and strategies regarding the case).[13]

Whatever local rules may or may not provide, the United States Supreme Court has made it clear that certain information must be disclosed to defendants, as a matter of constitutional principle. In *Brady v. Maryland*, the Court articulated the requirement of **mandatory discovery**, ruling that due process

---

11. *Berger v. United States,* 295 U.S. 78, 55 S.Ct. 629,79 (1935).

12. See, Federal Rules of Criminal Procedure. Rule 16: "Discovery and Inspection."

13. Federal Rules of Criminal Procedure. Rule 16(a)(2). See also, *United States v. Nobles,* 422 U.S. 225 (1975).

requires the prosecution to pro-actively make available to the defense evidence in its possession that strongly suggests the possibility of innocence, whether or not the defense even bothers to ask for any discovery.[14] (Naturally, defense attorneys need not turn over to the prosecution evidence that strongly suggests the possibility of guilt!)

Bill Miller often wondered what his duty "to see that justice is done" actually entailed. For example, could he ethically prosecute someone whom he believed to be guilty but regarding whose guilt he had some reasonable doubt? (He generally did prosecute but would offer a plea bargain that was more generous than normal.) Could he ethically use truthful evidence that he was aware the police obtained illegally just because the defense attorney was too stupid or lazy to challenge its legality? (He did not try to hide the illegality from the defense but usually used the evidence unless the defense bothered to object.) These issues were just the tip of the ethical iceberg that Bill Miller and his fellow prosecutors had to face.

Ethical Issues Confronting Prosecutors

Bill Miller liked being a prosecutor more than a criminal defense attorney because as such he thought he got to wear the "white hat." (Defense attorneys would take exception to that belief.) He did not have to defend people who were guilty. Sure, he sometimes worried about the awesome effect he had in the lives of others. He sent people to prison for years at a time. What if some of them were innocent? This bothered Bill a little but not too much. What was society supposed to do? Let every criminal defendant go unpunished in order to make sure that no innocent person ever went to jail? Bill did the best he could and took comfort in the fact that he never was expected to prosecute someone whom he personally did not believe to be guilty.

Nevertheless, Bill learned that keeping a prosecutor's hat "white" was not effortless. True, some wrongs were obvious and easily avoided. For example, Bill knew never to prosecute a person he believed to be innocent, knowingly allow a police officer or some other witness to commit perjury, or fail to turn over to the defense attorney any **exculpatory evidence** (evidence that might tend to completely exonerate the defendant—also known as mandatory discovery).

---

14. *Brady v. Maryland*, 373 U.S. 83 (1963).

But some "wrongs" were not so obvious. These issues were what Bill mentally labeled as his "personal gray areas." Bill liked to think in terms of black and white. But that was not always possible.

One "gray area" that Bill had to resolve involved a local criminal defense attorney named Nick Owens. This attorney was so incompetent and passive that Bill could not understand why anyone would ever hire him (he did manage to snare some unsuspecting clients from his advertisement in the phone book).

Bill first dealt with Nick a couple of months after he was hired as a prosecutor. Up until then, he had only heard courthouse gossip that "Nick is so afraid of trials that he will take any deal that is offered him—good or bad—no questions asked." Bill had thought that this must be a gross exaggeration, but to his unbelief, it was completely true. When in his first case with Nick, a residential burglary, Bill offered a pretty lousy deal, Nick just accepted it and somehow sold it to his client. After taking advantage of Nick in a couple of more cases, Bill began to wonder if what he was doing was wrong. Should he continue to take advantage of Nick's weak negotiating skills or should he start offering to Nick's clients what he would offer to those who hired a reasonably competent defense attorney? Bill decided to do the latter. Nick's clients would get the same breaks for pleading guilty that everyone else typically got.

Another ethical dilemma emerged for Bill when the victim in a rape case moved away without leaving a forwarding address. Bill could not find her. He was still personally convinced that she had been raped. "What should I do?" he wondered. "Do I have a duty to tell the defense attorney about the giant hole in my case? Would I be getting a fair conviction if I allowed the defendant to plead guilty? Is this 'exculpatory evidence' subject to 'mandatory discovery?' Or, would it be alright for me to bluff my way through a plea bargain?" (Some legal scholars argue that it is unethical to pretend to be giving someone a deal when the prosecutor knows for sure that such is not the case.) Bill put on a poker face and got the defendant to plea guilty to a reduced charge with a relatively light sentence.

A very similar dilemma confronted Bill in a residential burglary case which was heading for trial. The defendant who had a prior record of several burglaries rejected Bill's final offer of just a few months of jail time. Even though Bill had serious doubts about the victim's testifying abilities (he seemed a little odd), Bill felt he could not offer probation to someone with such a bad prior record. Bill had instructed the victim (the sole eyewitness to the crime) to come to his office an hour prior to trial to go over his testimony. When the victim showed up at Bill's door, Bill's heart sank. Bill had told the victim to wear his best clothes since he would be testifying before a jury. The victim showed up wearing a Swiss-style yodeler outfit, complete with white hose, knickers, clogging shoes, and a bizarre vest. Upon seeing him, Bill asked him what was going on. "I told you to wear your best clothes!" exclaimed Bill. The victim told Bill, "these are my best and most expensive clothes."

"What should I do now?" Bill agonized. "Drop the charges?" He really did believe that the victim had identified the right culprit, especially given the defendant's prior record. But, how could he go to trial with this laughing stock of a witness? Bill hid the witness in his office while he telephoned the defense attorney to ask if his client would take probation in exchange for a plea to a reduced charge. The client agreed and entered his guilty plea. Later that day, while talking to the defense attorney in the hall, the burglary victim walked by in the same outfit. Bill felt a twinge of guilt when the defense attorney asked Bill if he had seen "that weirdo who just passed by." Bill wondered if he had done the right thing in hiding the witness in his office while he worked out the new deal.

Another issue Bill wondered about was whether it was ethical to overcharge a defendant so as to soften the defendant up to plea guilty to what the person really did. For example, Bill had a case in which the defendant clearly committed a simple assault (a misdemeanor) but which was something of a stretch for the arresting cops to label aggravated assault (a felony)—which they did anyway. The defendant had a bad record including several crimes of violence. Bill had little sympathy for him and did not want him to be in a position to manipulate the plea bargaining system. Yet, Bill wondered if he had a duty, in the interests of justice, to drop the aggravated assault charge and thus render it useless as a potential bargaining chip. Bill really had to struggle with this one. In the end, he only offered to drop the felony if the defendant plead guilty to the misdemeanor. The defendant, given his prior record, could not take even a remote chance of another felony conviction, and capitulated.

Another ethical dilemma confronted Bill during a jury trial that took place towards the end of his first year in office. During the trial, Bill soon realized that the inexperienced defense attorney (a tax attorney who was representing a relative in a felony theft case and who never had done a trial in his life) never objected to any questions that Bill asked of witnesses, no matter how objectionable. Bill realized that he could ask for hearsay or anything else and it would probably not be objected to. Bill wondered if he would be getting an unfair conviction if he were to take advantage of the defense attorney in this way. After noticing the judge's dirty looks when Bill started going too far, his conscience got the better of him and he toned things down.

Sometimes Bill, a person who believed strongly in loyalty between family members and friends, took to wondering about the standard practice that prosecutors use in getting relatives and friends to turn on one another in exchange for a reduced sentence. He imagined the permanent damage it would do to his relationship with his brother if he were to **snitch** on him just to save his own neck. Bill privately adopted a personal policy of tempting friends to snitch on friends, but chose to avoid tempting close relatives to turn on one another.

Prosecutorial Pathologies

Picking the wrong shade of gray in an ethical dilemma is one thing, but sometimes prosecutors consciously choose what is unarguably inappropriate. They suffer from human weaknesses just like everyone else. Sometimes it is just a little act of hypocrisy, like the tendency on the part of many in Bill's office to routinely speed in their vehicles even though they regularly argued against defendants in their traffic appeals. (His speeding colleagues somehow all kept their driver's licenses tucked in the same small leather case that coincidentally happened to house their shiny district attorney badges.)

Other shortcomings were more significant. For example, in order to gain the support of the local chair of the Republican Party, Bill's boss had promised to give his son a job if Bill's boss won the primary and general elections. This is one of the dark sides of politically electing our chief local prosecutors: jobs are sometimes awarded more for political reasons than out of merit. **Nepotism** or something close to it can often take place.

What really irked Bill and his office friends was that this son of the party boss was not just made an assistant district attorney but was made the **first assistant district attorney** (the second in command). (The larger the prosecutor' office, the more supervisory slots exist between line attorneys and the chief prosecutor. Some large, urban offices not only have a first assistant, but other executive assistants, division managers, etc. Prosecutor offices can range from a couple of part-time prosecutors in a rural county to offices of several hundred full-time attorneys in a county like Los Angeles. All but the smallest of offices typically have at least one supervisory position below that of chief prosecutor.)

Two other pathologies that confronted Bill and his colleagues were **cynicism** (pessimism about human behavior) **and suspicion**. Police officers are believed to disproportionately suffer from these traits—not because people with such traits tend to choose police work but rather because police work tends to change people.[15] It should come as no surprise that prosecutors—who are

---

15. Langworthy, Robert H. (1987). "Police Cynicism: What We Know from the Niederhoffer Scale." *Journal of Criminal Justice* 15:17–35.

law enforcement officers—are also at occupational risk of acquiring such attributes.

Bill had been lied to by so many defendants and had dealt with so much filth that he started to believe that nearly everybody had a dark side to him or her. He began wondering about his own neighbors and was horrified to learn that several of them had prior criminal records (he typed many of their names one day into the computer out of curiosity).

In addition to fighting such misanthropy, Bill also had to deal with the **self-trauma** he experienced from time to time in witnessing the horrors that people do to one another. Meeting rape victims with swollen eyes, watching victims cry uncontrollably in his office, reading police reports of the disgusting acts fathers do to their daughters, all took their toll. The worst incident of trauma occurred one weekend when it was Bill's time to be "on call." Bill was paged by the police to come to a murder scene (district attorney policy was that someone in the office would always visit a murder scene before the evidence was removed). Bill, who before becoming a prosecutor did not even like to watch violent movies, was required to gaze upon the bodies of three small children, knifed to death by their unstable mother for apparently acting up at the dinner table. The smallest of the three was stooped over in her high chair. The mother's body was found next to her children (she had stabbed herself to death as well). Bill went home that day and cried in his wife's arms for half an hour.

Leaving Office

Bill Miller stayed with the district attorney's office for three years before moving on to do litigation work in a personal injury firm specializing in automobile accidents. As part of his new role as a civil litigator, he joined the "Trial Lawyers of America," but never again did the volume of trials he had done as a young assistant district attorney.

Bill had gained some valuable skills while working as a prosecutor. He was now very comfortable at public speaking. He knew how to think on his feet. He knew how to stay poised and articulate while under stress. He was even better at reading people than he was when he first started. Having negotiated hundreds of plea bargains, he was very good at negotiating prices and terms with real estate agents and car salespeople (his own wife was shocked at his skills when they went to buy a car together).

Bill would miss the job but he could take these skills with him. Some things he would not miss. He looked forward to the day when he would feel comfortable again about having his home address listed in the local phone book. He would not miss the hateful words victims would sometimes assault him with upon his losing a trial. He would not miss cops' anger at coming to court on their days off to testify in one of his cases that he told them was probably settled. He would not miss having to sit in silence and take crap from eccentric judges.

Yet, for the rest of his career, Bill Miller would look back on his days as a young prosecutor with pride and awe. He had seen more actual court time in the three years he served as a prosecutor than most lawyers ever do in a lifetime. He had worked as a true barrister. He had been where the action was.

Bill Miller rarely went to court after he left the D.A.'s office. He spent most of his days drafting civil complaints, writing interrogatories, doing depositions, interviewing clients, reading medical reports, and churning paper. He was lucky if he did a single trial in any particular year. The vast majority of people either settled or eventually dropped their law suit (only one percent of civil law suits in state courts ever go to trial).[16]

Sometimes, usually on a Monday morning, Bill would wake up after having the same dream. He dreamt that he lost his lucrative job with his law firm and was hired back with the district attorney's office. Somewhat to the surprise of Bill's conscious self, the dream was invariably a pleasant one.

*****

Questions for Class Discussion

1. It can be argued that prosecutors, often at very young ages, wield more power in the field of criminal justice that just about anyone else. What are some of the specific decisions that prosecutors get to make in our society?
2. In what ways does the principle of "separation of powers" protect prosecutorial discretion? Can judges order a prosecutor to prosecute someone? Can the state attorney general? The governor? If you were a head local prosecutor, are there certain types of cases you would decline to prosecute?
3. What are some factors that in reality limit the power and autonomy of local prosecutors?

---

16. Levine, James P. (1992). *Juries and Politics*. Pacific Grove, CA: Brooks/Cole Publishing Company, p. 34. See also, Friedrichs, David O. (2001). *Law in Our Lives*. Los Angeles: Roxbury Publishing Company, p. 208.

4. Would it be a good idea of the office head to deny assistant prosecutors a lot of discretion in carrying out their day to day duties? What might happen if assistant prosecutors are too tightly supervised? What implications does all of this have for the hiring decision?

5. Why are the vast majority of decisions made by local prosecutors invisible to the general public? Who besides prosecutors are aware of what is going on behind courthouse doors?

6. What sort of socioeconomic class do most prosecutors come from? What quality of law schools did they typically attend? Do they tend to graduate at the top of their class? Does any of this matter in how effective they might be?

7. What would you say is the stereotype out there of the prosecutorial personality? Is there such a thing as a prosecutorial personality or do prosecutors tend to differ greatly from one to another? If you were a prosecutor, how could we expect your personality to affect your job?

8. What traits, if any, should we expect all prosecutors to ideally share?

9. What is the best way to select chief local prosecutors? Should they be elected or appointed? Should assistant prosecutors have any job security or should their boss be allowed to fire them at will? Should we encourage assistant prosecutors to make a career of the job or expect them to leave after a few years?

10. In some countries local prosecutors work for the national government. In the U.S. they mostly work at the county level. At what level do you think most prosecutors should work: federal, state, or county? Why? Why do some prosecutors in our country work at the federal level? Why do some (in all states) work at the state level?

11. In what ways are prosecutors held to different standards of fairness than are defense attorneys? Do you agree that prosecutors should be held to a different standard? Why?

12. How much money should assistant prosecutors get paid? Should they get paid more, less, or the same as public defenders? Should they get pay raises based on performance rather than longevity? If so, what sort of factors should be included in performance-based raises?

13. How can spending time as a prosecutor help further a career in politics? Can you think of any former prosecutors turned politician? Is it good or bad that elected prosecutors sometimes have to concern themselves with politics in their decisions?

14. Are prosecutors more ethical than criminal defense attorneys? Less moral? Would helping to see to it that some people go to prison for long periods of time cause you any distress? Would it cause you satisfaction? Would you fear personal reprisals from people you helped send to prison?

15. Why might it not be so good an idea for a prosecutor to be overly adversarial with defense attorneys? Who tends to be more adversarial with defense attorneys: new prosecutors or veterans? Why?

16. According to the Table in the chapter, what are some of the different ways that "lay beliefs" can differ from "prosecutorial attitudes?"

17. Is it ethical for prosecutors negotiating a plea bargain to "bluff" when they know they have technical problems with a case. Is it ethical to overcharge in order to strengthen one's hand in plea bargaining? Is it ethical to judge shop? Would you do any of these things?

18. Many prosecutors seem to be somewhat cynical in nature. Is this because legally trained people who are cynical seek out jobs like this? Or, is there something about the work that twists people over time? Which other criminal justice professionals might you expect to be at risk for cynicism?

19. How might aspects of prosecution work lead to psychological trauma from time to time? What effect do you suppose it would have on your psyche to see a constant stream of crime victims (including molested children, rape victims, surviving family members of those murdered, etc.). How would you attempt to avoid becoming too traumatized?

20. What sort of general life skills can someone expect to take away from the job after working as a prosecutor for a few years? Would any of these skills be helpful to jobs outside of the law?

*****

Key Terms: U.S. Attorneys, local prosecutors, executive branch, chief law enforcement officer, nolle prosequi, local autonomy, decentralized system of prosecution, separation of powers, discretionary power, professional autonomy, public prosecutor, adversarial, socialization, vertical prosecution, horizontal prosecution, duty to do justice, discovery, work product, mandatory discovery, exculpatory evidence, snitch, nepotism, first assistant district attorney, cynicism, suspicion, self-trauma

Additional Concepts: power of prosecutor vs. judge, partisan hiring, elections, invisibility of decisions to public, supervising assistants, prosecutors' different personalities, lay beliefs vs. prosecutorial attitudes, wearing the white hat, duties of prosecutors, history of prosecutors, aggressiveness of new prosecutors, ethical issues, bluffing, over-charging defendants, prosecutorial pathologies, hypocrisy, leaving office, skills gained as a prosecutor, trial volume of prosecuting vs. civil law practice

CHAPTER SIX

THE JUDGE

Not all judges are created equal. This chapter shall look at two very different types of judges: magistrates (lower court judges) and trial-level judges. There are other types of judges as well, most notably appellate court judges. The study of judges is, as is the study of government in general, traditionally the domain of political science. The relatively small subset of political scientists who elect to study judges (as opposed to the many other areas of political science) have written quite a lot about appellate court judges, especially about members of the U.S. Supreme Court. Yet, very little has been written about the ordinary judges that most Americans deal with on a more intimate basis.

Appellate court judges will be examined in a later chapter discussing appeals. It will be the task of this chapter to cover the more ordinary judges whose decisions impact the lives of people as much as those of justices of the Supreme Court and other appellate judges. These every-day judges may not set national policy or strike down legislation, but they help decide the fate of so many human beings that their importance should not be overlooked. Let us begin by taking a look at lower court judges.

Part A: The Lower Court Judge

People called her "judge," but Rachel Bailey did not really feel like one. Like many lower court judges around the country, she had never gone to law school and never passed a bar exam.[1] She did not have the power to hold attorneys in contempt of court when they showed her disrespect. Her $60,000 per year salary was certainly no where near what "real" judges earned in her area.

Rachel Bailey was a judge of the Monroe County justice court. Her kind exists throughout the country. Her colleagues go by many different names in

---

1. See, Provine, Doris Marie. (1986). *Judging Credentials: Nonlawyer Judges and the Politics of Professionalism*. Chicago: University of Chicago Press.

different places: justice of the peace, district justice, city court judge, police court judge, municipal court judge, magistrate court judge, and (in the case of Judge Rachel Bailey) justice court judge.

Judge Bailey was appointed by the county commissioners with the consent of the president judge of the county (many lower court judges around the country are elected). She handled both civil and criminal matters.

Duties of Lower Court Judges

On the civil side, Judge Bailey presided over **small claims court**. She would listen to litigants each tell his or her side of things and then render a judgement in favor of one side or the other. The amount in controversy was limited in her court to matters involving less than $4,000—anything above that had to be taken to regular court.

In civil court, Judge Bailey saw lots of landlord-tenant disputes, unfulfilled minor contracts, petty damage to property, and unpaid consumer debts. Litigants rarely came with lawyers since their fees could not be justified given the small amount of hoped-for awards. They would show up at her office asking how to proceed and the judge's secretary would hand them a boiler-plate, civil complaint form to fill out. She would then schedule a hearing for them. Often times, the defendant would not even show up for the hearing (despite being notified via certified mail) and a **default judgment** would automatically be rendered in favor of the plaintiff.

When both parties did show up for a hearing, neither the litigants nor Judge Bailey worried much about formality or the rules of evidence. People just told their stories, Judge Bailey listened, and a ruling was made. If losers in court did not "pay up" as ordered, Judge Bailey would direct a deputy sheriff to go over to their houses, seize some assets, and auction them at a **sheriff's sale** to raise money for the winner. (Most litigants paid their debts before actual sale of their property, which would then be returned to them.)

Judge Bailey also had the power to marry people which she did on a routine basis. The actual legal ceremony was amazingly brief. So, Judge Bailey tried to add some of her own material to make it seem more substantive.

Apart from small claims court and marriages, the bulk of Judge Bailey's duties consisted of criminal court matters. She was the person who set bail in petty and serious crimes. At the request of police officers, she issued search warrants and arrest warrants. She listened to defendants who wanted to fight their traffic tickets. She conducted preliminary hearings on felonies and actually held trials on Class B and C misdemeanors (but not on the more serious Class A).

Judge Bailey set bail for people at what is generally called a "first appearance." (See chapter on "Justice Delayed" for a lengthy discussion of bail.) Judge Bailey personally liked to make use of **integrity tests** in deciding how much bail to require of someone. She would ask the accused a couple of questions to which she already knew the answers (e.g., regarding information she discretely noticed on their rap sheets). If they would tell the truth, Judge Bailey would be relatively charitable with them but if they lied she would set bail rather high.

Police officers came to Judge Bailey all the time seeking search warrants. She would have the police officer fill out a form in which the officer would particularly describe where the officer wanted to search, what he or she expected to find, and the **probable cause** he or she had for believing that contraband or criminal evidence would be there. She had a little section at the bottom of the form in which the officer would "swear or affirm" under penalty of law that nothing in his or her probable cause statement was invented or exaggerated.

Even though she required police officers seeking search warrants to go through the mechanical motions, Judge Bailey was not much of a check on the actions of police officers. In the four years of serving as a petty judicial official, Bailey had only once refused to grant a search warrant requested by a police officer. This was so despite the constitutional expectation that judicial officers granting warrants be **neutral and detached** (fair to both sides). Judge Bailey just figured that if an officer went to all of the trouble of coming down to her office to fill out the paper-work for a search warrant, he or she almost certainly deserved one.

Judge Bailey almost never issues arrest warrants. Arrest warrants are much rarer than search warrants. Search warrants are almost always needed to search homes and businesses—though not automobiles.[2] But arrest warrants are only needed to arrest people suspected of committing a subset of misdemeanors: those committed outside the presence of an officer. They are not required to arrest people suspected of committing felonies (unless the arrest will be made at home) nor for people who allegedly have committed a misdemeanor in the presence of an officer.[3] Almost everyone the police have interest in arresting either have committed a felony (in or outside of their presence) or a misdemeanor in their presence. Police usually just send a court summons to people whom they wish prosecuted for small crimes done outside of their presence.

---

2. See U.S. Constitution, amendment IV. See also, *Mapp v. Ohio,* 367 U.S. 643 (1961); *California v. Carney,* 471 U.S. 386 (1985); *California v. Acevedo,* 500 U.S. 565 (1991).

3. *United States v. Watson,* 423 U.S. 411 (1976).

A huge part of Judge Bailey's job was to handle "traffic court." She almost always found defendants guilty as long as the police officer showed up to testify. The problem was that many officers did not show up, especially if it was their day off. In that case, the judge would usually give a defendant two choices: have the case rescheduled for another day or else plead guilty to a lesser offense (e.g., a greatly reduced speed) and pay a much smaller fine. Sometimes, in matters involving police officers notorious for failing to appear for court, the judge would just enter a default judgment in favor of the defendant.

Traffic court was always a zoo. Every defendant was ordered to come at 9:00 a.m. or 1:00 p.m., even though his or her case might not be heard for hours later. Those few who came with attorneys were "bumped up" to the top of the list so that the attorney's time would not be wasted. The judge could afford offending citizens whom she would never see again but did not want to anger members of the bar with whom she regularly had to deal.

Plea bargains were encouraged in Judge Bailey's traffic court. Sophisticated people who got tickets (and who had the time) knew that by merely showing up for court and fighting the ticket, they would be offered a reduced penalty if they did not insist on going through with their hearing. Judge Bailey felt guilty about rewarding "sophisticated" people in this fashion (the honest, compliant folks who paid their tickets through the mail were given no breaks), but she felt she had no choice but to "bribe" those who came to court in order to reduce her load.

Another duty Judge Bailey had was to conduct preliminary hearings in felonies and Class A misdemeanors. Though some jurisdictions in the country have the same judge who will ultimately do the trial also handle the preliminary hearing, others allow the lower court judge to conduct the preliminary hearing.

The purpose of the **preliminary hearing** is for a neutral judicial officer to confirm that probable cause exists that a crime took place and that the defendant is the one who did it. Remember, arrest warrants are very rarely required. So, if it were not for preliminary hearings, police officers alone would get to decide probable cause and their decision would be final until a trial could take place. Cases often do not come to trial for months and it would be intolerable for a defendant to sit in jail (or worry while on bail) only to have charges belatedly dropped due to a lack of credible evidence. If pursuant to a preliminary hearing (a quick mini-trial) Judge Bailey found probable cause, she would bind the matter for a jury trial. If she did not find probable cause, she would dismiss the charges.

Judge Bailey rarely dismissed the charges. In fact, she bound cases over for trial about 98 percent of the time. This was not because Judge Bailey was more easily persuaded of probable cause than are most lower court judges. Preliminary hearings in this country almost never result in a dismissal of charges.[4] The burden of proof (probable cause) is very low and it is easy to "pass the buck" to a jury to decide the ultimate issue of guilt beyond a reasonable doubt.

One other criminal court chore Judge Bailey performed was to do misdemeanor trials. In her jurisdiction, lower court judges like herself were only authorized to do Class B and Class C (less serious) misdemeanors and not Class A (more serious) misdemeanors. She of course could not try any felony cases.

When Judge Bailey conducted a criminal trial it was always a **bench trial** and never a jury trial. These trials were very quick, almost as quick as a preliminary hearing in a more serious matter. Sometimes, defendants would simply use these trials as a way to make a lengthy sentencing argument, realizing that they had little hope for an outright acquittal. Most defendants who lost such trials were not punished very severely. Having felt like they had their "day in court" and pleased with a relatively light penalty, they accepted the verdict and the punishment. A few however, would want to fight on after their conviction. These few would appeal to the regular court with lawyer-trained judges who would give them a **trial de novo** (a re-trial of the case with a complete repetition of the witnesses and the evidence).

It is because defendants who lose in these lower courts of **limited jurisdiction** are given a "trial de novo" on appeal to a court of **general jurisdiction**, that the U.S. Supreme Court tolerates the use of non-lawyer judges in the lower courts. Some might argue that a non-lawyer like Judge Bailey does not know the rules of evidence well enough to conduct a fair trial. Even if one were to hire a lawyer in her court, what good would it do if the "judge" could not understand and competently rule on the lawyer's objections and legal motions. In the 1976 case of *North v. Russell*[5] the Supreme Court ruled that because defendants who lose their trials in lower courts are given a trial de novo on appeal, due process is not violated in the use non-lawyers as judges in these lower courts. (The dissent in that case argued that use of non-lawyers still is wrong since a trial de novo requires people to suffer multiple court appearances, delay, and financial burdens.)

---

4. The author, a former public defender and a former prosecutor in Pennsylvania, sat in on hundreds of preliminary hearings. Dismissals were almost non-existent. This was true in both counties he served in and true for all judges conducting the preliminary hearings. In many states (e.g., Utah where the author now resides), defense attorneys do not even bother with preliminary hearings. Rather, they routinely "waive" them, seeing them as wastes of their time.

5. *North v. Russell*, 427 U.S. 328 (1976).

Lower Court Advantages and Liabilities

Much can be said in favor of the lower courts. For one thing, they are local and close to the people. Once, in a preliminary hearing for theft, a local prosecutor was surprised when Judge Bailey refused to bind the defendant over for trial, despite the testimony of the alleged victim that a message therapist stole money from her purse while she was on the table. She explained to the prosecutor that the defendant's story that the alleged victim must be crazy and making this whole thing up had a lot of weight to it. The alleged victim was in fact mentally ill and was constantly accusing everyone from supermarket cashiers to gas station clerks of stealing money from her purse.

Another advantage of the lower courts is that due to their informal nature, people feel comfortable going there without hiring expensive attorneys. They are truly the "people's court," not just in civil matters but in traffic and minor criminal matters as well.

A third (huge) virtue of the lower courts is the great pressure they take off the courts of general jurisdiction. The National Center for State Courts has reported that for every four million criminal cases handled by courts of general jurisdiction, courts of limited jurisdiction handle over nine million. These figures do not count traffic and ordinance violations. For every eight million of those handled by courts of general jurisdiction, lower courts handle fifty-one million.[6] (Of course, one must add to all of this easing of pressure on the courts of general jurisdiction the many millions of civil cases processed in small claims court each year.)

Lower courts possess blemishes as well as virtues. Because so many judges in these courts are not legally trained, they sometimes fail to receive respect from lawyers who appear before them. In the case of some lower court judges this lack of respect given them may be justified. Some in fact seem indifferent to the written law even when they are aware of it. (The author remembers one time showing a lower court judge a statute in an attempt to convince the judge that his constant imprisoning of people for their financial inability to pay an entire fine at once was illegal. The lower court judge responded in a colorful way that he did not care what the law was; he was going to continue to send such people to jail anyway. A court of general jurisdiction did care what the law was and reversed him. Ironically, this same lower court judge was arrested a few months later for stealing his own court's fine monies. After his 30 days

---

6. Ostrom, Brian J. (1994). "State Court Statistics: Annual Report 1992." Williamsburg, Va.: National Center for State Courts, pp. 6, 8.

in jail—where he lived in protective custody—he took a job as a clerk in a 7-Eleven store.)

Other lower court judges are sensitive to the law but still get no respect. Some lawyers more graciously accept rulings of law-trained judges in courts of general jurisdiction much more readily than those of "mere" college graduates—or "mere" high school graduates—in lower courts. Add to this the fact that in many jurisdictions inferior court judges are not even given the contempt power, a situation exists in which some lawyers feel free to express their disapproval with decisions in abusive ways.

Another weakness of the lower courts is inequity concerning the volume of work confronting various lower court judges, even within the same county. For example, Judge Bailey's county was divided into eight judicial segments, each of equal population. Judge Bailey was given one of these divisions as her jurisdiction. On the face of things, this would seem fair since Judge Bailey's area contained the same number of people as that of any other lower court judge in her county. However, Judge Bailey's slice of the county consisted entirely of just one half of one town. This town was the only municipality of any real size in the county and one with a disproportionate amount of poverty and crime. Not only was Judge Bailey's turf confined to this one problematic town, but her half of the town was by far the poorer half, incorporating the local "drug zone" and "red light district." Whereas other lower court judges typically only worked twenty-five to thirty-five hours per week for their salaries (the one who worked twenty-five hours even had time to own and operate a Dairy Queen franchise on the side), Judge Bailey had to work fifty hours per week for identical pay. Courts of limited jurisdiction are often proportioned along lines of general population, but thought is not always given to the amount of business these various jurisdictions will generate.

Carving up a county into various segments for lower court jurisdiction also creates another problem: unprofessional environments. In many parts of the country lower court judges are required to physically locate their courts within their assigned geographical jurisdictions. Sometimes facilities that are both affordable and dignified are hard to secure. Many judges find themselves in strip malls or other facilities that were never designed to serve as a court.

Judge Bailey's own court was housed in a former dental office suite, right next to a "Blockbuster" store. There was no lock-up for the criminals brought there for court. Police officers often found themselves having to handcuff dangerous felons to heavy objects as they waited for their preliminary hearings. Lawyers had no place to confidentially speak with their clients. They were forced to talk to them in crowded hallways. Police officers and prosecutors politely declined to use as evidence anything that they might unavoidably overhear.

A final blemish on the face of the local courts is the **assembly line justice** that they are forced to engage in given their often massive caseloads. Judges working in rough jurisdictions with huge crime rates can face staggering volumes of work. This causes defendants sometimes to be treated as objects on a factory assembly line with little time for individualized attention. As one student of the lower courts once famously remarked, the assembly-line nature of these courts often means that "**the process is the punishment**" rather than any fines or other penalties imposed.[7]

In Judge Bailey's court, the "process" was indeed the "punishment." She remembers once overhearing a citizen who had come to her court to complain to a secretary about a grossly unfair parking ticket he had just received. He told the secretary that he was visiting a friend's row house on a crowded street in town that very afternoon. He said that as he parked he looked very carefully for signs forbidding him to park. There were no such signs. In fact, the sign right in front of his chosen parking spot said, "No parking Tues/Thurs from 4a.m. to 6a.m. for street cleaning."

Despite all of this he noticed a parking ticket on his windshield as he left his friend's house at 2 p.m. The police officer who had just written it saw him and hastily headed over to his squad car and left before the citizen could question him about the ticket. The citizen stared at the ticket, at the sign, at the street, at the curb, and for three or four minutes could not ascertain why he had received a ticket. Finally, he noticed a hand-crafted sign apparently made by a homeowner hanging obscurely in the window of a make-shift garage that had been added to the house. It said, "No parking—private driveway." The "driveway" was the public sidewalk complete with a high, unmarked street curb. A neighbor of this homeowner saw the citizen staring at the handmade sign and told the citizen that this homeowner was always calling the police to come and give unsuspecting people tickets, and the police always did just that.

The judge's secretary told the citizen that he could fight the ticket in court and he would no doubt win. He should come next Wednesday at 9 a.m. for his hearing.

The citizen said this would be a hardship as he would have to hire a baby sitter since his wife worked until 10 a.m. He further stated that he would have to be done by 10:30 a.m. or miss a class he taught at the university. The secretary told him that there was only a fair chance he would be finished by noon and she could not absolutely guarantee that his case would be called even by

---

7. See, Feeley, Malcolm. (1979). *The Process is the Punishment: Handling Cases in Lower Court.* New York: Russell Sage Foundation.

4 p.m. The man asked how much the fine was. She told him $25.00. Wisely (though unjustly) the man just paid it and left. He was unwilling to let the "process" be his "punishment."

The Lure of Money

Lower courts are not likely to go away because there is just no way that higher courts could ever absorb the caseload which they handle. In fact, in many areas there is an additional reason why lower courts will not only fail to disappear but will thrive: the profits they are capable of generating for local governments.

Lower courts have always been tempted by the lure of money. At one time, salaries of many lower court judges expanded or contracted depending upon the amount of fines such courts took in. The U.S. Supreme Court tried to put an end to this as far back as 1927 when it ruled that systems that based judicial salaries on the amount of fines judges collected were unconstitutional.[8] However, it was decades later before this decision was obeyed in many communities.[9]

Today the lure of money takes on a different form. In many states, fines collected by courts of general jurisdiction go to the state capitol. But, fines collected in lower courts are retained in whole or in part by local government. For example, lower courts operated by counties levy and collect fines for traffic offenses and petty crimes which occur in the particular court's jurisdiction within the county. Money collected winds up in the county treasury rather than that of the state.[10]

Cities and towns within a county can have their own municipal courts if they elect to do so. Fines collected in municipal court (e.g., from someone caught speeding in town limits) often are retained in whole or in part by the town or city that operates the court. Given the tens of millions of Americans who pay fines for traffic offenses, ordinance violations, and petty crimes every year, these lower courts can be a significant source of revenue for local governments, even after expenses of running the courts are deducted.[11]

---

8. *Tumey v. Ohio*, 237 U.S. 510 (1927).

9. Vanlandingham, Kenneth E. (1974). "The Decline of the Justice of the Peace." In John A. Robertson (ed.). *Rough Justice: Perspectives on Lower Criminal Courts.* Boston: Little Brown.

10. Steury, Ellen Hochstedler and Nancy Frank. (1996). *Criminal Court Process.* Minneapolis: West Publishing Company, p. 218.

11. Id.

Part B: The Criminal Trial Court Judge

The honorable Robert Moran took great pride in being a judge of the superior court, the trial-level court in which he first began practicing law as a prosecutor over twenty years earlier. As a superior court judge, Judge Moran handled more than just criminal matters. He heard everything from divorce cases to zoning issues to will contests. But, like his colleagues, fully half of his time was devoted to the criminal docket. This was fine with Judge Moran. As a former prosecutor he felt more comfortable with this side of the law. He also found it to be far more interesting than the civil matters.

Judge Robert Moran was not popular with the criminal defense bar. He was known as "Maximum Bob." He had a reputation for being self-righteous as a prosecutor and seemed even worse now that he wore the black robes. He routinely gave everyone whom he sentenced the maximum sentence allowed by law—no exceptions. This greatly reduced the negotiating power of defense attorneys in plea bargaining with prosecutors who would basically give them "take it or leave it" offers.

Of all the things that tend to stress defense attorneys, nothing bothers them more intensely than a perceived lack of judicial impartiality.[12] Though most lawyers find most judges to be impartial, there are exceptions.[13] Judge Moran was definitely one of the exceptions. Judge Moran would tell defense attorneys that "if you want to go to trial, go to trial. But if you lose the trial your client is going to get the maximum." Defense attorneys in Judge Moran's court complain that "in the four years that Judge Moran has been on the bench, only once has he failed to give someone the maximum when he is the one who got to decide the sentence."

For awhile defense attorneys thought that Judge Moran's tough approach was merely a desire on his part to create a "law and order" image for voters come election time. But after awhile they realized that it was not merely an image: Judge Moran was a "true believer" in maximum sentences.

Prosecutors appreciated Judge Moran for making their jobs as plea negotiators easier. Yet, even they did not like him. Many in the district attorney's office felt that Judge Moran was indiscriminately tough. He wasted precious prison space and tax payer dollars on relatively minor offenders. When it came to elections, few prosecutors voted for him in the secrecy of the booth.

---

12. Lynch, David R. (1997). "The Nature of Occupational Stress Among Public Defenders." *The Justice System Journal,* 19(1):17–34, p. 27.

13. Id.

The Selection of Judges

Like most judges in the country, Judge Moran was elected (just over half the states use elections to select their judges).[14] Judge Moran was elected to **long terms of office** (ten years). Long terms are typical in states that use elections. The thinking is that judges need to feel free to make correct though unpopular decisions without having to constantly worry about being re-elected every two or four years.

Once a judge is elected, it is almost impossible to unseat him or her even when the judge does finally come up for re-election. This is largely due to party politics coupled with voter ignorance. Few voters are qualified to assess the relative merits of judicial candidates. Most people may know how to cast their votes for president, governor, or senator, but how many people really know whom to vote for when selecting a judge? Judges are not allowed to campaign. It would be considered inappropriate for a candidate to openly advertise his likely views or positions as a judge, since judges are supposed to appear unbiased and "judicial." This leaves voters with very little information on which to base a decision. Often, voters are reduced to voting merely for a political party rather than for an individual. Democrats will vote for the Democratic judicial candidate while Republicans will vote for the Republican. Hence, judges in heavily Democratic counties often tend to be all Democrats while judges in heavily Republican counties often tend to be all Republicans. In other words, it is the local party apparatus and not the voters which often really decides whom the judges will be, and attorneys active in party politics often must pay their dues and "wait in line" before receiving party support.[15]

Judge Moran got his job as judge not though merit but because his father was the chair of the county Republican party (that is also how he got his job as prosecutor). Once elected, he seemed to be in for life. True, voters would have a chance to throw him out every ten years, but this did not seem likely.

A local criminal defense attorney learned the painful way how hard it was to unseat an elected judge. He told his best friend every horror story he could think of regarding Judge Moran just two nights before the election. He told him about how he was known as "Maximum Bob." He told him how Judge Moran was known to regularly sit half-drunk after lunch on the bench. He explained how this judge was rude to lawyers, police officers, victims and wit-

---

14. Council of State Governments. (1998). *The Book of the States, 1998–1999 edition.* Lexington, KY: C.S.G., p. 135.

15. For a classic study on this phenomenon, see Levin, Martin A. (1976). "Urban Politics and Policy Outcomes: The Criminal Courts." In Cole, George F. (ed.). *Criminal Justice: Law and Politics,* 2nd ed. North Scituate, Mass: Duxbury Press, 1976.

nesses to the point of being mentally ill. (Local attorneys were convinced he suffered from "Narcissistic disorder," as was evidenced by the fact that someone had written his name next to that term in an often-used book in the county law library.) The local attorney even told his friend how Judge Moran's old law clerk would vomit before coming to work each day, and how his current law clerk would hide from him for days at a time in the courthouse law library only to appear when the judge's secretary would tip the clerk off that the judge was looking for her. The friend became convinced that Moran should not be re-elected and promised the local defense attorney that he would not vote for him.

A few days after the election, the lawyer ran into his best friend in town. The friend asked the lawyer to remind him whom it was he was not supposed to have voted for the other day. When the lawyer said, "Robert Moran," the friend gasped that it was in fact Moran for whom he had voted. "Why?" asked the lawyer in frustration. "Because I could not remember the name of the guy you told me not to vote for, so I just voted Republican."

Because of the difficulty of voting for candidates who are forbidden to reveal their views and platforms to potential voters, many states choose to appoint their judges rather than to elect them. There are two types of appointments: political and merit.

Judges who get their jobs by way of **political appointment** are chosen either by the governor or by the state legislature. Merit may play a factor, but politics definitely matters. The best lawyer seeking to become a judge may not be selected if that lawyer is not politically connected. Why "waste" a judicial appointment on someone who has never helped the appointing power in any way? Nine states select their trial-level judges though political appointments.[16]

Twelve states opt for **merit appointment** of their judges.[17] A good way to illustrate how this works is to use the state of Utah as a case study.

In Utah, a lawyer who wishes to become a judge sends a resume to blue-ribbon "nominating commission" composed of seven members. One member of this committee is selected by the governor, one or two by the state senate, one or two by the state house, while the remainder are selected by the state Bar. Two or so of the committee members are typically lawyers while others are community leaders, business people, clergy, etc.

Typically this committee will receive applications from fifty or so lawyers who want the job and the committee will narrow the field down to five or

---

16. Council of State Governments, supra note 14, pp. 135–137.
17. Id.

seven finalists. The governor then interviews each finalist and picks one. The governor may have lawyers help him or her with the interviews, especially if the governor is a non-lawyer, but this really depends on the governor. Some governors actively telephone lawyers and say "if you can get by the nominating commission I'll appoint you, so why don't you try?" Other governors are more passive.

Once appointed, a judge must periodically stand for **retention elections** in which the voters are only given one candidate (the judge) and simply asked whether they vote "yes" or "no" to retain that judge. Local wisdom is that eighty percent of Utahans vote "yes" to retain every judge while twenty percent vote "no" in order to get rid of each and every judge. Very few seem to pick and choose retention based upon the merits of an individual judge. Only one judge has ever been "voted out" of office in Utah in a retention election. Judges defend this by saying that retention elections are only meant as a "last ditch check" or "failsafe," but many members of the state legislature question the validity of elections in which nobody ever loses.[18] (Other states apparently have had similar experiences with retention elections. Over a twenty year period looked at, only 22 judges failed to be retained out of nearly 2,000 retention elections held across ten states.)[19]

Judge Moran was grateful that his state used elections rather than merit appointments. He sensed that he might have a shot at a political appointment but not at one based on merit. He did not think that he could ever make it past a nominating commission. He remembers when he, as a young man, tried to gain entrance to the U.S. Air Force Academy. This required an appointment either by a U.S. Senator or a member of the U.S. House of Representatives. He had applied to both Senators in his state as well as to the Member of the House representing his area. He did not get anywhere with either Senator but did receive a letter from his Congressman asking him to come for an interview. He remembers the day when his father drove him to the interview at the Congressman's local office only to find a panel of three air force officers (all academy graduates) that the Congressman wisely had recruited to help him make a meritorious selection (and perhaps to take political heat off of him). This panel was not particularly impressed by young Moran's answers to tough questions, nor with his border-line grades and ACT scores, and did

---

18. This information was made known to the author in a Fall 2002 interview with a judge of the Utah Court of Appeals who was very familiar with the local process.

19. Hall, William T. and Larry T. Aspin. (1992). "Distance from the Bench and Retention Voting Behavior: A Comparison of Trial Court and Appellate Court Retention Elections." *Justice System Journal*, 15(3):801–813.

not recommend him. The Congressman personally telephoned Moran's politically connected father to apologetically explain that it was the panel of Air Force Academy graduates and not he who had rejected his fine son.

Duties of a Judge

As a judge, Judge Moran wore many hats. He presided in criminal court, juvenile court, and civil court. This was quite a change for the former prosecutor who only had to worry about adult criminal court. Judge Moran (as opposed to Assistant District Attorney Moran) had to worry about many areas of the law, not just the criminal side of things.

When he did wear the adult criminal court hat, Judge Moran performed various duties. One of the things he did was to hear and rule on pre-trial motions. These involved things like a motion to suppress illegally obtained evidence, a motion to quash an indictment that should never have been issued, a motion to change venue, or a motion to reduce bail. These hearings typically took a half hour or less each. One technique Judge Moran liked to employ with some motions (especially motions to suppress evidence) was to schedule the hearing on the motion right before trial was to start (and no time sooner) in the hopes that a plea bargain would make the hearing unnecessary. That is usually exactly the way things turned out.

Accepting guilty pleas was another big part of his job. Most guilty pleas involved plea bargains. His job was merely to accept or reject the bargain. He rarely rejected bargains, even ones that he did not like. He figured it was the attorneys' job—not his—to decide if an agreement was good or not for the people they represented.

Judge Moran did get to decide sentences himself when a person went to trial and lost. Few people went to trial, but nevertheless sentencing was an important part of his job.

The hardest thing Judge Moran had to do was to preside at trials. Like police work, presiding at trials consists mostly of finding ways not to be too bored while occasionally struggling not to panic. Lawyers do most of the work at trials, but judges earn their pay whenever one of the lawyers raises an objection that must be instantaneously and confidently ruled upon. Judge Moran was shocked the first time he presided as a judge at a trial at the number of times he guessed as to which way to rule on an objection. Now he finally understood one of the reasons why judges hate to do trials so much. He knew the rules of evidence. But it is hard to hear an objection (assuming one was paying attention to the testimony objected to), consider every possible nuance of every rule of evidence, and render an accurate decision—all in the course of a couple of seconds without consulting any law books. By his calculations, Judge Moran was guessing about whether to sustain or overrule an objection about one forth of the time. Usually if he knew he had to guess, he generally preferred to guess in favor of the defendant. This was not because he favored the defendant but because only defense attorneys (and not prosecutors) can get a verdict overturned due to judicial errors made at trial. When the defense appeals an error made by the judge, a higher court reviews it and sees the judge's mistake. When the judge's error hurts the prosecutor, it ends there (no appeal due to double jeopardy).

Pro's and Con's of Being a Judge

Judge Moran knew that being a judge had its rewards. The benefit that Judge Moran most cherished was job security. Even though he was not appointed for life like judges in some states, he knew that he had a job for ten year intervals before having to face re-election. Besides, since few voters know anything about judicial candidates, Judge Moran knew he had little to fear from elections as long as the letter "R" for Republican remained next to his name on the ballot in this heavily Republican jurisdiction. All of this was very important to Moran because he knew that being successful as a private attorney required tremendous patience and social skills which he was not sure he possessed. As a judge, he effectively had life tenure despite his ability or inability to get along with people.

Another perk of being a judge that Moran really liked was the salary. As a trial-level judge, Moran earned just over 140,000 dollars per year. Though many of his fellow judges whined about how hard it was to support a family on such a "meager" wage, Judge Moran secretly felt very satisfied. He realized that the legal profession was a glutted industry and to be able to make over 140,000 dollars per year while working less than 40 hours per week (Judge Moran usually took Thursday and Friday afternoons off) with tremendous job security was not too bad a deal. Judge Moran never had to worry about "making rain" (securing clients), and unlike the high-paid attorneys in private firms he was almost always home for an early dinner.

Another benefit of the job that pleased Moran was the prestige he held in the courthouse community by being a judge. People made paths for him in crowded courthouse corridors, rose when he entered rooms, and called him "your honor" when they addressed him in court. Court administrators and probation officers who rarely wore ties during the work day, put one on whenever they came to visit him in his office. Moran could say whatever he wanted to people in his courtroom (he was notorious for rudely correcting lawyers' choice of vocabulary and meanly insulting defendants' appearance), but should anybody say even the slightest rude comment he would slap him or her with a fine for **contempt of court**.

In our society, one may insult (though not threaten) the president or the pope or the governor to their faces, but one may not insult a judge. Judges are America's version of aristocrats, people placed on a high pedestal for life, and whom people must stand before while speaking and address at all times with deference. Judge Moran had the power to fine or even briefly imprison people for **direct contempt** (rudeness or disrespect shown in his presence) and the power to punish for **indirect contempt** (refusing to follow a judicial order outside the presence of the judge). Judge Moran even tried to have one lawyer temporarily suspended or at least publicly censored by the Bar for saying a joke about him at a private party at which the judge was not even present. He alleged in his complaint that the lawyer should be disciplined for "bringing the judicial office into public disrepute despite being an attorney and an officer of the court who had a legal duty to refrain from doing so."

Despite the benefits of job security, good pay, attractive work hours, and prestige, there were a few negatives to being a judge which Judge Moran did not appreciate. One negative was boredom. Clearing the docket week after week took time and mostly involved routine duties like rubber-stamping plea bargains that other people negotiated and signing proposed orders that other people (lawyers) had drafted. Even when Judge Moran got to do a trial, he realized that it was the attorneys who ran most of the show: they were the script writers, producers, directors, actors, and prop managers. He was just a referee, not a player on the field.

Another aspect of the job that bothered Judge Moran was a feeling he had that he was mainly a figurehead. Plea bargaining was done by prosecutors and defense attorneys. He merely accepted them in court. Case scheduling and management in his courthouse was handled by professional court administrators. Orders for him to sign were drafted by attorneys seeking the order—he was just a proof reader. Legal opinions he was expected to write were written largely by his law clerks. Sentences in cases not plea-bargained (e.g., when somebody pled guilty without a bargain) were usually recommended to him in the pre-sentence investigation report prepared by the probation office. It was only in those rare cases in which the defendant went to trial and lost that Judge Moran felt he had something to contribute (he chose to handle these sentences himself and did not rely much on pre-sentence investigation reports). Moran sometimes felt like the King in a chess set—a lot of prestige but not much of a real role in the game.

Though he was now used to the job, learning to be a judge was also something very hard for Judge Moran, as it is for new judges everywhere. In Europe, judges are groomed for the job by pursuing degrees that specifically train them to be judges (not just lawyers), and by working as assistant judges before becoming full-blown judges.[20] American judges on the other hand are given little if any specific training for the job. Luckily for Judge Moran, his county did pay for him to attend a few weeks at the **National Judicial College** located on the campus of the University of Nevada at Reno. But these crash courses were not enough. Judge Moran had to learn most of what he had to do as judge through on-the-job training. Luckily, as a former prosecutor, Judge Moran had a fairly good idea of how to conduct himself as a judge in criminal court. But, on the civil side of things, he felt quite incompetent for many months and made many embarrassing mistakes. One of the hardest things for Judge Moran was to no longer act like an advocate but to maintain a neutral stance on all cases. This was something the former prosecutor still had a hard time doing, especially in criminal cases.

The negative of the job that bothered Judge Moran the most was something that many lay people might not think of: loneliness. When one is put on a pedestal, it can be very lonely. Judge Moran's office was right next to the courtroom assigned to him which he did not share with any of the other judges. He had his own little fiefdom within the courthouse and had to go out of his way to socialize with other judges. Besides, there were not many other judges anyway, and he was not lucky enough to find one or two peers with whom he had a natural connection. Lawyers in the courthouse community were legion, but being a judge, Moran could not appropriately socialize with them. One time Judge Moran got so lonely in his chambers that he tried to make friends with a public defender who was assigned to his court and who had come to his office to get an order signed. The judge's secretary was out and Judge Moran invited the lawyer back into his personal office. The lawyer listened very deferentially as Judge Moran attempted to engage him in a conversation about the judge's lack of dating success, sports, and sore knee (which Judge Moran suffered from). After thirty minutes of awkwardness, Judge Moran signed the order and allowed the public defender to leave.

Ethical Dilemmas and Judges

Like all professionals who work in the criminal justice system, judges face many ethical dilemmas. For example, Judge Robert Moran was known as

---

20. Provine, Doris M. (1996). "Courts in the Political Process in France." In Herbert Jacob, E. Blankenburg, Herbert M. Kritzer, Doris M. Provine, and Joseph Sanders (Eds.), *Courts, Law, and Politics in Comparative Perspective* (pp. 177–248). New Haven, Conn.: Yale University Press.

"Maximum Bob" because he always gave people who went to trial and lost the maximum sentence allowed by law. Moran did this in order to send a message to defendants that they should not waste court time with trials unless they were pretty sure they would win. He also believed that criminals generally got off too easily and he philosophically agreed with harsh punishments. He thought people who victimized others should be severely punished.

One day Moran was forced to reconsider his ethics on sentencing when his law clerk asked if it was right to punish all robbers, drunk drivers, or thieves the same, even ones with similar prior records. Judge Moran explained to the clerk that in his view even the maximum penalties for these crimes were not severe enough—they all were getting less than they really deserved. But the law clerk's point that some robberies were worse than others, some drunk driving episodes were worse than others, and stealing from some people was worse than stealing from others, was not completely without merit. Some criminals are more culpable than others and should be punished more harshly even if they do the "same" crime and have a "similar" criminal record. Moran began to wonder if he should take less pride in being "Maximum Bob" and provide more individual consideration of those defendants whom he was to sentence.

Another ethical dilemma that confronts judges (at least the ones who do not give everyone the maximum) is whether it is ethical to punish a defendant who loses at trial after taking the stand in his own defense more than a defendant who does not take the stand and loses. Some judges believe that the former deserves extra punishment because he or she not only committed a crime but lied under oath about it (as evidenced by the jury's not believing the defendant). Some defense attorneys criticize judges who do this by suggesting that they are punishing people who exercise their right to stand up for themselves and that judges who punish defendants extra for testifying in their own defense are creating a "chilling effect" on the right to tell one's side of things. Despite this sentiment on the part of defense attorneys, appellate courts have ruled that because a defendant who is willing to lie under oath has less likelihood for successful rehabilitation, sentencing judges may deal with them more harshly than those defendants who go to trial and merely require the state prove its case against them.[21]

Another tough sentencing decision facing many judges, is whether or not it is ever justified for a judge to take into account what the judge believed a

---

21. See, *United States v. Grayson*, 438 U.S. 41 (1978); *State v. Smith*, 407 So.2d 652 (La. 1981); *People v. Adams*, 425 N.W.2d 437 (Mich. 1988).

defendant really did as opposed to what the jury convicted the defendant for. For example, suppose a jury inexplicably convicts somebody on trial for burglary and theft of the theft but not of the accompanying burglary. Suppose further that it would not be possible to have committed the theft without also committing the burglary. Judges might have to ask themselves whether they should give the defendant a more severe sentence than they ordinarily give thieves since the judge believes this particular defendant to be a burglar as well as a thief. Amazingly, taking into account at sentencing what the defendant probably did as opposed to what he did beyond a reasonable doubt may not be unconstitutional. One could argue that the reasonable doubt standard is relevant only to the guilt or innocence question. But, judges do not have to subject each and every factor used in determining a sentence to such a high standard (probability is an appropriate sentencing standard so long as a judge does not impose a sentence longer than the legal maximum penalty for the specific category of crime the defendant was convicted of).

There is one ethical duty that all judges have that is not subject to debate: the requirement to avoid all ex parte communications. An **ex parte communication** occurs whenever a judge discusses any aspect of a case with an attorney without the attorney for the other side also being present. The idea here is simple. In an adversarial system, judges should not be allowed to be lobbied in any way by one party to a case without the other party there to counter-lobby.

Judicial Personalities

Not all judges are the same. Robert Moran was known as "Maximum Bob" but it would be a huge mistake to assume that all judges are punishment-oriented. In fact, some are quite the opposite.

For example, a real life judge in Massachusetts was known as "Clueless K." for a series of extremely lenient sentences he meted out to defendants charged with various violent crimes including rape, assault, and child molestation. A judge in Philadelphia admitted to having cried in her chambers for having to sentence the rapist of a ten year old girl to a mandatory minimum sentence of five years in prison (the maximum sentence she could have given was twenty years).[22]

Judges superficially may tend to have similar backgrounds (middle class, law school graduates, born in the region where they now serve), but this does not mean that all of them have similar personalities. Especially in areas that still do not have mandatory sentencing guidelines for judges to follow, the

---

22. Levine, Daniel. (1999). "America's Worst Judges." *Readers' Digest* (August):78–84.

Table 1   Judges in Judge Moran's Courthouse

Judge	Nickname	Traits
Robert Moran	Maximum Bob	Very harsh sentences; verbally abusive to all; narcissistic
Gerald York	The Bear	Gets grumpy if attorney says the "T" word ("trial")—otherwise reasonable and friendly
Patricia Harper	Chatty Patty	Socially skilled; funny; political; popular; lenient sentences
John Cooper	Little Hitler	No nonsense; by the book; stern
Abraham Wood	Honest Abe	Decent; fair; smart; knowledgeable; humble
Kate Stevens	Even Stevens	Slow to anger; polite; fair
Leonard Cox	Big Hitler	Autocratic; aristocratic; imperious; does not suffer fools (attorneys or defendants)

Source: Fictional but based on author's experiences in two courthouses.

judge you wind up in front of can sometimes be as important as the crime that you committed. In Judge Moran's courthouse each of the seven judges had his or her own unique attributes, as illustrated in Table 1.

Conclusion

It cannot be disputed that defendants and lawyers who operate in the criminal courts are greatly affected by appellate court judges and most particularly by those of the U.S. Supreme Court. But it would be a mistake to overlook the huge impact that ordinary judges—both in courts of limited jurisdiction as well as at the trial court level—also have on the people who appear before them. All justice is not local but much of it is. An understanding of ordinary judges is critical to any profound understanding of the American criminal justice system.

*****

Questions for Class Discussion

1. What are the various responsibilities of lower court judges? Is serving as a lower court judge something you might enjoy as a career in criminal justice?

2. What are some of the advantages lower courts have over courts of general jurisdiction? What are some of the ways they are more handicapped than higher-level courts?

3. What happened in the case of *North v. Russell*? What were the arguments presented in its majority opinion justifying the use of non-law trained magistrates? What was the dissent's argument to the contrary? Which side do you think made the more persuasive case?

4. In some states, many lower court judges do not have law degrees yet rule on matters of law. Should we at least require them to be college graduates? Or, is that being snobbish? Should it be lawful (it is lawful) for an American president to appoint a non-lawyer to the U.S. Supreme Court? Can you think of any non-lawyers you would like appointed to the U.S. Supreme Court?

5. What do you think of the fact that some lower court judges give people a break just for showing up to court to fight their traffic ticket while less combative citizens just pay their fines in full? Have any of you ever been cut a break merely for showing up to traffic court ready to "fight?"

6. What do you think of the use by lower court judges of "integrity tests" in setting bail? Are such tests helpful? What questions might be posed in order to "test" a bail seeker's integrity?

7. How were lower courts in the past tempted by the lure of money? Today, the lure of money takes on a different form. How so?

8. Given that cases are almost always bound over for trial (more than 90 percent of the time), are preliminary hearings just a waste of the system's time? Are they a waste of the defense lawyer's time? Should we do away with preliminary hearings and just move straight to jury trial?

9. What is meant by "assembly line justice?" What is meant by the "process is the punishment?" If you were wrongly accused of a minor traffic violation that you felt you could beat, would it be worth it to you to go to court and fight it or would you be tempted to just pay the fine and get it over with? If traffic court were tomorrow, what plans would you have to cancel or arrangements to make in order for you to attend? Would it be worth saving a few bucks?

10. In the U.S. trial-level judges hear both criminal and civil matters. Would it be better for judges to specialize more? Why or why not? Which type of cases (criminal or civil) would you rather hear as a judge?

11. What are the advantages of giving judges very long terms (sometimes even life) on the bench? What are the disadvantages? Who else in our society has such job security?

12. Are elections the best way to select our judges, or is appointment better? How many judges who serve in your county can you identify by name?

Are you sufficiently informed as a citizen to know whom to vote for if asked to pick a judge from a list of candidates?

13. What is the difference between political appointments of trial-level judges and merit appointments? How are merit appointments carried out? Besides judges, do you know of any people who got some job by way of "politics" rather than being the best candidate for the job?
14. What sort of training do new judges receive? How do they learn their job? What sort of training do you think they should be given?
15. What are some examples of ethical dilemmas that judges might face?
16. What do you think of judges who always issue the maximum sentence for cases that go to trial and lose? Is that something you might like to do if you were on the bench? Do you admire "Maximum Bob" or look down on him?
17. The Table in the chapter lists various judges, their nicknames, and their judicial traits. Which of these judges do you admire the most? The least?
18. Judges are supposed to be completely neutral in the courtroom. Do you think this is possible, even at an unconscious level? Do you think referees in sporting events are capable of being completely neutral in contests, even at an unconscious level?
19. What is meant by an *ex parte* communication? Why is it so wrong? When have you ever been the victim of an *ex parte* communication outside of court in your own personal life?
20. How can it be argued with a straight face that lower court judges and trial court judges have just as great an impact on people's lives as do justices of the U.S. Supreme Court?

*****

Key Terms: small claims court, default judgment, sheriff's sale, integrity tests, probable cause, neutral and detached, preliminary hearing, bench trial, trial de novo, limited jurisdiction, general jurisdiction, assembly line justice, the process is the punishment, long terms of office, political appointment, merit appointment, retention elections, contempt of court, direct contempt, indirect contempt, National Judicial College, ex parte communication

Additional Concepts: types of judges, non-lawyer judges, duties of lower court judges, issuance of search warrants, issuance of arrest warrants, traffic appeals, advantages of lower courts, liabilities of lower courts, the lure of money, judicial impartiality, selection of judges, elections vs. appointments of judges, party politics, duties of a judge, rewards of being a judge, negatives of being a judge, ethical dilemmas and judges, judicial personalities

CHAPTER SEVEN

THE WITNESS

So far in this book, the various courthouse players discussed have all been professionals who inhabit the courthouse on a day to day basis: prosecutors, defense attorneys, judges, court administrators, etc. Another critical player in the courthouse is the witness who is brought in from the outside to testify either for the prosecution or for the defense. There are many different types of witnesses. Some of the more common types of witnesses typically appearing in court are: victim-witnesses, defendant-witnesses, eye witnesses, character witnesses, expert witnesses, and police witnesses. Each of these individual types of witnesses will be discussed below.

The Victim-Witness

Meg Willis understood what it could be like to be the victim of a crime and a potential witness in court better than anybody else who regularly worked in the courthouse. Her expertise was acquired before she was hired by the Lakeland County District Attorney's office as its first victim/witness advocate. She became an expert by having been a victim to a crime herself and a would-be witness in court.

Back when she was 28 years old, Meg was working in a group home for mentally handicapped adults while she was completing a bachelor's degree in social work. Early one evening, while Meg was driving home from work, her small car was broadsided by a repeat drunk driver who sped through a solid red light in his heavy vehicle. Meg's car was crushed and Meg was taken to the hospital in an ambulance. Meg's wrist was broken and her eye so damaged that she required plastic surgery. Her medical bills (she had no benefits at her job) totaled over $25,000. She wound up having to declare bankruptcy to stop the incessant hounding of bill collectors. Her credit rating was ruined for years.

Her car was only insured for liability to others and the repeat drunk driver had no insurance of his own. With no money to buy a car, she was forced to travel to work by way of public transportation. She lived and worked in two different suburbs with no bus links between them. She had to spend an hour and a half each morning and then again in the evening first commuting twenty five miles to downtown and then right back out again to a neighboring suburb.

Meg was **victimized twice**: once by the criminal and another time by the system. A few days after the "accident," Meg received a subpoena in the mail ordering her to appear for a preliminary hearing. Meg had to take off work the entire day without pay in order to attend the hearing which was inconveniently scheduled in the middle of her shift. After arriving for the hearing in a taxi, Meg was coldly told by a clerk that the hearing had been cancelled at the request of the defense attorney who called the other day mentioning a conflict with his schedule. She was told she would be notified by mail of the new hearing date.

Meg never heard another thing about the case. After waiting for weeks she called the district attorney's office and spoke with a secretary. She asked about the status of the case and was told that the defendant had waived the preliminary hearing and a trial would be scheduled in a few months. She asked about "restitution" and the secretary told her that since the case had not yet been disposed of she could not yet receive any. When she asked what steps if any she might have to take to make sure the court ordered restitution, the secretary merely repeated in an annoyed tone that she could not receive any money until the case was disposed of.

Meg never heard anything ever again. She tried several times to contact the prosecutor handling the case, but he was always in court and did not return her calls. She always wondered whatever happened with the case. After writing a letter complaining about how she was treated she went on with her life.

Meg had bitter feelings towards the district attorney's office and the justice system so she was surprised to find herself applying for a job with the district attorney's office after graduation. The advertisement in her college placement office attracted her interest however, since it suggested to her that the newly elected district attorney was perhaps trying to treat people like her better. The advertisement said that the district attorney's office sought to hire somebody with a bachelor's degree in social work or criminal justice who could work as a **victim/witness advocate** in order to:

"Provide emotional and moral support to victims of crimes; help prepare victims and other witnesses for court; provide witnesses with information regarding the current status of a case; act as a liaison between victims, police and prosecutors; assist victims in filing applications for the new victims' compensation fund; and help victims find professional counseling and support groups."[1] The pay was $39,500 per year plus benefits.

Perhaps life was not so unkind after all since Meg wound up getting the job. Meg would be working in a prosecutor's office but victim advocates like her also can be found working for police departments, sheriff offices, rape crisis centers, women shelters, and various private organizations. Some, like Meg, are paid. Others volunteer their time. Victim and witness advocates are people whose professions are still evolving. History has shown that their services however are very much needed.

In colonial America, victims were basically on their own when it came to the prosecution of crimes perpetrated against them. As mentioned in an earlier chapter, publicly paid prosecutors did not yet exist. Victims were expected to hire their own attorney to prosecute a criminal and even pay for any investigations and warrants themselves.[2] Though such practices now seem primitive, it should be pointed out that at least the victim controlled the process and had a huge say in anything that happened in court, including input into decisions regarding punishment and restitution.

In more modern times, publicly paid prosecutors stepped in to take control of processing criminal cases through court. These attorneys no longer worked on behalf of the individual victim however, but rather had the state as their client. Because of this, victims and other witnesses began to be seen by many prosecutors as mere tools to gain convictions. Whether a prosecutor cared for a victim as an individual depended on the individual conscience of a particular prosecutor.

In the latter part of the 20th Century, a **Victims' Rights Movement** took place in which victims and their allies began to demand better treatment by the courts. Most states passed legislation and even constitutional amendments which guaranteed a **Victims' Bill of Rights** which typically include such things as a right to:

1. timely notice of judicial proceedings they are to attend and timely notice of cancellation of any proceedings;
2. assistance in their role as a courtroom witness;
3. speedy disposition of the entire criminal justice process;

---

1. The elements of the job description were based on information regarding the local victim advocate's program found in the website of the Cherokee County, South Carolina Sheriff's Office: (August 2003). These duties of a victim advocate are typical of those listed around the country.

2. Stolzenberg, Lisa and Stewart J. D'Alessio. (1999). *Criminal Courts for the 21st Century.* Upper Saddle River, N.J.: Prentice Hall, p. 364.

4. clear explanations as to what is going on with a case;
5. full restitution ordered to be paid by the offender;
6. reasonable employer intercession services, including pursuing employer cooperation in minimizing loss of pay resulting from victim participation in court;
7. the speedy return of property when it is no longer needed as evidence;
8. a right to be heard in court during sentencing and other important proceedings.[3]

Victims' rights did not come easily at first. Though it now sounds strange, for a long time, victims even had a hard time securing the right to be heard during sentencing proceedings. In 1987, the U.S. Supreme Court ruled in the case of *Booth v. Maryland*[4] that so-called **Victim-Impact Statements** used by judges in sentencing decisions violated the provision against cruel and unusual punishment. The Court reasoned that such statements led to a real risk of sentences being imposed in an arbitrary and capricious manner. For example, two defendants being sentenced for two different murders carried out in similar manners might respectively receive life in prison vs. the death penalty based merely on the fact that a jury might conclude that one victim possesses more wholesome personal qualities than the other (i.e., some victims are "worth" more than others). Amazingly, only four short years and several personnel changes later, the U.S. Supreme Court completely reversed itself in the case of *Payne v. Tennessee*[5] in which it now reasoned that victim impact evidence is merely just a more direct method of informing the court of the harm a defendant has caused, something traditionally always taken into account by a judge meting out a sentence.

Today, victim participation at sentencing is no longer rare but it is far from commonplace. Because of plea bargaining, the vast majority of sentences are not decided at sentencing hearings at which a victim might testify or provide the court with a written statement but rather are decided during hurried private discussions between prosecutors and defense attorneys. Some prosecutor offices have developed policies requiring negotiators to attempt to "sell" prospective deals to victims first, but often such policies apply only to major felony cases (even then victims have no veto).

The victims right movement nevertheless has produced some good progress in the way victims are now treated in court. What happened to Meg when she

---

3. See, e.g., Utah Criminal and Traffic Code. (2003). Chapter 37—"Victims' Rights" and Chapter 38—"Rights of Crime Victims Act."
4. *Booth v. Maryland,* 107 S.Ct. 2529 (1987).
5. *Payne v. Tennessee,* 501 U.S. 808 (1991).

was a victim-witness might still take place much more frequently than it should, but at least there is now probably some shame about it among professionals in the courthouse when it does.

The Defendant-Witness

After the victim of the crime, the witness juries probably most want to hear from is the criminal defendant. Jurors tend to really perk up when a defendant walks up to the stand while the defense is presenting its case. Of course, whether or not a defense lawyer will allow his or her client to walk up to the stand is another matter.

Every defense attorney knows that allowing a defendant to testify is fraught with peril. The story of George Wagner is illustrative.

George was a young man in his early twenties who was hired by a family to provide a few handyman services for them in their home. A week or so after George had come and gone, the female head of home was robbed by a male wearing a nylon stocking mask who forced his way into the house and demanded the money he knew was located in a kitchen cabinet. The victim reported the crime to the police and told them she could "tell" it was George behind the mask. She recognized his face despite the distortions and clearly recognized his voice.

George was arrested and the case was bound over for trial. Legally George's lawyer could put George on the stand like the jury would want. This was because George told him that he was innocent—they had the wrong guy. George's lawyer did not believe him. George seemed to be lying and the lawyer was aware of his criminal history of two prior assaults and three prior thefts. But as long as George's lawyer did not know for a fact that George was lying, he could legally allow him to testify and tell his version of things. It is up to the jury (not the lawyer) to assess his credibility.

If George had told the lawyer he was guilty, the lawyer could still defend him by making the state prove his guilt. He could argue to the jury that the state did not prove necessary facts beyond a reasonable doubt. But the lawyer would be prohibited from putting George on the stand and thereby knowingly **suborn perjury** (that would not be defending George for a crime he may have already committed but would be helping George to commit a future crime).

If a client insists on committing perjury, the lawyer is expected to attempt to withdraw from the case if the trial has not yet begun citing unspecified "ethical dilemmas" to the court (the judge can usually guess what that must mean). If the case is too far along for the court to allow the attorney to withdraw, the lawyer is forbidden to help the client in any way with his or her planned perjury. For example, lawyers often tell judges at side bars that their clients insist on taking the stand against their strong advise and that for ethical reasons the lawyer will simply "play dead" the entire time the defendant is on the stand. Again, the judge usually gets the idea.

Since in George's case, the lawyer did not know for a fact that George was lying about his lack of involvement in the crime he could legally put George on the stand. However, there are other factors to consider.

First, the lawyer has to worry about George's prior criminal record. Generally, prior records are inadmissible as evidence since the prejudicial effect on the jury is so potentially great. However, if a defendant freely elects to take the stand, he is deemed to have **opened the door** to his truthful character. A prosecutor may then introduce evidence of prior crimes to show that he is a dishonest person who may be willing to commit perjury. Even then, evidence of prior criminal activity is limited in most jurisdictions to **crimen falsi** (crimes involving dishonesty) since dishonest people are thought more likely to commit perjury than other types of criminals.[6] In George's case, if he were to take the stand, the prosecutor could introduce evidence of his prior thefts (thefts are "crimen falsi") but not of his prior assaults (violent crimes have nothing to do with dishonesty and a related propensity to lie on the stand). The judge will caution the jury to use the prior theft convictions solely for the purpose of assessing the defendant's propensity to commit perjury and not as direct proof of the crimes for which he is currently on trial. Still, for the jury to hear of his prior thefts—even with a judicial admonition to be careful how they are considered—would be very damaging.

Second, the lawyer would have to worry about whether or not George would make a likeable witness or not. Jurors think with their hearts as well as their minds. Jurors have much less trouble convicting people they cannot stand then people they really like. Would George come across as a likeable person? Does he sound middle class and respectable? Does he have proper bearing and attitude? Does he seem harmless or threatening? Is he good looking? Does he groom and dress himself appropriately (this latter can be fixed prior to trial if the lawyer takes the time). In George's case, even after donning the suit and tie his lawyer provided him, he sounded rough and uneducated and had a problem looking people in the eye when he told his version of things.

Third, a lawyer usually will be reluctant to put a defendant on the stand if the prosecution's case is not going well. Why blow a good thing? In the famous

---

6. For a good discussion of the admissibility of prior records, see *United States v. Barnes*, 622 F.2d 107 (5th Cir. 1980).

O. J. Simpson case (the so-called "trial of the 20th Century"), Simpson was accused of knifing his ex-wife and her male friend to death on the sidewalk outside her apartment. During his trial, Simpson did not take the stand even though he was a very articulate and attractive person and even though the jury no doubt very much wanted to hear from him. Why not? One possible reason is that he had confessed the murder of his wife and her friend to his lawyers who would then be forbidden to assist him in committing perjury. But another likely reason is simply that the case for the prosecution was not going well (the murderer's glove was too small for Simpson's hand when he tried it on in court). Why take the chance of allowing Simpson to turn the tide when things were going so well for the defense? If anyone can ruin a defense, it is the defendant.

Even though George's lawyer could legally allow him to testify, he would probably be making a big mistake to allow him to do so. George had prior "crimen falsi" that would be introduced were he to open the door by testifying. Additionally, George's rough manner and poor ability to look people in the eyes would be enough for most lawyers to keep him off the stand. He simply did not make a likeable witness. In the end, George's lawyer decided to build a case without George's testimony by pointing out inherent reasonable doubt about any crime victim's ability to positively recognize the face of someone wearing a nylon mask and any victim's ability to recognize a voice while under extreme emotional stress.

The Eye Witness

In the middle of an August afternoon some years ago (true story) a man walked into a Kentucky Fried Chicken store in Balch Springs, Texas and robbed the workers at gunpoint of $615. Though no physical evidence of the crime existed that could tie the defendant, Lenell Getter, to the crime, Getter was nevertheless convicted. This conviction was based solely on the unanimous identification of him by five employees who picked him out of a photo lineup. Even though Getter had a good alibi (co-workers said he was at work at the time), the power of the five eyewitnesses' testimony was enough for the jury to convict him of the robbery and to sentence him to life in prison (the jury decided the sentence as well).

After serving 477 days in prison, authorities freed Getter at the district attorney's request. Another man matching Getter's description and carrying the same type of blue bag and long-barreled revolver that the original robber had been using had been caught robbing other stores in the area. When his photo was shown to the employees who initially had identified Getter, four of the employees changed their minds and identified the new robber as the man who had robbed them.[7]

Jurors love eyewitness testimony, especially from witnesses whom they feel would have no reason to lie. Eyewitness evidence is often given heavy weight by jurors, but perhaps too much weight. Scientific research has consistently shown for decades that jurors tend to place too much uncritical faith in the testimony of eyewitnesses. These studies show that inaccuracies unconsciously creep into the minds of sincere but misguided eyewitnesses at various stages in what scientists call the **memory process**. Witnesses may become more and more certain of imaginary details with the passage of time as the human mind attempts to fill in uncomfortable gaps in knowledge concerning important events.[8] As one state supreme court justice has stated,

"Although research has convincingly demonstrated the weaknesses inherent in eyewitness identification, jurors are, for the most part, unaware of these problems. People simply do not accurately understand the deleterious effects that certain variables can have on the accuracy of the memory process of honest eyewitnesses.... Perhaps it is precisely because jurors do not appreciate the fallibility of eyewitness testimony that they give such testimony great weight."[9]

Even the U.S. Supreme Court has tried to draw people's attention to the inherent fallibility of supposedly infallible eyewitness testimony. It has stated that the "vagaries of eyewitness identification are well-known; the annals of criminal law are rife with instances of mistaken identification."[10]

Some judges have refused to give **cautionary instructions** to jurors regarding the limitations and seductions of eyewitness testimony out of fear that to do so might be improper judicial commentary on the credibility of the evidence. However, others are now coming to the conclusion that "given the great weight jurors are likely to give eyewitness testimony, and the deep and generally unperceived flaws in it, to convict a defendant on such evidence without advising the jury of the factors that should be considered in evaluating it could well deny the defendant due process of law."[11]

---

7. Levine, James P. (1992). *Juries and Politics*. Belmont, CA: Brooks/Cole Publishing, pp. 137–138, citing Applebome, Peter. "Racial Issues Raised in a Robbery Case." *The New York Times* (May 31, 1983), p. A14.

8. For a long listing of empirical studies showing the weaknesses of eyewitness identification see *State v. Long*, 729 P.2d 483 (Utah 1986).

9. *State v. Long, supra* note 8 at 490.

10. *United States v. Wade*, 388 U.S. 218, 228 (1967).

11. *State v. Long, supra* note 8 at 492.

The Character Witness

Reverend Thomas Green of Saint Mark's Church felt very uncomfortable when he was approached by one of his congregants, Roger Billings, with a request that the good pastor testify at his upcoming trial on child molestation charges. Specifically, Billings wanted his minister to come to court and to tell the jury what a decent, upright and honest individual he was. Reverend Green knew (as did the entire congregation) that Billings, who had worked for the last eighteen years as a guard in the county jail, was charged with fondling two small children while they were being babysat by his wife in her home-based day care center.

Reverend Green did not feel entirely comfortable about testifying as to the virtues of Billings' character. True, Green had known Billings for about the last ten years and as far as he could tell Billings was honest and upright. Billings did not come to church very often but when he did he was always friendly and courteous. The minister recalled one time when Billings came to him with a twenty dollar bill that Billings had found in the hallway. When the minister inquired during services whether anybody had perhaps lost a twenty dollar bill, a dubious teenager raised his hand and claimed the money. Billings did not object in the least when the minister turned the money over to the boy.

Despite this past good experience with Billings as well as a few others (Billings for example never objected to his much more active wife's exceptionally generous donations to the church), the Reverend still was not sure that he should testify:

"What if Billings really had molested those two small children?" wondered the minister. "How would it impact the feelings and faith of these children and their families to see an ordained minister intervene on behalf of their abuser? Am I really confident enough of Billing's good character to testify in his favor?"

Sensing Green's hesitation, Billings' wife pleaded with her pastor to at least interview her husband before making a decision. For the sake of Billings' wife and all the many sacrifices she had made over the years on behalf of the church, Green felt an obligation to at least talk things over with Billings. After church one Sunday, he invited Roger Billings (now devout in his church attendance ever since his arrest) into his office for a private interview.

"Thanks for seeing me Reverend," began Billings upon sitting down in Reverend Green's office. "What those children said I did is horrible and I have never been so depressed in all my life. I really need your help as a witness at my trial but also as someone who can pray with me and help me get the strength to get through all of this."

Stiffly the minister responded, "Well, quite candidly I have not yet decided how to react to your request about court, Roger. Whatever I decide about that, I will certainly be here to help you in any way that I otherwise can."

"I really, really need you to believe in me Reverend so that you can testify as to my character!" There was a tone of panic in Roger Billings' voice as he spoke. "My lawyer says it is real important. What can I do to help you be sure that I did not molest those girls?"

Reverend Green fidgeted nervously in his chair. "I'm not sure why you need me to testify. Isn't there someone else who knows you better whom you could call upon. I do know you, but you really don't come out to church all that often." The minister was hoping that Billings would sense his unease and let him off the hook. To Green's disappointment, he was not going to get off that easy.

"Well, Reverend, my lawyer says that family and friends really don't count for much as character witnesses. Jurors just figure that just about anybody has family and friends who will say what a great guy they are. He said I need someone else, someone jurors can trust to tell it like it is—Someone like you. He specifically asked about you and said that people in small towns like ours really look up to ministers like you."

"I just don't know if I can be of all that much help," countered the Reverend. "To be frank, what if by some chance you did do what they say. I'm not saying you did but I really don't know."

With tears now appearing on his cheeks Billings replied, "I swear to you before God I did not do it. You have to believe me. I am facing prison time. I will be killed if I go to prison. I have worked for eighteen years as a guard and the inmates will target me. Even if by some miracle I got probation if convicted, I would get fired from my job just two years away from being eligible for a pension. That will destroy my wife and me financially. It just isn't fair for my wife to be destroyed for something her husband did not do. You got to help us Reverend. I beg you."

Reverend Green did not know what to think. He did not want to go to court, but what if Billings was telling him the truth? How could he refuse to help him and his wife in the very hour of their need? After two hours of grilling Billings about the charges, he became personally convinced that Billings must be innocent. He agreed to testify as a character witness on his behalf.

Character witnesses can be of great help to defendants charged with ugly offenses. However, defense attorneys must be very careful in using them. Evidence of bad character (including prior crimes) is generally not admissible unless the defendant "opens the door" by putting his **character at issue**. Once a defendant places his character at issue, the prosecution is then free to **rebut** the defendant's evidence with evidence of his true (bad) character. This can be most dramatic during a trial when an unsuspecting character witness for the defense is confronted with evidence of the defendant's bad character for the first time during cross-examination by the prosecution. This is exactly what happened to Reverend Green during Billings' trial.

It began when Green took the stand during the defense case-in-chief. Green, wearing his clerical collar as requested by the defense attorney, testified that Billings was "known to be honest and someone who would never hurt anybody." Green further told the jury that Billings was "gentle" and that he had "never heard anybody ever say a word against Roger Billings, ever."

When Reverend Green rose to leave the stand following his brief comments, the prosecutor asked him to remain seated for a "few additional questions." Green looked to the judge who indicated by his gaze and nod that Green needed to comply.

The prosecutor began her cross-examination with undisguised enthusiasm: "Reverend Green, you testified that the accused is gentle and honest. I hold here in my hand an official, certified, state police record regarding Mr. Billings. Would it surprise you to learn that Mr. Billings was convicted twice last year for shoplifting and once two years ago for exposing himself to a child in a park?"

Stung with shock and embarrassment, Green could hardly answer. "Yes, I'm, I'm very surprised. I had no idea." For a second it looked like Green was about to faint.

"Now that you know this information," continued the prosecutor, "does that change your opinion about the defendant's honest and gentle nature?"

"Yes, I would have to admit that it probably does," replied the witness.

"How does it change your opinion, Reverend?" queried the attorney.

Green took a few seconds and then in a hushed, saddened tone answered, "I suppose that Roger has some problems that none of us in his church family were aware of."

The prosecutor thanked Green for his honesty and excused him from the stand. The red-faced reverend walked from the courtroom glancing disapprovingly at Billings as he walked by him.

Of course in real life, a defense attorney representing someone like Billings would hopefully be careful enough to have acquired a copy of his client's criminal record before trial. The attorney also hopefully would know the law well enough to realize that opening the door to evidence of a flawed client's character would not be a smart strategic move. For this reason, defense attorneys do not put on character evidence in many (if not most) trials. But in those circumstances in which an attorney does represent someone with a spotless criminal record and reputation, character witnesses (especially credible non-relatives) can be of help.

The Expert Witness

Psychiatrist Alice Park was hired by a local defense attorney to evaluate a client, John Geist, who stood accused of deliberately killing his wife and her lover in anger when he discovered them having sex in his bed. Apparently Geist had come across the two when he returned home from work one afternoon much earlier than was the norm. Geist had returned because he was not feeling well. He had a bad headache. But something was much more wrong with Geist's mind than just a headache. The man was crazy.

Geist was charged with voluntary manslaughter for having killed the lovers while acting in the heat of a passion. The jury had to decide whether Geist was guilty or innocent of the charge. Geist was not contesting that he killed the couple. What Geist was claiming was that he should be found not guilty by reason of insanity.

This is where Dr. Park came in. The defense wished to call Dr. Park as an expert witness at trial to testify that in her opinion Geist was not legally responsible for the homicides. In other words, the psychiatrist would testify that in her view Geist was legally insane.

Dr. Park knew that mental illness by itself was no defense to a crime. Many people suffer from one of the many mental illnesses that afflict humanity. Most of these people do not commit crimes. Even profound mental illnesses do not necessarily qualify as forms of insanity. It depends. In Geist's jurisdiction, a jury could only find someone who was mentally ill, even severely mentally ill, not guilty of a crime (legally insane) if that person lacked the substantial capacity to appreciate the wrongfulness of the crime or the substantial capacity to obey the law.

Dr. Park had a rather strong view on the issue of whether or not Geist was insane. She believed that he was. Her evaluation determined that Geist was schizophrenic and paranoid. He had delusions that the U.S. Military was controlled by the United Nations and was planning to overthrow the President. She also had learned that Geist was a civilian worker at a local Air Force Base (he had not let his beliefs be known to anyone but his mother and father and best friend). Geist also had delusions of grandeur. He believed that the commanding General of the U.S. Air Force was on a personal mission to murder him before he could warn others. Dr. Park also knew that the man the military-phobic Geist stumbled upon having sex with his wife was a uniformed Air Force major from the local base.

Dr. Park was willing to testify that in her opinion Geist was not only paranoid and schizophrenic but unlike the vast majority of paranoid schizophrenics was unable to substantially appreciate that the act of killing his wife and her air force lover was morally wrong.

Expert witnesses like Dr. Park are used all the time in criminal trials, both as witnesses for the defense and for the prosecution. There are many different types of experts: psychiatrists, handwriting analysts, fingerprint experts, accountants, auto accident reconstructionists, blood typists, ballistics experts, drug analysts, coroners, voice print identifiers, and many more. All of these expert witnesses are used to express their opinions about something.

Ordinarily **opinion evidence** is not admissible. Witnesses should only provide jurors with the facts and let the jurors draw their own conclusions. Put another way, the role of most witnesses is to provide jurors with raw data, not to analyze the data for them. Analysis is the jury's job.

An exception is made however in the case of expert witnesses. Some things are **outside the ken of ordinary knowledge** and lay jurors may need help with making conclusions. Very few people for example, know how to match fingerprints or DNA. In order for experts to give their opinions about something two conditions must be met: "(1) The subject of the inference must be so distinctly related to some science, profession, business, or occupation as to be beyond the knowledge of the average lay person; and (2) the witness must have such skill, knowledge, or experience in the field or calling as to make it appear that his or her opinion or inference would probably aid the jury in its search for the truth."[12]

Before an expert may offer his or her opinion, the expert must first be **qualified as an expert** by the court. In order to do this, the attorney who calls the expert to the stand must **lay a foundation** in which the expert is asked about his or her credentials, training, and experience (of course the other side may cross-examine). If after this foundation is laid the judge agrees that the witness is an expert then the attorney may go on with his or her questioning which will ultimately result in the expression of the expert's opinion.

Geist's attorney had no problems laying a foundation regarding Dr. Park's qualifications. In response to the attorney's questions, Dr. Park stated that she had received an M.D. from Duke Medical School and was a board certified

---

12. Klotter, John C. *2000. Criminal Evidence*(7th ed.). Cincinnati, OH: Anderson Publishing Co. at 285.

psychiatrist with many years experience, including substantial work in the area of forensic psychiatry. She had published many scholarly papers on the subject of mental illness and the insanity defense. She had testified in many trials, both for the defense and for the prosecution. The judge ruled her qualified as an expert.

To Dr. Park's surprise (and Geist's dismay), the jury ultimately rejected Park's expert opinion and found Geist guilty. They in effect ruled that though he was severely mentally ill his illness was coincidental and not the cause of the homicides. They believed he did appreciate the wrongfulness of his misconduct and chose to disobey the law. In essence they concluded that he killed his wife and her lover out of plain old fashioned jealously and rage.

Dr. Park learned what every expert witness should know. Experts, despite their superior insights, are only there to aid the jury in its quest for the truth and not to decide **ultimate questions** of guilt and innocence. Expert testimony is only one piece of the many pieces of evidence that juries are free to consider in a case. Final questions of guilt and innocence are the unique **province of the jury**.

The Police Witness

Officer Mary O'Connell came to the burglary trial relatively unprepared. She thought that she would surely remember details of this case since she not only had been the arresting officer, but had already testified regarding the facts of the case at a preliminary hearing several months ago. O'Connell found out the hard way how one police officer can lose a case for a prosecutor.

Because O'Connell had investigated many crimes before and after the incident in question, she had forgotten many of the details of this particular burglary. The defense attorney, with transcripts of the preliminary hearing in hand and a fresh command of all the facts, was able to trap O'Connell time and time again with slight conflicts between what she now was saying and what she had earlier said at the preliminary hearing. O'Connell even said a few things that mildly contradicted her own police report, which the defense attorney was all too eager to point out.

O'Connell became embarrassed by her forgetfulness, and she became more and more defensive and belligerent toward the defense lawyer as he went about his cross-examination. None of this played well with the jury who began to see O'Connell as an angry, incompetent person who apparently did not know how to properly do her job. The final straw for the jury came when they heard O'-Connell admit to violating several standard operating procedures during the arrest of the defendant and the preservation of various objects of physical evidence.

Though not a "category" of witness normally discussed in law books, perhaps the most common witness to appear in criminal hearings and trials is a police officer. One might think that the most common witness would be either a victim or a defendant. But, defendants often do not testify for various reasons already discussed. Victims often do not testify since many crimes are "victimless" (e.g., drunk driving, drug possession, etc.). Unlike victims and defendants, police officers almost always take the stand at preliminary hearings and trials. For this reason the police officer as witness warrants its own discussion.

In some trials, the police officer may be one of only a couple of witnesses. For example, the prosecution's case in a drunk driving trial might only involve testimony from a police officer testifying as to a defendant's erratic driving, disheveled appearance, slurred speech, poor performance in field sobriety tests, and refusal to blow into a breath analysis machine. The defense case might consist of nothing more than a rigorous cross-examination of the same officer.

But whether a police officer is the sole witness to testify or one of many, most criminal trials probably involve some officer testimony. Officers are routinely called upon to identify physical evidence found at crime scenes, to relay the details of a defendant's incriminating statements, to testify as to what they saw and heard at a scene, to identify a suspect they saw fleeing, to debunk an alibi defense, to establish the chain of custody of physical evidence, etc.

What every police officer needs to understand is that because of the frequency with which police officers appear in court, testifying is a critical aspect of police work. It is therefore not true that it is an officer's job merely to investigate and to arrest, and the prosecutor's job to secure the conviction. It is also the task of any good police officer to help secure that conviction through competent courtroom testimony.

Police officers in the field should always be thinking ahead about how things will play out eventually in court. They should remember that defense attorneys who do not have the facts on their side will try to win favor with jurors by making them either like their client or else dislike the police. As stated in an earlier chapter, juries are reluctant to convict defendants they like or to reward police officers they dislike with a conviction.

Police officers can be liked by juries by acting professionally in the field, by performing their duties competently and according to standard operating procedures, and by refusing to allow defense attorneys to get under their skin during cross-examinations. It is probably a good idea for the officer to be polite with defense counsel no matter what the defense counsel does or says. This is not being weak. This will give the impression to the jury that an officer is a good person free of bias who can be trusted to tell the truth. An officer never wants to give the impression that he or she has an agenda of any kind at trial other than to be a detached witness relaying simple truths to a jury for analysis.

Of course, unlike most witnesses who come to court relatively unprepared, police officers should realize that they are key to a jury's impression of the rightness of a case. Hence, they should always prepare for a hearing or a trial by refreshing their memory of the details of a case by reviewing their reports of the matter beforehand. In this way, they can come across to the jury as more relaxed and sure of themselves. They also will be less prone to defense tactics of trying to put words into their mouths or to catch them in statements that contradict what they may have testified to in earlier settings.

As police officers gain more experience in testifying, their skills no doubt will improve. However, even though most police officers can expect to become in effect a **professional witness**, experience can never substitute for preparation and the right attitude.

*****

Questions for Class Discussion

1. Based on your reading of the chapter, name as many types of witnesses as you can. What is the role of each of these different types of witnesses?
2. Have any of you ever appeared in court as a witness? If so, what type of witness were you? What was it like to testify as a witness?
3. In colonial times crime victims were expected to hire a private attorney to act as the prosecutor in their case. Do you think crime victims today should be allowed to have this as an option? What would be the advantages and disadvantages of allowing this in modern courts?
4. What are some of the ways that victims have been historically mistreated by the criminal court system? What are some of the typical elements of a Victims' Bill or Rights?
5. What is meant by a victim-impact statement? What sort of things might you expect to see in such a statement from someone who was beaten and robbed?
6. Why were victim-impact statements initially seen to violate the Constitution? Why did the Supreme Court change its mind on their lack of constitutionality?
7. What are some of the duties of the victim/witness advocate? Would any of you consider such a job? How about doing it as an unpaid volunteer? A college intern for course credit?

8. Why is a allowing a defendant to testify in his or her own behalf such a hard decision for a defense attorney to make?

9. Before reading the chapter, did you know that defense attorneys are not allowed to aid their clients to lie on the stand? Why does this rule exist? What if the defense attorney believes the client is probably lying about his or her innocence but is not certain: should the defense attorney be required to keep the client off the stand? Knowing that attorneys are not allowed to suborn perjury, would you as a defense attorney press your client to come clean with you about the alleged crime?

10. If a client wishes to take the stand and commit perjury, what are the various steps a defense attorney could take to avoid suborning perjury and getting in trouble herself?

11. The prior criminal record of a defendant is not usually admissible in court. Does this rule make sense to you? If you were on a jury, would you find it helpful to know about someone's past criminal history, or do you think it would overly bias you? If you acquitted someone of rape after believing his consent defense, and then learned he had been to prison before for two earlier rapes, how would you feel?

12. Do jurors tend to put more trust in eye-witness accounts than is warranted? Why? What does the science and the "memory process" say about the reliability of eye-witness testimony?

13. Have you ever been falsely accused of misconduct in school, your neighborhood, or in your personal life by a sincere but mistaken eyewitness of some sort?

14. If you were a defense attorney in a case based solely on prosecution eye-witness testimony, what are some things you might try to do during the trial to properly defend your client?

15. Are character witnesses helpful in ascertaining the truth? How much credibility would you as a juror give such testimony? Do jurors probably put too much faith in such evidence?

16. Would you tend to give more weight to character testimony offered by clergy than by neighbors and co-workers? Would you give any weight to character testimony offered by close friends of the defendant? If asked to testify about the character of a close but dishonest friend, would you lie on the stand? Would your best friend be willing to lie about your reputation and character if it would help you in court?

17. If juries are the ones supposed to decide what truly happened in a case, why do courts allow experts to give their opinions? What is meant by evidence "outside the ken of ordinary knowledge?" What are some examples of expert witnesses?

18. How does an attorney go about qualifying an expert witness for court? Is there any field of knowledge that you know well enough that might qualify you as an expert witness?
19. Under what circumstances, if any, should mental illness be a defense to a crime? Should this issue be decided by a jury or by expert-witnesses well-versed in the science of mental health? What is meant by the "province of the jury?"
20. In what ways can it be said that a police officer is a "professional witness?" What sort of criminal cases would you expect to almost always involve police officer testimony?
21. Given that police frequently are asked to testify in court, should police departments give their officers training on effective testifying? What sort of things should this training involve?
22. How should police officers specifically "prepare for court?" What sorts of things might befall a foolish police officer who shows up to court without first preparing?

*****

Key Terms: victimized twice, victim/witness advocate, Victims' Rights Movement, Victims' Bill of Rights, victim-impact statements, suborn perjury, open the door, crimen falsi, memory process, cautionary instructions, character at issue, rebut, opinion evidence, outside the ken of ordinary knowledge, qualified as an expert, lay a foundation, ultimate questions, province of the jury, professional witness

Additional Concepts: the Victim-Witness, Booth v. Maryland, Payne v. Tennessee, the Defendant-Witness, considerations regarding defendant testifying, attorney playing dead if client perjures, admissibility of prior records, the Eye Witness, inherent fallibility of eyewitnesses, the Character Witness, the Expert Witness, the Police Witness, police preparation for trial, testifying as critical aspect of police work

CHAPTER EIGHT

THE STEPS OF DUE PROCESS

Rick Powell just finished his first year of law school and was looking for something useful to do for the summer. Unlike some of his luckier classmates, he was unable to find a paid summer position with a law firm. In fact, he really only had two job offers: working for his Uncle Jim's construction company or serving as an unpaid legal intern with the county public defender's office. Even though he resented working for no pay, he chose the unpaid legal internship. He was sick of working construction each summer. The pay was alright but he figured at this point in his life he should stick to situations that were law-related.

Rick's resentment at not being paid might have been mitigated if he had known how generous the public defender was in even allowing him to intern with her office. When Rick called the head public defender, Carol Hall, to inquire about summer opportunities, the public defender graciously offered him the chance to intern there. Immediately after the phone call, Hall regretted the offer. She was busy enough without having to find meaningful experiences for some law student all summer. Legal interns in her office in the past were never of much help. They could not practice law. They did not want to do secretarial work. It was hard to keep them busy and happy. But a promise was a promise and Hall would help Rick out as much as she could. At least Rick could have something on his resume that was law related and perhaps he could learn a little about legal life outside the phony ivory tower of academia. Besides, the public defender herself had benefitted by a legal internship with a public defender's office after her first year of law school. It was pay back time she figured.

Carol Hall almost had forgotten that it was time for Rick to begin his summer internship the day she glanced outside her office window and saw him parking his car in the county lot.

"Oh crap," muttered Hall. "That intern's coming in today. What am I going to do with him?"

Hall quickly started throwing together a schedule for him with the same quick wittedness that she was accustomed to using in preparing for spur of the moment court appearances. By the time Rick appeared at her office door, she was ready for him.

"Welcome to the public defender's office, Rick," began Carol Hall. "It's really good having you aboard. Have a seat."

After exchanging law school war stories for a few minutes, Hall presented Rick with his schedule for the day.

"Later in the summer, after you get your feet wet, I thought you could help us do 'intake.' What that means is you will meet with people applying with our office to have us represent them in court and you will determine if they are financially qualified or not to receive a government-furnished lawyer. Believe it or not, we get a lot of people who have money who are too cheap to hire their own lawyer. We'll teach you how to do all of that. But for the first couple of weeks, I thought it would be best for you to just learn the ropes of the office—give you the big picture of things. How does that sound?"

"It sounds good," replied Rick. "I had criminal law my first year but I really don't understand much about the mechanics of being a criminal lawyer, or any kind of a lawyer for that matter. It's been really bothering me."

"Great," the public defender continued. "I'm going to assign you to accompany various attorneys as they go about walking clients through the system. Today you will be attending some first appearances with Mel Thorpe, one of our staff attorneys. I'll hook you up with him in just a minute. Other days you'll be attending other types of proceedings and by the time the first two weeks are up, you'll have a real good idea of what we do around here."

"Sounds great, thanks for letting me do this," Rick humbly responded. His gratitude was now genuine. He was beginning to realize that this internship was more a learning experience for his benefit than anything else. He was grateful to Hall for the unrewarded mentor she was willing to be for him. She reminded him of his Uncle Jim who slowed down to teach him construction skills during his first confused summer working for him.

While the chief defender walked Rick over to attorney Thorpe's office, she handed him a sheet of the different court proceedings he would get to attend over the next two weeks. She titled this sheet, the "Steps of Due Process." The hastily drafted, hand-written sheet was hard to read but substantively it read like this:

Table 1   Steps of Due Process (By Carol Hall, Public Defender)

1. Arrest—Cops do this of course Rick. So I'll start you off observing number 2.
2. First Appearance—Rick, you'll be attending some of these today with attorney Mel Thorpe out at one of the magistrate courts scattered around the county. Mel will know exactly where.
3. Preliminary Hearing—Tomorrow I'll have you attend some prelims. I'll let you know with which attorney. In fact I'll probably have you attend these more than one day.
4. Grand Jury—You can't attend these. They're secret. But we'll let you stand out in the hall with one of the lawyers who oddly enough represents a subpoenaed witness rather than a defendant.
5. Arraignment—Goofy relic and a total waste of court time but you need to know what it is.
6. Pre-Trial Motions—We've got some good hearings coming up in motions court next week
7. Plea bargaining and entry of guilty plea—bread and butter stuff. Sparks can fly here, bud. This is the last stop for most of our clients.
8. Trial—Not everyone pleads guilty. Your choice to attend either a rape or drunk driving/ homicide trial coming up next week. You can sit at the defense table if the judge doesn't mind. I recommend the rape case but it's up to you.
9. Sentencing hearing—We'll get you in to see some of these. Check out the look on the defendants' faces when Maximum Jane hammers them.
10. Post-Verdict Motions—Purely legal arguments. Just like law school so you'll feel at home.
11. Appeal—We'll let you attend some oral arguments up in the high and mighty state court of appeals. Maybe you can even proof read some briefs for us before we submit them.

[*Author's Note*: Not all of the above "Steps of Due Process" will be explored in detail in this chapter. The latter steps richly deserve discussions of such length that separate, entire chapters will be devoted to them.]

The First Appearance

Rick and Carol Hall arrived at Mel Thorpe's corner office. It was a nice office, attractively furnished, but ruined by Mel's stacks of unfiled clutter.

"Hi Mel. This is a new legal intern who will be with us for the summer. His name is Rick Powell. He just survived his first year of law school. Before doing some work for us, he is going to be spending his first two weeks getting an overview of what we do around here. Is it ok if he hangs out with you at the First Appearances you're scheduled to do today? I'm trying to walk him though all of the steps of the process from First Appearance at one end through Appeals at the other."

"Glad to meet you Rick," the boyish looking Mel smilingly said as he rose to shake Rick's hand. "I'm Mel Thorpe." Looking towards Carol Hall he continued, "Sure, Rick can tag along if he'd like. Is it just for today?"

To Mel's extreme relief, Hall confirmed that it would just be for one day.

"I'll be leaving in about twenty minutes, Rick. You can drive over to Judge White's magistrate court with me. I'll round you up when it is time to go. Where will you be?"

Rick lifted his shoulders as he looked to Carol Hall. After a few moments of reflection, Hall stated, "We'll give him that small empty office by the file room. That will be his place to crash while here."

Hall felt a little embarrassed as she deposited Rick in the cramped, unloved office. She told him he could use the office law library down the hall during down times (like now). Rick was satisfied with the office—he never had an office before of any kind. Besides, he wanted a place to be able to go to get out of people's hair. He also noticed that the law library had some newspapers and popular magazines which he suspected would come in real handy during his intern days. Even better, the law library computer had internet access. If worse came to worse, he could pass time when feeling useless in some of his favorite chat rooms.

Soon it was time to leave for magistrate's court and the First Appearances that would take place there. Upon arriving at Judge White's court facility, Rick took a seat next to Mel Thorpe in the make-shift courtroom.

As far as Rick could tell, **the main purpose of a First Appearance** was for setting bail for those just arrested that day or the night before. (It is also used throughout the country to advise defendants of the charges against them and of their rights, including the right to a lawyer.)[1] Most of the bails being set were for minor amounts, with some defendants being released on no bail at all—just on their word to appear. Mel did not say much and spent a lot of time joking with the judge between "customers." Rick wondered what Mel was there for. "Maybe he speaks up when bail is set too high," figured Rick. But,

---

1. Stuckey, Gilbert B., Cliff Roberson, and Harvey Wallace. (2001). *Procedures in the Justice System* (6th ed.). Upper Saddle River, NJ: Prentice Hall.

even when bail was set really high, Mel didn't speak up. "They aren't our clients at this stage yet," explained Mel to a puzzled looking Rick.

"What is our role exactly?" inquired Rick.

"The main thing we're here for is to explain to defendants who indicate interest how they can apply for a public defender and how they don't want to represent themselves. I also tell anyone who expresses even slight interest in applying for a public defender to 'shut up' and not to do anything stupid like admitting stuff. If our office is going to end up with the case, we want to protect it from the start. If I'm rock certain that a defendant will financially qualify for a public defender, I'll sometimes ask the judge to reconsider the bail he just set if I think it was kind of high. Pretty routine stuff, unless you're the defendant heading for jail and scared crap-less."

"Is this your main job with the public defender's office?" asked Rick.

"What? No! I'd quit if they insulted my intelligence with this duty every day. We all take turns doing this, except for the senior trial attorneys. In fact, some public defender offices don't even send attorneys out to First Appearances.[2] If bail is too high on a client, they just file a motion to reduce it at the main courthouse later. I think Carol Hall is beginning to understand that we really don't belong here and will probably pull us from this duty soon. She's kind of new at the helm and started the job with a bit too much enthusiasm. It's wearing off and I'm sure she'll come to her senses soon. We do some good here but our time is better spent elsewhere."

Rick watched for several hours as various police officers ushered in defendant after defendant to have his or her bail set and to be told how to get a public defender. Apparently, this particular magistrate was designated for bail duty that day.

Rick was glad for the chance to see bail being set in the real world but was glad when it was time to leave.

"It's lunchtime," Mel said at noon. "We'll break until 1:30 and then resume. Let's head back to our office. Will you be coming back with me in the afternoon for more excitement?"

"No," replied Rick. "As an intern I'll only be working mornings, unless there is a trial to watch or something really big going on. Carol Hall told me to just go home when we're through here in the morning and she'll see me tomorrow at 9:00."

"What attorney are you going to be with tomorrow?" Mel inquired.

---

2. Some public defender offices do send attorneys to the First Appearance in light of the fact that it is considered a "critical stage" at which one has the right to an attorney present. Many other public defender offices do not bother. See, Emanuel, Steven. L. and Steven Knowles. (2000). *Criminal Procedure*. Larchmont, NY: Emanuel.

"I don't know yet. Ms. Hall will let me know tomorrow. But I think I'll be going to preliminary hearings."

"Oh, prelims are good to watch. Let me drive you back to your car."

The Preliminary Hearing

The next morning Rick arrived at Carol Hall's promptly at 9:00 a.m. This time she was fully prepared and quickly escorted him over to Julie McFadden's office. He would be accompanying Julie to a courtroom on the second floor where a preliminary hearing was scheduled to start at 9:30.

"We better get up there," Julie told Rick as soon as they were introduced. "I need to interview the client before the hearing starts. You can listen in on the interview."

Rick walked by Julie as they moved down the courtroom basement hall (where the public defender's office was located) and headed towards the elevator. He wanted to be friendly and talk but could see that the attorney was busy reading the arrest report. He wondered if she was simply re-reading it or if she were reading it for the very first time. He was too polite to ask.

The pair quietly rode the elevator to the second floor. Julie read while Rick stared at the control panel. When the elevator opened, Julie looked at Rick and smiled. "The client will wonder why two of us are interviewing him today. Let him think that he is getting two attorneys. He'll be impressed with our office."

Julie led Rick into Courtroom 2-C and both saw a sheriff sitting next to a young, visibly frightened woman sitting in a pew in an orange jump suit and leg irons.

"Wow," thought Rick. "This is the real thing." Rick had never seen a person in prisoner gear before.

Rick followed Julie over to the pew and they sat down next to their client. The sheriff left and stood by the exit door to give them privacy.

"Hello, I'm Julie McFadden with the public defender's office. This is my colleague, Rick Powell. I just want to go over your version of the facts before we have your preliminary hearing. Do you understand what a preliminary hearing is?"

"No, what is it?" asked the defendant.

"Well, it is not your trial. The **official purpose of a preliminary hearing** is for a judge to decide if there is enough evidence to have a trial.[3] The prosecu-

---

3. Miller, Frank W., Robert O. Dawson, George E. Dix, and Raymond I. Parnas. (2000). "The Preliminary Examination and the Grand Jury." Chapter 14 in *Prosecution and Adjudication* (5th ed.). New York: Foundation Press.

tor has to establish a **prima facie case** that you committed the burglary that the police say you did. If they can't do it, the judge will have to order your release."

"What is a prima facie case?" asked the defendant. ("Good question," thought Rick who also was listening. "I wonder if that is the same thing as probable cause?")

Julie did not mind explaining. "Well, a prima facie case simply means that there are enough facts to show you probably committed the crime—that there is **probable cause** as lawyers say. Later at trial, the prosecutor will have to prove you committed the crime beyond a reasonable doubt but today all the prosecutor has to prove is that you probably did it. If the judge thinks you probably did it, he will find that the state proved its prima facie case and will **bind the case over for trial**. He'll order the trial even if he has a lot of reasonable doubt that you did the burglary. Today, he only determines probability which is a very low standard. Once in a blue moon a judge will dismiss charges at this level but that is very, very rare. Most judges will pass the buck onto the jury even when the state's evidence is pretty lame. It is not right but that is what happens. Besides, usually there is probable cause or else the police would not have bothered to arrest someone in the first place. The purpose of this hearing is just for the judge to agree with the police that you probably did the burglary, not whether you did it beyond a reasonable doubt. That's for the jury."

"Will I get to testify today?" asked the woman. "I'd like to try to beat these charges today so I can go home."

"No. I won't let you testify," Julie told her. "I've read the police report and I can tell that there is enough evidence to bind you over for trial. It does not take much evidence at all for that. So, like almost always, the judge will probably order a trial whether you testify today or not. So, why give the prosecutor a chance to see our defense before trial? Your testifying won't help you avoid a trial. It will only help the prosecutor discover our defense."

"Well, if the judge is going to bind the case over for trial anyway, why don't we just **waive** [give up the right to] the preliminary hearing?" Rick objected. "It sounds like a waste of time."

Rick's challenge, made in front of the client, irritated Julie but her face did not reflect the emotion. "Well, Rick," the poised attorney countered, "a lot of public defenders do indeed waive these hearings all around the country calculating that they are wastes of time. They know that judges will normally bind cases over for trial no matter what is said or not said. But like some public defender offices, our office never waives the right to a preliminary hearing unless the state offers us something, like a great plea bargain up front, if we do. We use preliminary hearings as a **discovery tool**, to find out as much about

Table 2   Official and Unofficial Purposes of the Preliminary Hearing

Official Purpose: To require the prosecution to establish a prima facie case so that an innocent defendant does not have to agonize for months only to have a frivolous case dismissed at trial. If a prima facie case is established, the case will be bound over for trial. If one is not established, the judge will dismiss the charges.

Unofficial Purposes: Used by the defense to "discover" as much as it possibly can about the prosecution's case so as to better prepare for trial; to create a transcript that can be used to "impeach" state witnesses' credibility at trial should they deviate from their preliminary hearing testimony in any significant way.

---

the other side's case prior to trial as we can. We'll make them put on their witnesses to prove their case and then cross-examine the witnesses to find out all we can about the case. Our 'official' purpose for doing this is to force the state to show a prima facie case. But our 'unofficial' and real purpose is to discover as much as we can about the state's case in advance of trial. We also want to have a transcript of the testimony of the prosecution witnesses. That way, if they deviate in any way at trial from what they say at the preliminary hearing, we can **impeach** [discredit] them by pointing out the inconsistencies to the jury."

"Wow, you got it down to a science don't you," marveled Rick to Julie. Rick felt obliged at this point to explain to the defendant that he was brand new to the office. "You've got a good, experienced lawyer," Rick told the accused.

Julie went on to summarize the police report to her client and then to listen to her version of things. Basically, the client wound up admitting to Julie McFadden that the police report was accurate. She asked her attorney if she could work out a plea bargain. Julie said that a plea bargain could be negotiated in due course but right now it was time to discover more about the case than might be in the thin police report. "They aren't offering us any deals yet, so why not have the hearing?" Julie told her client.

As Julie was finishing up her interview with the client, a prosecutor came in and asked if Julie was ready to begin. "Let's do it," Julie told him.

The judge listened as the prosecutor put on his prima facie case. Prosecutors are not naive. They know that defense lawyers typically use such hearings as discovery tools. The **prosecutor's preliminary hearing strategy** therefore is to put on as little evidence as possible to prove the prima facie case—nothing more. They know that it does not take much for a preliminary hearing judge to bind a case over for trial. They want to limit as best they can the amount of discovery the defendant might obtain from this hearing. Often, prosecutors will only put on a **skeleton case** using a couple of key witnesses whose testimony they keep to a minimum with very narrow questioning. The rules of evidence are relaxed at this level and a few witnesses are usually all that is needed for probable cause to be confirmed (hearsay is even allowed at this level in many states).[4]

The **defense preliminary hearing strategy** is to use cross-examination to pump each state witness for information to the extent that the defense can get away with. Often, judges eventually tell a defense lawyer that it has become too obvious that the lawyer is only "fishing" for information and will eventually cut the lawyer off from further endless probing. Technically, defense lawyers at preliminary hearings have no right to **exceed the scope** of (go beyond matters raised in) the direct examination.[5] But, a lot of leeway is given to defense attorneys by judges who are afraid to cut them off too soon. This is the case even though everyone in the room knows the judge will almost certainly bind the case over for trial and that the defense is merely using the proceeding as a backdoor to discovery.

In rare circumstances the defense will try to beat the charges outright by putting on a full-blown defense at the preliminary hearing. But usually, the defense will put on no evidence whatsoever at this stage (sometimes to the shock of the defendant who must be told that there is no point letting the prosecution discover the defense case the way the defense is discovering the prosecution case).

In the case of Julie McFadden's client—the woman accused of burglary— the preliminary hearing played out exactly as Julie expected. The prosecution put on only two witnesses: the victim who testified briefly as to what was taken and to the fact that the defendant did not have permission to enter her home; and the police officer who testified that he caught the defendant with the stolen goods a few blocks from the victim's home during a legal traffic stop.

Rick and the accused then watched as Julie McFadden cross-examined these witnesses for a period four times as long as the prosecutor's direct examination, with a stenographer recording verbatim testimony as it was given.

---

4. Some states require magistrates to follow the usual rules of evidence at preliminary hearings while other states do not. See Saltzburg, Stephen A. and Daniel. J. Capra, (1992). *American Criminal Procedure—Cases and Commentaries.* St. Paul, MN: West Group. Most states do allow hearsay evidence to be admitted during preliminary hearings. See Carp, Robert A. and Ronald Stidham, (1996). *Judicial Process in America.* Washington, D.C.: CQ Press, A Division of Congressional Quarterly, Inc.

5. *State v. Russo,* 303 N.W.2d 846 (Wis. 1981).

When it came time for the defense to put on witnesses if it so desired, Julie told the court that there would be "no defense witnesses today." Julie did make a brief, hopeless argument asking that charges be dismissed (more for her client's benefit than for serious consideration by the judge). After listening politely, the judge declared that the state had "established a prima facie case and this matter will be bound over to a grand jury on the charges of burglary and theft."

"What happens now?" the defendant asked her lawyer.

"Well, the case will now go to a grand jury for an indictment and eventually will be scheduled for trial. I'll explain what that all means when I come out to the jail Thursday to see you and my other clients. In the meantime, I'll file a motion to get your bail reduced. I think it's kind of high."

"Thanks, that would be great," the woman told Julie as the sheriff came to take her back to jail.

The Grand Jury

After attending a series of preliminary hearings, the intern Rick Powell began to wonder more and more what grand juries were for. He read about them in the office law library and learned that their function was to verify that the state had a case that was strong enough to warrant a trial. "I don't get it," he told his mentor Carol Hall. "Isn't that the same thing a preliminary hearing is for?"

"You'll understand tomorrow," he was told by the chief public defender. "I've assigned you to accompany Abe Steiner who has a client going before the grand jury in the morning. Meet Abe at his office at 9:25."

Rick appeared at Abe's office ten minutes ahead of schedule. Abe and he talked about Abe's first year law school experiences for a few minutes before heading upstairs to the hallway outside of Courtroom 6.

"Tell me Abe," Rick asked as they parked themselves in the hallway outside of Courtroom 6. "I've got to know. What is a grand jury for exactly?"

"A grand jury is to make sure that there is enough evidence to have a trial. It would be wrong for some guy to wait six months for a trial only to have the charges dismissed for an obvious lack of sufficient evidence. The grand jury must believe the defendant at least probably did the crime before a defendant must wait months to learn whether a trial jury thinks he did it beyond a reasonable doubt."[6]

"Yes, but isn't that what the preliminary hearing is for?"

---

6. Miller, et al, *supra* note 3 at 695–697.

"Oh, I see your confusion Rick," replied Abe. "Well, in most states you either get a preliminary hearing or a grand jury, but not both.[7] It depends upon the state constitution. Older states back East tend to use grand juries, as does the federal court system—at least for felonies. Newer states tend to use preliminary hearings for everything—felonies or misdemeanors. A few states, like ours, give defendants charged with misdemeanors preliminary hearings but those charged with felonies both a preliminary hearing and a grand jury. I guess our state wants to give double protection to people charged with serious crimes."

"Why double protection? What good is that?" asked Rick.

"I guess the preliminary hearing gives a defendant the right to a detached, professional judge to decide things and the grand jury gives the defendant the right to a jury of his or her peers to decide things too. Both systems have their strengths, at least in theory I suppose. It is kind of dumb really since grand juries always bind over everyone for trial just like the preliminary hearing judges do. I read a study once that found that grand juries return an indictment in 99.5 percent of the cases submitted by the prosecutor.[8] Talk about a rubber stamp. In my experience, that is probably even worse than the statistics associated with preliminary hearings. And, at least with the preliminary hearing the defendant gets to do some discovery of the other side's case."

"Can't the defendant use the grand jury hearing to discover the other side's case?" asked Rick.

"No. The defendant has no right to cross-examine anybody that appears before the grand jury. In my personal opinion it really is a kangaroo court.[9] The prosecutor is even known as the **legal advisor to the grand jury**. The prosecutor gets to say who testifies and who does not and what questions get asked and which do not. Once I heard that a prosecutor was asked by a grand juror upstairs if a certain question could be asked of a witness and the prosecutor merely said, 'As your legal advisor I instruct you that such a question is not advisable.' What a kangaroo court."

---

7. For a listing of states that use grand jury indictments, see Popko, Sigmund G. (1987). "Arizona's County Grand Jury: The Empty Promise of Independence." *Arizona Law Review* 29:667–688.

8. Barkan, Steven E. and George J. Bryjak.(2004). *Fundamentals of Criminal Justice.* Boston: Pearson Education, Inc., p. 295, citing Saltzburg and Capra, *supra note 4.*

9. For condemnations of the grand jury as nothing more than a rubber stamp for the prosecutor, see Heilbroner, David. (1990). *Rough Justice: Days and Nights of a Young D.A.* New York: Pantheon, pp. 207–208. See also Blanche D. Blank. (1993). *The Not So Grand Jury: The Story of the Federal Grand Jury System.* Lanham, MD: University Press of America.

"Will I get to watch the grand jury today?" Rick thought that it might be interesting.

"No. I told you it is a kangaroo court. Nobody can go in there except the prosecutor, the grand jurors, and subpoenaed witnesses. The public cannot go in, defense lawyers cannot go in, even a defendant himself cannot go in. It is a secrecy thing. The original idea was that nobody who does not need to know is supposed to hear the dirt on someone who may be let off the hook by the grand jury."

"If we can't go in the courtroom why are we even here today?" asked Rick.

"Well, my client is a witness in a big felony drug dealing case. He was caught by the cops in a huge drug sting a few months ago. He was facing a minimum mandatory of ten years. The case was a slam dunk for the prosecutor so at the request of my client, we asked if he could 'do some serious work' for them in return for a greatly reduced sentence. He has been setting up and snitching on even bigger fish ever since. He is in the courtroom right now snitching to the grand jury about someone whom the prosecutor wants indicted. I told him I'd be waiting out in the hall in case he has a legal question. He is worried that they might ask him about other crimes that he has done that they did not give him immunity for yet. I told him if anything like that happens, he should ask for a recess to consult with his attorney outside the courtroom. The prosecutor said he would not object to his coming out to talk to me anytime he likes."

"Wow. I guess this client is glad for the secrecy. How much time will he get for all his cooperation?" asked Rick.

"He will be placed on heavy probation and put into a witness protection plan. In fact, he is already in witness protection. His old life is trashed but at least he won't be in prison. Don't discuss this with anyone, not even your wife or girlfriend or whatever. I really mean it, Rick"

"You have my word. I've forgotten all about it already," insisted Rick.

The Arraignment

The days were moving swiftly for legal intern Rick Powell. He noticed that next on his schedule of learning opportunities was the chance to observe some arraignments. This time he got to accompany Carol Hall, the chief public defender herself, to court. Hall liked to be present at arraignments and give her "speech" with all of the new clients and all of her assistant public defenders present. A few prosecutors too were usually present to help guide the paper work along. The judge usually showed up much later to actually arraign the few defendants who refused to follow the advice given by Hall in her "speech."

Table 3   Grand Juries vs. Preliminary Hearings

Grand Jury	Preliminary Hearing
Big—up to 23 people depending on state[1]	One judge
Proceedings closed to public	Proceedings open to the public
Bare majority vote decides	Judge decides
No right to a defense attorney	Right to legal counsel
No right to cross-examine state witnesses	Right to cross-examine state witnesses
No right to put on a defense	Defense can present its side of things
"Indictment" or "True Bill" returned	An "Information" is issued if bound over for trial

1. Federal grand juries use between 16–23 people. State grand juries range from 12–23 members. See, Saltzburg and Capra, *supra note 4.*

One of the first things that impressed Rick Powell with regards to arraignments was the mass of humanity present in just one courtroom. It was Friday at 10:00 a.m. in Courtroom 1, the largest courtroom in the courthouse. Defendants were packed into the room and a few even spilled out into the hallway. Private defense attorneys stood by their clients while public defenders and prosecutors huddled together in the front of the courtroom, beyond the "bar" which separated the sphere of lawyers from the domain of those not admitted to the legal profession. All sat quietly while Public Defender Carol Hall gave the "speech."

"Hello, my name is Carol Hall and I am with the public defender's office."

"Carol has a really loud voice for such a petite woman," thought Rick as he listened from his comfortable post up front. "I wonder if that comes naturally or if she picked it up on the job?"

Carol Hall continued with her speech. "Most of you are being represented by our office but what I am about to say applies to all defendants, even those with private attorneys. All of you are here for your arraignment. The **purpose of the arraignment** is to have your charges read to you, a brief summary of the facts that support those charges read to you, and for you to enter a plea of guilty or not guilty.[10] Now, I know almost all of you already know what the charges are. But the court wants to make sure that you know what precise charges survived the preliminary hearing and grand jury stages. Every once

---

10. Miller, et al., *supra* note 3 at 917.

and awhile people are surprised to learn that some of the charges they initially were told about were not actually bound over for trial.

"Another thing that will happen today is that your attorney, whether your private attorney or a public defender, will be asked to **enter an appearance** on your behalf so that the court will know who it is that is defending you from here on out. Some of you public defender clients may have used a private attorney at the preliminary hearing and then ran out of money. The court needs to know who will be representing you at trial. Once an attorney enters his or her appearance today at your arraignment, he or she cannot withdraw from the case without the judge's permission.

"Now, I'd like to explain something that can speed things up for all of you. You have the right to have the charges read to you word for word by a judge. This goes back to the olden days when people did not know how to read or write. Since almost all of you know how to read or have an attorney with you who knows how, there is really no point in wasting your time and the judge's time in having the charges read to you. So what we will be asking all public defender clients to do is to sign a form stating that you give up your right to have the charges read to you. This form will have the charges—the actual Information and Indictment—attached to it which you can keep and read.

"Now listen up because this is really important. I want all public defender clients to plead 'Not Guilty' which you can do on this same form. I want all of our clients to plead 'Not Guilty' even if four nuns and the Pope himself saw you do the crime, a videotape was made of you doing the crime, and a voluntary confession was given by you to the police.

"The reason you must plead 'Not Guilty' is that even if the state can prove your guilt, we might be able to work out a plea bargain of some kind—if for no other reason than you won't be taking up the prosecutor's time with a trial. But if you plead 'Guilty' we have no bargaining power whatsoever. They'll just move straight to sentencing.

"Now, what if you are here today without a lawyer and have not applied for a public defender? I advise all those who are representing themselves also to plea 'Not Guilty' at this point. In fact, if you are unrepresented by an attorney the judge will probably insist that you enter a 'Not Guilty' plea at this point for your own protection.

"Now, I believe that a secretary from the prosecutor's office will begin to call names. As you hear your name, proceed with your private attorney to the table where a prosecutor will raise his or her hand and they and your attorney will assist you with the forms I spoke about. If you are being represented by the public defender, our attorneys are already up here to help you. After you have signed the forms and entered your 'Not Guilty' plea, you are free to leave. You will receive notice in the mail when your next court date is. Our office will also notify you by mail when to come to the public defender's office for your next appointment.

"If anybody insists on having the charges orally read to them by the judge, you are just going to have to wait and go dead last. So I really think you should do it the way I have suggested. There is no advantage whatsoever to having the charges orally read to you by the judge unless you and your attorney do not know how to read. Thank you and we will begin calling names."

Rick Powell watched as name after name was called and defendant after defendant proceeded to a table, signed forms, and was given an appointment card. Rick was surprised at how casually a couple of the private attorneys dressed for this court appearance, apparently taking advantage of the fact that they would come and go before the judge came in. In a couple of instances he mistook an attorney for a defendant and vice versa.

As things began to wind down, Rick wondered what would happen to those few defendants who apparently were insisting on having their charges read to them by the judge. All of them were either public defender clients or people who showed up without any kind of an attorney. He watched as a judge eventually came in, took the stand, and mechanically read the charges to each of them. Some of the defendants tried to argue the merits of their cases but the judge would abruptly cut them off and tell them he was interpreting their comments as a Not Guilty plea. One exceptionally angry defendant not only insisted that his charges be read to him orally by the judge, but then refused to enter a plea of either Guilty or Not Guilty. He just stood there and refused to speak. Rick wondered how the judge would handle this. Would he hold this man in contempt of court? After asking the angry defendant several times how he wanted to plea, the judge told the stenographer to record that the defendant chose to **remain moot** and that the court would interpret this silence as a plea of Not Guilty.

As Rick was about to leave the courtroom at the apparent end of business, he noticed one defendant arguing with a private attorney in the back of the courtroom. The judge was waiting patiently on the stand reading some unrelated memo. After he and Carol Hall walked by the arguing pair on their way out, Rick asked Carol what that was all about.

"Oh, that?" remarked Carol. "That's a private attorney who has not been paid in full yet. He is not about to enter his appearance until the client pays him. The client is trying to get him to let him pay later but the lawyer is not keen on that. Remember, once an attorney enters his or her appearance, the attorney is stuck with the client unless the judge gives permission to withdraw."

"Won't the judge allow the attorney to withdraw if he or she hasn't been paid?" Rick sounded surprised.

"No way—not with most judges in this courthouse. They want cases disposed of. Clients can fire attorneys but once an entry of appearance has been made, attorneys cannot fire clients."

Pre-Trial Motions

It was a bright and early Monday morning of Rick's second week as an intern. It was also the day for **Motions Court** in Courtroom 4, the day that Judge Morrell scheduled hearings regarding various pre-trial motions filed in cases that she was assigned to eventually preside over at trial.

Pre-trial motions are typically filed well in advance of trial. Some judges review pre-trial motions promptly and make decisions well in advance of trial. Others put off ruling on pre-trial motions (except motions to reduce bail or other urgent matters) until a day or so before trial. They like to consider such motions just before trial in the hope that many of the motions will simply disappear with a last minute plea bargain. Pre-trial motions include such things as found in Table 4 below. If a defense attorney wishes to file more than one pre-trial motion in the same case, many courts expect all such motions to be drafted and argued together (rather than piecemeal) in what is known as an **omnibus hearing.**[11]

Rick walked upstairs to court with three public defenders all of whom were scheduled for morning motions arguments before Judge Morrell. As Rick and the attorneys entered the room, Rick took a seat while the attorneys briefly spoke with their waiting clients about what was about to be attempted on their behalf.

A few minutes later Rick found himself rising as the judge entered the courtroom. The judge nodded politely at the attorneys and at Rick, but cooly ignored the defendants. She invited all to be seated.

"I see we have three pre-trial motions scheduled for today," the judge began. "We've got a motion to suppress evidence, a motion for bail reduction, and a motion to quash an indictment. Let's start with the bail reduction."

"Thank you your honor," began assistant public defender Harmon as he rose from his chair behind the defense table. "My client has been in jail for three weeks on a misdemeanor theft case. He allegedly drove off without paying for some gasoline. He has two prior misdemeanor theft convictions. Bail was set by the magistrate at one thousand dollars. This is excessive. Though he does not currently have a job, he has lived in this county all his life. It is unlikely he will flee the jurisdiction. Why would he go to all the trouble? Even

---

11. Stuckey, et al., *supra* note 1 at 118.

Table 4   Common Pre-Trial Motions

Motion to Suppress	Request that certain illegally obtained evidence be kept from the jury.
Change of Venue	Request that a trial be moved elsewhere due to potential juror bias.
Motion to Quash	Request that decision made at preliminary hearing or by grand jury that enough evidence exists to justify a trial be reversed.
Bail Reduction	Request that bail fixed by magistrate be held as excessive and reduced.
Compel Discovery	Request that prosecution, in the interests of justice, be ordered to divulge to the defense before trial critical case information solely in its possession.
Motion in Limine	Request that prosecution be ordered before trial not to even attempt to introduce certain evidence at trial that would unduly prejudice the jury.
Continuance	Request that a trial date be postponed to allow more time to prepare or because attorney or witness is unavailable.

if he is convicted, it is likely he will not do much more time than he already has done."

"The bail does seem excessive, Mr. Prosecutor," the judge suggested as she looked at the other table.

"Well, your Honor," countered the prosecutor, "our position is that this is a third offense. He has been convicted before for theft—twice before. He just does not seem to learn and keeps victimizing the community. He should sit until these charges are resolved."

"How much bail can your client afford, Mr. Harmon?" asked the judge.

After whispering with his client for a few seconds, the defender replied, "He can probably come up with two or three hundred dollars, your honor."

"Very well, I am ordering that bail be reduced to two hundred and fifty dollars." The judge glanced over at a clerk to verify that her order was being made a part of the defendant's official case file. The clerk nodded back at the judge as she wrote down the instruction.

"Let us now hear the next case," the judge directed as she picked up another written motion on her desk. "The Motion to Quash was yours, was it not Mr. Templeton?"

"Yes, thank you your Honor," replied Templeton. "My client was bound over for a felony trial pursuant to a preliminary hearing and a grand jury decision. In this instance, both the preliminary hearing judge and the grand jury somehow claimed to find a case that was strong enough to warrant a trial. As I argued in my written memo, no reasonable judge or grand jury could have found a prima facie case given the set of facts presented to them. The only evidence they have against my client is that he was seen running away from a crime scene when the cops were coming to investigate an alarm. Flight alone is never enough to prove guilt and that is all the state has in the way of evidence. Innocent people often run when cops come, especially in poor neighborhoods like the one where this attempted store burglary took place. My client deserves to have this utterly frivolous case dismissed so he can move on with his normal life."

"Yes, I have carefully read your memo as well as that of the prosecutor's office that argues to the contrary. I also have the transcript of the preliminary hearing that both memos allude to. Is there anything else that you wish to argue that is not already in your memo, Mr. Templeton?"

"No, I think the memo covers things pretty well your Honor."

"Anything you wish to add, Mr. Prosecutor?"

"No, your Honor except to point out that the court should only overrule a preliminary judge and a grand jury if they acted completely outrageously. I don't think there was an abuse of discretion on their part here at all. There decisions were reasonable. A jury can and should decide this case."

"Very well, I will take your arguments **under advisement** and will render a written judgment later this week. Thank you for your memos and brief arguments."

Judge Morrell picked up another paper on her desk. "Let's move on to the suppression motion of attorney Wood. Ms. Wood are you ready to proceed?"

"Yes, your honor," replied the assistant public defender. "My client is charged with possession of cocaine. Basically, as my written motion states and my supporting **memorandum of law** supports, it is my client's position that drugs found in his car should be suppressed. The stop of his car, and hence the search of it, were completely illegal."

"Yes, I have read your memo. Very well, you may proceed with the evidence, Ms. Wood," instructed the judge.

"Thank you your Honor. I would like to call Officer Arthur McDermott to the stand."

"Oh I get it," Rick the intern thought. "Wood must have alleged things in her written petition about an illegal search, and now she is expected to prove what she has alleged. I guess that some pre-trial motions are simply legal arguments, while others also require that new facts be introduced and proven so that the judge can rule on the legal questions."

Officer McDermott was sworn in as a witness. Ms. Wood then had her hands full attempting to get the officer to admit facts that would lead the judge to conclude that the stop was illegal. If the stop was illegal, the judge would have no choice but to suppress anything found pursuant to the stop.

Ms. Wood put a lot of effort into grilling the officer. She knew that if her motion were granted this day, the state's case against her client would collapse. If her motion were not granted, she would have to seek a plea bargain because the state would certainly get a conviction at trial. This hearing was her client's real and only day in court as far as she was concerned.

Normally the efficient Judge Morrell liked to rule on suppression motions immediately after evidence is presented and brief oral arguments made. Usually the defendant lost and the prosecution won. However, to Ms. Wood's delight, the judge took this matter, like the earlier motion to quash, "under advisement." She said she would ponder the police officer's testimony as well as the legal concepts and render her decision in a few days. Though not a complete victory, Ms. Wood was beaming.

"Are you confident that the judge will eventually rule to suppress?" Rick asked the smiling Ms. Wood after she had finished speaking with her client.

"No, I think she could go either way on this one."

"But you seem so happy," said Rick.

"Well, the prosecutor whispered to me that if I withdraw the motion before the judge decides, he'll cut his last offer in half. I just told my client. My client wants to accept that offer."

"So in a sense you did win your motion," said Rick.

"My client thinks so," acknowledged Wood. "If my client is happy I guess I am too."

Remaining Steps of Due Process

Of course, due process does not end with pre-trial motions. There remain some crucial and complicated stages: plea bargaining; trial (for those few who don't plea guilty); sentencing (for those who go to trial and lose); and post-verdict motions and related appeals.

Each of these remaining steps of due process is so important and potentially so rich in discussion that each deserves its own separate chapter. It is enough for the reader to know for now that these remaining steps round out a defendant's due process voyage through the criminal courts. The reader is invited to read subsequent chapters for detailed information on each of the remaining critical due process steps.

*****

Questions for Class Discussion

1. An unpaid internship in a courthouse, as illustrated in this chapter, at first seems to be a "lose-lose" proposition: the intern is not paid and the office is burdened with a useless body to keep busy somehow. Why is a court intern rather useless to a public defender's or prosecuting attorney's office? Why would either party (intern or courthouse office) be willing to put up with an internship?

2. This chapter is entitled, "The Steps of Due Process." What exactly is meant by the term, "due process?" Where have you heard or read of this term before?

3. Some commentators have suggested that lawyers focus only on end results in terms of justice (e.g., a good plea bargain in the end), while clients often see justice more in terms of a fair process. What do you suppose is meant by this?

4. What happens at the "First Appearance?" Is this an important event or an unimportant event? How soon must the First Appearance take place?

5. What are some of the things that could happen to someone if we abolished the concept of "First Appearance?" Do you think that any societies exist that do not provide for a first appearance in criminal court? If so, what types of societies would you expect these to be?

6. What is the official purpose of the preliminary hearing? How often do judges fail to bind cases over for trial pursuant to a preliminary hearing? Why do you suppose that preliminary hearing judges almost always find enough evidence to warrant a trial?

7. Why do defense attorneys find preliminary hearings so useful? Is it fair that defense attorneys get a sneak peak at the prosecution's case in this manner?

8. By local custom, attorneys in some jurisdictions "waive" (pass up) the right for their client to have a preliminary hearing, figuring that the case will wind up being bound over for trial anyway. What would you say to such lawyers? What would the prosecutor have to offer you before you'd give up the right to a preliminary hearing?

9. What is the prosecution's typical preliminary hearing strategy? How long do most preliminary hearings take to conduct? How can probable cause be determined so swiftly?

10. What is the purpose of the grand jury? In what ways do grand jury proceedings differ from preliminary hearings?

11. Why do some states use grand juries and not others? Does your state use grand juries? If the U.S. Constitution speaks of the right to a grand jury, how do some states get around the apparent requirement?

12. Should defense attorneys be permitted to cross-examine witnesses in a grand jury proceeding? Do grand juries let defendants off more frequently than judges conducting preliminary hearings?

13. Why do grand juries seem so willing to do the prosecutor's bidding? Given the way that grand jury proceedings are conducted, do they really have much choice?

14. Suppose a grand jury or preliminary hearing judge insanely refuses to find a prima facie case (probable cause) and votes to set the defendant free. Is there anything a prosecutor can do or is the case forever terminated?

15. What does it mean for a lawyer to "enter an appearance?" Why are some lawyers so reluctant to take this particular step?

16. Should lawyers be permitted to "fire" their clients whenever they want to? Should it depend on what stage of the proceeding the case is at? Should it depend on whether the lawyer has been paid yet?

17. Some judges refuse to allow a defendant to plea guilty at an arraignment unless the person has legal counsel. Do you think such judges are coddling criminals or playing fair? If you were a judge, and someone foolishly wanted to plea guilty in a serious case without even consulting a lawyer, would you accept the guilty plea?

18. Is it immoral for a defendant who knows he or she is guilty to plea "not guilty" at the arraignment? Is this honorable? Why is it almost always a big mistake for someone to plea "guilty" at the arraignment stage even if the case is an eventual easy win for the prosecution?

19. What are some examples of "pre-trial motions?" Name and describe as many as you can. When are such motions heard by a judge?

20. List each of the following steps of the process in the correct order that they occur: preliminary hearing/grand jury, first appearance, arrest, pre-trial motions, arraignment, trial, plea bargain, post-verdict motions, appeal, sentencing.

*****

Key Terms: main purpose of first appearance, purpose of preliminary hearing, prima facie case, probable cause, bind case over for trial, waive, discovery tool, impeach, prosecutor's preliminary hearing strategy, skeleton case, defense preliminary hearing strategy, exceed the scope, legal advisor to grand jury, purpose of arraignment, enter an appearance, remain moot, motions court, omnibus hearing, under advisement, memorandum of law

Additional Concepts: steps of due process, official and unofficial purposes of preliminary hearing, grand juries vs. preliminary hearings, common pretrial motions, remaining steps of due process

CHAPTER NINE

The Plea Bargain

Plea Bargaining and the Defense Attorney

Claude Richards was frustrated. A summa cum laude graduate with a bachelor's degree in electrical engineering, he had turned down a lucrative job offer in the aerospace industry to attend law school. The reason: to become a trial lawyer. It was this lifelong ambition to do trials that also caused him to turn down two lucrative offers after law school with private firms specializing in patent law and to take a job as a public defender. "I want to do trials, not churn paper," he told himself. His starting pay with the P.D.'s office: ten thousand dollars per year less than the offer made to him years earlier by the aerospace firm.

But it was not the lack of good pay that frustrated Claude. It was the lack of doing trials. The main culprit derailing his dreams was the plea bargain. "I gave up a lot in time and money in the hope of doing trials," Claude would tell all friends who would listen. "But it seems that all I am is a wheeler and dealer. I want to be a trial lawyer, not a professional plea bargainer."

Claude did get to do trials—more than most lawyers admitted to the bar. But even though criminal lawyers probably do more trials than lawyers in any other legal specialty, studies show that over 90 percent of their cases will be plea bargained rather than tried.[1] Claude himself was only doing three or four jury trials per year. That would not be bad for a civil lawyer, many of whom are lucky to do twenty trials in an entire lifetime. But it was not enough to satisfy Claude. "I thought I'd be doing three or four jury trials per month. I was dreaming," Claude told his paper-churning former law school buddies. "I feel like a car salesman, only I sell guilty pleas for the right price rather than cars."

---

1. See, Bureau of Justice Statistics. (1983). *The Prosecution of Felony Arrests.* Washington, D.C.: U.S. Government Printing Office; Dawson, John M. (1992). *Prosecutors in State Courts.* Washington, D.C.: Bureau of Justice Statistics.

It was too bad for Claude that he was born a century and a half too late. There was a time in America (the first half of the 1800s) when plea bargains were relatively unheard of and most cases were resolved by way of jury trials. This period was known as the **golden age of trials**.[2] True, trials tended to be very short by today's standards (one jury might easily hear several trials or more in a single day). Technical rules of evidence were largely non-existent.[3] But defendants' cases were decided by juries rather than by attorneys negotiating with one another.

By the late 1800s all of this started to change. In many areas, plea bargaining became entrenched before the end of that century.[4] Yet despite the growing practice of plea bargaining, American lawyers and judges were reluctant to openly acknowledge its existence. It was as if it were the dirty little secret of American jurisprudence. Judges and lawyers were not sure what they were doing was constitutional. After all, the constitution called for a criminal court system based on due process gained through public trials, not guilty pleas. Plea bargaining, on the other hand, involved secret negotiations and arguably coerced guilty pleas. It was one thing for a defendant to voluntarily give up a right to a trial and to plea guilty. But could a system which resulted in so many defendants rolling over and admitting guilt be truly said to be non-coercive?

Finally, the U.S. Supreme Court itself put such fretting to an end when it ruled that plea bargaining was not only constitutional but commendable. In the 1971 case of *Santobello v. New York* it ruled that:

> "The disposition of criminal charges by agreement between the prosecutor and the accused, sometimes loosely called 'plea bargaining' is an important and necessary component of the American system of justice. Properly administered, it is to be encouraged. If every criminal charge were subjected to a full-scale trial, the States and the Federal Government would need to multiply by many times the number of judges and court facilities."[5]

So, here was Claude Richards, professional guilty plea facilitator, laboring in what seemed to him to be an Orwellian 21st Century legal world of near

---

2. Levine, James P. (1992). *Juries and Politics*. Belmont, CA: Brooks/Cole Publishing Company.

3. Id.

4. Sanborn, Joseph B., Jr. (1986). "A Historical Sketch of Plea Bargaining." *Justice Qurterly* 3 (June):111–138.

5. *Santobello v. New York*, 404 U.S. 257, 260 (1971).

universal confessions of guilt. "In China, the role of the defense attorney is not to get clients off. That would be considered ethically wrong. Rather, their role is to make impassioned sentencing arguments.[6] Is it any different here?" he often wondered.

Claude knew that plea bargaining has many defenders. Like the U.S. Supreme Court, many lawyers and legal scholars conclude that plea bargaining is indispensable to the system of criminal justice—that without it, the courts would be overwhelmed by a mass of trials they would be unable to handle. Others further argue that plea bargaining is morally legitimate since both sides voluntarily engage in and benefit from the practice. Still others suggest that the abolition of plea bargaining would be impossible because the parties would continue the practice even if higher authorities tried to curb it.[7]

Claude was aware of these arguments but did not personally agree with them. "I'm not so sure both sides benefit from plea bargains," he told himself. "The prosecution benefits, but do the defendants? If they do, then why does the U.S., with all the plea bargaining constantly taking place here, have a larger percentage of its population in prison than any other country in the world?"[8]

Claude similarly remained unconvinced that defendants voluntarily engaged in plea bargaining. He was not sure that having a judge pounce on a client for demanding a trial was conducive to real choice. He remembered how one trial-hating judge in his courthouse, after managing to go an entire year without a single trial, encountered a defendant who steadfastly refused to give up his right to a jury trial. The defendant lost his case and received a sentence so severe that attorneys reacted with stunned disbelief on hearing about it. It was the talk of the courthouse for months. That was the last time that anybody dared to have a trial before that judge for a long, long time.[9]

Claude was not even sure that plea bargaining was necessary to keep the sky from falling. "Why would we, as the Supreme Court said, have to build many more court facilities and hire many more judges if plea bargaining were

---

6. See, Lilly, Robert. (1986). "Forks and Chopsticks: Understanding Criminal Justice in the PRC." *Criminal Justice International* (March/April 1986), at 15.

7. See, Lynch, David R. (1994). "The Impropriety of Plea Agreements: A Tale of Two Counties." *Law and Social Inquiry*, 19(1):113–133, citing various academic sources defending plea bargaining.

8. See, Chaddock, Gail Russell. (2003). "Incarceration Rate in U.S. is World's Highest." *Christian Science Monitor* (August 18, 2003), citing an August 2003 report issued by the U.S. Justice Department.

9. This true story is found in Lynch, David R., *supra* note 7 at 120.

abolished? It seems to me that judges only spend two or three hours per day on the bench and most courtrooms sit idle most of the time?"[10]

Despite Claude's internal doubts about the legitimacy of plea bargaining, he put great effort and time into getting the best offers that he could from prosecutors and in getting clients to accept such offers. Claude felt that if he were going to be effective for his clients, he had to play the game. This was no time to be a revolutionary or a maverick. The revolution he would lead would be crushed and his clients punished.

Most of the time, prosecutors offered and Claude's clients readily accepted, plea bargains involving probation. Quite frequently though, Claude had to "sell" clients on the idea of doing a few months in the county jail. "Better months in jail than years in prison," he would sincerely tell them. They usually would come around with some gentle persuasion. The hardest "sale" though involved that small percentage of cases (which he always worried about) that would involve long years in prison even if the client agreed to plea guilty. Such cases more often than not required Claude to reach into what he liked to call his "bag of tricks." He used these "tricks" to save stubborn clients from themselves. "The worse thing a defense attorney can do to a client who is in big trouble is to passively acquiesce to their natural impulse for a trial," was his credo. He learned this lesson the hard way when he had his first murder case. The client killed his roommate in a drunken fit of anger over a disagreement regarding some money. The decedent's blood was found on the defendant's shirt and under his finger nails. The murder weapon, a brick used to smash the victim's head in, was found outside the defendant's house in the yard, carefully tucked away in a row of other bricks which formed a border for a garden. The prosecutor knew that no jury would believe the defendant's claims of non-involvement but was a little worried that they might return a manslaughter rather than a murder verdict. To avoid the hassle of trial the prosecutor offered Claude's client a seven year prison sentence if Claude could get him to plead guilty. Claude spent fifteen minutes trying to get his client to accept the proposal but was unable to persuade him to give up a trial. Claude

---

10. For a suggestion of how much excess capacity truly existed in courts about the time of the *Santobello* case in which the Supreme Court announce an indispensable need for plea bargaining, see Nardulli, Peter W. (1979). "The Caseload Controversy and the Study of Criminal Courts." *Criminal Law & Criminology*, 89:96–97. This study showed that Chicago judges spent only two or three hours per day on the bench and did not do much work thereafter. The 16 courtrooms looked at over a two-year period produced an average of only one disposition per day, even though 70% of the dispositions were dismissals or guilty pleas.

and his client went to trial and lost. The client was sentenced to life in prison with no chance for parole. Though some might feel that justice was done, Claude felt that he had let his client down. "I should have protected my client more from himself. I should have done whatever it took to get my guy to take that deal. I failed him as a lawyer," he told his wife after a sleepless night following the pronouncement of the life sentence.

Claude failed (or at least believed he failed) to exercise what criminal courthouse regulars refer to as **client control.** "You've got to control your clients," judges liked to say around his courthouse. "You've got to teach them when to accept a deal."

With time, Claude became much better at "client control." He realized that accepting a first or second or even a third decision to go to trial on the part of a client in serious trouble who was being offered a good deal was not effective lawyering. "I've got to wear them down," he figured. "I've got to make them understand the way things work around here."

When Claude got truly desperate, he would resort to the "tricks" in his "bag." One technique he sometimes used was **chair therapy.** This was particularly useful for relatively minor cases in which some knuckle-headed client on bail was offered a sweet deal (like probation or a little jail time) but had the "gall" to demand a trial even though he or she obviously was guilty. "Oh, judges around here just love to whack brazen people like them," Claude realized. "But I won't give them the chance." During trial weeks, Claude would have such clients sit in the courthouse corridor all day long waiting for a trial slot to open up for them. At the end of the day, he would send them home only to have them come back and sit all the next day. Probation started sounding better the longer they would wait. "If you want the probation, I could get you out of here in ten minutes," he would like to keep reminding them. "It's getting a trial that is hard. I can't tell you when or even if our trial slot will open up this term," he also liked to say.

For clients charged with serious felonies, chair therapy was not very effective. If Claude's usual pleading and eventual screaming did not work, he would bring in a colleague to help the client see the light. By this time Claude was the "bad guy" in his client's mind. So, what was needed was a "good guy" who could go in and befriend the client and try some gentle persuasion. Often, this **lawyer version of good cop/bad cop** resulted in a breakthrough that could not be achieved otherwise.

Usually though, Claude only had to contrast the prosecutor's offer with what the judge was indicating that he or she would give the client to get the client to agree to plea guilty. It might take a half hour or so of hand wringing, but usually the client came around in the end.

Some tactics Claude was very reluctant to use to get clients to come around, though at times he did succumb to temptation. For example, once he had a client who was firmly convinced that because he was a public defender, Claude must be both incompetent and in league with the government ultimately paying his puny salary. The client told Claude that he did not trust him to look after his interests and would demand a trial no matter what. Claude put his personal animosity towards this rude client aside, and as a true professional worked out a very attractive bargain. This consisted of three months of jail in exchange for a guilty plea to greatly reduced charges. Claude knew that this offer was a good one. In fact it was unusually generous. He also knew his paranoid client would reject any initial offer that was proposed to him outright. So when Claude presented the offer to the client, he told the client that the prosecutor had offered a good bargain of six months (not three). As expected, the defendant accused the defender of incompetency and worse. Claude acted surprised that the client did not want this deal and told him he doubted he could get a better one but would try. The defendant said he better try or else there would have to be a trial. Claude went to his office and attended to some unrelated matters. Claude came back an hour later looking jubilant and told the defendant of the "unbelievable" three months that the prosecutor said he might be persuaded to eventually offer. Later that day, the client happily entered a guilty plea.

Claude not only had what it took to "sell" good deals to clients, but also had what it took to negotiate good deals from prosecutors in the first place. The key to Claude's success was his personality more than his I.Q. Claude never scored extremely high on achievement tests, including the law school admission exam and the state bar exam. But Claude was emotionally stable (calm, confident, slow to anger) and likeable (friendly, reasonable, easy to talk to). Emotional stability and likeableness appear to be among the most **important traits of successful plea bargainers.**[11] Furthermore, Claude preferred to use a **joint problem-solving approach** in his negotiations with prosecutors, a style which most prosecutors identify as being more effective than an adversarial approach.[12] Probably much more so than in most areas of law, prosecutors and defense lawyers have a long term, close working relationship to preserve. A defense attorney, prosecutor and judge constitute what has been described as the **courtroom work group.** This work group has shared goals that can only be accomplished by working cooperatively, as if in a team. Such

---

11. Lynch, David R. and T. David Evans. (2002). "Attributes of Highly Effective Criminal Defense Negotiators." *Journal of Criminal Justice,* 30(5):387–396.

12. Id. at 391.

goals include reducing work, reducing stress, and reducing uncertainty (in short, reducing trials).[13] An adversarial approach would work against this.

The fact that Claude thought it most effective to be calm, friendly and co-operative did not mean that he ever "sold out" his client. In fact, in big cases Claude conscientiously prepared for plea bargaining by creating a game plan before even approaching the prosecutor's door. Claude thought through what concerns the prosecutor would reasonably have; what strengths and weaknesses both sides had; and what tactics he could use to abate the prosecutor's concerns while simultaneously emphasizing his side's strengths and the other side's weaknesses.[14]

As can be seen, Claude was good at plea bargaining. But he did not like it. He looked forward to the day when he would eventually leave the public defender's office. He was not sure where he would go. Perhaps it was not too late to get a job in a patent law firm. Yet, he still did not want to churn paper. Maybe he could get a job teaching paralegal studies or teaching criminal justice somewhere. Teaching would involve performing before a type of jury. It was a thought.

Plea Bargaining and the Defendant

Nick Santora did not mean to kill anybody. A short, slender, gentle man in his late twenties, Nick had a few beers one hot summer afternoon after work with some coworkers at the construction site before heading home. Nick was not sure how many beers he had consumed, but it was at least three and no more than five. Nick had a slight "buzz" but did not feel drunk. But his "buzz" (or whatever it was) was about to get him in the worst trouble of his life.

As Nick was driving home he rounded a sharp bend in the highway and slammed his heavy construction truck into the side of a small van carrying a man, his wife, and their two small children. The man and the two children were thrown from the car (none were wearing seat belts) and died within a few minutes from various head injuries. The woman somehow remained in

---

13. Ulmer, Jeffrey T. (1997). *Social Worlds of Sentencing: Court Communities under Sentencing Guidelines*. Ithica, N.Y.: State University of New York Press. See also, Eisenstein, James and Herbert Jacob. (1977). *Felony Justice: An Organizational Analysis of Criminal Courts*. Boston: Little, Brown.

14. For a good discussion on how to prepare for plea bargaining see, Herman, G. Nicholas. (1997). "Preparing for Plea Bargaining." Chapter 4 in *Plea Bargaining*. Charlottesville, VA: Lexis Law Publishing.

the car but wound up in a wheel chair, possibly for life. Nick was wearing a seat belt, but being very short had positioned his seat very close to the air bag in the heavy vehicle he was driving. The small man was stunned when the bag deployed. This caused him to have amnesia. He did not remember running the red light that several witnesses said he ran.

Police responded to the scene within minutes of a witness's cell phone call. One of the officers smelled beer on Nick's breath and had him do several field sobriety tests on the spot. Perhaps still stunned from the air bag (or perhaps because of the alcohol), Nick was unable to concentrate and failed all of them. Nick blew into a breath alcohol measurement device and registered a .079 blood alcohol level (barely below the automatic drunk driving conviction level of .08 in his state).

Nick was charged with homicide by vehicle while driving under the influence. Though he blew under .08 (too low for an automatic conviction) the state still thought it could prove drunk driving based on Nick's poor driving and failed field tests. If convicted he faced a minimum mandatory sentence of three years per death (nine years total).

Nick was not sure why he ran the red light. Maybe he did so because he was drunk. But he was not sure that he actually was drunk. He had felt the effects of the beers but had not felt drunk. His coworkers claimed he did not seem drunk when he left them ten minutes before the accident. And, Nick found out that the curvy intersection where the impact occurred was one of the most accident-prone in the county. Nick was willing to pay for his crimes, but was not sure what crimes, if any, he had committed.

The prosecutor was sure. She was convinced that Nick was a drunk killer. She met with the surviving wife and mother and promised the sobbing woman she would not go easy on Nick. In the minds of the prosecutor and surviving victim, Nick's callous recklessness killed the poor woman's entire family.

The prosecutor at first refused to make Nick's attorney, a private lawyer who specialized in drunk driving cases, any deal at all. "That's fine with me," Nick told his lawyer. "I'm not sure myself I was drunk. I think I want a trial."

Nick's attorney met with the prosecutor and laid out the case for the defendant. "You've got tainted field sobriety tests due to my client's severe air bag injury; a low breath alcohol score; a notoriously dangerous intersection; and a defendant with no record who comes across as someone's cute, little, helpless, baby brother. What if he is acquitted? How will the wife feel about that?"

The prosecutor saw the defense attorney's points and eventually offered a six year sentence. "Too high," the defender countered. "You've got to give me something I can realistically sell to my client. He is itching for a trial." The prosecutor knew the defender long enough to know he was sincerely trying to reach a bargain that might work.

"What would your client take?" the prosecutor curiously asked.

"Maybe if you offer three years, he might go for that," the defender honestly replied.

"No way!" the prosecutor responded with visible anger. "With the minimum mandatories he would be getting three lives for the price of one."

"Then come down to five years. Your case could go either way and you know it," suggested the defender. "You could sell that to the victim. Five years of hard time is a major whack."

"OK, tell him five years firm," the prosecutor instructed after thinking it over. "Tell him juries don't like hearing about three dead bodies, especially when two are kids. Tell him nine years is just the minimum he'll get if he loses, not the maximum. I wouldn't be surprised if the judge gave him double that and neither would you."

"I'll see if he'll go for it," the defender answered. "I'll let you know."

The defense lawyer knew he had a strong shot at a complete acquittal. He also knew that the prosecutor had a strong chance of complete victory. Juries are just too unpredictable for either side to ever be sure. It is always "a crap shoot," a defense attorney once said. "You don't know what the jury is going to do."[15]

Nick's defense lawyer also knew that if his client were convicted, the judge assigned the case might very well sentence beyond the minimum mandatory sentences. Suppose the judge did sentence his client to six years per dead body instead of the minimum of three years each—that would be eighteen years, not even counting the injuries to the mother.

The defendant was lucky he had a private lawyer in this case. His luck was not due to any superior skill on the part of his attorney. Most of the public defenders in his county could have probably negotiated a similar plea offer. Rather, the defendant was lucky because he was more apt to trust the private lawyer with a good deal like this than a public defender. Public defenders who propose deals to clients, even wonderful deals, are often told that "this does not look very good. I think I need to hire a real lawyer."[16]

---

15. Lynch, David R. (1998). "In Their Own Words: Occupational Stress Among Public Defenders." *Criminal Law Bulletin*, 34(6):473–496, at 487.

16. Lynch, David R. (1999). "Perceived Judicial Hostility to Criminal Trials." *Criminal Justice and Behavior*, 26(2):217–233, at 226.

Many defendants want plea bargains. But some do not. Defendants who are obviously guilty and who are being offered probation or light jail time often are happy to plead guilty. Defendants whose guilt is not so obvious or who are being offered years in prison are often reluctant, even adamantly opposed, to entering a guilty plea. They tend to want trials.

Defendants grow up watching television like everybody else. They watch fictional lawyers going to trial and getting fictional people off. They hear about celebrated cases in the media that often go to trial (because they are so non-routine). What they don't usually grasp from television is the true extent that plea bargaining takes place. Even in shows that depict plea bargaining, many more defendants wind up turning down the bargain and going to trial than what actually takes place in real courts.

Defendants often have a hard time understanding why their lawyer would want them to passively accept prison time in a case that is not air tight. In the case in which their lawyer is a public defender, they think they know why. Public defenders are incompetent pseudo-lawyers who are too scared, lazy, or compromised to go to trial. As one public defender put it:

"When you're in private practice your clients tend to respect you more and respect the advice given. I think anytime someone has to pay for something they tend to listen a little better. And as it is now, a lot of them out there don't even think public defenders are lawyers."[17]

Another public defender once said:

"I find it … offensive when we have the case, and I can tell you of two instances where we got them plea bargained 1 to 3, and they say 'you guys stink. Oh P.D., I'm going to get a real lawyer.' He pays the real lawyer $1500 and gets the exact same plea bargain. They listen to the private lawyer because they're paying him money, the P.D. is not, doesn't know anything."[18]

As mentioned earlier, the vast majority of defendants wind up accepting plea bargains. It just takes some lawyers, especially public defenders, longer to convince certain clients to plead guilty than others. Those defendants who refuse to accept plea bargains are sometimes made examples of as a warning to presumptuous future defendants. For example, in one real life case a robbery defendant with no prior record was offered probation by the prosecutor. As reporters covering the case noted, "The public defender assigned to handle his case urged him to accept the offer. But Baker, a delivery man with no prior convictions, pleaded innocent and asked for a chance to prove it in a

---

17. Lynch, *supra* note 15, at 478.
18. Id., at 477.

jury trial. Eventually he was convicted, and the same judge who had earlier approved the probation offer sentenced Baker to six years in prison."[19] Many judges like to put it this way: "He takes some of my time, I take some of his."[20]

This **trial tax**[21] (substantial trial penalty) apparently can indeed have a chilling effect upon the right to a trial. Even a prosecutor has admitted that "the threat of heavy sentences and the promise of one-time lenient offers must have coerced some innocent men and women into pleading guilty."[22]

Amazingly, despite the perceptions among lawyers that a trial tax exists, very little interest has been shown among academic researchers in exploring coercion from defendants' viewpoints. One English study found that defendants often believe themselves to have been "ordered," "forced," or even "terrorized" into pleading guilty.[23] Such studies are apparently rare in the United States, although one exception was Jonathan Casper's classic study called" *American Criminal Justice: The Defendant's Perspective.*" In this study, Casper noted that a defendant does not see the decision about the punishment received as being based on "abstract notions of morality," but rather as the result of a game in which courthouse actors use the same "hypocritical and manipulative ways" that the defendants themselves use in dealing with people.[24]

Nick did not have to be coerced or terrorized into accepting the attractive offer. Despite doubts about his own innocence, Nick was rational enough to realize that going to trial was a potentially life-shattering mistake. There were three dead people and a broken woman. He did not want to risk a conviction and raw exposure to a sentencing judge without a deal of some kind.

Unlike Nick, why do some defendants choose trial over a plea bargain? Several possibilities present themselves. First, some defendants who sense that the case against them is shaky are willing to roll the dice despite the risk of po-

---

19. Tybor, Joseph R. and Mark Eissman. (1985). "Judges Penalize the Guilty for Exercising the Right to Trial." *Chicago Tribune* (October 13):1,6, at 1.

20. Uhlman, Thomas M. and N. Darlene Walker. (1980). "He Takes Some of my Time, I Take Some of His: An Analysis of Judicial Sentencing Patterns in Jury Cases." *Law and Society Review,* 14(Winter):323–341.

21. The term "trial tax" for a substantial trial penalty was coined by David Brereton and Jonathan Casper. (1981–82). "Does it Pay to Plead Guilty?" *Law & Society Review,* 16:45–65.

22. Heilbroner, David. (1990). *Rough Justice: Days and Nights of a Young D.A.* New York: Pantheon Books, at 243.

23. Baldwin, John and Michael McConville. (1979). "Plea Bargaining and Plea Negotiation in England." *Law & Society Review,* 13:287–308, at 296.

24. Casper, Jonathan. (1972). *American Criminal Justice: The Defendant's Perspective.* Englewood Cliffs, N.J.: Prentice-Hall, at 80–81.

tentially greater penalties for losing. Even some judges can understand this and reduce the "trial tax" accordingly. They become less angry at a defendant for taking up court time with a case that presents "a good fight, a fair shot at a fair trial that's going to be interesting," than they do with a case that is a **dead bang loser**.[25] Many defendants in Nick's shoes (a defendant whose case arguably had reasonable doubt) choose a trial despite what is offered them. If they win, they win big. Even if they lose, some judges will punish them only for the crimes they did without any additional penalty for "wasting" court time.

Some defendants who go to trial do so simply because even with a plea bargain they still would be required to serve spectacularly long sentences. It is easy to "sell" probation to almost any defendant. It takes a special kind of defendant who is willing to voluntarily sign away decades of his or her life without a major fight.

A third category of defendant who is likely to insist on going to trial is the innocent defendant. It is much easier to convince a culpable person to take a deal than it is to convince someone to plead guilty to misconduct they simply did not do. Fortunately for Nick, he was not certain of his innocence. If he had been, he would have had a very difficult time convincing himself to plead guilty, even if that were the most rational path to take. Remember, juries are unpredictable. Innocent people can get convicted (after all, if they did not appear to be guilty they likely never would have been arrested). One defense attorney spoke of how stressful the high stakes can be to defend at trial the rare client whom the attorney actually believes is innocent:

"I did a trial with a guy. They offered him 2–6. He steadfastly maintained his innocence and I personally believed him which made it even worse. He got convicted. He got 18–54 and I still wake up rehashing that trial. That's over a year ago. It's tough."[26]

Because of plea bargaining, we live in a strange country where the guilty can sometimes be better off than the innocent. Guilty people take plea bargains and get reduced sentences. Innocent people who fight it out and lose get punished much more severely than the guilty who accept a bargain. In some situations, it is better to have done the crime than to be innocent of it.

A fourth category of defendants likely to go to trial are irrational defendants. These have been around for a long, long time.[27] Even when offered a

---

25. Lynch, *supra* note 15, at 485.

26. Id., at 483.

27. Neubauer, David W. (1974). *Criminal Justice in Middle America.* Morristown, N.J.: General Learning Press.

great deal despite obvious guilt they turn the deal down, thus forcing themselves and their reluctant attorney into trial mode. Sometimes they are so irrational that they fire their legal counsel and proceed to trial **pro se** (representing themselves). In such cases the old saying that "a defendant who represents himself has a fool for an attorney," applies quite well.

The time came for Nick to enter his guilty plea and to be sentenced pursuant to its terms. Before a judge could accept Nick's (or anybody's) plea of guilty, the judge must be convinced that the guilty plea is being **knowingly and voluntarily entered.**

In order to be knowingly entered, the defendant must possess "a full understanding of what the plea connotes and of its consequence."[28] Hence the judge must be sure that the defendant understands exactly what crimes and facts he is admitting[29] and the maximum sentence for the offense (in other words, how good the deal may or may not potentially be).[30]

In addition to being "knowingly" entered, a guilty plea must also be "voluntarily" entered. In order for the guilty plea to be voluntarily entered, the court must be satisfied that the defendant was not induced by way of threats or coercion to give up his or her right to a trial.[31] This last point created a stir in the courtroom when Nick was entering his guilty pleas to the homicides. The judge asked Nick the routine question of whether he had been "coerced or threatened in any way to enter the guilty pleas and give up the right to a jury trial." Nick sincerely replied, "Well, yes sir, I really wanted a trial because I'm not sure I was even drunk. But my lawyer told me if I did not take this deal I could be an old man before I got out of jail. I'm too scared to go to trial but I do think I might be innocent. I guess you could say I feel intimidated about not having a trial. Yes, definitely I'm intimidated."

The irony here is that many believe that plea bargaining by its very nature is often necessarily coercive. Lawyers get clients to admit guilt through ways of bribes and threats, carrots and sticks. Judges want to have it both ways. They want defendants to be scared out of going to trial yet they don't want them to admit that they feel coerced and intimidated. Because Nick did not say "No" to whether he felt coerced and intimidated, the judge could not accept his guilty plea nor give him the plea bargain. "I'm sorry, counsel but I cannot accept this plea," the judge told Nick's defense attorney. Motioning

---

28. *Boykin v. Alabama*, 395 U.S. 238 (1969).
29. *United States v. DeFusco*, 949 F.2d 114 (4th Cir. 1991).
30. *Hart v. Marion Correctional Institute*, 927 F.2d 256 (6th Cir. 1991).
31. *Walker v. Johnston*, 312 U.S. 275 (1941).

them to proceed to the corner of the courtroom, the judge told the attorney, "Perhaps you should talk some more over there with your client."

After a few minutes of hushed, angry and anguished whispering (the tone of which could be heard by all in the courtroom), Nick's defense attorney indicated to the judge that his client was now ready to finish entering his plea. "Very well, you and your client may approach the bench," the judge directed.

Once again the judge asked Nick the critical question, "Have you been coerced or intimidated in any way to enter a guilty plea today?" There was a long pause in the courtroom. Then Nick responded, "No, sir." Ignoring the long pause and pleased with his vocal response the judge continued, "Are you giving up your right to a jury trial of your own free will and voluntary choice?" After an even longer pause, Nick replied that he was. "Are you sure?" the judge inquired, as if by asking this question the judge could erase any lingering stigma from Nick's earlier botched attempt to plead guilty. "Yes, I'm sure," Nick sadly confirmed.

Entering a guilty plea is not easy for many defendants to do. To help "grease the skids," courts have devised a couple of alternative guilty pleas that can make the process less painful for reluctant defendants. These are not used in the course of ordinary business but rather reserved for times when really needed.

One such alternative to the traditional plea of guilty is the **nolo contendere plea**. Literally, these words mean, "I will not contest it." In effect, a defendant who is entering such a plea is neither admitting guilt nor denying it. It is a face saving mechanism that some have criticized as a "foolish concept"[32] which some prosecutors and judges resist using. Legally, in criminal court it has precisely the same effect as a straight plea of guilty without the defendant having to ever say he or she is in fact guilty (though it cannot be used as evidence of guilt in a subsequent civil suit for the same act). Trial-level courts are given great leeway by higher courts as to whether or not to allow a defendant to plead "nolo" rather than "guilty." Simply put, courts may accept such pleas as long as it is in the "public interest" to do so.[33] Too bad for Nick that his lawyer did not tell him of the option to enter a "nolo" plea. This plea seems to fit Nick and his circumstances quite well. But, Nick did not sufficiently protest his entering of a straight guilty plea for either the judge, the prosecutor, or even his own lawyer to bring up this option reserved only for special occasions.

An even stranger alternative guilty plea is the **Alford plea** which many prosecutors are forbidden by their superiors to use "except in the most unusual of circumstances."[34] Judges also feel uncomfortable with such pleas since they

---

32. Herman, *supra* note 14, at 125 citing comments of Judge Learned Hand.
33. *United States v. Chin Doong Art*, 193 F. Supp. 820 (E.D. N.Y. 1961).
34. Herman, *supra* note 14, at 118 citing policies of the U.S. Department of Justice.

seem to turn the guilty plea hearing into something of a farce. Nevertheless, such pleas are legal and used from time to time, especially in cases in which a defendant absolutely refuses to plead "guilty" or even "nolo contendere." Unlike a "no contest" plea, an "Alford plea" involves a defendant who is affirmatively asserting that he or she is innocent but will nevertheless accept the punishment. The plea comes from the case of *North Carolina v. Alford*[35] in which a man was charged with first degree murder. Alford flat out told the court that he was innocent of any crime but that he was willing to plead guilty to the reduced charge of second degree murder in order to avoid the threat of the death penalty. The court accepted Alford's plea and sentenced him to thirty years in prison, the maximum sentence for second degree murder. Later at prison, Alford changed his mind about doing the thirty years and tried to take back his "guilty plea" by pointing out the fact that he never actually admitted guilt. Indeed, he even had told the court he was innocent. The U.S. Supreme Court ruled that such a plea was lawful because it could see no real difference between a "nolo contendere" plea in which a defendant refuses to admit guilt and a plea such as this in which a defendant protests his innocence. Like the standard in accepting any type of guilty plea, a court can accept an Alford plea as long as it finds that there is a **factual basis** that links the defendant to the crime and as long as the plea is being voluntarily and knowingly entered.

Like Alford, Nick changed his mind about his guilty plea soon after arriving in prison to begin his five long years at hard time. He met with his lawyer to ask what could be done. "The judge does not have to let you withdraw your plea," the lawyer told him. "We could ask but it is unlikely this judge will disturb the conviction at this point."

"Under what circumstances can a person withdraw a guilty plea?" asked Nick.

"Well, the judge only has to let you withdraw your guilty plea after sentence has been imposed for a very limited number of reasons, none of which apply." Nick's attorney then handed him a list of valid reasons—outlined in Table 1.

Nick and his attorney went over each and every possible basis for withdrawing the guilty plea. Nick was told that it was unlikely the judge would rule that Nick's plea was involuntarily or unknowingly entered given Nick's responses to the judge's oral questioning in court. Additionally, the court would no doubt point out that Nick had initialed every item on the **Boykin Form** (form that summarizes a defendant's trial rights which lawyers are required to go over with the client prior to entering the guilty plea).

---

35. *North Carolina v. Alford*, 400 U.S. 25 (1970).

Table 1   Withdraw of a Guilty Plea — Legal Grounds

Plea not voluntarily entered

Plea not knowingly entered

Defendant denied effective assistance of counsel

Sentence exceeded the legal maximum for the offense

Court lacked jurisdiction over the offense

Statute criminalizing the conduct was unconstitutional

Conviction constituted double jeopardy

Source: Various legal cases cited in Herman, G. Nicholas. (1997). "Withdrawing the Guilty Plea." Chapter 11 in *Plea Bargaining.* Charlottesville, VA.: Lexis Law Publishing.

"If we go to court, the judge will get a transcript of your day in court and confront you with your testimony that you were sure that you were doing this voluntarily. He will also show you the Boykin form we filled out with all the items you initialed before going to court. We can't win on that angle, not with this judge."

"What about the other grounds?" asked Nick.

"Well, the court had jurisdiction since the accident occurred in this county and not some other one. The sentence is well below the legal maximum for the offense. There is no double jeopardy here. And there is nothing unconstitutional in making homicide by vehicle a crime. I'm telling you there are just no grounds to withdraw your plea."

"What about ineffective assistance of counsel?" asked Nick. Offended, the lawyer abruptly left without ever replying.

Plea Bargaining:
The Victim and the Prosecutor

Opponents of plea bargaining make strange bedfellows: civil libertarians who oppose it due to the chilling effect they believe it has on a defendant's right to a trial, and "law and order" advocates who oppose it due to the lenient sentences they believe the practice generates. Victims tend naturally to fall more often into the "law and order" camp than the one concerned about due process rights of the accused. Hence, prosecutors often have to "sell" deals to victims in much the same way that defense attorneys must "sell" deals to clients. The only difference, of course, is that defendants have the power to veto a defense lawyer's bargain whereas a victim has no veto over a prosecutor's plan. Nevertheless, prosecutors for political and other reasons naturally prefer to have the victim "on board" with any plea bargain, especially if the case is a serious one. Victims may not have veto power, but they can and often do influence the outcome of a negotiation.

Some victims who see defendants bargaining down their charges and sentences might wish that plea bargaining were abolished altogether. They, like the civil libertarians who also would support such an abolition, are unlikely to have their hopes met. Efforts to abolish plea bargaining are not new. Decades ago, the National Advisory Commission on Criminal Justice Standards and Goals recommended that plea bargaining be eliminated nationwide no later than 1978.[36] That never occurred. Part of the problem is the fact that it is not just defendants and defense attorneys who are addicted to plea bargaining. Prosecutors like it too.

In addition to cutting down their work (trials are time-consuming), a system of institutionalized plea bargaining greatly exalts the power of prosecutors. It could be said that although judges might hold the most prestige in the criminal courthouse, the prosecutor wields the most power. This is because plea bargaining turns the prosecutor into the judge, jury and sentencer. Due to plea bargaining, sentencing decisions are transferred away from the bench and onto the prosecutor's desk. There, prosecutors have nearly total discretion. Many prosecutor offices do not even have internal office guidelines regarding how assistant prosecutors are to go about negotiating deals, other than to avoid creating bad press or bad relations with judges.[37] Prosecutors sometimes "work through a pile of cases in machine-gun fashion, making snap decisions as to appropriate punishments in just a few minutes per case."[38] With frightening efficiency, prosecutors make judgements regarding the strengths and weaknesses of the evidence, check the prior criminal history of the accused, decide upon an appropriate sentence, and write down the offer to be later sent to the defense attorney in a form letter. Such reviews can take fewer than ten minutes per case, even though some cases involve substantial periods of incarceration.[39]

Twenty-nine year old Amy McDonald sometimes sat amazed as she reflected on the awesome responsibility that a young person like her had in deciding the fate of hundreds of human beings each year. She realized that she,

36. Miller, Frank W., Robert O. Dawson, George E. Dix and Raymond I. Parnas. (2000). *Prosecution and Adjudication.* Fifth Edition. New York: Foundation Press.

37. Lynch, *supra* note 7, at 125.

38. Id., at 126.

39. Id.

like all prosecutors, generally had the upper hand in negotiations with defense attorneys. After all, most people charged with crimes are guilty and can be proven to be such. Still, Amy felt a little strange being the one who was expected to weigh the evidence (a job she always was taught was that of a jury) and to decide upon an appropriate sentence (a job she was always taught belonged to a judge).

Though Amy was getting used to the awesome power that she had, she still could vividly remember her first few months on the job. Working in a county of moderate population, Amy's office could not afford the luxury of long apprenticeships. After just two months on the job, she was handling a full caseload including everything from shoplifting to non-capital homicides. She remembered the first few times she offered prison time as part of a plea bargain. In all but one of those cases the defense attorney and the defendant agreed to the offer without any further discussion. This scared her at first. She did not like knowing that she was the one who "sent people away" for such long periods of time. On the other hand, she also wondered if she was offering sentences that were too lenient. "Could that be why the defense attorneys accepted them so readily?" she would ask herself.

Eventually Amy got a feel for what students of the court refer to as **going rates** (appropriate sentences for a standard case that defense attorneys, prosecutors, and judges all expect).[40] She learned for example that shoplifters got probation unless they had awful prior records and that residential burglars could expect to do a few months in jail even if they had no prior convictions. She also learned that defense attorneys in her jurisdiction expected to be given "sentence bargains" rather than "charge bargains" or "count bargains." Judges expected this too.

In a **sentence bargain** the prosecutor "recommends" to the court the actual sentence a defendant will receive (in addition to the charge he or she will plead guilty to). If the court rejects this "recommendation," the defendant is free to withdraw his or her offer to plea guilty. In practice, judges rarely reject the prosecutor's recommendation since to do so could very likely produce a time-consuming trial. As long as the prosecutor and the defense attorney are both satisfied with an agreed-upon sentence, the judge normally is happy to go along.

In a **charge bargain** the prosecutor does not negotiate an actual sentence but rather allows a defendant to plead guilty to a lesser charge in exchange for

---

40. Feeley, Malcolm M. (1979). *The Process is the Punishment: Handling Cases in a Lower Criminal Court.* New York: Russel Sage Foundation.

giving up the right to go to trial. For example, a person charged with burglary may be permitted to plead guilty to theft or a person charged with aggravated assault may be permitted to plead guilty to simple assault. The judge is then expected by all concerned to give a sentence appropriate to the reduced (not the original) charge. It would be against the judge's interests to surprise everyone with too severe a sentence given the reduced offense since that would only encourage more trials in the future. In some areas, judges are bound by **sentencing guidelines** which basically box the judge into a very narrow range of potential sentences based upon the crime pled to and the prior record score of the defendant. Hence, attorneys in such areas can very accurately predict what the sentence will be.

In a **count bargain** a defendant charged with multiple offenses pleads guilty to one or more of them in exchange for the rest of his or her crimes being dismissed. For example, a defendant charged with six burglaries might plead guilty to one of them in exchange for the others being dropped. The judge would then be expected to give the burglar a sentence that a person would ordinarily receive who had only committed one offense, not six.

As mentioned, Amy's jurisdiction used sentence bargains. Having to "sentence" defendants in routine cases no longer bothered Amy. She realized that she had to follow the "going rates" and it was her job merely to offer them. However, not every case was routine. In such non-routine cases, Amy had to think for herself and do some real negotiations with opposing counsel.

Cases could be non-routine for one of several reasons. First, a state's case might be weak rather than strong like cases normally were. In this situation, defense attorneys would expect an offer below the standard one. The greater the likelihood of an acquittal, the more generous the offer had to be. Amy remembers once finally offering a 90 day jail sentence to an alleged rapist because her case was so weak. The victim was upset with Amy's decision but Amy offered the deal anyhow. There was no physical evidence. The victim waited a week before reporting the rape to the police. The victim was raped while drinking heavily and voluntarily playing strip poker with the defendant, facts Amy believed would not favorably impress a middle class jury.

A case could also be non-routine due to the seriousness of the charges combined with a very serious prior criminal record. For example, Amy once prosecuted someone for robbing a store clerk at gunpoint. The case was a fairly strong one for Amy though not a "slam dunk." The defendant had a horrendous prior record, including three prior burglary convictions and a conviction for arson. There was no "going rate" for a case like this. The defense lawyer knew that his client would have to eventually plead guilty. The judge could easily give him decades if convicted. Amy initially offered the defendant fifteen years which eventually was negotiated down to nine years. Was it a good deal or a bad one for the defendant? Who could say? Certainly Amy could not.

A third way a case could be non-routine has to do with unusual circumstances involving either the victim or the defendant. Suppose for example that an adult rape victim or the child victim of a molester adamantly did not want to go through the additional trauma of having to testify. Or, suppose that a defendant had a terminal disease with just a short time left to live—expensive time for a correctional facility. Or, suppose that someone accused of selling drugs had cooperated extensively with the police in doing drug stings after his arrest and subsequent bail. Such unusual characteristics regarding either the victim or the defendant extinguish any hope of finding an obvious "going rate." Clearly the seriousness of the current offense and the severity of the prior record (the two prongs usually used for a "going rate") are sometimes accompanied by other powerful factors that must be considered.

Amy did not even like the term "going rate." "Sure, I have lots of cases that are routine, but I always have many that are not," she once told a lawyer friend who sued insurance companies for their customer's automobile accidents.

"I know just what you mean," the civil lawyer agreed. "The norm in my area of practice is that an insurance company who wants to settle should offer lost income, medical expenses, plus pain and suffering. The pain and suffering piece is generally agreed upon by lawyers to be about three to five times the dollar amount of the medical expenses. That is what you criminal lawyers would call the 'going rate.' But a huge number of my cases are not routine. For example, in some cases it is not clear which driver was negligent and the insurance companies rightfully expect to pay a lot less. Others involve victims who permanently lose their good looks or maybe have to give up a loved hobby for life. In those cases I expect more for pain and suffering. Lots of my cases are non-routine."

"It's almost like it is routine to have non-routine cases isn't it? At least that's how it is in my world." Amy suggested.

"Exactly," replied her friend. "That is why they pay us—I guess at least me—the big bucks."

Amy had to do more than struggle with non-routine cases having no "going rates." She also was confronted with ethical dilemmas on a weekly basis. With huge discretion comes a huge responsibility not to abuse that discretion. Amy sometimes found herself tempted by various seductions made possible by the system's vast dependence on plea bargaining.

For example, Amy wondered whether or not it was ethical to plea bargain a case in which she believed the defendant was probably guilty but in whose guilt she herself had reasonable doubt. "If this went to a jury and I was on it I would vote to acquit," Amy would sometimes tell herself with regards to a weak state case. "Given my own doubts is it ethical for me to vigorously pursue a guilty plea. Or should I drop the charges?" Amy generally just offered a better than normal deal but was not sure that was the right moral course. As scholar Lynn Mather opined long ago, with regards to plea bargaining, that "one important consequence of this simultaneous consideration of the guilt and sentencing issues is that information which is only supposed to pertain to one issue may become relevant to the other."[41]

Another question Amy morally agonized over was whether or not she should ever over-charge so that she could later give things up more easily during negotiations. It would certainly make her negotiating life easier. Some in her office did this. But Amy refused to play that way. "I'm not a used car salesman," she once told an office-mate.

Something Amy was willing to do was to bluff defendants into entering guilty pleas even though she knew she no longer had a case. Sometimes, Amy would discover a couple of weeks before trial that a key witness was lost, dead, or moved away to a place too far to expect the witness to return for a trial. Amy wondered if she had an ethical obligation to tell the defense attorney that she no longer had a case. Usually she handled such matters by making an unusually "generous" offer which generally precipitated the desired guilty plea.

The hardest ethical dilemma for Amy though had to do with incompetent defense attorneys. One in town was particularly ineffective. Amy learned that this attorney was so trusting and gentle that he would urge his clients to accept almost any deal that Amy proposed. At first Amy took advantage of him by consistently driving very hard bargains, especially in non-routine cases. Later though she started feeling guilty. "Is it fair for me to beat up on a nice guy like that?" she asked herself. "Is it fair that his clients get punished more than the others?" In the end she decided to offer him the same deals which she estimated she would eventually offer a reasonably competent attorney. She felt better about herself after that. She directed the hard bargaining towards those who could put up a fair fight.

*****

---

41. Mather, Lynn. (1979). *Plea Bargaining or Trial?* Lexington, Mass.: Lexington Books, at 141.

Questions for Class Discussion

1. Did it surprise you to learn how few trials most attorneys (civil or criminal) do in the U.S.A.? Why do you suppose most Americans believe that many more cases (civil and criminal) go to trial than actually do?

2. What do you think about the "golden age of trials" in which nearly everyone was given a trial, but a short one without much use of formal rules of evidence? Was that era closer to the spirit of due process or is our current era, characterized by very few trials with a lot of formal rules requiring a lot of time?

3. Do you agree with the U.S. Supreme Court that plea bargaining, if properly administered, ought to be encouraged?

4. What are the advantages of plea bargaining to the defendant? What are the advantages to the prosecution? What are the advantages to the crime victim? What are advantages to society?

5. How do each of the following benefit on very personal levels as human beings from a system based primarily on plea bargains: defense lawyers, prosecutors, judges?

6. One plus of a system based on plea bargaining is that it saves a lot of money. Is this a valid constitutional reason for basing our criminal court system on the institution of plea bargaining? Do we have any choice in the matter to do otherwise? Would you support higher taxes or cuts in military defense spending to bring back a golden age of trials?

7. What is the difference between a charge bargain, a count bargain, and a sentence bargain? Which would you prefer to be offered as a criminal defendant?

8. What types of people tend to go to trial even though they have been offered plea bargains?

9. What is meant by the term, "client control?" What do you personally think of attorneys who cannot or will not achieve "client control?" What do judges think of such attorneys?

10. What do you think about tactics such as "chair therapy" to get clients to take a deal? Would it be OK to do this to a client in order to get him or her to accept a plea bargain that truly was in the client's own best interests?

11. What is the purpose of a Boykin Form? What sort of things does it specifically cover? Do you have much faith that such an instrument protects people from being coerced by the system into pleading guilty?

12. What should judges do to ensure that guilty pleas are being "knowingly and voluntarily entered?" Are judges currently doing enough in your opinion to ensure this is indeed the case?

13. Would you ever accept a plea bargain regarding a crime you did not commit but which it looked like you did? Objectively speaking, is there ever a time when the rational thing would be to accept a plea bargain despite actual innocence?

14. Given that innocent people are less likely to accept plea bargains than are actual wrong-doers, and therefore more at risk of getting hammered when and if convicted, are the truly innocent worse off than the guilty in a system so in love with guilty pleas?

15. Many defendants apparently do not trust public defenders in part because they are paid by the government. If you were on trial, could you ever trust a defender who is being paid by the same government that is attempting to put you in jail? What, if anything, can be done to minimize this problem?

16. Are private criminal lawyers more effective overall that public defenders when it comes to plea bargain negotiations? How can it be that public defenders do as good a job (if not better) at negotiating plea bargains for their clients?

17. Should victims be given the right to veto plea bargains being offered to the criminals who have hurt them? If not, how much input, if any, should crime victims have?

18. In your opinion, is it ethical for a prosecutor to negotiate a plea bargain concerning someone whom the prosecutor believes is probably guilty but not guilty beyond a reasonable doubt? Or, should the prosecutor just drop the charges entirely in such a situation?

19. What are some of the legal grounds for withdrawing a guilty plea after it has already been entered? Should judges just allow anybody to withdraw a guilty plea for any reason as long as they do so fairly promptly after it was entered?

20. What is meant by "nolo contendere?" What is an "Alford plea?" How does "factual basis," the standard for accepting a guilty plea, differ from guilt beyond a reasonable doubt? How sure should we as a society be of someone's guilt before we allow the person to enter a plea of guilty?

*****

Key Terms: golden age of trials, client control, chair therapy, lawyer version of good cop/bad cop, important traits of successful plea bargainers, joint problem-solving approach, courtroom work group, trial tax, dead bang loser, pro se, knowingly and voluntarily entered, nolo contendere plea, Alford plea, factual basis, Boykin form, going rates, sentence bargain, charge bargain, sentencing guidelines, count bargain

Additional Concepts: omnipresence of plea bargaining, legality of plea bargaining, arguments supporting plea bargaining, criticisms of plea bargaining, "selling" deals to clients, wearing clients down, public defenders and plea bargaining, defendants' perspectives on plea bargaining, reasons some defendants choose trials, legal grounds for withdrawing a guilty plea, difficulty in abolishing plea bargaining, prosecutorial power in plea bargaining, negotiations in non-routine cases, prosecuting despite personal reasonable doubt, overcharging, bluffing after case falls apart, negotiating with incompetent defense attorneys

CHAPTER TEN

THE TRIAL (PART 1)

Right to a Jury Trial

Nobody knows when the first jury trial occurred. The event has been long lost in the mists of time. It is known that jury trials took place in ancient Greece. The great Socrates himself was convicted of corrupting the youth several centuries before the birth of Christ.

America inherited this western tradition of trials directly from the English. But early English trials were strange. One strange early practice was **trial by battle** in which the alleged victim fought the accused in a contest of physical strength. The winner was vindicated and the loser punished. It was believed that God would help justice prevail in this solemn ritual by siding with the truth-teller. Sometimes man helped God a little by evening the odds. For example, a man accused by a female of a crime might be required to fight the woman barehanded while she was allowed to use weapons; or the man might be required to fight a woman while he was buried up to his waist in a pit.[1] Despite such attempts at making things fair, imagine the poor victim who lost the fight despite telling the truth. First, the victim is beaten by the very person who had already victimized him or her earlier. Next, he or she is branded a liar by the village and punished accordingly. Finally, the victim's religious faith is maimed because God failed to be there as promised in the hour of need.

Another strange practice was **trial by ordeal**. Once again it was believed that God would help one survive the ordeal, but only if one were innocent. Ordeals could include such things as being forced to walk successfully over a bed of hot coals or having one's hand placed in boiling water to see if the skin would later blister. Trials by ordeal occurred not just in the Old World but in

---

1. Gruberg, Martin. (2003). *Introduction to Law*. Lanham, Maryland: University Press of America, p. 9.

America as well. In Salem, Massachusetts women suspected of being witches would be thrown into the lake. If a woman survived she would be hung as a witch because it was believed that witches repelled water. If she drowned the villagers would know that they had accused an innocent person.[2]

Trials took a huge leap forward in 1215 thanks to the **Magna Carta**. The Magna Carta was a sort of early constitution in which the noblemen of England forced the king to accord them various rights. One of these rights was the right for "freemen" to be tried by a jury of their free peers instead of by a crony of the king. Of course, noblemen at that time cared little for the rights of the common man. "Freemen" and their peers only included the land-owning nobles (the rest of us were inconsequential serfs).[3]

As the centuries clicked by, the right to a jury trial eventually trickled down to common people. This right crossed the Atlantic with the British colonists who fiercely resisted any attempts on the part of the crown to water it down.[4] Today, anybody accused of a "**serious crime**" (one theoretically punishable by at least six months in jail) has the right to a jury trial.[5] Hence one who wishes to contest a petty offense (e.g., a speeding violation) will have the right to a hearing before a judge, nothing more. But those charged with most misdemeanors and all felonies will have the right to a full-blown jury.

Jury Selection

Assistant District Attorney Dan McGuire watched nervously from his seat in the front of the courtroom as a bailiff led the **jury panel** into the room. From this panel of thirty or so souls, twelve would be selected to serve this day in the case McGuire was about to prosecute. McGuire knew that this panel of prospective jurors was a subset of folks taken from a larger body of prospective jurors known as the **venire** (those summoned for jury service who actually show up at the courthouse).

McGuire did not subscribe to the cynical view of some of his colleagues that potential jurors are merely those citizens too stupid to get out of jury service. He realized that many of the people here today wanted to come. Teachers, government workers, and others often liked to come since they still got

---

2. Id.

3. Levine, James P. (1992). *Juries and Politics.* Belmont, CA.: Brooks/Cole.

4. *See, Duncan v. Louisiana,* 391 U.S.145 (1968), for a discussion of the history of the right to a jury trial in America.

5. *Baldwin v. New York,* 399 U.S. 66 (1970).

paid by their employer while getting a break from the dull routine of their jobs. Retirees often liked to come since it gave them something important to do. But some who had assembled did not want to be there: students who were missing lectures, small business owners who were not taking care of business, corporate executives whose work would merely pile up rather than be done by others, homemakers whose small children were being babysat by others. McGuire knew that these busy people would expect to have their valuable time put to good use. He figured that his case, a prosecution for bigamy, was not likely to be seen by them as a boring time-waster.

McGuire, the son of a mid-western wheat farmer, prosecuted cases in the same county in which he had been born and raised. Today, he had his work cut out for him in helping to ensure that the twelve ultimately selected from the panel to hear the case at hand would give him a fair shot at a conviction. The defendant in this case was a twenty two year old Muslim immigrant who had married two women in a private religious ceremony four years ago in the county seat. Both of his "wives," two daughters of a friend from the old country, had consented to the union. Normally McGuire would not have cared what these folks did in the privacy of their homes. But he could not ignore one critical fact: the wives were both underage when they "married" the defendant. One was fifteen at the time and the other only fourteen. Though the marriage was performed in a private religious ceremony with no pretense of a civil union, the trio did live together as "man and wives," which in his state was enough to constitute the crime of bigamy. But would the jury be willing to convict people in a day and age of tolerance, sexual liberation and "live and left live?" McGuire decided he did not want to wait until the trial began to enlighten the jury on the reasons why this man should be prosecuted. By then it might be too late.

McGuire would have the chance to "educate" the future jury during what is known at the **voir dire**. The voir dire (a French term meaning "to see/to say") is the process by which the jury panel is whittled down to just twelve actual jurors. The idea is that lawyers and the judge will question the prospective jurors so as to ferret out any who are too biased to serve in a fair and impartial manner. Any juror who answers a question in such a way as to expose bias will be **challenged for cause** by the lawyer wishing to eliminate that prejudiced juror. If the judge agrees that the prospective juror is biased, that juror will be excused to rejoin the venire waiting for other trials elsewhere in the courthouse. For example, a juror who admits knowing one of the parties or who admits that they are too upset with the charges to think straight would be successfully challenged for cause. There is no limit to the number of challenges for cause in a voir dire. If so many members of the jury panel turn out to be biased that twelve are no longer remaining, additional prospective jurors will be summoned to the courtroom. It has happened that due to extensive pre-trial publicity hundreds of prospective jurors in various high profile cases have been successfully challenged for cause after admitting that they already had formed a fixed opinion of the case. Even in such extraordinary cases, twelve jurors are eventually chosen however.

In addition to challenges for cause, lawyers are also given a limited number of **peremptory challenges**. Using a peremptory challenge, a lawyer (either the prosecutor or defense attorney) may ask to have a potential juror excluded for any reason or for no reason whatsoever. (The sole exceptions are that race[6] or gender[7] alone cannot be the basis for the challenge. The trial judge will watch carefully for any suspicious patterns and will demand a credible explanation if any systematic exclusions emerge.) The idea behind the peremptory challenge is that a lawyer might strongly sense that a juror is biased yet be unable to prove it. Thus, a challenge for cause would not be successful. A certain number of peremptory challenges are allowed to help assure a fair jury (e.g., a lawyer could get rid of someone who looks eccentric without having to prove what those looks mean).

Of course, lawyers often wish to use peremptory challenges to shape the jury in ways benefitting their side only. Unfortunately for lawyers who wish to thus **stack the jury** with those biased for their side, such challenges are limited in number by local rules (perhaps five or so for a misdemeanor case, seven for a felony, twenty for a capital case).

In some courthouses, judges do all the voir dire questioning (though lawyers are usually allowed to submit appropriate questions to the judge ahead of time). McGuire's courthouse followed a different procedure. In his courthouse, lawyers did all of the questioning while a judge sat waiting to rule on any challenges for cause that might be advanced.

Since McGuire was the prosecutor, he got to begin the voir dire questioning. McGuire stood up and introduced himself to the citizens seated in the courtroom's well worn, wooden benches.

"Good morning ladies and gentlemen. My name is Dan McGuire and I will be prosecuting this case today. On behalf of Judge Brown seated on the stand and defense counsel Mary Temple seated just over there, I would like to thank you for your sacrifice as jurors. In a moment I will be asking you some questions. After I am done Attorney Temple will ask you some questions. The pur-

---

6. *Georgia v. McCollum*, 505 U.S. 42 (1992).
7. *J.E.B. v. Alabama ex rel. T.B.*, 114 S. Ct. 1419 (1994).

pose of these questions is to make sure that all who sit on the jury are free from any problems that might interfere with weighing the evidence fairly and impartially. Both the prosecution and defense deserve a fair and impartial jury. We will be asking our questions to you as a group. If anything I or the defense attorney raise in our questions applies to you personally, just raise your hand so that we may inquire further.

"First question: Do any of you know either me, Ms. Temple, Judge Brown, or the defendant Omar Mustafa seated next to Ms. Temple?" (Nobody raised a hand.)

"Very well," continued McGuire. "Have any of you ever been convicted of a crime?" (Again, nobody raised a hand.)

"I'll tell you now straight up what this case will involve. The defendant is charged with the offense of bigamy. The state will attempt to show that he engaged in sexual cohabitation with two women at once. In other words, he both resided with and had ongoing sexual relations with more than one woman at the same time. The state legislature has made this a crime. If I prove beyond a reasonable doubt that Mr. Mustafa is guilty of this crime, would any of you have difficulty in convicting him?" (The jurors just sat there in cold silence. This did not bother McGuire. He was just trying to get a public commitment out of them to apply the law.)

"Would any of you have any philosophical problems convicting someone of bigamy given that he is an immigrant to this country from a land where such a practice is acceptable?"

McGuire noticed a man in the back wince a little, but the man did not raise his hand. McGuire asked him his name and in a very gentle manner asked him if he had any concerns. The man claimed he had no concerns. McGuire made a note to himself to strike him when the time came with one of his seven peremptory challenges.

McGuire continued the questioning. "In addition to bigamy, Mr. Mustafa is charged with statutory rape in that it is alleged that he had sexual intercourse with two underage girls whom he claimed to be religiously but not legally married to. Would any of you feel bad about convicting someone of statutory rape even though the victims—and even their parents—consented to the sex?" One juror, a woman, raised her hand. McGuire asked her for her name and asked her what her concerns were. "Well, I don't see how it is rape if the victim consents," the woman replied. McGuire explained that statutory rape was not forced sex but sex with a minor who is not deemed legally old enough to give consent. McGuire did not want this juror chosen so he carefully crafted his next question to her. "Do you not like this law ma'am?" he asked the woman. "No, I don't like it," she confided. "It does not seem right to me."

McGuire was about to make a challenge for cause but thought it best to seal the woman's fate first. "Ma'am, is it fair to say that because of your disagreement with the law on this point that you would have difficulty in returning a guilty verdict even if the state proves that the defendant had sex with a minor?" "Yes, I guess so," the woman admitted. "Your honor," McGuire said as he now turned towards the bench. "I would challenge this honest juror for cause." "Granted," the judge ruled. "Ma'am you are excused from this trial. You may leave now and rejoin the jurors downstairs in the jury waiting room. Hopefully, you will get to serve in a trial that you feel more comfortable about. The bailiff will show you the way back to the waiting room." The woman left with one of the bailiffs.

McGuire felt lucky that he did not have to use one of his precious peremptory challenges on that juror. He knew that unless a juror openly admitted to this particular judge that he or she were biased, the judge rarely granted the prosecution a challenge for cause.

After a series of additional questions designed to uncover potential bias, McGuire shifted strategy. He began asking questions clothed as inquiries into bias but which were in reality designed solely to **educate the jury**. McGuire was about to use voir dire to make some closing arguments in advance.

"Ladies and Gentlemen, the judge will instruct you at the end of the trial that you are the judges of the facts—the judges of what happened—and not the judges of the law. The court will explain to you that bigamy and statutory rape are crimes in this state. He will also explain to you that ignorance of the law is no excuse. Would any of you refuse to follow the judge's instructions with regards to the law of our land by acquitting someone whom you believe beyond a reasonable doubt to be guilty?" McGuire already got rid of the juror who obviously had problems with this and did not really expect anybody else to volunteer to be kicked out of the room at this point. Sure enough, no jurors raised a hand. McGuire though was satisfied. He just got all of them once again to make a public commitment to uphold the law as long as he proved the elements of the offenses. This might help cut off discussion during jury deliberations at the end of the trial as to the propriety of convicting a man from another culture with the crimes charged.

McGuire decided he would make one more educational point (no affirmative responses were expected): "Ladies and gentlemen, I must prove each element of bigamy and statutory rape beyond a reasonable doubt. That does not mean that I must prove each offense beyond all doubt or to a mathematical certainty. Would anyone hold me to such an impossible standard?" McGuire pretended to wait for a possible hand to be raised. After a few seconds he sat down, having made his point.

Ms. Temple, the defense attorney now stood up and introduced herself. She too raised various questions designed to uncover potential bias. She too asked a couple of questions designed merely to educate the jury. She concluded her questioning by asking exactly such a question:

"Ladies and gentlemen. My client is presumed innocent until proven guilty. It is the state that has the burden of proof. My client does not have to prove his innocence or anything else. He certainly does not have to take the stand. If I choose to protect my client from the indignity of taking the stand and to force the state to meet its very high burden of proof on its own, would any of you hold this decision against Mr. Mustafa in any way whatsoever?" Ms. Temple pretended to wait for a possible hand to be raised. She then sat down.

The time came for the two opposing attorneys to begin exercising their peremptory challenges. Each was allowed seven. Only one challenge for cause had been raised and it was advanced as soon as the apparent bias was exposed (as was the usual practice in this courthouse). The peremptory challenges were saved until the end of the voir dire. It was now time to begin striking jurors for any reason or no reason at all.

A bailiff walked over to McGuire's table with a sheet listing all the names of the prospective jurors that had just participated in the voir dire. By design, the listing of the jurors' names correlated with the order in which the bailiff had sat them in the courtroom benches. Because of this, the attorneys could easily match a name with a courtroom face. One of the names already had a line drawn through it by the bailiff (the name of the woman who had been successfully challenged for cause). McGuire took out his pen and put a line through the name of the person who had winced at him. "P-1" he jotted next to the crossed-out name (standing for prosecution strike #1). The bailiff then approached the defense table and handed the sheet to Ms. Temple. Temple smiled to herself as she saw whom McGuire had chosen to strike first. Temple took her pen and struck out the name of a dour, conservatively dressed retiree who looked to her like an unliberated and intolerant man. She inked in "D-1" next to his blotted out name (standing for defense strike #1). The bailiff then continued this ritual, going back and forth between the two tables allowing each side to strike names in turn.

Both McGuire and Temple had their own prejudices regarding whom to strike with a peremptory challenge. Some people were obvious to strike. The prosecutor always liked to strike anybody who looked "bleeding heart," or "anti-establishment." Social workers, liberal college professors, biker-types, and left-over hippies were all candidates for one of his peremptory challenges. He also got rid of anybody with a criminal record, even if it only involved a misdemeanor long ago. "You never know if they might still hold a grudge," he

Table 1   McGuire's List of Pro-Prosecution and Pro-Defense Potential Jurors

Potential Jurors to Keep	Potential Jurors to Strike
Republicans	Democrats
Conservative dressers	Minimum wage workers
Old people	Unemployed people
Relatives of cops	Long haired men
Church goers	Young people
Home Owners	Apartment dwellers
Family men	Freaks
Stay at home moms	Flamboyant dressers
Business owners	Agnostics
Non-drinkers	Party Animals
Men who wear ties to court	Butch women/effeminate men
Women who wear dresses to court	Stupid people
N.R.A. types	Trailer Trash

figured. Attorney Temple on the other hand liked to routinely strike anybody who had any relatives in law enforcement or anybody who seemed too intelligent to be easily confused (confusion often leads to reasonable doubt, she reasoned).

Sometimes, after striking several obviously undesirable prospective jurors, attorneys like McGuire and Temple still have one or two peremptory challenges left that they hate to fail to use and hence just see go to waste. On such occasions attorneys sometimes resort to personal superstitions or prejudices as to the categories of people who tend to be pro-prosecution or pro-defense. McGuire even had developed his own "confidential" list which he very discretely showed to every new attorney who joined his office. McGuire was proud of this list which he kept in his desk drawer and refined from time to time. A copy of McGuire's list is found in Table 1.

After McGuire and Temple had finished striking seven names each, the bailiff brought the list to the judge. The judge reviewed it for a little while, more out of curiosity than for any legal reasons.

"The following people have been selected to serve on the jury," the judge solemnly began. "As your name is called, you are invited to immediately take a seat in the jury box on the side of the courtroom. I will call twelve names, then a thirteenth. This thirteenth juror will also sit in the jury box and will serve as an alternate in case someone gets sick during the trial. If nobody gets sick by the end of the trial, the alternate will be excused just prior to deliberations."

The judge then started reading the names of the jury who would hear the case. As usual, he simply began with the first name on the list that had not been stricken and continued in order down the list until the thirteenth name was read. Everyone whose name had not been read (those against whom challenges had been exercised plus a few more deep down at the end of the list) were invited to return to the juror waiting room for possible service in another courtroom. The judge then had the bailiff administer the juror oath to those in the box. After smiling at the sworn jurors, the judge looked seriously at the prosecutor at nodded. "Show time," McGuire said to himself as he rose.

Opening Statements

Since McGuire was the one seeking a conviction, it was he who got to begin the contest. McGuire knew that for something that did not constitute evidence, the opening statement certainly could have a dramatic effect on the outcome of any trial. McGuire figured (and some psychologists have confirmed) that most jurors in most cases irrevocably decide guilt or innocence during or right after the opening statement.[8]

The purpose of the **opening statement** is to give the jury a sort of road map to help it avoid getting lost or confused during the presentation of the evidence. During the statement, attorneys attempt to give the jury a very simplified overview of the evidence which they plan to offer. This is necessary because during the trial evidence is presented one witness at a time. This piecemeal presentation can become very confusing unless jurors have an initial understanding of the big picture. A trial is like a jigsaw puzzle. It helps to see the picture on the box before one starts attempting to make sense of each individual piece.

The opening statement is not an opening argument. Lawyers are not supposed to use it to argue the merits of their own case or to comment on the quality of what the other side will present.[9] Neither are they supposed to use it as a vehicle to instruct the jury as to the intricacies of the law (though some light references to law will be tolerated).[10] Rather, the purpose of the opening statement is merely to give the jurors a preview of the evidence which will be presented, that is, to provide it with an outline of the testimony about to come.

---

8. Perrin, L. Timothy. (1999). "From O.J. to McVeigh: The Use of Argument in the Opening Statement." *Emory Law Journal,* 48:107–167.

9. *State v. Bleau,* 649 A.2d 215 (R.I. 1994).

10. *State v. Martinez,* 613 P.2d 974 (Mont. 1980).

Dan McGuire stood before the jury in his shined shoes and crisp suit and began to speak. He made certain to make eye contact with members of the jury as he spoke to them, taking turns with each one. He believed that establishing rapport with the jury was critical.

"Ladies and gentlemen, as I mentioned during jury selection my name is Dan McGuire. I will be prosecuting this case today. Thank you again for your service. Allow me to take a few minutes to walk you through the evidence which I shall shortly be presenting. As you already know, the defendant Omar Mustafa is charged with bigamy and statutory rape. I intend to prove that he lived in a state of sexual cohabitation with two young girls whom he supposedly made his spiritual wives in an illegal, private religious ceremony four years ago. At the time, Mustafa was twenty two years old and the girls were only fifteen and fourteen.

"In order to prove bigamy it will be necessary for me to prove two elements: 1) that Mustafa resided with two women at the same time; and 2) he had an ongoing sexual relationship with each of them at that time. It is not necessary to prove a legal or even an illegal marriage—the sexual cohabitation is what constitutes the crime of bigamy.

"In order to prove statutory rape, I will have to prove that Mustafa had sexual intercourse with someone who was under the age of consent, that is, under the age of sixteen and that Mustafa was at least four years older than the child.

"To prove these things I shall be producing four witnesses. The first witness you shall hear from is Connie Meadows who is a close neighbor of the defendant and his unusual family. She will testify that Mustafa held out both of these girls as his wives and that they held themselves out as such as well. She will also testify that they all lived together under the same roof for the last four years. She will also testify that each of these girls had a son born to her during this period, whom Mustafa constantly referred to as his sons.

"The second witness I shall present is an official from the social security administration. He will testify that official records show that Mustafa was twenty two at the time he started to live with these two children, and that one girl was fifteen and the other fourteen at the time.

"The third witness shall be Hassan Zaifnejad. Mr. Zaifnejad will testify that he was the Muslim cleric who married Mustafa to both of these young girls four years ago in a private ceremony without a valid marriage license. He will tell you that all present knew that this ceremony was against the law but believed they were following a higher law. Mr. Zaifnejad will also tell you that he has pled guilty to being an accessory to bigamy and received probation in exchange for his truthful testimony today.

"The fourth witness you will hear from is one of the so-called wives of Mustafa—the younger of the two girls. She will testify that she moved out of the house last Spring after an argument and now lives in government housing with her son. She will testify that both she and her sister married Mustafa in a private religious ceremony four years ago at the urging of their parents who had arranged the marriage. She will testify that at the time she was only fourteen and her sister fifteen. Mustafa told her he was twenty two at the time. She will tell you that Mustafa had sexual intercourse with both her and her older sister regularly thereafter. She will tell you that he is the father of both of their sons. She will also tell you how Mustafa told various male neighbors how he was lucky to have two young beautiful women to sleep with and suggested that American, monogamous marriages were unnatural and inferior.

"After you have heard all of the evidence I will be asking you to return guilty verdicts on the bigamy charge and also on the statutory rape charges. Thank you for your attention."

McGuire returned to his desk and sat down. The judge looked at the defense attorney and gave a nod. After patting her client kindly on the arm, Mary Temple rose from her chair and addressed the judge and jury.

"Your honor, the defense would like to exercise its right to present an opening statement at the conclusion of the state's case and the commencement of the defense case-in-chief," Temple informed the court. Temple knew that she had the legal right to wait until midway in the trial to present her opening statement, but knew that it was usually a bad idea to hold back. She knew that if a defense attorney waited until the opening of the defense case to give an opening statement, it might be too late to turn things around. Unless there were some extraordinary reasons to wait, it was almost always better to come out swinging right from the start before the jury had made up its mind. But, in the bigamy and statutory rape trial of Omar Mustafa, Mary Temple felt she had extraordinary reasons to wait. Her client was guilty and she knew there was no way to get around that. She could not put him on the stand since he told her he had done what was alleged in the indictment. He was a bigamist. He did have sex with these girls while they were underage. His excuse was that he did not appreciate the moral wrongfulness of his actions. He was from the old country. It was legal there. It was customary there. Temple knew that this type of defense was legally objectionable. But the judge might allow it and the jury might accept it. She could try to paint a picture of overzealous prosecution. Sure, Mustafa was guilty in a technical sense but she knew that juries are not always rule-minded. Some juries are reluctant to convict people they feel sorry for. She could force the state to prove its case and through cross-examination try to garner sympathy for her client. She would wait and see how the prosecution case went and tailor her opening statement accordingly. She would give the opening statement later when she could better match it to the flow and mood of the trial.

Prosecution Case-in-Chief

Assistant District Attorney Dan McGuire had to bite his lip to keep from laughing at Mary Temple's unorthodox delay of the opening statement. "She doesn't have a clue of what to say, does she?" he told himself. His smugness soon evaporated when it occurred to him that Temple was no fool and might have something up her sleeve. His thoughts were abruptly interrupted by the judge: "You may call your first witness, Mr. McGuire."

"Thank you your honor," the prosecutor said as he took control of the drama. "The state calls Connie Meadows to the stand." Connie's testimony was straightforward. She confirmed that she was Mustafa's neighbor and that he did live under the same roof with the two sisters for the past four years. She further confirmed that he portrayed himself in the neighborhood as the husband to both females and the father to both boys. She also testified that Mustafa on one occasion expressed concern to Connie that Connie's husband might be missing out on true marriage by limiting himself unnaturally to just one woman. He never brought up that point again after being put in his place by Connie's angry response.

The time came for Ms. Temple's cross-examination. Temple decided not to try to paint this truthful witness as a liar. To do so would not garner the sympathy she was seeking for her client. Instead, she tried to get Connie Meadows to admit that Mustafa was not such a bad guy.

"How long have you known Mr. Mustafa, Ms. Meadows?" Temple began.

"About four years," was the reply.

Since this was cross-examination, Temple knew she could lead the witness from here on out. On **direct examination** (the questioning of a witness by the lawyer who called the witness to the stand) **leading questions** (questions that suggest the answer) are not permitted since it is inappropriate for a lawyer to put words in a friendly witness's mouth.[11] The witness, not the lawyer, is supposed to be testifying. However, during **cross-examination** (the questioning of a witness by the lawyer who did not call the witness to the stand) leading

---

11. Federal Rule of Evidence 611(c) states in part that "Leading questions should not be used on direct examination of a witness except as may be necessary to develop a witness' testimony ... When a party calls a hostile witness, an adverse party, or a witness identified with an adverse party, interrogation may be by leading questions."

questions are permitted since hostile witnesses are less likely to let an attorney put words in their mouths.[12] Mary Temple knew, like all criminal lawyers know, that since leading questions are permitted on cross-examination, an attorney should take advantage of this by channeling the witness's testimony down the narrow path the attorney wants it to go. Asking an **open-ended question** (one that cannot easily be answered with a simple "Yes/No" response) of an unfriendly witness is very dangerous as it is an invitation for a long and hostile narrative.

"Ms. Meadows," the defense attorney continued. "Is it fair to say that Mr. Mustafa did not imprison these women in any way—that they came and went as they pleased?"

"Yeah, I guess that's true," the neighbor replied.

"Is it not also true that Mr. Mustafa provided for his household by working hard at two jobs?"

"Yeah, he works full-time at a warehouse and at a convenience store on weekends."

Temple knew this next question was risky but if she did not take some risks she would lose anyway: "Ms. Meadows, isn't it true that you never saw Mr. Mustafa abuse these women in any way?"

"Yes, I'll give him that," agreed the witness.

Temple would take one more gamble: "He was loving, was he not?"

"Yes," came the hoped for response.

Mary Temple realized that any second the prosecutor would probably object on the grounds of relevancy. Relevancy is just one of many potential **objections** that attorneys can make during a trial. An objection is an assertion that a particular question violates one of the official rules of evidence that has developed over the centuries to ensure a fair contest. When an attorney makes an objection, a judge must either **sustain the objection** (agree with the attorney who objected) or **overrule the objection** (rule that the question is allowed). Unlike trials in continental Europe in which witnesses more or less speak in a narrative style with few rules to hinder the free flow of communication, American trials are tightly controlled and lawyers are bound by many evidentiary rules. Some of the more common bases for objection are found in Table 2.

Even if McGuire did not object any time now on the grounds of relevancy, Temple figured that bad points about her client might come up if she kept

---

12. Federal Rule of Evidence 611(c) states in part that "Ordinarily leading questions should be permitted on cross-examination."

Table 2   Common Objections

Irrelevant (does not aid to resolve any helpful point—time waster)

Prejudicial (evidentiary value is outweighed by the prejudicial effect it will have on jury)

Inflammatory (evidence or closing argument will inflame the passions of the jury)

Calls for a Conclusion (invites witness to analyze facts rather than just report them)

Calls for Speculation (invites witness to testify to facts he/she does not know about)

Calls for an Opinion (invites non-expert to testify to matters jury can figure out by itself)

Privileged Communication (secrets legally protected from disclosure by witness)

Incompetency (witness is too young or has some other handicap that renders witness unreliable)

Hearsay (calls for second hand information which the witness is asked to repeat)

Leading the Witness (question suggests the answer desired by the lawyer asking it)

---

treading in such dangerous waters. A rule followed by many criminal lawyers is to "never ask a question that you don't already know the answer to." But, this was no ordinary trial and Temple had to take a few risks to win. Even so, she sensed it was time to quit while she was ahead. She had got more than she had hope for. "No further questions, Your Honor," Temple told the court.

"Very well, if there is no re-direct you may call your next witness, Mr. Prosecutor."

"Thank you, Your Honor. The state calls Jack Burton to the stand."

After being sworn in, Mr. Burton testified that he worked for the social security administration and was a custodian of official records there. He went on to state the ages of Mustafa and his two "wives" both now and what they would have been four years ago. It was obvious that he had no reason to lie. "You may cross-examine the witness," the judge told Temple when Burton had finished giving his testimony. "No questions," Temple replied.

Hassan Zaifnejad next took the stand at the invitation of the prosecutor. He admitted that he was indeed the cleric who had performed the illegal marriage ceremony four years earlier. He also confirmed that both he and Mustafa knew it was a crime to have more than one wife but neither they nor anybody in their close immigrant community particularly cared. The prosecutor knew the jury would wonder why this witness was being so cooperative, so he got the cleric to explain that he was allowed to plead guilty to being an accessory to bigamy and given probation on condition that he give truthful testimony. McGuire knew that Temple might try to make this plea bargain appear somehow sinister on cross-examination, but thought it prudent to try to take some of the sting out of her questions by bringing up the matter during direct examination.

Sure enough, Temple pounced all over the cleric during cross-examination. She got him to admit that probation was a very attractive offer. She made it look like maybe he would say anything the state wanted if it would keep him from being put in jeopardy of going to jail. She even managed to **impeach** (cast doubt upon) his testimony by getting him to admit that he had a prior criminal conviction for theft (she had done her homework prior to trial). "This trial could be going worse," she whispered to Mustafa after she ended the cross-examination.

The state saved its best witness for last. The jury perked up as Sabah Falak, the younger "wife" of Omar Mustafa, took the stand. Sabah testified that she was the one who had turned Omar in to the authorities. She did so because she had grown up and realized how he had abused her by marrying her at such a young age with the blessings of stern and sexist parents who failed to protect her. She testified that she finally stood up to Mustafa last Spring, and ran away after he had threatened to "corporally discipline" her—something husbands still did to wives in the old country. She confirmed that he first had sex with her after the "marriage" when she was only fourteen, and that she and her sister both lived in the same house with him, taking turns "servicing" his high sexual needs. She also testified that she heard Mustafa telling other men in the neighborhood the same thing he had told the neighbor Connie Meadows: that his kind of marriage was better than the American kind.

Defense attorney Temple knew that she had to be careful with her cross-examination. Her goal was to get sympathy for her client, not to alienate the jury by attacking this young victim. With this in mind, she used carefully crafted leading questions to get Sabah to admit that though Mustafa had threatened "corporal discipline" one time, he never actually hit her. Temple also got Sabah to confirm that Mustafa did not pick his wives but rather they were picked for him by his parents and her parents. Finally, Temple got Sabah to remind the jury that she and Mustafa only had one child in four years. Temple left this line of questioning quickly without ever bringing up the possibility of birth control or fertility problems. Temple hoped that this last point might cast some doubt on Sabah's portrait of Mustafa as a person making high sexual demands.

Dan McGuire saw what Temple was trying to do. "She is trying to make this sexist, child rapist look like a sweet guy," he told himself. "She can't win on the facts or the law so she is going for the sympathy angle. I'll debunk that crap during my closing argument," he reassured himself. With these thoughts in mind he informed the court that "the **prosecution rests its case.**"

Attorney Temple was about to take control of the trial by putting on her defense of Mustafa. But first, her legal mind raced as she quickly analyzed the possibilities of a quick and dirty win. "Did Dan McGuire put into evidence some facts regarding each and every element of bigamy and statutory rape?" she asked herself. Every once and awhile a defense lawyer gets lucky when a prosecutor forgets to introduce some evidence of some essential point or another. For example, Temple herself could remember one time when she was defending a drunk driver. The prosecutor was being pressured by the judge to present her case quickly because the judge had a social appointment he needed to get to in the early evening. The prosecutor raced through her case as quickly as she was able to do. She proved that the car in which the defendant and his friends were traveling was being driven in an extremely erratic manner; that the defendant failed all the field sobriety tests; and that the defendant's blood alcohol limit was well over twice the legal limit. What she forgot to ask her police witness was to verify that it was the defendant who had actually been behind the wheel and not one of the others present in the vehicle. Once the prosecutor informed the court that the prosecution had rested its case, Temple stood up and told the court that the defense demurred. A **demurrer** is a request for the court to dismiss a case on the grounds that even if a jury believed all of the evidence that was presented by the state, something that was required to be proven was not even brought up. In the trial of the drunk driver, the court had no choice but to grant the demurrer. The judge later apologized profusely to the prosecutor for having rushed her so.

For a brief instant Temple once again toyed with the idea of telling the court that the defense demurred. She knew her request would be denied, but prosecutors always miss a heart beat whenever they hear such a request: "Oh, crap what did I forget?" she imagined poor Dan McGuire thinking in panic. She decided not to be cruel. She would have to work with Dan in the future.

Temple next considered asking the judge for a directed verdict. A judge will grant a **directed verdict** when the evidence is so weak that no reasonable jury could return a verdict of guilty.[13] The standard is not how the judge would vote if he or she were a thirteenth juror but rather whether any reasonable jury could possibly return a verdict of guilty. Temple gave some serious thought to asking for this. She did not expect the judge to direct the jury to return a verdict of "not guilty." But, at least her motion might suggest to the jury that the prosecution's case was weak enough for her to try. However, Temple quickly reasoned that the potential for the jury seeing a shocked judge and prosecutor might have an effect on it opposite of the one she desired. She decided to stay cool and quiet.

"Ms. Temple," the judge called out upon hearing the prosecution rest its case. "Do you have any motions to make at this time?"

"No, Your Honor," Temple responded after pausing to consider the options as outlined above. "The defense is ready to present its case at the court's pleasure."

"Very well," noted the judge. We will break until 2:00 p.m. at which time this court will again be in session. The jury is admonished not to discuss this case with anybody under any circumstances. You are not even allowed to discuss this case with fellow jury members. It is not yet time to deliberate anything. Talk about the weather, the economy, or sports but do not discuss this case. I will see you all back here at 2:00 p.m. Have a nice lunch. This court is in recess."

*****

Questions for Class Discussion

1. What was "trial by battle" and "trial by ordeal?" What cultural factors perhaps facilitated belief in such strange notions at the time?
2. How did the Magna Carta represent a huge leap forward in the history of trials? Who were given the right to a jury of their peers under the Magna Carta? Who got to serve on such juries as "peers?"
3. Who gets to have a jury trial today, that is, how serious a crime does one have to be charged with before being granted the option of having a jury trial?
4. Given the fact that courts are so congested, should we consider scaling back the right to a jury trial by granting it only to those accused of having committed a felony?

---

13. Levine, *supra* note 3, at 25.

5. What is the venire? Would you try to get out of jury service if asked to serve?

6. What is the difference between a "challenge for cause" and a "peremptory challenge?" How many challenges for cause are allowed each side? How many peremptory challenges are typically given?

7. In what ways do lawyers use the voir dire process to "educate the jury?" What should the prosecutor attempt to educate the jury about? What should the defense attempt to educate the jury about?

8. How do lawyers attempt to use the voir dire process to "stack" the jury? Is this unethical or good lawyering? Would you insist that your lawyer attempt to stack the jury if he or she could?

9. Should peremptory challenges in jury selection be abolished in America as they have been in England? What are the pro's and con's of continuing to allow peremptory challenges?

10. If you were a defendant like the one in this chapter charged with bigamy and statutory rape, what sorts of potential jurors would you want selected to serve on your jury? What sorts would you want your lawyer to get rid of using peremptory challenges?

11. Look at the Table in this chapter entitled, "McGuire's list of pro-prosecution and pro-defense potential jurors." Which of McGuire's hunches do you agree with and which do you disagree with?

12. What is the purpose behind the "opening statement?" Why is it called a "statement" and not an "argument?"

13. What options does a defense attorney have in choosing when to deliver his or her opening statement? Why is it generally not such a good idea to postpone giving a defense opening statement until the prosecution rests its case? When is it a good idea to postpone giving a defense opening statement until the prosecution rests?

14. What is the difference between direct examination and cross examination? How can cross examination play an important part in getting to the truth?

15. Would you feel comfortable as a defense attorney cross examining a witness who you know just told the truth but whom you probably could make look like a liar through aggressive cross examination tactics?

16. Give an example of a "leading question" versus an "open ended question." When, if ever, are leading questions allowed during trials?

17. Why are lawyers forbidden to lead witnesses on direct examination, but allowed to do so on cross examination? Given that lawyers may lead on cross examination, how often should their questions on cross be leading ones?

18. According to the Table in the book, what are some examples of common objections made by lawyers during trials?

19. Some democracies make very little use of formal rules of evidence and hence testimony is more free-flowing. For example, witnesses are freer to speak their minds but can often introduce hearsay, other bad acts of the defendant, personal opinions, etc. The fact finders are expected to sift through what is relevant and credible from what is not. Would you prefer getting rid of our heavy use of formal rules and just let witnesses more freely speak their minds?

20. From a defendant's point of view, are jury trials always preferable to bench trials? When might a defendant prefer a judge to a jury in deciding his or her guilt or innocence?

21. Some countries utilize professional jurors (legally trained people who hear and rule on cases). Do you think that the advantages of using such sophisticated jurors rather than lay people outweigh the disadvantages?

*****

Key Terms: trial by battle, trial by ordeal, Magna Carta, serious crime, jury panel, venire, voir dire, challenged for cause, peremptory challenges, stack the jury, educate the jury, opening statement, direct examination, leading questions, cross-examination, open-ended question, objections, sustain the objection, overrule the objection, impeach, prosecution rests its case, demurrer, directed verdict

Additional Concepts: mechanics of jury selection, purposes of opening statement, abuses of opening statement, defense delay of opening statement, prosecution case-in-chief, calling and questioning of witnesses, common objections, admonishing jurors not to discuss case

CHAPTER ELEVEN

THE TRIAL (PART II)

Theory of the Defense

One of the basic rules of defending someone at trial is to have a have a plan and to stick with it. This plan is known as the **theory of the defense**. In some cases the theory is based on an alibi. In other cases the theory centers on eyewitness error. In the defense of Omar Mustafa for bigamy and statutory rape, defender Mary Temple's theory was based simply on creating sympathy for Mustafa.

Temple knew that sympathy was not technically a legal defense like insanity or self-defense. But, she also knew something that most criminal defenders know: juries are reluctant to convict people whom they like or feel sorry for. Temple knew that Mustafa was legally guilty of the crimes with which he had been charged. After all, he was a bigamist, as this state chose to define the term. He did cohabit with two women at once in a sexual, "man and wife" style relationship. Temple also knew that Mustafa was a rapist. Sure, he did not force his two young "wives" to have sex with him. But their tender years automatically made them legally incapable of consenting to sex with a full-blown adult like her client.

Temple did not believe that she could win if she merely tried to argue that the state failed to prove the technical elements of these crimes. She would have to try to go with a sympathy angle and hope the jury would somehow conjure up reasonable doubt—whether consciously or unconsciously.

Temple had wisely saved her opening statement until midpoint in the trial, as was her right. She wanted to see how the state's case went before she fully committed herself in front of the jury to a particular set of facts regarding her sympathy defense. But the time had now come for her to draft an opening statement. There was no more time to delay.

Mary Temple decided that before drafting her opening statement it might be a good idea to interview her client one more time. Now that the prosecutor's case-in-chief was over, she was curious as to what Mustafa thought about the trial thus far.

The trial was in recess until 2:00 p.m. so Temple had a couple of hours to get her defense case-in-chief all mapped out. This was not a lot of time but there was not much to map out. She had decided to call just a couple of character witnesses whom she anticipated could vouch for her client's gentle ways. She also planned on calling a couple of witnesses who could explain to the jury the cultural norms that guided Mustafa and his community. She figured that these could be the same as the character witnesses. As she saw it, Mustafa and his relatives lived like the Amish do in Pennsylvania: in the world but not of the world. They had their own values, beliefs, morals, and standards—none of which Mustafa had violated. Mustafa was not a bad person. He just was caught between the tide of two civilizations.

Temple had already made the decision not to call her client, Omar Mustafa, to the stand. "What could he possibly add to his defense?" she reasoned. "All he'll wind up doing is admitting that he is in fact legally guilty of everything the state claims. I'll introduce the sympathy stuff through other people."

As Temple sat down with Mustafa in her office to go over his impressions of the prosecution's case, she listened with compassion as Mustafa began to moan about how horrible his future life in jail would be.

"It's all over, isn't it Ms. Temple?" Mustafa asked as he sat down across from his lawyer's desk. "How much do you get for statutory rape and bigamy?"

"Don't give up yet, Omar," responded Temple. "I had a case once in which a husband was on trial for murdering his wife. He had confessed to the police that he had purposely given his wife an overdose of sleeping pills in her cocoa to put her out of her misery. The poor woman had been crying herself to sleep every night begging the Lord to take her due to all the pain she was constantly experiencing. My client could not take it anymore so out of mercy he 'helped her to find rest' as he put it. Well, mercy killing is not legal in this state and he was tried for homicide. The jury acquitted him of all charges even though he was guilty according to the law books. You see, Omar, juries are reluctant to convict people they feel sympathy for."

"Are they allowed to do that?" Omar wondered out loud.

"Well, whether they are allowed to or not, they do. Juries let people off for all sorts of reasons that aren't technically legal. Sometimes juries let people off because the defendant was acting unselfishly. You may have heard the story of Robin Hood. The guy was a thief—actually he was an armed robber—lying in wait in the woods to rip people off. Yet, he is considered a hero in our culture. Nobody would feel comfortable convicting Robin Hood if he were tried today.

"Sometimes juries let people off because the victim deserved what the defendant did to the victim. The battered wife syndrome exists as a defense in many states. Even in a state that refuses to recognize the battered wife syndrome defense, juries often acquit women who kill their pig of a husband—even if they kill the jerk while he is sound asleep. The woman is not in imminent danger from the monster. She could walk out the door to safety. Yet, the jury lets her off even though the judge explains to them that the battered wife syndrome defense is not available.

"What I'm trying to say is that juries don't leave their hearts outside of the deliberation room. But there are two things our jurors will need from us. First, we need to get them to have a lot of sympathy for you. I think we can do that by hyping up the virtue of having tolerance for other people's customs. The second thing is harder. It's true they don't leave their hearts outside of the jury room, but they don't leave their minds outside either. I need to give the jury some legal rationale to find you not guilty. The jury needs to have something to intellectually hang its hat on. Even if they want to acquit you, they will probably need something to legally justify the verdict. Even if it is a little far fetched, we probably should give them something."

"Well, you're the lawyer. I don't know anything about that sort of stuff," Mustafa admitted. "I never finished high school let alone law school."

Mustafa's reference to law school caused a bell to go off in Mary Temple's head. She reflected back to her law school days and to a law review article she had edited as a student. The article was on justifications and excuses to crimes. She could not remember all of the creative points the article's author had come up with but she thought she could remember the basic defenses to any crime. She took out a yellow legal pad and a jelly sandwich from her drawer. As she ate, she jotted down all of the potential legal defenses she could think of. Her ideas are found in Table 1.

What all the defenses Mary Temple wrote down had in common was that unlike an alibi defense or a "they got the wrong guy" defense, these defenses do not involve challenging the fact that the defendant did the harm the state claims occurred. Rather, they propose that even though the defendant did do the harm, the defendant was either justified in doing it or should be excused for having done it. A **justification defense** suggests that a defendant did the right thing and there is nothing to apologize for. For example, killing is usually evil but killing in self-defense is a justifiable homicide. An **excuse defense** suggests that a defendant did the wrong thing but should be forgiven because there is something wrong with the defendant. For example, killing someone while insane may not be justified but it is excused (forgiven).

Temple realized that the state had clearly proven that the defendant had committed bigamy and statutory rape. It would do no good to argue that the state had the wrong guy or that he had never had sex with these girls.

Table 1   Legal Defenses to Crimes

Justification Defenses

Self-defense (reasonable force was used to protect oneself from bodily harm)

Defense of Others (reasonable force was used to protect third parties from bodily harm)

Defense of Property (reasonable, non-deadly force was used to recover property just taken)

Execution of Public Duties (reasonable force was used to prevent suspect from escaping)

Necessity (breaking the law was choosing the lesser of two evils)

Resisting Unlawful Arrest (resisting a bogus arrest—defense no longer recognized in most states)

Excuse Defenses

Insanity (mental illness made one unable to judge right from wrong or to conform to the law)

Mistake (reasonable mistake of fact negates the mental element of a crime)

Duress (threats of bodily harm causes one to do another's bidding)

Entrapment (police tempt somebody to commit a crime that he/she was not predisposed to do)

Age (youths are adjudicated delinquent and rehabilitated rather than punished for a crime)

Involuntary Intoxication (crime occurred due to spiked punch or weird reaction to a prescription)

Rather, she needed to come up with either a justification or an excuse. Even a lame defense could work with a sympathetic jury, though the less lame the better.

Temple quickly ruled out all of the defenses but two: necessity (a justification) and duress (an excuse). "Maybe if I explain these two defenses to Omar, he might be able to come up with some facts which I could advance to the jury in support of one of them," Temple told herself.

"Listen, Omar," began Temple. "I was wondering. There are two possible defenses I'd like to explore with you. One is called 'necessity' or the 'lesser of two evils defense.' This means that even though you had sex with these underage girls and lived with them as a husband would, you might be justified in breaking the law if by doing so you saved the girls from an even greater evil."

"What do you mean?" Omar asked. He was confused.

"Well, suppose someone were freezing to death in the woods in winter and trespassed into a cabin that said 'No Trespassing.' Even though that person broke the law, a jury could find that the individual was justified in violating the law because it is better for someone to trespass than to freeze to death. If we could convince the jury that by marrying these girls you saved them from a worse fate of some kind, maybe the jury could feel alright about acquitting you. What would have happened to these girls if they had refused to marry you like their parents insisted? Would they have been beaten or sent back to some horrible fate in the old country or anything like that?"

Omar looked into the hopeful face of his attorney but shook his head back and forth. "Their parents wanted them to marry me but would not have punished them all that much for refusing. I wasn't exactly the catch of the century. They are very pretty girls. The parents would have found somebody else for one or both of them."

"Crap," Temple thought to herself. "This guy is not making it easy for me."

"Alright, Omar," continued Temple. "Let's focus on you. Could it be that you were acting under duress? The defense of 'duress' occurs when someone does a crime because he or she is being threatened with bodily harm. For example, if I am an accountant and help a drug dealer to cheat on his income taxes because he is threatening to break my legs, my helping him break the law might be excused because I can't think straight under such conditions. I am thought to be under his control and my actions are his, not mine. Now, think very hard Omar before you answer this. Is there any way that maybe you married these girls under duress? Did anybody coerce you into marrying these girls?"

Temple watched Omar sit up straight as a rod and his eyes get big. She knew right away she had hit a nerve.

"Well, the cleric who married us told me that if I refused I would burn in hell as an infidel. He told me that only someone brainwashed by the Americans could refuse to marry such two beautiful young women of the faith. He told me that God would surely withdraw all influence from me and that in a few years I would lose my faith entirely. Hell is not a happy place in my religion."

"Did you believe him?" asked the attorney.

"Oh yeah. I've seen it happen before. Someone turns their back on some of the old ways and before you know it they have become completely Westernized. There is only one path to God and it is not the way of the West."

Mary Temple realized that she was on to something. Duress only works as a defense if the jury believes that someone feels so threatened by another that he or she believes there is absolutely no choice but to do a crime. "This could work," she thought. "The cleric was not threatening him with physical harm but with the certainty of eternal damnation. In a sense that is physical harm. That is even scarier to someone like Omar than a physical threat." Temple's optimism quickly was tempered by one sobering realization, however. She realized that duress no longer operates as an excuse for committing crimes once the threat is over. Once the threat has dissipated, one is required to conform one's conduct to the law. For example, a prisoner who is being threatened by a guard might be forgiven for escaping, but would be required to turn himself into other authorities once he is safe. He cannot just continue "escaping" the rest of his life. The question now was how to convince a jury that Mustafa's duress never went away, not even after several years.

"Do you still believe you'll go to hell if you stopped being a husband to your wives?" Temple asked. She had no idea how he would answer.

"Well, not really. I've kind of outgrown those fears. But I was already father to their children by the time I doubted the cleric's threats. What was I supposed to do then? Just walk away?"

Mary Temple realized she had something now for the jury to hang its hat on. She would argue duress. She would hope that the jury would ignore the fact that Omar outgrew his fear of the cleric over time and acquit him anyway based on sympathy for his having followed his culture's norms. It was not a perfect defense but it was not hopeless either. She realized that for her to advance the duress theory she would probably now have to put her client on the stand—something she earlier swore to herself that she would not do. "That's alright," she soothed herself. "Let them get him to admit that he slept with underage girls and acted as their husband. I'll argue that he did so out of duress. If they are sympathetic to him, they might acquit him despite the fact that he continued to live with them even when no longer afraid of going to hell."

Of course, Temple realized that all of this could go either way. She could already imagine the prosecutor arguing to the jury that religious belief hardly excuses people who take the law into their own hands. But she had a chance and would take it. After suggesting to her client where he could grab a cheap but good lunch, the attorney swiftly began to outline the specifics of her opening statement.

Defense Opening Statement

Two o'clock in the afternoon soon arrived. Both the defense and the prosecution stood up as the jury solemnly entered the courtroom. They stood up again (as did the jury) when the judge entered the courtroom a half a minute

later. Judge Brown pleasantly greeted the jury and asked the jurors collectively
if they had a good lunch. A few jurors nodded as the judge switched his gaze
towards Mary Temple and her client Omar Mustafa.

"Ms. Temple, I believe you had reserved your opening statement until you
were ready to present the defense case. You may now proceed with your opening remarks."

"Thank you, Your Honor," began Temple as she stood up. Temple walked
over to the jury box, stopping just four feet in front of the center. It suddenly
occurred to her that Mustafa was lucky to have a woman for a lawyer in a case
like this. She thought it must be an advantage for a man accused of victimizing women to have a woman as his advocate. Even though juries are supposed
to understand that lawyers represent people regardless of their personal opinions of them, she suspected that at some level most jurors probably see the
lawyer as a sincere ally of the accused.

Before beginning her speech to the jury, Temple glanced back at Mustafa
and gave him a warm, friendly smile. It seemed to have a good effect upon
the jurors since several of them smiled as well. Prosecutor Dan McGuire tried
to restrain himself from rolling his eyes in disgust. But, he was not entirely
successful. The defendant Mustafa noticed a couple of jurors making sympathetic eye contact with the displeased McGuire.

Temple stood before the jury with her hands folded reverently in front of
her mid-section. She had rested her notes on the bannister of the jury box but
knew that she would refer to them only rarely. She wanted to speak to the jurors, not read to them.

"Good afternoon, Ladies and Gentlemen," Temple began in a confident
voice much larger than her petite frame seemed to warrant. "The defense has
waited patiently for the chance to present its version of things. You have heard
the state's side of things. But there is another side to all of this—a side that I
suggest will cast things in a totally different light."

Temple paused for dramatic effect. She could tell that the jury was keenly
interested in what she would say next. She decided to ratchet up the drama
even further by boldly being blunt.

"Ladies and Gentlemen, my client did indeed religiously marry these two
young women just as the state has alleged! I'd be insulting your intelligence by
trying to deny that. But that is not the whole story—far, far from it.

"The very first witness that I will call this afternoon is my client Omar
Mustafa. Omar will tell you how he has lived his entire life isolated from mainstream American society. His parents, devout fundamentalist Muslims from
the Old Country brought him up in traditional Islamic culture, even going so
far as to home school him themselves. Ever since he was a little boy, the only

friends Omar had were members of his faith, all of whom lived with families that were culturally identical to his own. Omar's family did not have a television nor the internet. In Omar's society, he was taught that marriages were arranged and that it was right and proper for a young man in his early twenties to marry young women in their early teens. This is the way of his people.

"When Omar married these women, he will tell you that he did not know that he was doing anything wrong. But, there is something else you will learn. Omar will tell you how he was threatened by Hassan Zaifnejad, his spiritual leader and the cleric who performed the marriage. He will tell you that Zaifnejad told him that if he were to refuse the arranged marriage—one agreed to by not only his parents but the parents of the young women as well—that he'd be damned to burn in hell.

"Most Muslim clerics help people to live better lives than they would otherwise live. However, just like in any religion, a few extremist preachers do more harm than good. All of you are aware from world events how intimidating some so-called holy men can be. I am not going to suggest that Omar's cleric is a terrorist—far from it. However, you will learn that although Omar was never physically threatened by this cleric with earthly harm, this young and unworldly man was emotionally blackmailed and mentally coerced by this intimidating older man into breaking the law.

"In addition to hearing from Omar, you will also hear from two other witnesses. Both of them are members of Omar's cultural and religious community. They will both testify regarding the cultural norms and expectations of their community. They will also vouch for Omar's peaceful ways.

"After you have heard the rest of the story, not just what the prosecution has thus far tried to portray, I will be asking you to return a verdict of justice—a verdict of 'not guilty.' Thank you."

Having concluded her remarks, Mary Temple began walking back to the defense table where her client sat in the business suit she helped him pick out at the mall. She could not resist glancing at prosecutor Dan McGuire as she passed in front of his table. Their eyes met briefly and she could tell by his gaze that he was sincerely impressed with her defense strategy. She also saw no weakness in his eyes. She could tell that he was up for the challenge she had just lain down.

Categories of Evidence

Mary Temple remembered being taught in law school nothing but deep doctrinal legal theory. That was perhaps as it should have been. But upon graduating and after practicing awhile in the real world, Temple came to quickly learn that most trials do not turn so much on fancy, academic legal debates as they do on the factual evidence that is presented and the spin that skilled lawyers can put on that evidence. Before trying to spin the evidence, Mary first wanted to present some of her own. The prosecutor, Dan McGuire, had already put enough facts into evidence to convict her client. Approaching the case purely from a legal theorist perspective, Temple would have to admit to herself that Omar Mustafa was guilty. Temple's job was now to try to put into evidence some defense facts that she hoped might alter the course of things. She would establish a duress defense as best that she could, then spin her closing argument in a way to create as much sympathy for Mustafa as she possibly could muster. Temple hoped the jury would not base its verdict just on legal theory but also on a human sense of right and wrong.

As an attorney Temple was not allowed to testify. Neither the opening statements nor the closing arguments of attorneys are considered legal evidence. All evidence that is introduced into a trial is done through the testimony of witnesses. As she promised in her opening statement, Temple would call just three.

Temple knew that she had to be clever. McGuire was no fool. He could see what she was up to. In order to prevent McGuire from successfully objecting to relevancy, she had to dress her sympathy evidence up as evidence material to a duress defense. The rule with regards to irrelevant evidence is quite simple: it is always and without exception inadmissible. **Relevant evidence** is evidence "having tendency to make the existence of any fact that is of consequence to the determination of the action more probable or less probable than it would be without the evidence."[1] The evidence does not have to make the fact at issue a lot more or a lot less probable, but it does have to at least contribute something to the truth-finding enterprise. It is possible for evidence to be relevant (in that it adds or subtracts from the probability of some issue of consequence) but not material (in that it adds or subtracts so little that it is merely trivial and a waste of time). Nowadays, most lawyers have probably forgotten this subtle distinction and just equate the two terms.

One might ask why any lawyer would wish to present irrelevant evidence in the first place, especially those like criminal lawyers being paid by the case and not by the hour. As Mary Temple would confirm, there may be strategic advantages in trying to do so. Lawyers sometimes attempt to introduce irrelevant evidence in order to confuse juries, prejudice juries, distress and upset

---

1. Federal Rules of Evidence 401.

the witnesses for the other side, or to unduly prolong the trial in an attempt to cause lack of attention to what is truly important.

Mary Temple would try to get Mustafa's jury to become prejudiced in his favor, using as much irrelevant evidence as she could get introduced. She remembered the first drunk driving case she tried in her earlier days as a prosecutor before becoming a defense attorney. The erratically driving defendant had failed all the field sobriety tests and the breath machine and had even urinated in the road in front of the police officer who had pulled him over. It seemed like an open and shut case until the crafty defense attorney asked his client why he had been drinking that day. The defendant explained that it was his daughter's wedding day and he had been celebrating. He was on his way home from the reception. Though irrelevant, the jury heard this testimony and acquitted the defendant. They told Temple after the trial that they felt it would be wrong to punish someone for drunk driving on such a momentous occasion.

McGuire would be watching and objecting but Temple thought she could get a lot of legally irrelevant but helpful evidence introduced. She had the right to put on a duress defense. If in doing so some irrelevant evidence happened to necessarily come in as well then so be it.

Temple's case would rely heavily on sympathy evidence. But, sympathy evidence is not technically a formal classification of evidence. There are different types or categories of evidence which lawyers attempt to introduce in trials. Once category is known as direct evidence. **Direct evidence** is testimonial evidence which if believed to be truthful requires no inferences or reasoning to be made on the part of the jury. Often this type of evidence is referred to as "eyewitness testimony" but this is perhaps a bit simplistic since "ear witness," "smell witness," and "taste witness" also qualify.

If a police officer testified on the stand that she responded to a domestic call and upon arriving saw the defendant slam his fist into his wife's nose, the jury would not have to infer whether or not the defendant punched his wife. The jury would only have to decide whether or not it believed the police officer was giving truthful and accurate testimony. If the jury concluded that the officer was accurately telling the truth, then in could directly conclude that the defendant punched his wife. If on the other hand, the officer testified that he did not see the defendant hit his wife but merely saw blood both on the defendant's fist and the wife's broken nose, the jury would have to infer that the defendant punched his wife even if they believed the officer to be truthful. This would not be direct evidence but rather circumstantial.

Circumstantial evidence is evidence which even if believed by the jury to be truthful still requires the jury to infer a conclusion. For example, if I hear a gunshot and run into a room and see you holding a smoking gun over a dead body, I would still have to infer that you shot the victim. After all, it is possible that the victim shot himself and the individual holding the gun merely picked it up after the fact.

Criminals do not wait around for an eyewitness to be present before they commit their crimes. Hence, some cases can only be proven by way of circumstantial evidence, if they can be proven at all. A case relying entirely upon circumstantial evidence can properly result in a conviction as long as the circumstantial evidence of guilt is beyond a reasonable doubt.

A third type of evidence is known as "real evidence." **Real evidence** consists of tangible physical objects (e.g., a gun, torn underpants, alleged burglar tools, etc.) or traces of physical things (e.g., blood spots, fingerprints, semen, etc.). This type of evidence is introduced through a witness on the stand who is familiar with its context and can testify to its relevancy. The side wishing to have the evidence admitted usually asks the **court reporter** (the stenographer who is using a phonetic keyboard to take dictation of everything being said in court during a trial) to first mark the physical evidence as either a state's exhibit or as a defense exhibit (which is usually done with a tag or a little sticker that the court reporter keeps on hand). The moving attorney then usually shows the object to the opposing counsel as a courtesy so that the other side can examine it up close. Next, the attorney approaches the witness on the stand, shows the witness the object, and asks the witness to identify it and explain how it relates to the case (e.g., a police officer witness might say that it is the knife which the officer found next to the murder victim). Finally, the attorney will ask the judge to allow admission of the object into evidence as "State's exhibit number 3" or "Defense Exhibit number 14" (or whatever number one is up to at that point—the sticker or tag will indicate this to the attorneys). Once admitted, the object will be later sent to the jury room as the jury deliberates the verdict. Jury members will be able to hold it and closely inspect it to their satisfaction.

One ground for objecting to physical evidence is that it is irrelevant. Another common objection involves challenges to the **chain of custody** (proof that the object is the very one found at the crime scene—chain of custody is not that critical when an object is so unique that a witness can confidently identify it on the stand just by looking at it). Absent a documented chain of custody, the analysis of some evidence (e.g., semen or blood or hair that has been sent and analyzed at a crime lab) cannot be introduced into evidence since how can one be sure that the right physical evidence had been analyzed? Such evidence is considered **fungible**, meaning it cannot be readily identified by the witness unless there is some documented chain of custody to rely on.

Another type of evidence is "opinion evidence." **Opinion evidence** consists of conclusions or analysis by the witness of facts, rather than just the reporting of facts to the jury. With rare exceptions (e.g., expert witness testimony or character witness testimony), opinion evidence is inadmissible. It is generally the witness' job to provide the jury with the data but not to analyze it for the jury. That is the jury's role.

The final type of evidence is documentary evidence. **Documentary evidence** consists of writings or recordings of some kind. Examples of documentary evidence include such things as written contracts, wills, ransom notes, and suicide letters. Of course, the best proof of the contents of such documents would be the original document itself rather than some reader's interpretation of the contents. For this reason, documentary evidence is subject in many jurisdictions to the "best evidence rule." The **best evidence rule** provides that in order to prove the contents of a writing, voice recording, videotape, or photograph, the original is required unless it has been innocently lost or destroyed.[2] Oral testimony regarding the contents of any document or recording which a witness has reviewed is generally admissible only if the original is genuinely unavailable. In addition to documents that have been innocently lost or destroyed, unavailability could include situations in which the document is in the hands of someone who refuses to produce it or in the hands of a criminal defendant who does not have to give it up due to the 5th Amendment right against self-incrimination.[3]

Of course, nothing would prevent a person from orally testifying as to what she saw or heard with her own senses even if a recording of the event was also made. For example, if a police officer both heard and tape recorded a confession as it was being made, the officer could testify to what he heard with his own ears even if the tape recording is also available. Here, the officer would not be testifying about the contents of the tape recording but rather testifying as to what he heard with his very own ears. If he were not present at the confession and was only relying upon his review of the tape recording, he would have to produce the tape recording in order to satisfy the best evidence rule.

The best evidence rule does not apply to physical objects such as guns, knives or hair but rather just to documents or recordings of some kind. The reasons for the rule are obvious: to prevent fraud and to limit innocent misinterpretations of the document or recording.

---

2. Federal Rules of Evidence 1002.
3. Federal Rule of Evidence 1004.

Defense Case-in-Chief

Mary Temple's defense case would rely on just three witnesses. One witness would be Mustafa himself who would be giving a lot of "direct evidence" of the events that occurred as witnessed by him as an eye and ear witness. Among other things, he would tell the jury what he heard the cleric say, the parents say, and the girls say. The jury would have to judge whether or not Mustafa was telling the truth.

The other two witnesses Temple would call would give "opinion evidence." As expert witnesses, they would testify about the local fundamentalist Islamic culture which they shared with Mustafa. As close acquaintances of Mustafa, they would also testify about Mustafa's character.

Mary Temple took a discrete but deep breath. Her courage thus summoned, she announced to the court that "the defense calls Omar Mustafa to the stand."

Omar slowly walked to the stand trying not to look like the complete nervous wreck of a man that he was. He felt his knees actually buckle under him as he mounted the small step to the slightly elevated witness chair. He sat down and looked straight at his lawyer where he hoped to find comfort in an ally's face. He was trying hard not to vomit the small lunch he partially had just eaten.

A bit of confusion occurred when the bailiff instructed Mustafa to place his hand on the Christian bible as part of the swearing-in ceremony. Mustafa was reluctant to do so out of concern that it might be an act of heresy on his part. The judge sensed Mustafa's concern and wisely instructed the bailiff to have Mustafa take the oath without any scriptural props.

After being sworn in, Mustafa was ready to be interrogated. Temple decided to get Mustafa to relax a little bit by starting off her questioning with simple, even boring, questions. Mustafa was asked to give his name, address, and the names of the two women with whom he lived. He was asked their ages. After a few more such questions, designed as much to put Mustafa at ease as they were to provide the jury with information it did not already know, Temple began to engage Omar Mustafa in a more interesting dialogue.

"Omar, how did you choose these two young women to marry?" Temple asked.

"I didn't choose them," was the reply. "My parents and their parents did all the choosing."

"Did you ever pursue or court these women?"

"No," the defendant responded. "That would have been immoral."

"Did you know them before marrying them?" asked the defender.

"Not really. I knew who they were and that they were to be my wives. But I never really had much to do with them before Mr. Zaifnejad married us. We don't date in my culture. We just get married to whomever our parents decide."

"Why would your parents decide and not you?" Temple inquired.

"Because they know best. Look at all the divorce in this country. It's because young people pick their own spouses. Parents know best about these sort of matters."

Temple liked what she was hearing. Mustafa's answers were strange sounding but it was obvious he was no typical pervert trying to prey on young girls. He did not even get to pick his wives.

"Omar, did you ever consider not marrying these two young women?"

"Well, at first I did object a little bit. I told my Mom that maybe I should marry someone whom I knew better—someone who I was in love with."

"How did your mother react to that?" asked Temple.

"She coldly stared at me. Great sadness was in her eyes. She went upstairs and told my Dad. I could hear him yelling at her and her yelling at him. My mother and father left the house and came back with the cleric, Mr. Zaifnejad."

"Did Mr. Zaifnejad talk to you?" Omar acknowledged that he did.

"What did Mr Zaifnejad tell you?" At this point the prosecutor tried to object to Temple's question on the grounds of hearsay. His objection was overruled.

"He said that only foolish people marry out of love. He told me that these girls were chosen for me and I had no choice but to marry them. He told me that I was lucky that they were pretty since lots of men are asked to marry ugly girls. He said if I refused to marry such two pretty girls chosen for me I would not only be ungrateful but sinful. He said I was on the road to leaving the faith and if I did not repent I would become sinful just like most of the Americans."

"Did he speak of hell?" Temple asked. McGuire objected strenuously on the grounds of leading the witness. This time McGuire's objection was sustained. Temple rephrased the question. But, Omar knew by then what direction she wanted him to go and he obliged her.

"I was told by Mr. Zaifnejad that if I did not marry these girls I would go to hell. Not maybe go to hell but definitely go."

"What was your reaction to that?" asked Temple.

"It scared the hell out of me," Omar reported without even realizing his pun. The jury laughed. Omar was confused. Temple smiled broadly. McGuire was not amused.

The testimony continued with Omar explaining in some detail the norms of his culture. He spoke of how he knew no other world except the close knit community in which he was raised. He spoke of how his mother schooled him at home for religious reasons and how his friends all shared his faith. Most importantly, he came across as a gentle, devout Muslim boy who was merely following the ways of his people.

On cross-examination, McGuire led Omar through a series of specific questions designed to show that McGuire had broken the law.

"You married these girls in a ceremony when you were twenty two and they were only fourteen and fifteen years old and you knew how old they were didn't you?" suggested McGuire.

"Yes, but I …"—McGuire cut him short. "Yes or No will do," he told the defendant. "Yes." confirmed Mustafa.

"And, Mr. Mustafa, you had sex with them shortly thereafter, right?"

"Well, yes of course. We were married."

"You knew you were breaking American law by marrying these girls so young? Isn't that also correct Mr. Mustafa?" McGuire waited for an answer.

Mustafa hesitated. He looked at his lawyer. She just looked back. "Well, not really," Mustafa said.

"What do you mean, 'not really?'" McGuire smelled blood. "You did not get a marriage license did you? You did not get one because you knew that you could not."

"My marriage was religious not civil," Mustafa tried to suggest.

"Yes, but don't members of your community usually get marriage licenses so that their marriage is both religious and legal?"

"Some do," Mustafa admitted.

"But not you. You knew you would not be given one."

"How would I know that?" asked the defendant. "I was not a part of your world."

"Oh come on Mr. Mustafa," McGuire sneered. "Do you mean to tell this court that you did not know that it was illegal to marry two women at once in this country? Do you mean to tell this court that you did not know or at least suspect that there were age requirements for marriage in this country?" Temple objected on the grounds that McGuire was asking two questions at once and was also being argumentative. The judge instructed McGuire to ask his questions one at a time and to soften the tone of his questioning. When McGuire calmly re-asked the question about having two wives at once, Omar admitted he knew that was not legal. As to the question regarding age requirements, he continued to maintain ignorance but seemed somehow to be lying.

McGuire continued to hammer Mustafa. "Mr. Mustafa, did you not brag to neighbors about how you got to sleep with two beautiful young girls?" Mustafa paused before replying, "I'm not sure. Anything's possible. I say lots of things." He sounded like somebody trying to evade the truth without directly lying.

McGuire even got Mustafa to admit that he no longer lived by all the precepts of the religion that supposedly coerced him into breaking the law. "Didn't I see you drinking a beer with your lunch today?" asked McGuire. Temple objected on the grounds of relevancy—she pointed out that the prosecutor himself had been known to occasionally drink a beer at lunch. After a brief **side bar conference** (a private, hushed discussion between the lawyers and the judge up at the podium where the judge sits), the judge overruled Temple's objection. After reluctantly admitting he did have just one beer to help wash the food down, McGuire inquired, "Isn't that against your religion?" Mustafa admitted that it was.

McGuire followed up by getting Mustafa to admit that he no longer feared going to hell for things like refusing to marry people the cleric insisted that he marry. "But, I did fear such things when I got married," Mustafa pointed out.

McGuire continued his assault by getting Mustafa to admit that he thought American marriage was culturally inferior and against nature. Temple tried to object to this line of questioning on relevancy grounds, but the judge overruled her after McGuire pointed out that she had opened the door to this by injecting the issue of Mustafa's culture into the trial. Pursuant to McGuire's relentless attack, Mustafa told the jury that "men need more than one wife. It's better for the wife to share wifely duties. They don't have the same frequency of needs that men do." Even Temple felt a little disgusted by this last statement, though her face gave absolutely no sign of anything but calm confidence.

By the time McGuire had finished cross-examining her client, Temple could see that she indeed had a worthy adversary with whom to deal. McGuire had managed to make her client look as much like a sexist opportunist as a victim of parental and clerical oppression.

To prevent McGuire from doing too much more damage, Temple decided to keep the testimony of her next two witnesses short and simple. She called two of Mustafa's neighbors to the stand. They were both middle-aged women. Temple had purposely chosen women rather than men to testify on behalf of Mustafa. Since the alleged victims were female, Mustafa's supporters in court would be female as well.

Guided by Temple's questioning, both women confirmed that marriages were always arranged in their community. Both confirmed that it was believed sinful for someone to resist parents' reasonable choice of spouses. Both confirmed that going to hell was inevitably what happened to those who disobeyed parents and religious leaders on matters so important as marriage. Both confirmed that bigamy was an accepted practice within their community and that marriage of a man in his early twenties to young teens was normal and done all the time in the "old country." Both testified that they were very familiar with Mustafa's reputation in the community and that he was known as somebody who was honest and non-violent: a "gentle boy of good will," as one of them put it.

On cross, McGuire skillfully managed to get both women to admit that everyone in the community knew that it was illegal to marry more than one spouse. He even got them to admit that Mustafa bragged prior to his wedding how lucky he was to marry two beautiful young girls. "I never saw a groom so excited as Omar to get married," one of the women confessed.

Having done much to undercut the defense assertion that Mustafa married these two underage girls only out of fear of going to hell and not for any selfish reasons whatsoever, McGuire saved his best question for last. He asked one of the women, "Did Mustafa know that it was against American law to marry even just one girl this young?" McGuire was not sure how this witnesses would respond. Perhaps for this reason he should not have asked the question. But, McGuire figured that if the witness responded unfavorably he could point out to the jury later that "ignorance of the law is no excuse." If the witness answered favorably, then he would have scored a huge point. Temple did not want to take a chance on a response favorable to McGuire. She objected on the grounds that the question was undoubtedly out of the ken of knowledge of the witness. The judge asked the witness if she knew the answer. "Yes," the witness told him. The judge went on to overrule Temple. Temple next thought about objecting on the grounds of relevancy since "ignorance of the law is no excuse" anyway, and Mustafa's knowledge or lack thereof would not matter. Temple wisely realized that was not a path she wanted to go down. The witness was allowed to answer McGuire's question. To Temple's deep disappointment the woman affirmed that Mustafa had known that it was illegal to marry someone that young. In fact, the witness even recounted Mustafa opining that "Americans are prudes when it comes to age and promiscuous when it comes to anything else." "Ouch," was the only word Temple could think of upon hearing that revelation.

It was now time for Temple to rest her case. Before McGuire had done his handiwork with her witnesses, Temple felt confident that things were going her way. Now it appeared that McGuire might be getting the upper hand. But it was perhaps too close to call. Temple realized that the ultimate fate of Mustafa might rest upon who gave the better closing arguments.

Closing Arguments

Closing arguments are quite different from opening statements. Whereas opening statements merely give a concise overview of the evidence that witnesses will present, closing arguments are arguments, not statements. During **closing arguments** both sides are allowed and indeed expected to comment on the quality of the evidence and the credibility of the witnesses.

A critical question is which side should go first and which should go last in making a closing argument. Obviously, both sides would prefer to have the last word. The decision as to who goes last varies from place to place. Some states designate that the defense attorney should be allowed to speak last since the state is the one seeking to take away someone's liberty. Other states allow the prosecutor to go last to make up for the fact that the state is the one with the heavy burden of proof.

Like opening statements, closing arguments do not constitute evidence. This does not mean, however, that these monologues are completely unregulated. They are subject to rules of fair play, just as the presentation of the official evidence is.

For example, inflammatory language falls outside the acceptable bounds of closing argument. **Inflammatory language** is language that tends to significantly harm the ability of the jury to remain objective, rationale and dispassionate.[4] In a drug case, for example, it might be alright for a prosecutor during closing argument to briefly refer in a mild tone to "society's drug problem."[5] But, it would be unacceptable for a prosecutor to refer repeatedly and emphatically to how marijuana is "poison that is destroying our children in our schools and is bringing and end to our youth."[6] When a prosecutor's inflammatory remarks have "so poisoned the well that the trial's outcome was likely affected,"[7] a reversal of a conviction will be required.

Of course, defense attorneys also are forbidden from inflaming the passions of the jury. However, even if they do so it is sometimes difficult to know what the court can do about it other than to sustain the prosecutor's objection and reprimand the defense attorney. Even if the defense lawyer's comments were to "poison the well" it is unlikely that the prosecutor would want the judge to declare a mistrial and start the whole trial process over again.

---

4. *Agressot v. United States*, 3 F.3d 525 (1st Cir. 1993).
5. *United States v. Ferguson*, 935 F.2d 1518, 1530–31 (7th Cir. 1991).
6. *United States v. Doe*, 860 F.2d 488, 494 (1st Cir. 1988).
7. *United States v. Mejia-Lozano*, 829 F.2d 268, 274 (1st Cir. 1987).

Another very important rule of fair play governing the presentation of closing arguments is the prohibition against directly expressing personal opinions regarding the evidence.[8] For example, Hawaii demands that "a lawyer shall not … assert his personal opinion as to the justness of a cause, as to the credibility of a witness, … or as to the guilt or innocence of an accused; but may argue, on his analysis of the evidence, for any position or conclusion with respect to the matters stated herein."[9] The reason for rules like the above is that, as the United States Supreme Court noted decades ago, lawyers' "assertions of personal knowledge are apt to carry much weight against the accused when they should properly carry none."[10]

The fact that lawyers are forbidden from directly expressing their personal opinions about a case might come as a surprise to jurors who listen to lawyers zealously making closing arguments in which the lawyers seem to express personal opinions. But if one were to listen to lawyers carefully, one would realize that few ever technically give an actual opinion. For example, defense lawyers cannot permissibly come right out and state something like, "My client told you he is innocent and I for one believe him. I am sure he did not do this crime." However, they might say something more hypothetical like, "My client told you he was innocent. Doesn't his testimony have the ring of truth to it? Did he not seem like someone who was being honest with you?" To jurors there might seem little difference between the two approaches. But, legally the later is permissible while the former is not.

In McGuire's and Temple's jurisdiction, local rule dictated that the defense attorney was the first to present his or her closing argument while the prosecutor got to go last. Defense counsel Mary Temple was ready. Since she knew McGuire would speak after her, she could not afford to give a meek argument. She knew she had to come out swinging.

Swinging is just what Temple did. She first pounded on the sympathy angle, reminding the jury of how Omar Mustafa was basically a nice guy who was a victim of his own culture, parents, and clergy. She pointed out his reputation in the community for honesty and non-violence. She reminded the jury that he did not choose his wives but they were chosen for him. She stressed the fact that marrying younger women was normal in the old country and normal to Omar and his immigrant community. Omar was not like most statutory rapists, Temple noted. Unlike others charged with such a crime, he had

---

8. *State v. Marsh*, 728 P.2d 1301 (Haw. 1986).

9. *Hawaii Code of Professional Responsibility* DR 7-106(C)(4).

10. *Berger v. United States*, 295 U.S. 78, 88 (1935).

permission from the girls, their parents, his parents, his clergy, his entire community, and his ancestors.

Temple went on to tell the jury that Omar did not try to legally marry these girls. He just religiously married them. This was unlike many a bigamist who pretends to legally marry a new woman while hiding from the new wife the fact that he was already married to someone else. Nobody was tricked or lied to here. If someone was being manipulated, it was Omar as much as the young women.

After pounding the sympathy angle, Temple next argued the defense of duress. This was the "excuse" the jury could find to let the sympathetic Omar off the legal hook. Temple argued passionately that though Omar may have married these two minors religiously in violation of state law, he did so out of fear. "Sure, he may have found them attractive, but that is no crime," she told the jury. "His primary motivation for marrying them was to avoid going to hell. He was acting under duress, and duress is an excuse to a crime. Can you see how someone home-schooled by religious parents and completely cut off from television and the outside world might fear going to hell if he disobeyed religious traditions? Can you imagine the pressure he felt to marry these girls when the community holy man told him he'd go to hell if he did not do that? If duress can excuse someone who did a crime out of fear of being subjected to grave bodily harm, can't we also excuse a young person who is being threatened with the terrifying flames of hell? What is the state requiring of my client? Does it expect him to go to hell rather than marry two willing young women? Does it expect him to be an outcast to his own family and society? Isn't the state trying to punish Omar for following his traditions?"

Temple paused a few seconds to collect her thoughts before continuing. She realized that McGuire, who would get to speak last, would no doubt tell the jury that duress is no longer an excuse once the threat has dissipated. Yet, Omar continued to have sex with these minors long after he reasonably could have remained in a state of fear. To try to take some of the sting out of such anticipated remarks, Temple concluded by asking, "Ladies and Gentlemen, once married, what does the state expect of Omar Mustafa? That he walk away from these women after fathering their children? That he walk away from the children? Members of the jury, I suggest to you that justice dictates that you find duress and that it was ongoing. I propose to you that is the only just verdict you can render. Thank you."

As Temple sat down, a wave of relief flooded her. Sitting down after closing argument always had this effect on Temple when she did a trial. For her this trial was now effectively over. Win, lose or draw, there was nothing more she could do to affect the outcome. There was no more pressure on her at this point. Her sole role now—except for the remote possibility of objecting to something outrageously inappropriate that McGuire might say—was to sit back and look dignified. That required no effort. Temple was naturally dignified-looking in her expensive trial suit.

Before the jurors had a chance to completely digest what Temple had just told them, McGuire was on his feet approaching them. His gate reflected an odd mixture of deference to the jury and confidence in what he was about to say. He was glad that he would have the final word since Temple could be so convincing. He was looking forward to giving his spin on things.

McGuire realized that he had to argue against the duress defense. But like Temple, he knew that a jury could always find some legal pretext to acquit someone if it really wanted to acquit. If it wasn't duress, it could somehow conjure up reasonable doubt. McGuire had seen this happen before. What McGuire really had to do was to undo the sympathy that Temple had no doubt just created for Omar Mustafa. That was not a task that McGuire felt uncomfortable taking on. McGuire would not even have to act. He really did have little sympathy for Mustafa and (what he considered to be) Mustafa's self-righteous and arrogant community.

Looking straight into the faces of the jury, McGuire began his speech. "Ladies and Gentlemen, I am very grateful for the opportunity to address you. Let me begin by assuring you that nobody is trying to punish Mr. Mustafa for holding particular beliefs. Thoughts are not crimes. Beliefs are not crimes. Mr. Mustafa is free to believe anything that he wants to believe. But, he is not free to do anything that he wants to do. The judge will instruct you in a few minutes that 'ignorance of the law is no excuse.' I would add to this that religion is no excuse either—especially to statutory rape.

"When people come to our country they are expected to live by our laws—not French laws, not Chinese laws, not Israeli laws, not Arab laws, but our laws. Immigrants get a lot of benefits from joining our society. In return, we expect certain things from them. One of these things is respect for our laws. If I go overseas, I am expected to obey the laws of that country. I would not drink beer for example in Saudi Arabia. It is against the law. If I were to do so, I would expect to be punished if caught. Well, Mr. Mustafa has been caught having sex with two children. He is not a child. He is a fully grown man. He is not a victim. He is a perpetrator, is he not? He did not have to rape these girls, for that is what I propose to you the law says he did—he raped them. Due to their tender age they were not capable of giving their consent to sex. Having sex with someone unable to give consent is a type of rape. The defendant did not have to marry these girls or get them pregnant. He chose to do these things. Now, he wants to hide behind his culture. But there is no such thing as a 'my culture says it's ok' defense in this country. There never has been such a defense, and for good reason.

"All of us—except native Americans—are immigrants or the descendants of immigrants. Ours ancestors all gave up certain things when they moved here. They all promised to obey American law. And that is by and large what they all did. If you acquit Omar Mustafa, what kind of message will you be sending back to his immigrant community? Will you not be saying, 'Go ahead, break the laws of your adopted country. Go ahead, grown men, have sex with young teenage girls if you want. Go ahead, have multiple wives if you want. You can do whatever your culture says is ok despite what the law of your new chosen home says.' This is not the message we dare send.

"Defense counsel has argued that you should acquit Mustafa because he had sex with these girls out of duress. She argues that he was afraid of going to hell and is not responsible for his crimes. I suggest to you that he is responsible. Surely a grown man like Mustafa is free to reject unreasonable religious advice. What religion would order a man to have sex with underage girls under threat of hell? Islam? How likely is that? Even if Mustafa's cleric gave him this ridiculous advice, he should have seen it for the extremist view that it was.

"But even if Mustafa could not bring himself to reject the religious advice, he still is responsible for bigamy and sex with underage girls. As the judge will probably instruct you, the defense of duress only is valid as long as the threat is ongoing. You cannot continue to break the law forever just because you initially were afraid of something. If I am ordered to smoke marijuana or else be beat up, I don't have the right to continue to smoke marijuana the rest of my life. Just because Mustafa was once afraid of the cleric does not mean that he continued to be. And, once the fear had subsided—which we heard that it did from the defendant himself—Mustafa could not continue to justify having sex with these girls anymore. They had the right to be free of his advances. They had the right not to be his ongoing victims. One of the girls continued to be victimized right up until the time she was old enough to run away. That was not right.

"Defense counsel has tried to paint Mustafa's case as not the ordinary statutory rape and bigamy case. She has brought up the fact that his culture is different, that he was home-schooled, and that parents gave permission. But all of these are sentencing arguments, not arguments relevant to guilt or innocence. Let these kind of arguments be considered by the judge at sentencing. It is not your job to sentence Mustafa. That is the judge's role.

"Ladies and Gentlemen, if my arguments make sense to you I am asking you to do the right thing and to convict Mr. Mustafa. Hold him accountable for his actions just like you would hold any American accountable. Mr. Mustafa is an American. He is responsible to obey his country's laws, even the one's he and his community may not like. Thank you."

McGuire sat down and felt the same sense of relief that Temple had felt following her summation. He glanced at her as he poured himself a glass of water from a pitcher on the table. Their eyes met briefly and they fought the urge to give each other a smile. Why shouldn't they be friends again? The battle was over. It was now merely up to the judge to instruct the jury and for them to await the verdict.

Instructing the Jury

Judge Brown dutifully took control of the trial. Up to this point, he was a passive figure waiting to rule on objections advanced by the litigants. Unlike judges in some countries, American judges do not run trials. The lawyers do. Lawyers are the actors, screen writers, producers, directors, and prop managers. But now that closing arguments were over, it was up to Judge Brown and nobody else to teach the jury the law. It was time for him to deliver his **jury instructions.**

"Ladies and Gentlemen, I have a few instructions to give you," began Brown. "In order for you to do your job, you must know what the law is. You will be the judges of the facts but I will give you the law. Your job will be to figure out the facts-what took place—and to apply these findings of fact to the law as I will now give it to you."

Judge Brown began by defining the elements of bigamy and the elements of statutory rape to the jury. He explained that bigamy involved the cohabitation of a man with more than one woman at the same time, when such cohabitation involved an ongoing sexual relationship with each. He explained that it was this intimate cohabitation that constituted bigamy. It was not necessary for the parties to believe themselves to be legally married. The sexual cohabitation was enough.

Judge Brown went on to explain that statutory rape was consensual sex with someone who was too young to give that consent. He explained that local law required the alleged victims be under seventeen years of age and that the defendant be at least four years older than the alleged victims.

Judge Brown next instructed the jury about the duress defense. He told them that a defendant who did wrong could be excused by the jury if the jury felt that he was being coerced into doing a crime due to threats of physical violence. The judge told them that once any alleged threats no longer clouded a defendant's mind, he could no longer be excused in disobeying the law.

After giving the jury several other minor instructions, the judge concluded by telling the jury about the presumption of innocence and the need for the state to overcome this presumption with proof beyond a reasonable doubt of every element of the crimes charged (including proof beyond a reasonable doubt that the defense of duress should not excuse the defendant).

As Judges like Brown surely know, proof beyond a reasonable doubt is not easy to define. How sure should jurors be before taking away someone's liberty for an alleged criminal offense or stigmatizing them with a criminal record? Obviously, they should not require proof to a mathematical certainty. That would not be possible. On the other hand, should jurors be allowed to send someone to prison—perhaps for very long terms—out of belief that the person is probably guilty though they are not quite certain?

In most civil cases, one only needs to be convinced by a **preponderance of the evidence** that someone is responsible for a wrong in finding judgment against him or her. That means that if the fact finder (judge or jury) believes that the defendant is probably culpable (more than a 50 percent chance), a judgment in favor of the plaintiff should be granted. Hence, if John sues Mary for conversion (wrongful taking) of his money, and a jury is convinced that Mary more likely than not did wrongfully take John's money, then Mary can be ordered to give John his money back. This payment to John would not constitute punishment of any kind. Mary is not being told to go to jail, to live under the rules of probation, or even to pay a fine to the state. She is merely being asked to pay back a debt that she apparently owes John. If Mary is forced to pay restitution which in reality she does not owe John, a harm is done to Mary. But at least society never meant to punish Mary in any way—just get her to pay what it thought was a debt owed. Mary is not stigmatized as a criminal and never lost her liberty either through a jail sentence or by having to live the rules of probation.

On the other hand, if a police officer wishes to charge Mary with the crime of theft, the officer may arrest Mary based on a mere likelihood of guilt (**probable cause**—something quite akin to preponderance of evidence in civil court). But, a final conviction in criminal court requires much more. To convict, punish, and stigmatize Mary for a crime, the fact finder must be convinced of her guilt **beyond a reasonable doubt** (in other words, firmly convinced). Though this standard does not require proof beyond all doubt, it clearly requires something much more than mere probability or likelihood. Courts have struggled for many decades with a precise definition of reasonable doubt that judges could use to instruct juries. Some legal scholars have suggested not even trying to define it precisely for juries. They think the words should be left alone to speak for themselves. However, Judge Brown did not believe that the phrase "reasonable doubt" was self-defining to lay jurors. He wanted to explain it to them. Following a definition proposed by Justice Ruth Ginsburg of the U.S. Supreme Court,[11] he instructed the jury as follows:

"Ladies and Gentlemen, the state has the burden of proving the defendant guilty beyond a reasonable doubt. Some of you may have served as jurors in civil cases, where you were told that it is only necessary to prove that a fact is more likely true than not true. In criminal cases, the government's proof must be more powerful than that. It must be beyond a reasonable doubt.

"Proof beyond a reasonable doubt is proof that leaves you firmly convinced of the defendant's guilt. There are very few things in this world that we know with absolute certainty, and in criminal cases the law does not require proof that overcomes every possible doubt. If, based on your consideration of the evidence, you are firmly convinced that the defendant is guilty of the crime charged, you must find him guilty. If on the other hand, you think there is a real possibility that he is not guilty, you must give him the benefit of the doubt and find him not guilty."

Following this instruction, Judge Brown explained to the jurors that they were now excused to go deliberate. He told them that their verdict needed to be unanimous. He told them that they had a duty to try to come up with a verdict that was unanimous unless to do so would do violence to their conscience. He told them that they should be polite and to listen to one another's arguments with an open mind. He told them to elect a jury foreperson to direct their deliberations and to tally the votes. He then excused them to deliberate.

As the jurors left the jury box, both lawyers stood out of respect. Mustafa stood as well. Mustafa's fate now rested in the hands of people as strange to him as music television: twelve ordinary, fellow Americans. (Mustafa's fate will be decided in the next chapter, "The Jury Deliberates.")

*****

Questions for Class Discussion

1. What is meant by a "theory of the defense?" Why is it so important for a defense lawyer to have one even though there is no requirement for a defendant to prove his or her innocence? What would juries think if there were no theory of the defense ever presented to them?

---

11. See, *Victor v. Nebraska*, 511 U.S. 1 (1994) (Justice Ginsburg, Concurring opinion).

2. The chapter talks about justification defenses and excuse defenses. What is the theoretical difference between the two?

3. Identify as many justification defenses as you can. Identify as many excuse defenses as you can.

4. Which defense did Mustafa try to use during his trial? What did you think of this attempt?

5. What is meant by relevant evidence? Can you give some examples of irrelevant evidence in a hypothetical trial?

6. Defense lawyers often try to get irrelevant evidence admitted during a trial. Why would they want to do this? Is it unethical to try to confuse juries or arouse prejudice by introducing irrelevant evidence—or is that merely smart lawyering?

7. What is the difference between direct and circumstantial evidence? Would you ever be willing to convict someone of a serious crime based solely on circumstantial evidence? If so, could you come up with an example?

8. Suppose a lawyer wishes to have a piece of "real evidence" like a knife admitted during a trial? How exactly does a lawyer go about this?

9. What is meant by "fungible evidence?" Can you give some examples? Why is it so important for witnesses to present a "chain of custody" when evidence is fungible?

10. Why do we allow expert witnesses to testify as to their opinions when we forbid ordinary people to do this? Should we allow any witness to present his or her opinion and let the jury just give it the weight it deserves? Do juries have to follow the opinion of the expert witness? Why not?

11. What is the "best evidence rule?" Do you agree that such a rule makes sense?

12. What is a "side bar conference?" Why was one needed in the Mustafa case? Should side bar conferences be taken down by the court reporter?

13. How do closing arguments differ from opening statements? If you were on a legal defense or prosecution team, would you rather be assigned to give the opening statement or the closing argument in a trial? Why?

14. States in the U.S. differ as to which side (prosecution or defense) gets to give the last closing argument. Which side would you hope your state gives the nod to go last? What does your choice have to say about your due process vs. crime control value preference?

15. Why not allow lawyers to use inflammatory language during closing arguments? Is there really such a thing? Can you give an example of inflammatory language in a hypothetical homicide case? In a child molestation case? In a drunk driving case?

16. Are lawyers allowed to express their personal opinions as to guilt or innocence during closing arguments? Why not? How do lawyers go about

making impassioned closing arguments without technically expressing their personal opinions?

17. Who instructs the jury at the end of the trial? What were some of the things the judge in the Mustafa trial instructed the jury regarding?

18. What did the judge in the Mustafa case mean when he told the jury during jury instructions that they were the judges of the facts but not of the law?

19. After some trials, jurors complain that they could not understand the jury instructions that the judge had given them. Why do you suppose some judges find it difficult to express jury instructions in simple English? If judges stray too far from legal language in their instructions, what could be the result on appeal?

20. If you were on the jury, would you have convicted Mustafa in this case of both bigamy and statutory rape, just one of the crimes, neither of the crimes? Why? What sort of sentence, if any, do you think Mustafa should receive?

21. For those of you who would normally feel uncomfortable representing people whom you know are legally guilty, would you have felt dirty representing Mustafa in this case even if you were personally convinced of his legal guilt?

*****

Key Terms: theory of the defense, justification defense, excuse defense, relevant evidence, direct evidence, circumstantial evidence, real evidence, court reporter, chain of custody, fungible, opinion evidence, documentary evidence, best evidence rule, side bar conference, closing arguments, inflammatory language, jury instructions, preponderance of the evidence, probable cause, proof beyond a reasonable doubt

Additional Concepts: reluctance to convict sympathetic defendants, examples of justification defenses, examples of excuse defenses, duress defense explicated, demonstration of defense opening statement, categories of evidence, strategic reasons for soliciting irrelevant evidence, defense case-in-chief, demonstration of direct examination, demonstration of cross-examination, demonstration of closing arguments, prohibition against lawyers expressing personal opinions, demonstration of judge instructing jury

CHAPTER TWELVE

THE JURY DELIBERATES

Jury deliberations are marvelous things to contemplate. Though seven out of ten juries find themselves disagreeing on a verdict after the initial vote, only one jury in twenty remains split until the end.[1] Somehow, in 95 percent of the cases, juries are able to eventually reach a consensus. In other words, deliberation really works.

Even so, the first vote usually predicts the ultimate outcome.[2] Hence, the function of jury deliberations appears to be not so much one of changing the inevitable outcome as it is of getting the minority somehow to come on board with the majority. Rational persuasion, peer pressure, compromising, leadership, and fatigue all can play roles in achieving the sought after harmony.[3]

In the jury deliberations regarding the trial of Omar Mustafa for bigamy and statutory rape (see preceding two chapters), all of these factors would come into play. But, one of the jurors in that trial would have a pivotal role to play in the jury's discussions.

Rick Young was surprised that his fellow jurors elected him as their **jury foreperson**. As is the case with most juries, electing the foreperson was the very first item of business that the defendant Mustafa's jury addressed upon retiring to deliberate. Some juries simply elect "juror number one" (whomever that happens to be) as the foreperson. In Rick's case, however, he was likely selected due to an aura of leadership and a look of intelligent confidence that he naturally tended to project.

Rick's job as foreperson was to manage the debate and to keep the discussion focused on delivering a verdict. Rick also would be responsible for tallying up the votes and reporting the verdict to the court when the jury had finished.

---

1. Levine, James P. (1992). *Juries and Politics.* Belmont, CA: Wadsworth, at 150–151.

2. Tanford, Sarah and Steven Penrod. (1986). "Jury Deliberations: Discussion Content and Influence Processes in Jury Decision Making." *Journal of Applied Social Psychology,* 16:322–347.

3. For an excellent discussion of these factors, see Chapter 9, "Jury Room Politics," in Levine, *supra* note 1, at 150–168.

After selecting a jury foreperson, the second thing many juries do is to take an initial vote in order to see where things stand. This is what happened with Mustafa's jury as well. Rick Young suggested that everyone vote "so that we can see whether or not there is even anything really to argue about." This decision on the part of Rick was regrettable. Once people take a public position on something it is often harder for them to change positions quickly without looking flippant or weak. Though this last point never occurred to Rick, he did realize that things would probably not be resolved quickly: the initial vote resulted in seven in favor of conviction on all charges, and five in favor of complete acquittal.

The lack of agreement was cause for concern. Like many states, the state Mustafa was tried in required an **unanimous verdict** of either guilty or not guilty. Even if the vote had been eleven to one, the jury could not have gone home without trying to win the holdout over. And, here the tally was a disappointing seven to five. That meant in order to return a verdict, a large group of people would have to defect to one side or the other—not something that can be pulled off with minimal effort.

Not all states require unanimous verdicts. True, the tradition of unanimous verdicts dates back to the middle ages and had become an accepted feature of American justice no later than the 1700s.[4] But, when a few states in the twentieth century finally chose to break with this long tradition, the U.S. Supreme Court backed them. Defendants tried to argue that **non-unanimous verdicts** were unconstitutional in that they permitted convictions despite the apparent presence of reasonable doubt. But the highest court ruled that though a weak majority (e.g., seven to five or eight to four) would not be enough to support a conviction for a crime, a super-majority of nine jurors out of twelve would suffice. In the case of *Johnson v. Louisiana,* the Court ruled that:

> "Of course, the State's proof could be regarded as more certain if it had convinced all 12 jurors instead of only nine; it would have been even more compelling if it had been required to convince and had, in fact, convinced 24 or 36 jurors. But the fact remains that nine jurors—a substantial majority of the jury—were convinced by the evidence. In our view disagreement of three jurors does not alone establish reasonable doubt, particularly when such a heavy majority of the jury, after having considered the dissenters' views, remains convinced of guilt."[5]

---

4. See discussion in, *Apodaca v. Oregon,* 406 U.S. 404 (1972).
5. *Johnson v. Louisiana,* 406 U.S. 356 (1972).

Despite the generous views of the U.S. Supreme Court, the Mustafa jury was required to arrive at a unanimous verdict, leaving no room for even a single dissenter—no matter how irrational. (Mustafa's state, like most, also required the use of twelve people on a criminal jury—no fewer—despite the fact that juries as small as six have been held to be permissible as long as all six agree on the verdict. The Supreme Court does not know where the number twelve first came from (the twelve apostles perhaps), and has ruled that there is nothing in the constitution requiring twelve member juries (though at least six would be required to constitute a deliberative body.)[6]

So, foreperson Rick Young had his work cut out for him. Somehow, he had to guide twelve people to eventually think as one. Young himself believed Mustafa to be guilty. "The law is the law," he thought, "and Mustafa broke it." But, why couldn't all of the jurors see this? Rick decided to open the case up for discussion. He suggested that all jurors "take turns and briefly explain" why they held the positions they did. Rick hoped that by reasoning with one another, a consensus could be achieved.

Certainly, reasoning does sometimes cause people to change their minds. Everybody can probably think of a situation in which he or she changed a strongly held view in the face of arguments not previously considered that seemed very persuasive. Rick, like the other jurors who sought to convict, believed that those jurors wishing to acquit could be made to change their minds through the process of calm, rational discussion. Rick was wrong.

Rick began the discussion by expressing his views that the state clearly proved its case. "Did Mustafa sexually live with more than one woman at a time?" he asked. "Yes, Mustafa himself admitted that he did," Rick confirmed. "That is the crime of bigamy in our state, just like the judge explained. Did Mustafa have sex with two females who were under the legal age of consent? Yes, he did. He admits it. That is statutory rape. Mustafa's attorney wants us to feel sorry for this guy because he was living his religion or because of his culture or whatever. But feeling sorry for someone is not a defense. We are only here to decide if the state proved its case and it clearly has."

Other jurors quickly agreed with Rick. One said, "I like Mustafa but there is no denying that he is guilty." Another said, "I don't like Mustafa. I think what Mustafa did is disgusting. Who does he think he is having sex with two young girls? I don't care if they agreed or their parents agreed. It is wrong. And, where does he get off marrying two females at once? He lives in America and has to obey our country's laws whether he likes them or not."

---

6. *Burch v. Louisiana,* 441 U.S. 130 (1979).

Jurors wishing to acquit quickly raised the issue of duress. "Mustafa was told by the cleric that he would go to hell if he did not marry these two women," one of them emphasized. "Mustafa believed him just like you or I would if we lived in that community. The judge said that when people are threatened to the point that they can no longer think straight, then that can be a defense. Omar Mustafa acted under duress just as surely as someone being threatened by the Mafia with physical violence. Mustafa's parents, the girls' parents, and the cleric are all more guilty than young Omar. It would be wrong to convict Omar. I won't be party to that."

A couple of other jurors expressed approval with these comments and added to them. Jurors wanting to convict tried to point out that duress is a temporary condition but Mustafa continued to break the law even after he no longer feared going to hell. They also pointed out the fact that most Muslims live in monogamous relationships and that most marry adults, not underage girls. They suggested that this entire duress defense was just made up. But it was all to no avail. It began to dawn on foreperson Rick Young that rational persuasion was not going to get the job done. Something else was needed to get a consensus.

One of the best tools that juries have in bringing about a verdict is peer pressure. Nobody likes to look like a fool, not even in a group as temporary as a jury. There is a strong human instinct to conform. As the Japanese like to say, "the nail that sticks up will be hammered down." Classic movies like "*Twelve Angry Men*," that portray one juror using logic and reason to convert the other eleven to his enlightened ways propel the myth that reason can easily defeat peer pressure. In the real world, the one deviant juror nearly always caves in. The same apparently holds true when there are just two or three disagreeing with a large majority.[7] (In the late 1990s, Kevin Moore of Wilmington, North Carolina was convicted of first-degree murder pursuant to a botched armed robbery outside a local mall where the victim had been waiting in his car to pick up his daughter after work. After convicting Moore, several jurors claimed that they had been "pressured by other jurors into voting guilty." In fact, a couple of them had even cried while the verdict was being announced in court.[8] Pressure gets verdicts.)

The fact that jurors may feel pressured to convict is little grounds for an appeal. If appellate courts were to overturn every verdict in which peer pressure

---

7. See, Hastie, Reid, Steven D. Penrod and Nancy Pennington. (1983). *Inside the Jury.* Cambridge, Mass.: Harvard University Press.

8. Wilmington Star News. (1997). "Jurors Say They Were Pressured." March 25, 1997, p. A-4. See also, *North Carolina v. Moore*, 558 S.E.2d 189 (1998) in which the appeal was dismissed.

played a role there would be little certainty in verdicts. Appellate courts view jury verdicts like many people view sausages. The final product is nice but nobody wants to delve too deeply into how the product was made.

Of course, peer pressure works best when a small minority is pitted against a large majority. Things turn much more complicated when the two groups are nearly equal in size. In the case of Mustafa's jury, the vote was split seven to five. Peer pressure in such a circumstance is much less effective than would be in the case of a jury split eleven to one or ten to two.

Fortunately, another factor can play a helpful role in achieving a consensus. Not all jurors are created equal. As the deliberations continued, Rick began to notice an interesting pattern. Four of the jurors seemed to be dominating the discussions—two wanting to convict (including himself) and two wanting to acquit. The others seemed to sheepishly be looking to these four for guidance. Rick's observations were very astute. In fact, studies show that leaders play a key role in jury deliberations. Often, cases are decided by only a small handful of jurors. The others fall into line once these leaders are all on board one with another. This has been known for a long time. Early research on jury behavior found that leaders in the jury room—often people of high social status in the outside world—exert an influence disproportionate to their numbers.[9] Rick realized that it was not necessary to get all twelve of the jurors to agree on a verdict. It was only necessary to get the leaders to agree. Then everyone else might just capitulate to their collective judgment.

The challenge was how to get four opinionated, strong-willed, confident people to agree on a verdict. Both sets of two understood the other set's positions: all the rational persuasion in the world would likely prove ineffective. Neither set could be bullied by peer pressure: both sides had their followers among the remaining jurors, with neither group able to claim a strong majority. At this point the jury was **hung** (unable to reach a verdict). If the jury were to remain hung, the judge would have to eventually declare a **mistrial**. From the point of view of judicial economy, mistrials are about the worst thing that could happen. When a judge declares a mistrial, the case must be tried all over again from scratch with a brand new jury. If that jury remains hung, the process repeats itself until some jury is able to reach a verdict of either guilty or not guilty (of course, plea bargaining often takes place to bring closure in the interim).

---

9. Strodtbeck, Fred, R. James, and Carl Hawkins. (1957). "Social Status in Jury Deliberations." *American Sociological Review*, 22:713–719, as cited in Cole, George F. and Christopher E. Smith. (2004). *The American System of Criminal Justice*, 10th edition. Belmont, CA: Wadsworth/Thomson Learning, at 363.

This jury did not want to remain hung but its members were not sure how to proceed. While listening to the unfruitful discussions, juror Rick Young had a flashback to his youth when he applied for a job with the U.S. Foreign Service. Shortly after finishing college, Rick had taken the written exam to become a U.S. diplomat. He had wanted to pursue a career as a political officer in U.S. embassies around the world. Being very bright, Rick passed the written exam and was invited to Washington for oral interviews. Part of this interview process included a "leaderless group discussion." Rick was seated at a round table with five other candidates who were instructed to reach a group decision regarding how a fixed amount of money should be spent by a mythical governmental agency wishing to engage in charitable endeavors overseas. Six different charities were given as options to be funded. There was enough money to fund one or two charities but not enough to fund six different ones. Rick and the five other candidates each argued for a charity that he or she thought was most deserving. Each argued his or her individual positions brilliantly for the entire hour allocated without ever agreeing to any particular course of action. Rick later learned that he did not score very high on this exercise. Upon returning home, he was telling a friend of his with a graduate degree in organizational behavior about this when the friend suggested that what the Foreign Service was really looking for was somebody who could build a consensus, not just someone who could intelligently defend a position. "All six of you probably failed that exercise," he suggested. "They were looking for a particular kind of leader—one who could build a consensus." Rick never again tried for a job with the Foreign Service, but always swore that if he ever did, he would seek to be a consensus builder like his friend suggested. Well, it suddenly occurred to Rick that ultimate leadership in the jury room also boils down to the ability to build a consensus, that is, the ability to forge a compromise. Compromise is the essence of any democracy. It is the grease that keeps the machinery of Congress humming. Like the Congress, the American jury is a tiny democracy. Sometimes, compromise is the only way to get something accomplished.

Rick decided that he would suggest that everybody consider what legal scholars would call a **compromise verdict**. A compromise verdict is one in which juries agree to a middle position in order to reach a verdict that everyone can accept. For example, if some jurors want to convict someone of murder while the others want to completely acquit the defendant, a potential compromise might be to convict the defendant of manslaughter. Or, jurors wanting to convict someone of burglary might agree to a lesser theft conviction if that is what it takes to get those wishing to acquit of all charges to convict of something. In addition to compromising on charges regarding a single defendant, juries also sometimes compromise in a multi-defendant case by letting some less malicious defendants go free while convicting their more malicious accomplices.

Compromise verdicts have been blasted by some as cop-outs that allow convictions despite the apparent presence of reasonable doubt among some of the jurors. Such criticisms reach their zenith when juries compromise in such a way as to return what are obviously **inconsistent verdicts** (e.g., finding an alleged armed robber not guilty of robbery but guilty of theft when it would have been impossible to have stolen the goods without also committing the robbery). Nevertheless, the U.S. Supreme Court has ruled that compromise verdicts, even ones which result in inconsistent verdicts, are completely legal.[10] It is sausage being made.

Because of the potential for compromise verdicts, prosecutors sometimes have to make a very important strategy decision. Should the prosecutor only charge a suspect with one serious crime thus forcing a jury to either convict of that crime or else acquit? Or, is it better to give the jury a menu, thus allowing some wiggle room if that is needed in order to ensure a conviction of some type? For example, a prosecutor can charge a defendant who breaks into a home and steals something with burglary (a felony) and nothing else. This cuts off any possibility of the compromise verdict of theft (a misdemeanor). Of course, in this situation the prosecutor is basically telling the jury that if it wants to convict the defendant, it has no choice but to return the felony conviction. The prosecutor is banking on the hope that rather than let the defendant off entirely, the jury will convict on the sole serious charge. The downside is that by forcing a jury's hand in this manner, a prosecutor may also be increasing the odds for a complete acquittal. A more conservative but less glitzy strategy would be to charge the defendant with both burglary and theft.

The dilemma of whether or not to cut off the possibility of a compromise verdict is most dramatic in a homicide case. In a first degree murder case, a prosecutor can either charge a defendant with the generic crime of "criminal homicide" (allowing for the jury to pick between murder — including what degree of murder — and manslaughter) or the sole, specific charge of first de-

---

10. See, *United States v. Powell*, 469 U.S. 57 (1984), ruling that there is no constitutional right to a consistent verdict in a trial of a single defendant charged with multiple counts in which some counts result in convictions while others inconsistently result in acquittals; and see, *Harris v. Rivera*, 454 U.S. 339 (1981) ruling that there is no constitutional right to a consistent verdict involving the trial of multiple defendants in which one defendant is acquitted inconsistent with the conviction of another.

gree murder (forcing the jury to return a verdict of murder and thus a life sentence or else to acquit entirely).

In the case of Omar Mustafa, the prosecutor assigned the case chose to charge Mustafa with both statutory rape and the less serious crime of bigamy. The rape charges involved two different victims. All of this allowed for the possibility of a compromise verdict in the form of a conviction for the less serious bigamy charge, with the jury returning an acquittal for the more serious charges of raping the two girls. It also allowed for the possibility of a conviction of rape regarding one of the girls (e.g., the younger one who no longer wishes to be Omar's wife) with an acquittal regarding the rape of the other girl (who wishes to stay with Omar). Most prosecutors probably prefer not to gamble. Any conviction is better than none—at least this is how the prosecutor in Mustafa's case saw things. The Mustafa jury was given a full menu of charges. It could pick and choose and compromise how it saw fit.

One of the things helping Mustafa's jury to be in the mood for a compromise was fatigue. After hours of fruitless arguing the jurors wanted closure. The room began to feel oppressive. Boredom had sunk in. Many jurors were tired of fighting and wanted to go home. Even the most opinionated among them were now softened up for a compromise.

Yet, the leaders of the group who favored conviction on all counts were not sure they could ethically and legally acquit somebody of crimes that they were convinced had been committed. Furthermore, even some of the jurors who favored a complete acquittal of all charges felt guilty about their desired verdict. These jurors believed that the state had proven its case beyond a reasonable doubt but disagreed with the law itself. As one of them put it, "I think we should let Mustafa off even though he is guilty of statutory rape and bigamy. But, I don't know what to do because the state has proven its case. I usually agree that bigamy and statutory rapes should be punished. But in this particular instance, I just think it would be unjust to punish Omar for living according to his culture. Can we legally acquit Omar even though he technically did the crimes the state says he did? If we did convict him, would that be justice?"

What the jury was now struggling with was the concept of **jury nullification**. Jury nullification is the power that every jury possesses to find a defendant not guilty even though it is convinced that the state has proven the defendant's guilt beyond a reasonable doubt. Whether one sees jury nullification as an act of jury mercy or as an act of jury lawlessness, the U.S. Supreme Court has stated that tolerance of nullification is required because the existence of the practice is a "recognition of the jury's historic function, in criminal trials, as a check against arbitrary or oppressive exercises of power by the Executive Branch."[11]

There are many examples of jury nullification in American history. For example, Pennsylvania juries often balked at convicting local farmers living on the Mason-Dixon Line of violating the fugitive slave laws when they helped slaves escape to freedom by allowing their farm to be used as a stop on the underground railroad. Of course, jury nullification has its dark side as well. All white Southern juries in the late nineteenth century were notorious for refusing to convict members of white lynch mobs for meting out vigilante "justice" against African American victims.

Despite the existence of abuses, the argument could be made that jury nullification is not just a power that juries have, but a right. In fact, one could argue that even if it could be shown that judges are better than lay jurors at determining the facts of a case, lay juries should be retained precisely because of their power to act as a check on the government by nullifying laws with which they disagree. Yet, if nullification is a right, it is one that is almost always kept secret from juries. Only juries in two states (Indiana and Maryland) are told by trial judges that under their state constitutions the jury is the judge of the law as well as of the facts.[12] Judges in other states will give an opposite instruction. They instruct juries at the end of a trial that the jury's sole role is to determine the facts (what happened), not the law. (These states apparently believe that though juries have the power to nullify the law, that power does not necessarily give them a right to do so.) Judges in these states will lay down the law to the jury, and instruct the jurors to apply the facts as they find them to the law precisely as it has just been explained to them.

Whether one sees jury nullification as a virtue or as a vice, as a democratic right or as an act of anarchy, the fact remains that juries do have this power. Nobody can punish a jury in any way for exercising it. If, at the end of a trial resulting in an acquittal, a jury were to admit that it acquitted despite the state's having proven its case, the judge could not find the jury in contempt nor could the prosecutor charge its members with any crime. The power to nullify the law is absolute and double jeopardy bars any re-trial of the matter before another, supposedly more law-abiding, set of jurors.

The reason that juries do not more often consciously engage in jury nullification is simply because they are never told that they have the power to do so. Hence, juries lacking in boldness are left to nullify the law unconsciously

---

11. See Powell, *supra* note 10, at 65.
12. Levine, *supra* note 1, at 102.

by finding reasonable doubt in ridiculous manners. Such was the situation of the jury in the Omar Mustafa case. Not knowing that they had the power to nullify the law, those jurors convinced of technical guilt sought for ways to justify an acquittal based on manufactured reasonable doubt.

The compromise verdict that was taking shape involved the crafting of not guilty verdicts regarding the statutory rape of the two young brides, but a guilty verdict regarding the bigamy charge. The jury correctly sensed that in their state, the maximum punishment for bigamy was no where near as great as the maximum penalty for the statutory rapes of two young women. Yet, how could those jurors who felt obliged to follow the letter of the law acquit on the rape charges knowing that both girls were well below the age of consent? This is where the defense of duress would ultimately come in handy. But not until some other drama first played out to grease the skids for the duress argument to work its magic. This drama was that of the **Allen charge**.

The "Allen charge" gets its name from the 1896 case of *Allen v. United States,* which declared its legality.[13] Typically, an "Allen charge" works as follows. A hopelessly deadlocked jury gives up any hope of ever reaching a consensus. The jury, ashamed of its inability to return a verdict, sends a note to the trial judge explaining that it is hopelessly deadlocked and does not know how to further proceed. The judge then calls the jury back to the courtroom. At this point the jury probably feels defeated, yet is greatly relieved that the ordeal is finally about to end. Believing the judge has called it back to excuse it from any further deliberations, the jury learns to its horror that the judge has actually called it back to stress to it the importance of returning a verdict one way or the other, that it has a duty to do so if it possibly can, and that each juror should reconsider his or her positions unless by so doing so he or she would be doing violence to his or her conscience.

Allen charges work quite well. When the Mustafa jury got its Allen charge, it only took 45 minutes for it to return with a verdict, albeit a compromised one. Jurors who did not believe the defense theory of Mustafa acting under duress suddenly changed their mind. Perhaps he did feel coerced into having sex with these two young women. They could see how that might be possible. They could support an acquittal of the rape charges, especially since the bigamy charge would remain. They were not making up their own laws. They were finally finding some reasonable doubt.

Once again the jury in the Mustafa case sent a note to the judge by way of the bailiff. This time the note announced the good news, "We have a verdict."

---

13. *Allen v. United States,* 164 U.S. 492 (1896).

The judge had the bailiff telephone prosecutor Dan McGuire and defense attorney Mary Temple to summon them back to court. Both had offices nearby (in the case of McGuire, in the courthouse).

Upon hearing that there was a verdict in the case, both McGuire and Temple became nervous. The jury was out too long for the verdict to bode obviously well for a conviction (McGuire's experience was that juries who deliberate a very short time usually convict). But the jury had not deliberated so long as to bode obviously well for an acquittal (it was thought that very long deliberations often indicate the presence of reasonable doubt). McGuire and Temple ran into each other at the courthouse elevator as they were anxiously returning to court. Both looked at each other with the sympathetic eyes of fellow sufferers, not as adversaries. Jury verdicts are always high stakes events for attorneys.

When the bailiff saw that both attorneys had taken their seats in the courtroom, he opened the door to the deliberation room and had the jury come in. Once the last juror had sat down, the bailiff crossed the courtroom to a door that led to the judge's chambers. A few seconds later, the bailiff announced, "All rise," as the judge came in and took his seat.

"I hear that the jury has reached a verdict," the judge began. "The bailiff is instructed to retrieve the verdict slip from the jury foreperson."

Prosecutor McGuire and defense attorney Temple tried not to look too anxious as they studied the judge's face as he read the verdict slip to himself. The poker-faced judge gave no reaction whatsoever regarding what he read. Handing the verdict slip back to the bailiff, the judge asked the bailiff to confirm the verdict with the jury foreperson.

"Mr. Foreman," the bailiff began. "In the case of State vs. Omar Mustafa, on the count of statutory rape allegedly involving the underage female Sabah Falak, how do you find, guilty or not guilty?"

"Not guilty," Rick Young solemnly announced.

"Regarding the count of statutory rape allegedly involving Omar Mustafa and the underage female Hawaidah Falak, how do you find, guilty or not guilty?"

"Not guilty," the foreperson again confirmed.

At this point Omar Mustafa's heart began to soar just as prosecutor McGuire's began to sink. But it was not yet over.

"Mr. Foreman," continued the bailiff, "Regarding the count of bigamy allegedly involving Omar Mustafa and the females Hawaidah Falak and Sabah Falak, how do you find, guilty or not guilty?"

At this point not a single juror's eyes were looking at the defendant. Up until this point several always had been eyeballing Mustafa. "Oh crap," thought Temple as she noticed this. "Here comes some bad news."

"Guilty," Rick Young announced. He continued to look straight ahead at the bailiff even after he had delivered the news.

The bailiff continued the ritual by summarizing to the jury that it had just found the defendant not guilty of those counts involving statutory rape but guilty of the charge of bigamy. "So say you all?" the bailiff asked the jury collectively after he summarized the verdicts. The jurors all seemed to nod their heads in the affirmative.

"Would you like to poll the jury?" the judge asked Mary Temple. "No Your Honor, that will not be necessary," she replied. If the jury had convicted her client of the rapes she probably would have asked the judge to **poll the jury** (individually ask each juror separately if he or she agreed with the verdict). But since she could claim some measure of victory, she was not in the mood for what was virtually always an exercise in futility.

Dan McGuire was not unhappy with the verdict. He too could claim a measure of victory. "A conviction is a conviction," he always liked to say. Besides, McGuire did not hate Mustafa like he hated some defendants. He was not particularly upset that the jury chose to exhibit some level of mercy, however irrational he thought that mercy to be. The bottom line for McGuire was that he got a conviction that he could add to the "win" column of the win/lose trial score card he kept in his office desk top drawer. Like most prosecutors in America, McGuire could claim he won more often than he lost. (Studies suggest that prosecutors typically win between two-thirds and four-fifths of cases they try in terms of a conviction on at least one count charged.)[14]

Functions of the Jury Trial

A. Fact Finding

The jury trial of Omar Mustafa, like all jury trials, served many functions. The most important official function of the jury trial is to determine the facts of a case. In assessing whether or not the criminal jury trial is an effective in-

---

14. See, Vidmar Neil, Sara Sun Beale, Mary Rose, and Lewis Donnelly. (1997). "Should We Rush to Reform the Criminal Jury?" *Judicature,* 80:286–290 which cites that about two-thirds of trials result in a conviction; See also, Reaves, Brian A. and Timothy C. Hart. (1999). *Felony Defendants in Large Urban Counties, 1996: State Court Case Processing Statistics.* Washington, D.C.: Bureau of Justice Statistics, U.S. Government Printing Office, which cites that 84% of jury trials result in a conviction.

strument in determining what really happened in a case, one must distinguish the concept of "truth" and the concept of "**legal guilt**." Because juries are instructed to find that critical case facts exist only if they are convinced of them beyond a reasonable doubt (an extremely high standard indeed), one is struck with the reality that their goal is not the heroic one of finding the truth, but rather the more manageable task of deciding whether the state has proven essential facts beyond a reasonable doubt. This means that many times facts are not found to have been legally proved, although the jury believes them to be probably true, and although in fact they are true. Because of this reasonable doubt standard, juries may do a poor job at convicting the guilty, but hopefully a good job at acquitting the innocent.

Of course, several negative factors interfere with the ability of the jury to do its formal function of fact finding. Too often, the jury selection process is used by defense attorneys to peremptorily strike from the panel all jurors of assumed high intelligence in the hope that jurors of lower intelligence are more easily confused (hence, possessing reasonable doubt). If one believes that higher intelligence facilitates accuracy in determining the facts of a case, the fact that peremptory strikes can be used in this manner is distressing, especially when one remembers that many highly educated people are clever enough and busy enough to somehow avoid jury duty to begin with.

Another negative factor interfering with fact finding is the lack of diversity that can exist on some juries. As any statistician knows, twelve people is hardly a large enough sample to adequately produce a true cross section of any diverse community. Minorities, who constitute a disproportionate percentage of criminal defendants, all too often see few of their own sitting in the jury box. The same holds true for young defendants. To the degree that a truly diverse and **representative cross section of the community** produces a synergy that helps determine what happened in a particular case, we have cause for concern. Juries also, can bring with them biases based on factors other than race and age, such as gender and economic class, which a mere sample of twelve might find difficulty in smoothing over.

Other problems with the jury's fact finding mission may be attributable to inequality of legal representation. Much more so than plea bargaining, trials are based on the notion of an **adversarial contest**. However, some attorneys are better adversaries than others. Resources at the parties' disposal also are often unequal. The state has the resources of police investigators and crime labs, while most criminal defendants are lucky just to have a devoted and competent lawyer. In addition to having the police available to do much of their leg work for them, prosecutors also have the advantage of polished, experienced witnesses such as detectives, crime lab officials, and other **professional**

witnesses, while defendants must often rely solely on rough presentations made by witnesses unaccustomed to public speaking.

Not all the aspects of the jury trial, however, combine against criminal defendants when it comes to the trial's fact finding function. Truthful but illegally obtained evidence is sometimes suppressed and kept from the jury entirely. Prior records, though of great potential interest to a jury, are kept secret out of fear of undue prejudice (though what jury would not want to know that the drunk driver who claims he refused the breath test merely out of moral outrage was convicted of drunk driving four times in the past two years). Witnesses, vital to the case, often cannot be relied upon to show up for court as summoned . Such witness "**no shows**" probably plague the prosecution side more than the defense since the prosecution has the burden of proof.

B. Other Functions

As important as the fact finding function of the jury trial is, the jury trial performs a multitude of other functions as well. One things juries do is that they **correct the law** by simply refusing to apply it. This is, in a sense, a very democratic thing to do as no doubt de Tocqueville would agree. In the case of the Omar Mustafa trial discussed in this chapter, ordinary people with no connection to the government were provided with a mechanism to show mercy to someone whom they found somewhat sympathetic though technically guilty. Though some are offended by the notion of juries nullifying law, it can be argued that this mechanism acts as a check on not just the government securing an unjust conviction (as earlier discussed), but also causes government officials to think twice before even bothering to charge somebody in the first place. What prosecutor would even want to bring someone to trial on a charge that jurors think is no big deal or on one which causes jury members to consider, "but for the grace of God, there go I."

Another function that jury trials arguably perform is that they help bring a **false aura of legitimacy** to the court by reassuring people that they—and not professional elites like lawyers and judges—are the ones who typically decide guilt or innocence of their fellow citizens. Because most lay people are ignorant of the magnitude of plea bargaining, the mere fact that jury trials sometime take place produces a belief that the judicial system is directly accountable to the people. It is unfortunate that this belief is somewhat misplaced, but the fact that trials do occasionally occur does help uphold the comforting myth.

Jury trials also help to affirm to prosecutors, defense counsel, and judges the attractiveness of plea bargaining. Whether one wins or loses, trials are stressful and time consuming endeavors. Like Dan McGuire and Mary Temple in the Mustafa story, one feels relieved when they are finally over. These necessary, occasional experiences with stress and time consumption no doubt serve to reinforce the tremendous advantages of plea bargaining to the courthouse community.

Jury trials also are very educational. They school lawyers as to the frequent unpredictability of juries. Neither prosecutor McGuire nor defense attorney Temple could guess as to how the jury in the Mustafa case would ultimately rule. To the degree that lawyers, like other human beings, value certainty of outcome, jury verdicts can serve as strong reminders of the preferability of processing cases via plea bargains.

Finally, jury trials serve one enormously important role. They bring finality to a case that simply cannot be negotiated or disposed of by any other means. Some defendants simply will not plead guilty no matter how compelling the evidence against them is, or how attractive an offer is made them. The trial then acts as a final escape for defense counsel, prosecutor, and judge.

In sum, the jury trial serves a multitude of functions, of which accurate fact finding is just one, albeit an important one. This cannot be any other way, for the trial is a ritual rich in meaning, and for most people too powerful a symbol to ever serve just one purpose.

*****

Questions for Class Discussion

1. The book points out that the first vote in jury deliberations usually strongly suggests the ultimate outcome. Why do you suppose this is so? Does this mean that deliberations are meaningless in most cases? What does the book suggest is the main purpose of the deliberation process in most cases?

2. Seven out of ten juries find themselves disagreeing on a verdict after the initial vote. About what percentage of cases do eventually go on to reach a consensus? What are some of the factors that come into play that help a consensus to be forged?

3. The Supreme Court has ruled that unanimous verdicts are not required by the Constitution. Do you think that was a good ruling? If some jurors are not sure of guilt, does that suggest reasonable doubt in the case over-

all? According to the Supreme Court, what percentage of a jury must agree in order to have a verdict?

4. What is meant by the following factors which the chapter suggests play important roles in helping juries achieve verdicts: rational persuasion, peer pressure, compromise, leadership, and fatigue?

5. How does rational persuasion play a role in helping juries reach consensus? Can you think of a time when you held a strong view about something only to change your mind based on someone's rational arguments?

6. The book discusses the important role that peer pressure plays in helping juries to achieve a consensus. Is peer pressure a good thing or a bad thing for the process? If you were on a jury, would you likely give in to peer pressure?

7. What does the book say is the "fallacy" of the movie, "Twelve Angry Men?" Do you agree that the movie is probably not very true to life?

8. Why is leadership so important in helping the system get its verdicts? If you were on a jury, would you more likely be a leader in the deliberations or more likely remain disengaged from the debates? What types of people do you think tend to emerge as leaders in the deliberation room?

9. What is meant by a "hung jury?" What happens to the case if it is "hung?" Why do you suppose defense lawyers often consider a "hung jury" to be a victory of sorts?

10. What is the "Allen charge?" Is it generally effective? Should judges even resort to "Allen charges," or just let the jury go home?

11. What is a "compromise verdict?" Are compromise verdicts legal? Are they fair?

12. How does fatigue play a role in helping juries reach consensus? Have you ever "given in" to some person arguing with you due to fatigue? Can you give an example?

13. What is meant by the term, "jury nullification?" Why does it take place? Can you give some historical examples, both good and bad, of jury nullification? Do you think jury nullification is a right juries have or merely a power?

14. Should juries be explicitly told of the opportunity they have to nullify the law? What are the pro's and con's of that?

15. Now that you know of jury nullification, what types of crimes, if any, do you disagree with to the point that you would be tempted to nullify the law as a juror?

16. Do juries truly represent a fair cross section of the community? Is it statistically likely for them to do so when a sample of only twelve people are chosen? Should we, at least in serious cases, make juries larger in order to increase the odds for a fair cross section?

17. Does diversity on a jury help the verdict process or hinder it? How? Does diversity on a jury help the truth-finding mission? How?

18. What is meant by the concept of "legal guilt?" How does it differ from "factual guilt?" Would you feel comfortable as a defense attorney defending someone who you knew was guilty in fact but perhaps not "legally guilty?"

19. The book suggests that juries serve functions other than mere fact-finding. What does it mean when it suggests that juries also help "correct the law," bring a "false aura of legitimacy" to the court, and help affirm to lawyers and judges the "attractiveness of plea bargaining?"

20. Are juries competent to do the job we ask them to do? Do average Americans have what it takes to do the job or are lay jurors too easily misled by crafty attorneys? Who, if anyone, could do a better job of deciding guilt or innocence? Even if it could be somehow proven that judges would do a better job at deciding guilt or innocence, might we still want to use juries for some other reason(s)?

*****

Key Terms: jury foreperson, unanimous verdict, non-unanimous verdicts, hung jury, mistrial, compromise verdict, inconsistent verdicts, jury nullification, Allen charge, poll the jury, legal guilt, cross section of the community, adversarial contest, professional witnesses, no shows, correct the law, false aura of legitimacy

Additional Concepts: effectiveness of deliberations, rational persuasion, peer pressure, leadership, juror fatigue, fallacy of *Twelve Angry Men,* consensus building, prosecutorial strategy of not giving jury a choice, relevance of length of deliberation regarding probably verdict, percentage of trials resulting in convictions, fact-finding function of jury trial, impediments to jury's fact-finding function, other functions of the jury trial

CHAPTER THIRTEEN

SENTENCING

Judge Liz Winters of the Court of Common Pleas of Jefferson County enjoyed many things about her job. She liked the prestige her office gave her. She enjoyed the $145,000 yearly salary she pulled down for a mere forty hour work week. She appreciated the job security, the paid holidays, and the generous pension plan. She kind of liked people calling her "Your Honor." What she did not enjoy was the heavy, post-trial responsibility she had of sentencing people convicted in her courtroom. Unlike some of her colleagues who eventually became accustomed to meting out life-altering sentences, Winters could never get used to messing with people's lives. She felt a profound moral duty to be careful.

Most sentences did not cause even the sensitive Liz Winters much pause. Fines, probation, and even short jail sentences were meted out by her in somewhat assembly-line fashion. But the big cases calling for the possibility of long imprisonment turned Winters into a deeply reflective person. This was not because the pudgy, middle-aged judge was soft on crime. Indeed, she sometimes punished defendants in excess of what the prosecutor argued for. Judge Winters simply did not want to make an error when it came to playing God.

A lot can be learned about a society by the way it sentences its criminals. As Winston Churchill once said, "the mood and temper of the public with regard to the treatment of crime and criminals is one of the most unfailing tests of the civilization of any country."[1]

In Singapore, minor mischief makers are sometimes beaten with a cane.[2] In Saudi Arabia, a thief's offending hand is cut off, and fornicators can receive one hundred lashes.[3] In 1997, a Yemeni court sentenced two murderers to be

---

1. Krantz, Sheldon and Lynn S. Branham. (1991). *The Law of Sentencing, Corrections and Prisoner's Rights.* St. Paul, MN: West Publishing Co., p. 2.

2. Readers may recall the celebrated news story of the 1990s in which an American teenager caught vandalizing cars in Singapore was sentenced to be beaten with a cane for his misdeeds.

3. Souryal, Sam S., Dennis W. Potts, and Abdullah I. Alobied. (1994). "The Penalty of Hand Amputation for Theft in Islamic Justice." *Journal of Criminal Justice,* 22(3):249–265.

publicly crucified.[4] At the other extreme, Norwegians like to pamper their inmates with bowling alleys.[5]

In the United States it is unconstitutional to use corporal punishment in any way against someone convicted of a crime, yet, executions—including the potentially torturous electric chair and gas chamber—are lawful. Imprisonment is a very popular sentence in America. It is so popular that America, despite a perception among its public that courts are far too lenient on crime, leads the world in the percentage of its citizens incarcerated (the American prison population quadrupled between 1980 and 2003, giving it the dubious honor of world per capita incarceration leader).[6]

Judge Winters was not particularly worried about what was going on in the rest of the country or the rest of the world. But she was very concerned about the appropriateness of the sentences she gave out. Her goal was to be neither too harsh nor too lenient.

On a sunny, cold November day, Judge Winters sat stiffly in the old leather chair in her chambers pouring over the files of three defendants whom she would be sentencing the next day. Other files involving obvious minor penalties sat on the floor by the judge's desk, having been already mentally processed by her.

Judge Winters knew that virtually any sentence that she were to give the three remaining serious defendants would be upheld on appeal. Living in a state that did not use mandatory sentencing guidelines, their fates were entirely in her hands. Appellate courts in such states grant enormous deference to the discretion that trial judges have in crafting appropriate sentences.[7]

One case Judge Winters was contemplating involved Adam Seltzer, the seventeen year old son of a drug dealer who worked as a reluctant "mule" for his Dad. The boy turned down a plea bargain of six months in jail because it was contingent upon his testifying against his father. Under local law the youth was tried as an adult (sixteen was the age of adult accountability), and was reluctantly convicted by a jury of sympathetic grown-ups. The state sentencing guidelines (more on this later) recommended but did not mandate a sentence of somewhere between 48 and 54 months in prison.

The second serious sentencing case involved Gus Hall, a pathologically lazy thirty-two-year old who lived in his parents' basement and had a long record

---

4. "Yemeni Court Uphold Crucifixions." (1997). *Associated Press Wire Service*, August 31.

5. Conversation with a Norwegian criminal justice student, Spring 2001.

6. "Incarceration Rate in U.S. is World's Highest." (2003). *Deseretnews.com*, August 18.

7. *Solem v. Helm*, 463 U.S. 277 (1983).

of thefts and burglaries (but not of employment). Gus had been in and out of the criminal justice system his whole adult life. Lately, his crimes had become much less frequent ever since he learned that he was dying of liver cancer. At first he avoided criminality due to wanting to behave during whatever time he had left. But, soon his law-abiding ways were probably due mostly to being too tired from chemotherapy to do crimes. Despite having gone "straight" for more than two years, Gus was eventually caught stealing vodka out of a neighbor's house when the neighbor came home unexpectedly sick one Tuesday. Judge Winters felt that Gus, the incorrigible thief and prowler, deserved a lengthy prison sentence. Yet, to impose one would likely result in the correctional system having to pay for Gus's expensive, end-of-life medical treatments.

The third case which occupied the judge's thoughts concerned Claudette Norris, a twenty-two-year old convicted of voluntary manslaughter for having shot her woman-hating husband in the back as he walked out the front door following a heated argument. Earlier that night, the husband had slapped Claudette around for having forgotten to pick up some beer for him at the grocery store on her way home from work. Claudette, suffering from many bruises and fractured bones from earlier beatings, was expected to bring home the couple's sole paycheck, do all of the domestic chores, and to comply with her husband's every command, including sex whether she wanted it or not. What finally led to the shooting was the poor woman's discovery that her chronically unemployed husband was having a daytime romance with his old girlfriend, whom he was lavishly entertaining with his wife's hard-earned money. The sentencing guidelines for voluntary manslaughter coolly recommended a period of incarceration of somewhere between 72 and 81 months.

In deciding an appropriate sentence, Judge Winters needed to take into account what she was trying to accomplish. Traditionally, there are **four classical goals of criminal sentencing**. These are rehabilitation, deterrence, incapacitation, and retribution.[8]

Rehabilitation assumes a medical model of crime. Crime is seen as a social illness which can and should be "cured." If Judge Winters were to think that Adam (the reluctant drug "mule"), Gus (the incorrigible thief), and Claudette (the desperate, battered husband-killer) suffered from social diseases that once cured would put them on the path of virtuous conduct, she would probably

---

8. There are many discussions regarding the goals of criminal sentencing. For one such discussion, see LaFave, Wayne R. and Austin W. Scott, Jr. (1986). "Purposes of the Criminal Law—Theories of Punishment." In (same authors) *Criminal Law (2d ed.)*, pp. 22–29.

want to punish them only to that degree that was minimally necessary to effectuate the "cure." There would be no point in inflicting pain beyond that which was necessary to prevent future occurrence of crime. If Judge Winters were indeed to embrace rehabilitation as the primary goal of her sentencing, perhaps she would give a short jail sentence to Adam (who seemed unlikely to recidivate), a long prison sentence to Gus (whose many past stays in prison apparently had yet to produce the desired curative effect), and a relatively soft sentence to Claudette (since she no longer had an abuser to neutralize).

Deterrence has as its goal the convincing of people that crime is not in their best interests. It assumes people are rational and can intelligently do a costs-benefits analysis. Who would risk not wearing a seat belt if the penalty were life in prison?

If Judge Winters had deterrence as her primary sentencing goal, she would have to decide if she were interested in specific deterrence, general deterrence, or both. **Specific deterrence** seeks to convince the actual, individual offender to refrain from repeating the misconduct in the future (e.g., Judge Winters might give Adam the drug "mule" a taste of jail so that he is scared out of ever transporting drugs again). **General deterrence** seeks to convince the general population to avoid committing a crime (e.g., Judge Winters might make Adam the drug "mule" serve time as an example to the rest of us of what happens to drug couriers). For deterrence to work, the likelihood and severity of the punishment must exceed the potential benefits of the crime enough to scare people out of committing it.

Incapacitation has as its goal the removal of an offender from society so that the offender cannot do any more harm, at least as long as the incapacitation lasts. Incapacitation does not seek to rehabilitate or deter, it simply seeks to "remove the problem" and thus provide relief. This relief can be temporary (as in a five year prison sentence). The relief could also be permanent (as in the case of life imprisonment, execution, or banishment). In the case of cancer-victim Gus Hall, Judge Winters might wish to give him a lengthy sentence so that he will die in prison. Perhaps she will not care if he gets rehabilitated or learns that crime does not pay. At least he will never have the opportunity to burglarize again.

With regards to incapacitation, some critics (including defense lawyers) like to argue that prison without rehabilitation is merely "**warehousing**" defendants who will simply re-offend when they get out. They say that "warehousing" does nobody any good. The counter-argument to this is that having a respite from someone for awhile is much better than having no respite at all. Critics of the "warehousing" argument also point out that it is important to remember that many types of crime are strongly correlated with youth. If we incapacitate a person during his or her youthful years, the person may to a large degree "age out" of crime by the time he or she is released.

Retribution is the fourth classical goal of criminal sentencing. Bluntly put, retribution is revenge. Diplomatically put, retribution is **just deserts**. But, either way, retribution has as its goal the settling of a score: "an eye for an eye, a tooth for a tooth" or "you do the crime, you do the time." Retribution assumes that criminals are not just mere victims of bad genes or bad environments, but have free will to choose right from wrong (and they choose wrong).

Some people believe that retribution is an old-fashioned, unenlightened reason to punish people and cannot be ethically justified. However, courts have consistently ruled that (ethical or not) it is a legal basis for crafting a sentence (e.g., even if the death penalty does not deter murder it still could be justified as lawful retribution). If Judge Winters had retribution as her primary sentencing goal, she might feel a greater desire to punish Gus the burglar than to punish Claudette the husband killer, even though manslaughter is generally thought to be a much more serious crime than burglary. After all, the judge might feel that Claudette's victim (unlike Gus's neighbor), had it coming.

In deciding the appropriate sentences for Adam, Gus, and Claudette, Judge Winters had a lot of things to consider, not the least of which was whether she favored rehabilitation, deterrence, incapacitation, or retribution (or some combination of these) as her primary objective(s). Typically, Judge Winters tended to lean towards rehabilitation in non-violent crimes and retribution in violent ones. But none of the three of the cases before her today was typical. Claudette's homicide was violent but the judge did not feel an impulse toward retribution. Gus's burglary was non-violent but Winters was sick of seeing him in court and wanted some just deserts. Adam's reluctant drug transporting was a case unique in its own way. Fortunately for Judge Winters, she had something in each file which she found to be of enormous help in reaching a tentative, pre-hearing decision. This helpful something was the "pre-sentence investigation report."

The Pre-Sentence Investigation Report

Like Judge Winters, Phil Moore of the Jefferson County Adult Probation and Parole Office took his duties (as a pre-sentence investigator) very seriously. Phil first started with the probation and parole office just out of college, supervising a standard caseload of about 120 **probationers** (people who are not sentenced to a period of incarceration) and **parolees** (people who are sentenced to a period of incarceration but who get out early). He spent most of his time ensuring that clients had not been rearrested for any new crimes, pestering them to find jobs, serving as a collection agent for their fines and restitution payments, and checking them for potentially "hot" urine. After five years he wanted to try something different without having to find a new employer. He asked his manager if he could join the probation office's pre-sentence investigation unit the next time a vacancy occurred. One did occur a few months later and Phil switched hats.

The first time Phil did a report for a judge he was meticulous and thorough. He knew that judges about to sentence someone relied heavily upon such **pre-sentence investigation reports** (documents prepared by specialized probation officers at the request of a sentencing judge to provide background information on a defendant as an aid in sentencing). Early in his new role, Phil was taught by his office colleagues that sentencing judges need to be familiar with the **whole person**. Judges need to know all relevant facts about every facet of a defendant's life in order to avoid turning the sentencing decision into a mere game of chance.[9] Phil was told that though he should not bore judges with too much detail, it was better to err on the side of providing too much background than too little. He took all of these instructions to heart.

Every pre-sentence report was unique but Phil tried to include certain things in nearly every report he wrote for a judge. These standard aspects are found in Table 1.

Phil quickly became accustomed to writing pre-sentence reports for judges. However, there was always that unusual case that presented itself now and then that called for something much more than formulaic writing and standard contents. Even so, an occasional unusual case was part of the job and was to be expected. What really surprised Phil one Monday morning when he perused the new files just assigned to him was getting three unusual cases in his lap all at once: the cases of Adam Seltzer, Gus Hall, and Claudette Norris.

Phil read each of the three files with interest. "Holy crap," he said to himself when finished. "These will take some extra thought." Phil usually liked extra thought but not on Monday mornings. Fortunately, his first interview with any of the three was not scheduled until the next day (Tuesday), with the other two scheduled for Wednesday and Thursday, respectively. That gave Phil all of Monday to get a head start on these files. He noticed that his supervisor was thoughtful enough not to assign him any other new reports to prepare that week.

---

9. See, *United States v. Grayson*, 438 U.S. 41 (1978).

Table 1   Standard Contents of a Pre-Sentence Investigation Report

Defendant Characteristics	Victim Impact
Age, education, employment history, prior record, drug and alcohol issues, family background, medical condition, probation/ parole history, past attempts at rehabilitation, defendant's version of crime, acceptance of responsibility, remorse, cooperation with law enforcement, whether or not defendant committed apparent perjury, current rehabilitation efforts, compensation efforts, degree defendant's conduct was induced by another	Victim's version of crime, pain and suffering, victim provocation if any, relationship to defendant, desire for compensation, desire for justice, ongoing injuries, age and other demographic information

Miscellaneous	
Sentencing guidelines recommendations, investigator's recommendations and reasoning	

Source: Author's professional recollection and Chapter 25 ("Sentencing") in F. Miller, R. Dawson, G. Dix and R. Parnas, *Prosecution and Adjudication (5th ed.),* New York: Foundation Press (2000).

Phil spent the rest of Monday organizing police reports, collecting rap sheets, telephoning victims, telephoning arresting officers, and otherwise preparing for the interviews with the defendants themselves. Tuesday came soon enough. At 2:00 p.m. sharp, Phil went out into the office reception area to find Gus Hall, the prowler with liver cancer, smoking a cigarette as he waited to be summoned to the back offices.

"Gus Hall?" Phil inquired.

"Yeah, what's up?" Gus replied. Gus put his cigarette out on the floor with his shoe as he rose to meet Phil. Gus flicked the butt into a trash receptacle as he rose to full measure.

"Follow me please," Phil said. "By the way, for future reference, this is a smoke free building."

"Oh, sorry, sir," Gus responded. Phil could not tell if Gus was being sarcastic or respectful. He was used to respect on solemn occasions such as this, yet Gus's deferential words did not quite match his strangely confident manner.

"Please sit down, Mr. Hall," Phil requested as he motioned Gus to a seat in front of his functional, metallic desk. Phil saw Gus heave an unrestrained sigh of boredom as both took their seats.

"Do you have somewhere more important to be right now?" Phil curtly asked. Phil was not in the mood to put up with any disrespect.

"No, I'm sorry," Gus apologized. "It's my cancer medication. It makes me drowsy."

"Oh, I see," Phil contritely acknowledged as he eyeballed Gus. Phil felt some shame regarding his lack of sensitivity until he saw what appeared to be a smirk appear on Gus's face. Now he did not know what to think. "Is this guy playing with my head?" Phil wondered.

Phil hoped that he could gain mastery of the interview by explaining his role in the pre-sentence stage of Gus's case. He informed Gus of what a pre-sentence report was and how the judge might use it to help determine Gus's sentence. He explained that though the judge ultimately decided the sentence, he often used the pre-sentence report as an important resource.

Phil went on to tell Gus that he would need to ask him some questions so that he could write his report to the court. He told Gus to answer each question honestly and that honesty impressed Phil very favorably. This little speech, though routine and generally calming to Phil, did little to dispel the awkwardness he felt in the presence of Gus Hall. Gus unbelievably seemed to alter between states of boredom and amusement as Phil soberly lectured. Phil cleared his throat and began his questioning.

"Tell me about the crime the jury convicted you of," began Phil.

"They say I broke into my neighbor's house and stole some vodka. The neighbor claimed he recognized me when he came home from work. The jury refused to believe my testimony that I was at home at the time watching television and that the neighbor simply confused me with someone else."

"Are you still claiming that you did not do the crime?" asked Phil incredulously.

"Look, the jury said I did it so legally I did," Gus said. "That's all that really matters, right?"

"Are you sorry for what you did?" asked Phil.

"Well, even if someone did steal some vodka from a neighbor I don't see what the big deal is. Besides, I got bigger problems to worry about. The doctor says I've got 12 months at most to live, Phil."

"Please don't call me Phil. I am the man writing your pre-sentence report. You may call me Mr. Moore."

"Sorry, Mr. Moore, sir," Gus hastily responded. Somehow, his use of the word "sir" seemed to swing the pendulum too rapidly in the other direction to seem sincere.

The interview continued for thirty more minutes. At times, Gus seemed to be very cooperative. He readily confirmed the former offenses on his rap sheet, his spotty employment history, and his life history of alcohol abuse. He showed appropriate embarrassment when Phil Moore went over his failed attempts at past rehabilitation. He exhibited signs of sympathy when Phil mentioned how his neighbor felt the need to purchase a gun and an alarm system after the break-in and theft of the vodka. But when Phil asked Gus about his cancer, Gus seemed to get cocky again, as if the fact that he had a terminal illness somehow empowered him. When Phil asked Gus what punishment he felt would be appropriate in his case, Gus just smiled and said, "surprise me."

Following the interview with Gus, Phil was uncharacteristically at a loss of how to proceed. He looked to his state's sentencing guidelines to give himself some guidance in this matter. **Sentencing guidelines** typically take the form of a grid created by a state legislature which indicates to a sentencing judge the penalty that the state legislature deems appropriate for a particular crime in light of a defendant's particular criminal history. The pre-sentence investigator determines the proposed sentence from the grid and includes it in his or her report to the judge. (Such grids work better in determinate sentencing states rather than in indeterminate sentencing states since the latter rely on a parole board to determine the ultimate time to be served.)

To understand how a sentencing guidelines grid works, picture a graph produced by X and Y axes just like in a high school geometry lesson. The X-axis (the horizontal one) represents the seriousness of the current offense on a scale of one to ten—with shoplifting perhaps being a one, burglary of a non-residence a five, armed robbery an eight, and murder a ten. One can look up the score for any crime by looking at a detailed list of "crime scores" also published by the legislature.

The Y-axis (the vertical one) on this graph represents the prior record score of the defendant, often on a scale of one to six or so. Each prior felony conviction might generate one point towards the overall prior record score, while every two misdemeanors together might generate one point (for a maximum score up to six points).

Once having determined both numbers, the scorer plots the defendant's position on a graph included in the sentencing guidelines materials (e.g., to the right six on the X-axis and up two on the Y-axis). This point will land in a cell (a box on the graph) with numbers in it. These numbers (e.g., 13 to 18 months) represent the presumptive range of months in jail or prison which the legislature deems appropriate for this perpetrator (in this case, the legislature is saying it believes a sentencing judge should give the perpetrator somewhere between thirteen and eighteen months of incarceration, the precise number of months depending upon the facts of the particular case). In other words, the judge still has some discretion at sentencing, but if he or she follows the legislature's wishes, not very much. Obviously, the farther a defendant's score proceeds horizontally and vertically from the "0,0" point of origin, the longer one's incarceration will be (those who have tiny scores for current offense seriousness coupled with low prior record scores fall into cells indicating months of probation rather than months of incarceration time).

In some jurisdictions, legislatures have developed **mandatory sentencing guidelines,** meaning that judges absolutely must follow them. In these states, almost all sentencing discretion is transferred away from judges to the state legislature (much to the chagrin of judges who feel their traditional powers eroded). In other jurisdictions, legislatures have developed **non-mandatory sentencing guidelines,** which judges must consider before passing sentence but which they are then free to deviate from if they so choose (if they do deviate from the guidelines, however, many states require the judge to state on the record why he/she chose to do so). In still other jurisdictions, state legislatures have not developed any type of sentencing guidelines whatsoever, leaving it completely up to judges to use their traditional powers to give any sentence they feel appropriate (as long as the statutory maximum sentence allowed for a particular offense is not exceeded).

In pre-sentence investigator Phil Moore's state, sentencing guidelines existed but the legislature chose to make them merely advisory to judges rather than mandatory. In practice, Phil noticed that most judges most of the time gave sentences harmonious with what the local state guidelines suggested, but deviations from the guidelines (including some whoppers) did regularly occur.

Phil Moore sat down and carefully calculated Gus Hall's sentencing guideline scores. First, he calculated his current offense gravity score by looking up "burglary" on the list provided by the legislature. Under "burglary" he saw several sub-listings and scanned down until he saw a subcategory labeled "residence—victim home at the time" right below "residence—victim not home." He wrote down the number next to "residence—victim home at the time," which was the number "seven." Next, Moore calculated the prior record score. This did not take long. The maximum anyone could get was a six and it took Moore two seconds to establish that Gus Hall earned a six (with all his prior felonies and misdemeanors he could have earned a twelve if that were possible).

With the two scores in hand, Moore plotted Gus' results on the sentencing grid and saw that he landed in a box that suggested a sentence anywhere from 80–87 months in prison. "Gus should know better than to commit a felony with a prior record score of six," Phil told himself. Moore immediately realized that such a sentence would constitute a life sentence for the cancer-stricken Gus. Moore did not feel that Gus deserved to finish out his life in prison but neither did he feel that a sentence under twelve months (the maximum amount of time Gus's doctors estimated Gus had left to live) was a fit punishment for Gus's crime. Complicating the matter further, Moore knew that the strapped prison (rather than private insurance or federal medicaid) would have to pay for Gus's expensive treatments, including hyper-expensive, end-of-life care, if Gus got the sentence he really deserved.

"Why do I have to have a case like this?" Phil Moore lamented to his boss.

"That's what we're paying you the not-so-big bucks for," the pleasant but unhelpful supervisor told him.

Moore did not know what to recommend to the judge. He suddenly became intensely jealous of colleagues in another county who told him once that, "our judges do not want us to recommend actual sentences. They say that it is their job—not our job—to decide the sentence. They just want us to give them the background information, nothing more."

Moore's judges wanted "more." Though the local judiciary did not feel in any way bound by the specific sentencing recommendations of Moore and his office colleagues, they nevertheless wanted recommendations.

The longer Phil Moore thought about his recommendation, the more he worried. Sure, he cared about recommending a just sentence, but he also wanted to recommend something that the judge would not think was crazy. But what could that be? If he recommended years in prison (like Gus deserved and the guidelines suggested), the judge might think he was a fool to advance such a medically expensive proposal. On the other hand, if he recommended a few months in jail, the judge might balk at such leniency. In the end, Moore decided to recommend the minimum number called for in the sentencing guidelines: 80 months in prison. He could always plead "guidelines" if the judge criticized his suggestion. Besides, this arrogant burglar with his smirks, cockiness, and phony "yes sir's" might very well deserve to spend whatever time he had left locked up.

The "Gus Hall report" took a lot out of Phil Moore. Luckily, the reports on his remaining two "difficult" cases proved much easier than he had anticipated. Though the facts of the two cases were peculiar, the interviews with the defendants proved calm and straightforward.

Adam Seltzer, though electing not to testify at trial, readily admitted to Moore that he had transported drugs for his father. He explained that his father begged and finally "ordered" him to do it. Adam was only seventeen and asked his mother what he should do. She tearfully told him to "mind your father." Adam's father wanted Adam to take a package containing twelve individually wrapped, tiny bags of cocaine and deliver it to a contact in a nearby housing project. Adam's father explained that he could not do it himself since he was would be recognized by competitors there and prevented from making the delivery. Adam was very hesitant to do this. He was scared of getting beat up or arrested. But when his father angrily insisted, he agreed.

Unknown to Adam or his father, the "contact" was a snitch working undercover for the vice cops in exchange for a reduced sentence on other drug charges. When Adam tried to deliver the drugs, he got busted. Just before making the arrest, cops heard Adam explaining to the wired-up snitch why he, rather than his father, was delivering the goods. "Hey, my Dad's making me do this crap but I don't like it one bit. It really, really sucks," Adam could be heard saying on tape.

Phil Moore noted in his report to the judge that Adam had several things going for him that suggested a sentence below the guideline range of 48 to 54 months. First, he was very young. Though 16 was the age of adult criminal responsibility in this state, Adam was only 17 and still really just a minor for most purposes in society. Second, Adam had no prior record whatsoever. Third, Adam was unduly influenced by his father (and mother) to do this crime. Fourth, Adam was unlikely to recidivate. Fifth, Adam showed real remorse for his crime and readily admitted responsibility. Sixth, Adam did not commit perjury during the trial by taking the stand to deny involvement. Instead, he remained silent which he had every right to do. Moore recommended eleven months in the local jail, noting that it was five months longer than the plea bargain Adam was offered in exchange for testifying against his father, something Adam understandably could not bring himself to do.

Claudette Norris's case also found Phil Moore suggesting a sentence below the legislature's sentencing guidelines' range. Like Adam Seltzer, Claudette admitted her guilt to Phil. She tearfully acknowledged that she had caused her husband's untimely demise. In addition to this acceptance of responsibility, Moore noted in his report that psychologists hired by the defense diagnosed Claudette as suffering from "battered wife syndrome," and would be testifying at Claudette's sentencing hearing. Phil indicated in his report that the psychologists planned to testify that this is a condition that causes one to believe that an abusive husband is all-powerful and will seek out and destroy any wife who dares go to the police or who dares tries to leave the marriage. Moore noted that though the "battered wife syndrome" was not recognized in their state as a legal excuse to homicide (hence its inadmissibility during the trial), it is recognized in many other states as a defense and should at least be a factor considered at sentencing. Moore also pointed out that though the jury could have found Claudette guilty of murder, it only returned a guilty verdict for manslaughter, strongly suggesting sympathy for the defendant's condition. Moore recommended 60 months in prison, somewhat less than the 72–81 months generally deemed appropriate by the legislature for voluntary manslaughter involving a defendant with no prior criminal history.

Though Phil Moore felt better about his recommendations to the judge regarding Adam Seltzer and Claudette Norris than he did about those regarding Gus Hall, he still felt on shaky ground on all three. The judge could think him either the fool or the sage on one, two, or all three recommendations. Phil decided to turn his reports in and to wait and see what Judge Liz Winters would actually do come the sentencing hearings.

The Sentencing Hearings

Judge Liz Winters felt nervous as she waited in her chambers for the first of the day's six scheduled **sentencing hearings** (hearings in which a judge listens to attorneys' arguments and then announces the sentence of the court). Three of the hearings would be merely perfunctory. Winters would take care of them first to get them out of the way for the real work at hand. Judge Winters knew exactly what sentence she would be rendering with regards to these first three cases. She would politely listen to arguments of counsel (no witnesses were expected to testify), take a few seconds to "reflect" on the arguments, then move on to announce the sentences which she had already decided. She knew that these relatively minor cases (involving second offense drunk driving, simple assault, and misdemeanor theft) were routine and she would waste no time or brain power giving them each short sentences in the middle of the recommended guideline range.

What made Judge Winters nervous were the three more difficult cases on the day's court docket: Adam Seltzer, Gus Hall, and Claudette Norris. The judge had read the pre-sentence investigation reports on each of them with great interest. Like Phil Moore, she had mixed emotions regarding each of them. She took some comfort in the fact that Phil Moore had been required to come up with some numbers. "At least someone else out there besides just me has had to struggle with these three sentences," she thought. In a more collegial courthouse, Liz Winters might have felt at ease discussing these cases with other judges to get their opinions. But, judges in her courthouse somehow felt very restrained burdening others with decisions that courthouse culture considered their own alone to make.

After reading the three pre-sentence reports, Judge Winters eventually came to some tentative sentencing decisions. Though she wanted to hear arguments from counsel, she was leaning toward following Phil Moore's recommendations of leniency with regards to youthful Adam Seltzer and battered Claudette Norris. As to Moore's recommendations regarding the prowler Gus Hall, she would not be following the sentencing recommendation of 80 long months in prison. "Moore is nuts!" she whispered to herself when she had read the recommendation for the first time. "The medical report in the file says that this guy will be bedridden within six months and dead within twelve. That's just what the warden wants: an inmate to nurse at county expense," she thought sarcastically. Winters was thinking of giving Gus Hall four months in prison. "Let's take away his liberty just long enough until he gets real sick, then get him out of our hair," she decided.

As Judge Liz Winters entered the courtroom punctually at 9:30 a.m., all present in the room arose on cue. Winters outlined the order that she would hear sentencing arguments, making sure to put the three easy matters first. She did this for the aforementioned reason, but also to get rid of an unnecessary audience of lawyers before she had to make the really tricky decisions.

Winters quickly processed the first three cases. As usual, she followed the recommendations found in the pre-sentence report, which in turn reflected the sentences recommended in the legislative sentencing guidelines. Winters generally followed the pre-sentence report's recommendations in uncomplicated cases, believing that "the P.S.I. people usually know what they are doing," as she liked to put it.

After a ten minute recess, Winters returned to court to start tackling the three remaining, difficult cases. She was pleased to notice that much of the original audience had left. She decided to hear the matter of Claudette Norris first, since not only attorneys were waiting but a psychologist-witness as well.

Winters listened as the psychologist summarized her findings regarding battered wife syndrome. Winters then asked the defendant's attorney if there were any inaccuracies in Phil Moore's pre-sentence report that he would like to point out to the court. When the attorney answered that he saw no inaccuracies, the court invited the defendant to speak. Normally defendants say little of value but this time things could be different, so Judge Winters perked up.

After crying for twenty uninterrupted seconds, the defendant Claudette Norris told the court how sorry she was for what she did. She apologized to her in-laws who kept their heads bowed as they sat motionless in the benches. (Judge Winters was impressed by the fact that the victim's family members did not glare back angrily during the apology as they often do. This suggested to the judge that they would not act with disgust if some leniency were extended.)

Claudette went on to tell the court that she just "went crazy" on the day of the homicide and "wasn't thinking straight." None of these comments surprised Judge Winters, yet she still felt touched by the obvious sincerity of Claudette's remorse.

To help grease the skids for a lenient sentence matching that suggested by Phil Moore (a sentence below the bottom of the one recommended in the state guidelines), Judge Winters invited Claudette to explain to the court how she got to be "so crazy" that day. As Winters expected, Claudette spoke movingly about her abuse and own victimization at the hands of her husband.

Following Claudette's remarks, the judge invited the prosecutor to give his recommendations, followed by arguments of the defense counsel. Both attorneys spoke eloquently, but added nothing useful to the decision of the court.

Following the remarks of the attorneys, the judge showed even more leniency than Phil Moore had called for in his report. Audience likely matters at sentencing.[10] If Winters had sensed a strong desire for retribution toward Claudette from the prosecutor and the victim's family, she might have felt obliged to mete out a sterner sentence. Having no desire for retribution herself, and having sensed an unspoken sympathy for Claudette from all who were present, the judge announced a sentence of just four years in prison: a long time for someone with no criminal history but not so long for an un-negotiated case involving a dead body. To the judge's secret relief, nobody seemed upset, and Claudette was taken away to serve her four years. Though the law did not require it, the judge gave Claudette **credit for time served** to be applied toward her sentence.

Four years in Claudette's state meant four years. This is known as a **determinate sentence**, a sentence that is plainly set by the judge at the sentencing hearing, with no adjustment of the sentence by a parole board possible. (It should be noted that even when determinate sentences are used, there is still such a thing as **good time**. This is a type of prison-rules incentive program providing for time—varying widely from jurisdiction to jurisdiction—to be automatically knocked off one's sentence for every month that one goes without disciplinary "write-ups.")

States that do not use determinate sentences use **indeterminate sentences**. For example, an indeterminate sentence might take the form of "two to six years." A defendant given such a sentence might, like Claudette, get out after four years. But, it would be up to a parole board to determine exactly when the defendant would get out (the defendant could get out as early as two years if the parole board sees evidence of rehabilitation, or the defendant may have to serve the full six years if there are no such indications).

---

10. The author found out the potential importance of an audience at sentencing following the loss of his first jury trial as a young defense attorney. The judge sentenced the defendant, convicted of robbery, very harshly before a courtroom of only the two lawyers, the defendant, and the judge. Defense counsel filed for a reconsideration of sentence which generated a second hearing. This time the lawyer personally insisted that many members of the defendant's family come to watch. The judge reduced the sentence at this second hearing by several years, citing how impressed he was that the defendant had such support.

Indeterminate sentences used to be the norm in America, but the trend since the 1970s has been to abandon indeterminate sentences in favor of determinate ones. Critics of indeterminate sentences claim that they are based on a mistaken notion that parole boards can somehow diagnose who is rehabilitated and who is not. Defenders of indeterminate sentences argue that rehabilitation should be encouraged and rewarded by correctional authorities. By and large the critics of parole have been winning out. By the end of the 20th century the majority of states had made the switch from indeterminate to determinate sentencing schemes.[11]

With Claudette Norris's sentence now determined, it was time to decide the fate of Adam Seltzer, the reluctant drug-delivery boy. Judge Winters liked Phil Moore's recommendation of just eleven months in the local jail. This kid was no threat to society. The judge could imagine many kids she personally knew feeling pressured to do their parents' bidding if pushed hard enough. But could she possibly justify giving Adam a mere eleven months when the bottom of the sentencing guidelines called for four long years?

Transporting drugs was considered a very serious crime in this state. In fact, the state legislature was even now debating the creation of **minimum mandatory sentences** (sentences which judges must impose with no exceptions whatsoever) for drug offenses such as this. The talk around the state capitol building was that the minimum sentences being considered for selling or transporting drugs were very draconian. Judge Winters did not like mandatory sentence laws. She already had to deal with them with regards to repeat drunk drivers and handgun crimes. The "no exceptions whatsoever" nature of such laws offended her. She knew that some of her colleagues in the federal courts have been known to recuse themselves from taking drug cases rather then being forced to mete out mandatory sentences that violate their consciences. She hoped that defense counsel was smart enough today to help set her up in a position to justify showing extraordinary leniency to Adam Seltzer. She would not be disappointed.

Defense counsel made a simple but very persuasive argument for the granting of a sentence well below the sentencing guidelines. Reminding the judge that the guidelines in their state were just suggestions and not mandates, the attorney went on to state the obvious: this poor boy was not a willing participant but rather someone cruelly torn between obedience to parents and obedience to the government.

---

11. Hunzeker, Donna. (1995). "State sentencing systems and truth in sentencing." *State Legislative Report*, 20(3). Denver: National Conference of State Legislatures.

The judge could tell that even the prosecutor thought that the sentencing guideline recommendations were way out of line. When the prosecutor had her chance to speak and used it to argue for a sentence of "at least several years for such a dangerous crime," the judge asked her bluntly why her office had earlier offered the defendant a mere six months in a plea bargain if this kid were such a societal menace. The prosecutor's embarrassed attempt to justify the six months as an incentive for the kid to testify against his own father made things worse rather than better for the state. The judge sentenced young Adam to eleven months just like Phil Moore had suggested.

The court was nearly empty by the time Judge Winters turned her attention to the sentencing of Gus Hall. Only Hall, his mother, the victim, the lawyers and Judge Winters herself were left (plus the omnipresent clerk, stenographer, sheriff, and bailiff).

As Judge Winters eyeballed the defendant Gus Hall, she reminded herself of her firm intention to give this man a light sentence. It occurred to Winters that this was shaping up to be "light sentence day" in her courtroom. But, unlike the other light sentences she had given that day, this one would not be based on sympathy for the defendant but rather on sympathy for state taxpayers: end-of-life care was very costly and this man had little time left. "Why did Phil Moore recommend 80 long months in his stupid report?" the judge again questioned herself. "What could he have been thinking?"

The judge began the hearing by asking the defense attorney if the report contained any inaccuracies that should be noted. The defense attorney replied, "Nothing worth bringing up Your Honor."

"Very well," noted the judge. "I would like to first hear from Mr. Hall and then from defense counsel and finally from the prosecution. Mr. Hall, do you have anything you would like to say today before I hear arguments from the attorneys?"

Judge Winters was hoping that Hall would come across as a pathetic dying man that would facilitate the granting of leniency which Winters wished to shortly give. As Hall stood up, the judge took courage in his pathetic appearance. He looked awful, even corpse-like, despite the new, charcoal suit he was wearing. Rather than making Hall look better, the suit only served to magnify the pale, sickly look of the face sticking out of the top of it. "Ten to one odds that will be his coffin suit," Winters thought as she waited for Hall to speak.

Fighting off what appeared to be an impulse to vomit, Hall began to speak. Every soul in the courtroom listened with reverence, as if expecting to hear something deep and philosophical from a man who at this very moment seemed more to belong to the next world than this one.

"Your Honor," began Hall, "I have lived a life of self-serving laziness, sponging off my parents and engaging in a constant stream of various petty and not so petty offenses."

"So far, so good," thought Winters. "He's about to give us his prayer of contrition."

"Authorities have no idea of the extent of my different crimes," Hall continued. "Some will look upon my life and see nothing but wasted opportunities and unfulfilled potential. I took an IQ test back in high school. They said I had an IQ of 135, putting me in the top two percent of the population. I could have done anything with my life—been a doctor, business executive, architect, who knows? Instead, I chose to sit around, drink, do drugs, listen to music, and watch TV."

"Good, all good," Winters told herself. "But I did not know about the drugs."

The sickly Hall heaved pathetically twice, before he continued. "As I was saying, I have lived a life of laziness, a life of giving the finger to the world so to speak. Today, my lawyer tells me that I should come here to the court and say that I am truly sorry for all that I have done, especially for the most recent burglary that brings me here today. He says I need to apologize to my neighbor for trying to take his vodka. But I am not sorry! I had just the life I wanted. It was great. The alcohol was good. The drugs were even better. The crimes I got caught doing were worth it, especially since I figure I must have done ten crimes for every one I got nailed for. Even when I was nailed for something, you guys gave me probation over and over again, followed finally by a bunch of easy jail sentences. I liked jail. I got to sit around, talk with the guys, lift weights, watch television, and read *Prison Life Magazine* while all of you were at work. I did miss my drugs, but nothing's perfect, right? I had a wonderful life and my only regret is that I'll now die and cease to exist. I don't fear God. I don't fear jail. I don't fear you, your laws, or your silly punishments. I am a dead man walking and I expect you to pay all of my death bills. Go ahead, give me a life sentence, make my day."

Judge Winters sat stunned for a few seconds as if just hit by a club. She looked at the prosecutor, now her ally, and saw anger in her eyes. She looked at the defense attorney, who appeared red with deep embarrassment. She looked back at the defendant who just smiled arrogantly at her. She looked at the sheriff, who, having just taken a position inches from Hall, looked as though he were ready to tackle him at the first legal opportunity.

Judge Winters's first inclination was to lash back at the defendant and slam him with the maximum prison sentence possible. But wasn't that just what Hall was baiting her to do? Winters decided not to play this agent provocateur's game. "Thank you Mr. Hall," she stated in a flat, dismissive tone. "Would defense counsel now like to make an argument?"

The defense attorney rambled on for a brief minute with insincere, barely comprehensible argument and sat down. It was obvious, he did not care what the judge did to his rebellious, uncontrollable client.

The prosecutor followed with her comments. She passionately asked for the maximum sentence. She told the judge that if this defendant did not deserve the maximum, then nobody would ever deserve the maximum.

Judge Winters enjoyed the arguments of counsel, not so much for their substance but for the chance she had to completely compose herself. She now saw clearly what she would do.

"Gus Hall, it is the sentence of this court that you serve eight months in the county jail. Given what the medical reports say, not to mention your deeply disturbing physical appearance, this sentence should be long enough to safely incapacitate you until the disease you suffer from totally takes over that duty from us. At that low point you will be released to die at the expense of someone other than the state correctional system. I know you thought I would be awed by your childish, little outbursts but you aren't important enough to impress me or anybody else in this courthouse. Adieu, Mr. Hall. You just aren't worth any unusual reactions from this court. Sheriff, please escort this sad man to his new home."

This time it was Gus Hall who was genuinely surprised. He coughed uncontrollably as the sheriff escorted him in chains from the courtroom.

The day's business now over, Judge Winters left the bench and returned to the comforts of her chambers. She hung up her robe, took a soda pop from her small office refrigerator, touched a key on her sleeping computer, and began checking out the latest national news. She just played God in the lives of three different people. But, now it was time to move on.

*****

Questions for Class Discussion

1. What sorts of things can we tell about a society by the way it punishes its criminals? What can we specifically say about our own country by the way it punishes (or fails to punish) its criminals?

2. Our country incarcerates a larger percentage of its people than any other country. One fourth of the world's prison inmates are in American prisons. Are we too punitive a society or are we merely wealthy enough to be doing the right thing? Are there any alternatives to prison you think we should be using more of?

3. Can you identify by name the four classical goals of sentencing?

4. What is meant by "rehabilitation?" Is crime an "illness" that can be cured by the correctional system? Do we have an ethical duty to try to rehabilitate the people we lock up?

5. What is meant by "deterrence?" What is the difference between specific deterrence and general deterrence? Are you personally deterred by the law from committing certain crimes or violations? How fast would you travel on your local freeways if there were no speed limits to deter you?

6. What is meant by "incapacitation?" Is it a helpful thing? Is it fair to categorize this goal of punishment as merely "warehousing" people?

7. What is meant by "retribution?" Is revenge a morally justifiable criteria for punishing criminals? Is it a lawful criteria to consider?

8. Which classical goal of sentencing do you suspect you would lean more heavily towards achieving if you were called upon to start sentencing people: rehabilitation, deterrence, incapacitation, or retribution?

9. What is the difference between probation and parole? What sort of conditions are probationers and parolees expected to live by?

10. Who writes the pre-sentence investigation report to the judge? According to the Table in the book, what sort of information do such reports typically contain?

11. Do you believe that judges should punish some violators more harshly than others based on the crime's subjective impact on the victim? For example, is it logical to punish one residential burglar much more harshly than another because one burglar randomly chose the house of a hypersensitive victim who developed chronic nightmares from the crime, while another randomly chose the house of a thick-skinned person who easily moved on with her life?

12. What do you think about mandatory sentencing guidelines? Are they a good idea or are they legislative encroachments upon the judicial function? Can judges be trusted to sentence people correctly without mandatory guidelines?

13. What does a typical sentencing guidelines grid look like (at least in states that use determinate rather than indeterminate sentencing)? What two factors play a role in deciding what box or cell on the grid a defendant lands in?

14. Sentencing grids are a lot like the admissions grids that some universities use in deciding who gets admitted and who does not, or who gets a scholarship and who does not. At such universities, two things determine where on the admissions grid a prospective student lands: SAT (or ACT) score and high school GPA. Is it fair to categorize students based on just

these two criteria? Or, would it be unfair to use "squishy" criteria rather than such straightforward, standard criteria in making judgments?

15. Does your state use determinate or indeterminate sentencing? Which system do you like better? Why?

16. More and more states have adopted minimum mandatory sentences for more and more crimes. Why do you suppose this is so? Is it a good thing or a bad thing?

17. If you were the judge, what sentence would you have given to the teenager who was pressured to be a drug mule for his dad? What sentence would you have given the cancer-stricken burglar? What sentence would you have given the woman who executed her abuser?

18. What do you think about the "battered wife syndrome" defense? Is it a valid defense or simply a license to commit murder?

19. Studies show that women are consistently sentenced less harshly than men for the same crimes even when they have similar prior records. Why do you suppose that is so? What, if anything, should be done about this?

20. Do sentencing hearings contribute anything that cannot be put down in writing without a hearing? Do sentencing hearings favor the articulate over the inarticulate? The good-looking over the ugly? Those with good acting skills over the more honest? Should we do away with sentencing hearings and just have judges rely on the written pre-sentence report, along with defense lawyer's written input?

*****

Key Terms: four classical goals of criminal sentencing, rehabilitation, deterrence, specific deterrence, general deterrence, incapacitation, warehousing, retribution, just deserts, probationers, parolees, pre-sentence investigation reports, whole person, sentencing guidelines, mandatory sentencing guidelines, non-mandatory sentencing guidelines, sentencing hearings, credit for time served, determinate sentence, good time, indeterminate sentences, minimum mandatory sentences

Additional Concepts: routine nature of most sentencing, stress of non-routine sentencing, playing God, Winston Churchill, sentences in other countries, standard contents of a pre-sentence investigation report, the pre-sentence report interview, mechanics of sentencing guidelines, societal shift to determinate sentencing, judicial dislike of mandatory sentences, illustration of sentencing hearings

CHAPTER FOURTEEN

THE APPEAL

Joan Wade was a thirty-nine year-old mother of two junior high school students when she finished law school and passed the bar exam. Trapped in the local area (a very tight legal job market) due to her husband's career, she felt fortunate to have been taken on by the local public defender as one of two new hires. Due to her limited mobility, it was the only job offer she received. But, she was excited to have it. There had been nineteen applicants for the two positions, including one with an Ivy League law degree (who was the other new hire).

Joan was very nervous on her first day at work but relaxed when her boss told her that she would be spending most of her first two weeks accompanying more senior attorneys to their various assignments so that she could "get a feel for how things are done in the real world." Imagine her surprise when, on the third day, her boss personally delivered to her an incredibly expansive file (actually a box of files all labeled "Randy Harris") and told her that this was something she should start working on when not shadowing others to their court appearances.

"What is all of this?" Joan politely inquired as she looked at her boss smiling somewhat sadistically at her.

"These are the records of a big trial that some private criminal defense attorney lost last month. The defendant wants to appeal. The private lawyer has started having some serious health problems and is cutting back on most of his legal work. Since the defendant is now broke no other private lawyer wants him. So, we are the lucky folks who get to do this appeal, or rather, you get to do it. You'll have the help of Stuart who will officially be the lead attorney of record. But, I expect you to do most of the research work, not Stuart, OK?"

"OK, I understand. So, what was the guy convicted of?" Joan reluctantly asked as she stared at the crammed box. She had a feeling it was going to be something really, really big. Her boss's smile grew larger.

"Capital murder," he mischievously announced with a spooky chuckle. "A jury found him guilty of killing his parents in their own bed with an axe while they slept. The jury sentenced him to death. The motive apparently was money, an inheritance. It's all in the file. Anyway, your job will be to research the issues that you and Stuart identify as appealable, and then write the brief to the appellate court which Stuart can polish if necessary. You will also help Stuart make oral arguments before the appellate panel when it comes to that."

"But, shouldn't someone with more experience be doing this?" Joan was trying to sound matter-of-fact rather than nervous, but she was very nervous.

"No, you can handle it," her boss assured her. "Look, there is only one thing law school prepares students well for and that is how to draft **legal briefs**. Using the law to advocate for a position in a paper was about the only thing I knew how to do well when I graduated. You've written and argued briefs in school, right?"

"Well, yes in the moot court competitions which we all had to participate in. But those were just pretend."

"Well," quipped her superior, "This is for real. I always give my brand new lawyers an appellate brief to draft right after they get hired. It's my policy. It gets their feet wet and gives them something familiar to do. Be grateful Stuart will be there to back you up. I'm only assigning both of you to the appeal because it is a capital case. Normally, my new attorneys do their appeal all alone from first written sentence in the brief to final spoken word before the panel. You can do this Joan, it really is not any more complicated than that high brow stuff done in moot court in law school. It probably is even less complicated. If you ask the secretaries, they can show you where old briefs from other cases are on file. There are even four or five old capital homicide appeal briefs around. You can take a look at them to help kick-start you."

"When is the brief due?" Joan was hoping she would have a couple of months.

"Check the documents in the file, but I think in about four weeks. Plenty of time. But right now, I think Stuart wants you to accompany him to a preliminary hearing on a burglary case. It will be a good opportunity for you to get acquainted. Don't screw up on the due date for the brief. That's a **drop dead date**—figuratively for us, maybe literally for our client if we screw this up. If I were you I'd have the brief filed at least three days before it's due just to be careful."

"Don't worry, I'll take care of it," Joan insisted. "I guess I better get over to Stuart's office."

As Joan walked to Stuart's office she felt tingles of excitement (chills of fear?) in her stomach. She was proud to begin her legal career with something as consequential as a capital murder appeal, even if she would have Stuart looking over her shoulder. She replayed in her mind the part about her boss saying that she was the one to do most of the legal research. "This is it," she thought. "This isn't doing endless proof-reading of thick contracts written by more senior attorneys at some uppity corporate law firm. I'm doing something important from day one. Public defending is going to be really neat."

Stuart was polite when Joan knocked on his door but it was obvious he did not have time to talk about the appeal right then. He was too busy reading the burglary file which he evidently had never seen until just a few minutes earlier. "Well," he said after a couple minutes of silent, swift reading, "let's get down to Courtroom Six for the prelim on this burglary. You can watch how it's done. It's no big deal really."

"For me it's still a big deal," Joan admitted.

After the preliminary hearing, Joan returned with Stuart to his office hoping to discuss the murder appeal. She was surprised when he told her that it was really her appeal, and she should just get started by familiarizing herself with the case file. "I'm just here as an attorney of record because it's a capital case. But I'm guessing your brief will be super. Just go through the case file. Everything is in there including the original police reports, the preliminary hearing transcript, the lawyer's trial prep notes, and of course the transcript of the trial itself. Look at some of the old briefs our office has written on other capital murder appeals, and you'll get the idea. The hardest part of writing an appellate brief is just getting the first sentence done. After that your law school training will guide you, it really will. It's like riding a bike, you never forget how to write a brief. Just pretend it's for a class at school and you want an 'A.' That's what I did when I wrote my first appellate brief. It worked. Too bad I didn't have a clue about how to get someone's bail reduced or how to do an arraignment, but law school did teach me how to research and write a dynamite brief."

Joan thanked Stuart for his advice, limited though it was, and returned to her office to start reading through the case file. As she sat down, she saw a note from her boss on the desk telling her that he was reducing her "tag along" learning experiences with other attorneys for the next few days. He wanted her to have a few days to really get into the appeal.

Joan spent the rest of the day reading the police reports and the preliminary hearing **transcript** (word for word recording taken down phonetically in court by a court stenographer and later reproduced in standard English). By the time Joan finished reading the transcript, she had a good grasp of the facts of the crime. Apparently, the defendant Randy Harris was a twenty year old spoiled, lazy, self-absorbed young man whose parents had made a fortune in nursing home businesses in Arizona. After spending the year after high school "finding himself" in Europe (which to him meant nightclubbing with various unsavory friends) his parents convinced him to attend an expensive, private, liberal arts college where he majored in frat parties, drugs, womanizing and television. After one semester, Randy was placed on academic probation for earning three D's and two F's. After the second semester the college threw him out for failing to improve, despite his parents' ability to pay full asking-price tuition.

Randy stayed in the college town after expulsion and continued his life of non-stop pleasure-seeking until his parents finally cut off his funding. Infuriated, Randy called them repeatedly insisting that they send him money. According to Randy's friends, the calls became more and more heated. At first the parents sent Randy money now and then, but when it became clear that Randy had no intention of "working for chump change like losers," they told him that he was completely on his own.

Randy claimed he was nature-hiking in the area of the college town a thousand miles from his parents' home on the day that his wealthy parents were found axed to death in their bed. Yet, two of his parents' neighbors and an old high school buddy swore in court that they were certain that they saw Randy in town the night before the murder at various low-profile locations. A college-town woman whom Randy had been pursuing for months back where he lived told the court that Randy had stood her up on a date scheduled to take place two days after the murders. When she asked Randy why he did not keep their date, he angrily told her to mind her own business. Of course, there was also the fact of the inheritance for the jury to consider. Randy as an only child was entitled to get his parents' entire fortune of six million dollars, enough money to finance the selfish lifestyle to which he had long become accustomed.

Keeping Randy off the stand and arguing that the state's purely circumstantial case failed to establish guilt beyond a reasonable doubt, the defense lawyer hoped for an acquittal. Instead, the jury not only returned a finding of guilt but went on to sentence him to death.

In appealing the conviction and the sentence, Joan had her work cut out for her. She knew that the first order of business in any appeal was to **spot issues** that could be later developed and argued to require dismissal of the charges or (failing that) the granting of a new trial. This would require reading the lengthy transcript of the trial itself. She would begin reading the transcript the next day, but for now she thought it prudent to telephone the private attorney who had represented Harris at trial. Familiar with the trial, this lawyer was an excellent starting off point for looking for appealable issues. He probably would have some good ideas.

It was a good thing that Joan telephoned the lawyer the very next day. The lawyer pointed out to Joan that nothing could be appealed until post-trial motions were first argued before and denied by the judge who had presided over the trial. The lawyer was surprised that nobody had called him yet from her office to get his input about what could be argued. "I was just about to call your office about this," he told her. (Joan was not entirely sure what he meant by "post-trial motions" so she decided to see Stuart right after she finished the conversation.)

Before getting to what he thought were potential appealable issues, the attorney wanted to explain to Joan why Randy Harris never took the stand at his trial. "This is just between us, lawyer to lawyer," he emphasized. He explained that he could not put Harris on the stand because Harris had more or less confessed the murders to him. He told Joan that Harris had gone to argue with his parents in person about giving him more money but wound up killing them when they still refused to assist him. He wore surgical gloves during the killing which he had purchased before the trip and which he later discarded in a gutter elsewhere in town. The axe he used belonged to his father. He also admitted to the attorney that he had entered town "very discreetly" and left town "very discreetly." "This guy is scary," the attorney told Joan. "He killed his own parents for money."

When asked what issues he thought should be argued on an eventual appeal, the trial attorney told Joan that he had jotted down some preliminary ideas for post-trial motions and that these could be found in the thin blue file in the box. Joan ended the phone call by thanking the attorney and assuring him that she would see to the "post-trial motions" right away. She then scurried down to Stuart's office.

"Stuart, do you have a few minutes?" Joan inquired after rapping gently on Stuart's mostly-open door. "Not really, but go ahead anyway Joan," Stuart suggested. "How's the appeal coming?"

"That's what I wanted to talk to you about. I just spoke to the private attorney who handled Harris' murder trial. He asked why nobody has filed any post-trial motions yet. What exactly is he talking about?"

"Oh crap!" Stuart exclaimed. "What were we thinking! We can't just appeal this case to a higher court without first filing post-trial motions. Since we took this case over without having done the trial—something very unusual for us—I guess we just forgot about the post-trial motions. They are a usually a waste of time but something that must be done."

"But I was told the appellate brief is due in just four weeks," Joan responded. "Are we too late to do post-trial motions?"

"No, I'm sure you were just told wrong. It is true that appellant briefs are held to a four week time-table in our jurisdiction but the four weeks don't even start until a judge first denies the post-trial motions. Since this trial just ended ten days ago, we've still got time to file the post-trial motions."

"What are post-trial motions?" asked Joan.

"Let me explain," Stuart replied. "The first step in appealing a conviction and a sentence is to file post-trial motions. **Post-trial motions** are basically a listing of all the errors which you allege occurred in the trial which warrant that the charges be dismissed outright (like when a jury returns a ridiculous verdict) or warrant that a new trial be given the defendant (like when the judge allows bad evidence to be admitted over objections of defense counsel). Basically, your post-trial motions are what you will eventually argue to the appellate court, but you first have to give the trial judge a crack at correcting the mistakes himself or herself. Appellate courts don't want their time wasted if a trial judge is willing to resolve errors at his or her level."

"Do trial judges frequently give relief pursuant to post-trial motions?" asked Joan.

"Does it rain very often in Death Valley?" asked Stuart. "Only twice in my seven years with this office have I ever had a judge grant any of my post-trial motions. Judges in theory grant such motions but when they do they are basically admitting that they as the trial referee screwed up during the trial so big that a new trial has to be given. Obviously, judges aren't very keen on admitting that they messed up justice that bad."

"Oh, I think I follow you," Joan acknowledged. "For example, if I object to hearsay during a trial and a judge overrules me and allows the evidence in, I could ask for a new trial in my post-trial motions based on the judge's erroneous ruling on my objection."

"Exactly," Stuart agreed. "Of course, every judge makes mistakes in every trial so the mere fact that an error was made will not get someone a new trial. That's why we have the **harmless error doctrine**, which you learned about in law school.

"Oh yeah," Joan acknowledged. "That's the rule that says that even if a judge makes a bad ruling during a trial a defendant won't get a new trial if the error did not likely have a profound impact on the overall outcome of the trial.[1] I remember that rule."

"Right," responded Stuart. "Without the harmless error doctrine, every defendant would get a new trial because mistakes are made by judges in every single trial."

"So, I should get working on the post-trial motions, trying to find non-harmless errors," noted Joan.

---

1. See, *Arizona vs. Fulminante*, 499 U.S. 279 (1991).

"Yeah, but remember to do a good job because they won't let you make any arguments on appeal that you do not let this trial judge have a chance to correct himself in your post-trial motions. What I am trying to say is that the post-trial motions will frame your eventual appeal."

"So, I basically am writing my eventual appeal when I write my post-trial motions," Joan said.

"Precisely. You'll raise various issues in your post-trial motions. The trial judge will probably ask you to write a **memorandum of law** regarding each of them. This memorandum of law will be sort of a preliminary sketch of what you'll eventually argue more thoroughly in your full-blown appellate brief. After the trial judge reads your memorandum of law, he will have you orally argue your motions in court before him and then almost certainly deny each and every motion That is how the game is played. After the trial judge denies your motions, you can then appeal the same issues to the appellate court who will give them real consideration. I'm hardly ever successful on my post-trial motions, but I figure I win about one out of eight appeals. Of course, that usually just means a new trial, not a dismissal of the charges."

Joan listened with interest to all that Stuart was telling her until Stuart happened to look at his watch and realize he was soon due in court for a bail reduction hearing on another case. Before taking his leave, he told Joan that since this was a capital murder case, he better be the one primarily responsible for spotting potential appealable issues. "I'm used to spotting issues," he told her. "Let me take care of that. You can research and write the full-blown brief that will lay out the legal arguments regarding the issues. How does that sound?"

"Sounds good to me," Joan said. "Oh, before I forget, the lawyer who did the trial says he wrote down what he thinks are appealable issues. He says they're in a thin blue file in the box."

"Super," Stuart acknowledged. "Nobody is more on top of potential winning issues than the lawyer who got burned at trial."

"Maybe I should call the defendant and see if he has any ideas for the appeal," Joan suggested.

"Not necessary," Stuart insisted. "Clients control the decision of whether or not to appeal but lawyers are the ones who get to decide what issues to appeal. Appellate courts have ruled that lawyers control the development of the appeal, not the client. Clients don't know enough about the law to spot issues or to develop them. We'll send the defendant a copy of our post-trial motions later as a courtesy before the hearing before the trial judge. Got to get to court before the judge sends for me." Joan nodded goodbye as Stuart hustled down the hall.

Mechanics and Functions of Appeals

After talking to Stuart, Joan realized that she was not as versed in the intricacies of appeals as she thought she should be. She decided to do some very basic research on the mechanics and functions of appeals. When nobody was looking, she discretely went into the office law library and began reading about basic appellate procedure in one of the legal encyclopedias.

To her amazement, she started off learning that there is apparently no federal constitutional provision requiring states to provide criminal appeals.[2] Nevertheless, states generally require (either by way of statute or state constitution) anybody convicted at trial of a crime to be provided at least one appeal. This one certain appeal is known as an **appeal of right**. All defendants are entitled to one appeal, no matter how solid and air-tight their conviction seems at first blush to be. Because defendants have this appeal of right, nearly every trial-conviction in this country is appealed at least once (there is much for a defendant to possibly gain and virtually nothing to lose—especially if a free lawyer is being used).

Since defendants control the decision of whether or not to appeal, attorneys confronted with trials that appear to be free of meaningful errors often have to resort to picking the least frivolous of the frivolous issues and arguing those as best they can. Often only standard, generic, **boiler-plate issues** are argued and nothing else. Such "boiler-plate" issues include assertions that the "sentence given was disproportionate to the crime" or that the "verdict was against the weight of the evidence." These are easy and obvious issues to attempt to advance but are not well received by the appellate courts. Though they appear in many (if not most) briefs, appellate courts are weary of such arguments. Briefs that contain standard, "boiler-plate" issues with nothing else are probably viewed by reviewing courts as lawyer "code" for "my client is making me appeal but there is nothing really worth appealing."

Joan found it hard to accept that lawyers can be forced by clients to argue frivolous issues on appeal so she tried to find more information on this subject. Reading more deeply, she discovered that there was something called an **Anders Brief** which an attorney being forced by a client to advance a hopeless appeal can file in lieu of an ordinary brief.[3] In an "Anders Brief," the lawyer defends his or her assertion that there are no legitimate issues that could possibly be advanced and asks the court to excuse the attorney from having to write a regular brief. When Joan asked Stuart about "Anders Briefs" later on,

---

2. *Abney v. United States,* 431 U.S. 651,656 (1977).
3. *Anders v. California,* 386 U.S. 738 (1967).

he told her that their office had no use for them. "It's much, much easier just to argue the least frivolous, boiler-plate issue and lose than to write an Anders Brief," he told her. "Anders Briefs require a lot of work to justify no legitimate issues. Basically you have to raise all possible issues and explain how each is frivolous. And, these briefs really piss the defendants off."

Joan read other things about appeals, but it was mostly facts she readily remembered from law school. She read that after the appeal of right, appeals in most states become **discretionary appeals**, meaning that higher appellate courts (such as the state supreme court and the U.S. Supreme Court) do not have to accept the appeal unless they find the issues to be raised interesting or of great public interest. (Lawyers submit a tiny summary of what the interesting issues would be in an attempt to convince the court to invite them to submit a full-blown brief .) For example, in Joan's state any person who is convicted in a trial can appeal as a matter of right to the state's **intermediary appellate court** (the court between the trial court and the state supreme court) and that court must consider the appeal. But, the appeal to the **state supreme court** (the highest appellate court in a state system) is almost completely discretionary (with few exceptions the state supreme court only has to hear cases that it finds really interesting or which it believes involve issues that will affect many people rather than just one defendant). Joan knew that the same rules apply in the federal court system. Clients insisting that they'd appeal "all the way up to the U.S. Supreme Court" do not know what they are talking about, Joan realized. In fact, the U.S. Supreme Court grants **certiorari** (permission to appeal and to be fully heard) in fewer than one percent of the cases it receives.[4] Ninety-nine percent of the time, the High Court "**denies cert**" rather than "**grants cert**." In fact, Supreme Court justices admit that they do not even have time to read most of the petitions seeking "cert" and instead ask their law clerks to do an initial review and call to their attention those few petitions that the clerks believe will be interesting to the Court. The small percentage of cases that survive law-clerk screening are then collectively discussed by the justices in a conference and a vote is taken on whether or not to hear the appeal.[5] (The state and federal appellate systems referred to above are outlined in Table 1.)

Joan stopped her reading briefly to reflect upon the nature of appeals. Joan, like any law school graduate, knew that all post-trial appeals are advanced by defendants, never by prosecutors. Prosecutors cannot appeal an acquittal even

---

4. Maguire, Kathleen and Ann L. Pastore. (1994). *Sourcebook of Criminal Justice Statistics—1993*. Washington, D.C.: U.S. Government Printing Office, at 554.

5. O'Brien, David M. (2000). *Storm Center: The Supreme Court in American Politics*. New York: W. W. Norton & Company, at 140, 200.

Table 1   State and Federal Appellate Systems

State System (processes most crimes)	Federal System (processes federal crimes)
Trial-level court (name depends on state)	U.S. District Court (federal trial-level court)
Intermediate Appeals Court ("appeals of right" go here. In small states "appeals of right" go straight to state supreme court)	U.S. Court of Appeals (also known as Circuit Court since the U.S. is carved up into twelve appellate regions or "circuits")
State Supreme Court (appeals in most states are discretionary at this level and rarely heard)	U.S. Supreme Court (nearly all appeals to it are discretionary. If the Court agrees to hear a case it grants what is known as "certiorari" or permission to appeal).

if huge errors fatal to the prosecution's case were made by a trial judge in his or her rulings. There are no exceptions to this rule that only defendants can appeal the outcome of a trial.[6] The only matters prosecutors can appeal are unfavorable pre-trial rulings (e.g., the wrongful pre-trial decision to suppress physical evidence or confessions). Such pre-trial or **interlocutory appeals** are permitted since double jeopardy does not attach until the first member of the actual trial jury has been selected and sworn.

Joan remembered from the hundreds of case studies read in law school that appeals advanced by defendants convicted by way of trial basically serve two functions. These are **error correction** and **policy review**.

Policy review is exemplified by such cases as *Roe v. Wade* (the famous abortion rights case) or *Miranda v. Arizona* (which gave us the famous "Miranda rights" that police must read). Judges in such cases actually use a constitution to create new law and new policies rather than to correct everyday errors made during trials. Any appellate court can engage in policy review by interpreting the state or federal constitution to strike down a particular law or practice and thus in a sense make new law. Constitutional issues of national importance usually wind up being decided by the U.S. Supreme Court. The U.S. Supreme Court's current members and their philosophical leanings are found in Table 2.

---

6. U.S. Constitutional Amendment V. See also, *United States v. Ball*, 163 U.S. 662 (1896).

Table 2   U.S. Supreme Court Justices and Their Philosophical Leanings

Justice	Appointed by/Year	Philosophical Leanings
John Roberts	Bush/2005	Conservative (devoutly religious Chief Justice, attended Catholic boarding school, Harvard Law grad)
Clarence Thomas	Bush/1991	Conservative (African American against Affirmative Action, relatively quiet during oral arguments)
Antonin Scalia	Regan/1986	Free-Wheeling (former law prof who tends to dominate oral arguments)
Samuel Alito	Bush/2006	Conservative with libertarian streak (former federal prosecutor)
Anthony Kennedy	Regan/1988	Conservative to Moderate (most likely the swing voter in close cases)
Sonia Sotomayor	Obama/2009	Liberal (grew up in NYC housing project, attended Ivy Leagues)
Stephen Breyer	Clinton/1994	Moderate to Liberal (court's consensus builder and legal technician)
John Paul Stevens	Ford/1981	Moderate to Liberal (considers himself judicial conservative but often sides with liberals on court)
Ruth Ginsburg	Clinton/1993	Liberal (former law prof, women's rights advocate and ACLU leader)

Sources: U.S. Supreme Court official Web Site (2009); Wikipedia (2009); The Supreme Court's Current Cast," *Deseret News* (Salt Lake City), Sunday, September 30, 2001, p. 8A; and David M. O'Brien, *Storm Center: The Supreme Court in American Politics.* New York: W. W. Norton & Company (2000).

Most appeals do not involve the creation of new law and policy. They usually involve error correction. Errors that need correcting can be made either by juries or by judges. If a jury convicts somebody on evidence so weak that no reasonable jury could possibly have found guilt beyond a reasonable doubt the appellate court will overturn the verdict and set the defendant free. Joan realized that the chances of an appellate court doing this are very slim. The standard is not how the appellate judges would personally have voted if they had been on the jury but whether the verdict was utterly ridiculous given the quality and quantity of the evidence. Appellate courts often say they do not like to sit as the **thirteenth juror** in second-guessing a jury as to the facts of a case. The jury had the opportunity to observe the witnesses as they presented their stories. Appellate judges have nothing but cold transcripts at which to stare.

Errors can be made by judges as well as juries. For example, if a defense lawyer at trial objects to certain evidence or testimony and the judge erroneously **overrules** the objection rather than **sustains** the objection, an appellate court may grant a new trial with the directive that such unfair evidence not be presented next time. Most successful appeals involve such judge-made errors (bad rulings on objections or motions) rather than jury-made errors (unconscionable verdicts). They usually result in new trials rather than in the charges being dismissed (the new trial is not deemed to violate double jeopardy since it is understood that the court is merely giving the defendant what he or she is requesting).

With regards to judge-made errors, Joan, like every law school graduate, knew all too well that lawyers who fail to **object** (protest) during a trial to improper testimony or other evidence being admitted forever lose the right to argue the admission of that evidence later on appeal. In order to **preserve an issue for appeal**, a trial lawyer must object during the trial and give the judge a chance to correct the mistake right then and there. Failure to object at trial cuts off the right to appeal later. The only exception to this rule involves what is known as "plain error." Simply put, **plain error** is error so huge that it completely and dramatically taints the entire trial to a degree which makes the process fundamentally flawed. Lawyers can appeal plain errors even if they failed to object to them during the trial.[7]

In contemplating all of this, Joan remembered the time that she served as a "judge" while still a law student during a regional "mock trial" tournament involving pre-law undergraduates competing against one another at a local university. Joan had just taken a course entitled the "Law of Evidence" and was up to date on the many nuances of what was admissible in courts and what was not. While serving as judge during one of the tournament's simulated tri-

---

7. *United States v. Young*, 470 U.S. 1 (1985).

als, she was genuinely surprised how often she guessed while ruling on the objections of bright and well-coached students playing the role of lawyers in the contest. "I was guessing about one-fourth the time," she later confided to her husband. "Some of these objections were hard to field. You only have a few seconds to figure out the law before looking like a total fool. It's not like you can take three minutes to review the many exceptions to the hearsay rule in some law book while the contestants wait for your ruling on a hearsay objection. Sometimes I wasn't paying attention and didn't even understand the objection and just totally guessed. Trial judges must really hate doing trials. Fielding objections is really stressful."

Joan's comments to her husband probably have more than a grain of truth to them. Joan remembers talking to a real judge visiting her law school who confirmed to her that "we really fly by the seat of our pants" when fielding objections during trials.[8] Joan found it fascinating when this judge further admitted to her that when he was in real doubt about how to rule on an objection, he generally leaned towards a ruling favorable to the defense. "Why?" asked Joan, "Is it because you want to protect defendants' rights?" "Not entirely," the judge confessed. "It is also because prosecutors cannot appeal my mistaken rulings. Bad rulings made against the state are not subject to embarrassing review by my superiors. If the prosecution wins the case despite my potential mistake in favor of the defense, there is no reason to appeal. If the prosecution goes on to lose at trial, double jeopardy prevents my mistake in favor of the defense from being appealed. Defendants who lose can and will appeal—I guarantee it. They will comb the transcript for any erroneous ruling I might have made. If I'm going to guess wrong, I'd rather guess wrong against the prosecutor than the defendant. I think a lot of trial judges probably feel this way."

Before finishing her self-study, Joan wanted to make sure she had a strong grasp of the actual steps or mechanics of an appeal. The information was not exciting but important. What she learned is found in Table 3.

Stuart's Post-Trial Motions

Now that Joan had refreshed her memory regarding the fine points of appellate procedure, the only thing she could do was to wait for Stuart to iden-

---

8. See, Carp, Robert and Ronald Stidham. (1990). *Judicial Process in America*. Washington, D.C.: Congressional Quarterly Press. (In which a trial judge is cited as admitting that "We often have to shoot from the hip and hope you're doing the right thing. You can't ruminate forever every time you have to make a ruling.")

Table 3   Steps of an Appeal

Step	Purpose
1. Objecting during trial (or raising motions)	Allows for immediate resolution and preserves the issue for later appeal to higher court
2. Post-trial Motions	Gives trial judge chance to correct own bad rulings or jury's unconscionable verdict
3. Notice of Appeal	Makes higher court aware of appeal/ signals clerk of court to send trial transcript and other trial records to the higher court
4. Submitting Briefs	Provides appellate court with a detailed presentation of the issues and legal arguments. Appellant files brief first then other side files a responsive brief presenting the other side.
5. Oral Arguments	Attorneys appear in person before appellate judges and orally present their arguments. Judges have the opportunity to quiz the attorneys regarding points of concern to them.
6. Opinion Issued	Informs parties of the Appellate Court's decision and gives court's reasoning

tify the issues that should be raised in the post-trial motions. Since she had a lot of time on her hands, she began to research one issue she was certain Stuart would identify on appeal: the appropriateness of the jury's sentence of death.

While still taking notes on death penalty jurisprudence a few days later in the law library, she looked up to see Stuart handing her an official-looking document entitled "Commonwealth vs. Randy Harris: Post-Trial Motions." "Here is what I came up with Joan. Look them over. Let me know if you have anything else you think we should throw in the pot."

Joan at first thought Randy meant to look over the motions and to get back to him. But when he just stood there silently, she realized that he meant for her to give him feedback right then and there. Joan took a few minutes and read Stuart's motions. She was impressed that he had identified two good issues that she had not thought of in addition to his having spotted the seven issues that she had spotted during her own review of the case.

"I think you have spotted everything that I did plus two more," she finally announced.

"Are you sure I didn't miss anything?" Stuart's question seemed sincere.

"Well, yeah. I've had little to do around here but think about this case and hang out in the office library. I spotted nine potential issues but two I dismissed later as dead bang losers that would only detract from our arguments. Of the seven I kept, you nailed them all. You also came up with your own eighth and ninth issues which are pretty good and which I never thought of." Joan looked at Stuart to assess his reaction to her comments. He looked pleased.

"Well, like we were all taught in law school, I always put my strongest issues first and my weakest last, Joan. So, I guess if your seven final issues correspond to the first seven I put down in the motion, I think we are probably on the same wave length. My eighth and ninth issues are legitimate but I don't think they'll carry the day for us."

"Where do we go from here, Stuart?" Joan wanted to know. She was anxious to get cracking.

"Why don't you go ahead and start researching the memorandum of law which we'll submit to the trial judge on these issues."

"OK, I'll start to get on it right now," Joan said. "When is it due?"

"We've got until a week from Thursday. But don't do more than a nice, little outline of the law on each point. Number one, the trial judge probably won't want to read a full-blown brief, not even in a capital murder case. Number two, we'll probably lose the post-trial motions anyway and will want to do our major legal writing for the appellate court."

"OK, a tight little memo it is then," Joan concurred. "I'll have it done by next Tuesday. That will give you a couple of days to look it over before it is due, OK?"

"Good deal," confirmed Stuart. "I'll look forward to what you come up with."

Tuesday came soon enough. Joan and Stuart discussed the legal arguments outlined in Joan's memorandum for the trial judge. Stuart told Joan she had done an outstanding job. Stuart meant it. He could see that the cutting-edge legal research skills that Joan had acquired as a law student had not yet been dimmed by the trench warfare of everyday legal practice. Stuart told Joan he was going to submit her memo "as is." He did just that by sending the memo to the D.A.'s office with a copy sent to the trial judge.

No surprise to Stuart, the prosecutor's memorandum of law in response was nowhere near as cerebral as was that written by Joan. But it was good enough to convince the judge that any erroneous rulings made during trial by the judge were harmless errors and that the verdict and sentence returned by the jury were completely reasonable (oral arguments did nothing to alter the judge's opinions regarding these matters). Upon being told by the trial judge in writing that Randy Harris' post-trial motions were "very carefully considered but denied," Stuart and Joan promptly filed a Notice of Appeal. The ball was now in the state's intermediate court of appeals.

Joan's Brief to the Court of Appeals

Joan had four weeks to write a full-blown brief to the court of appeals. She finished writing it in three. The brief had several sections to it. The first section presented the facts of the alleged crime and the procedural history of the case. This section required some thought. Joan did not want to insult the intelligence of the reviewing court by sugar-coating the horrors of the alleged crime by leaving critical facts out. But, she did not want the court to be prejudiced against her client by presenting the facts in an unnecessarily gruesome manner. Joan chose to present the story of the crime in as matter-of-fact a tone as possible without omitting facts obviously critical to an understanding of the alleged crime. (Joan was all too aware that the prosecution would be writing a brief as well in which it would be sure to cite all relevant facts using a somewhat different tone.)

The second section of the brief listed the "issues" to be presented on appeal. Like Stuart had done in the post-trial motions, she prioritized her listing beginning with the strongest issues first and the weakest issues last, with two exceptions. She listed the three issues being raised regarding the appropriateness of the death penalty at the end since to list them earlier would have been chronologically awkward.

The third section of the brief was the section of real substance, taking up a voluminous forty-five pages (adding to the time-honored wisdom that the word "brief" is a misnomer in the law). In this section, Joan laid out the legal arguments regarding each of the nine issues listed in the section before. To back up her arguments, Joan cited **primary legal sources** (laws themselves) and **secondary legal sources** (learned commentary on the law).

The "primary legal sources" Joan relied upon to support her legal assertions consisted of **statutes** (laws passed by the state legislature or by Congress), **constitutional provisions** (word for word phrases found in either the state or federal constitutions), and (most importantly of all) huge amounts of **case law** (written opinions of appellate courts which serve as binding precedent for all new, similar cases).

Joan's "secondary legal sources" included references to **legal treatises** (scholarly books which claim to describe and analyze a body of law) and **law review articles** (published articles written by law professors and others which explore and critique the law).

Joan was careful to never cite an appellant court case as precedent without first **Shepardizing** it (looking up the case in *Shepard's Citators*, a series of reference books which indicate whether the case is still good law or has been overruled). Joan remembered the time in law school when she failed to "Shepardize" a case she cited as precedent in one of her papers. The professor lowered her grade on the paper by a full letter even though the case was not central to her argument. He told her it was "unacceptable, unethical and sloppy lawyering to ever cite a case without first checking to see if it is still good law." How the professor knew that the obscure case had been overruled Joan still wondered to this day. Did the professor or perhaps one of his research assistants take the time to "Shepardize" all of his students's citations mentioned in papers?

In researching the primary and secondary sources used in her brief, Joan not only relied upon traditional books physically found on the shelves of the law library, but also made use of computerized legal research tools like **LexisNexis** and **Westlaw**, which charge a stiff fee but which save huge amounts of time. These computerized search engines not only can find statutes and cases exactly on point once a few key words are provided, but can "Shepardize" what is found as well. Joan was lucky her public defender's budget allowed her to access these wonderful tools. Unlike internet sites like **Findlaw.com** (the free, poor man's version of the above), full-blown "LexisNexis" and "Westlaw" (not the watered down versions also available) can be too expensive for many public defender's offices to afford. Joan was accustomed from law school to having free access to these expensive computerized tools. For a small fee, law schools are allowed to subscribe to the services in what many suspect is an attempt by the companies to "addict" future (paying) lawyers to their charms. Large, private law firms have no trouble affording such luxuries. Small firms and government firms like Joan's must often make do with "old economy" products.

The final section of Joan's lengthy "brief" was a summary of her arguments and a statement of what she was asking the court to do. After the recapitulation of her arguments she asked the court to do one of three things. First, she asked the court to set her client free due to a lack of evidence sufficient to support a verdict of guilty. She argued that no reasonable jury could have convicted her client on the circumstantial evidence presented. After all, there were no eye-witnesses to the murder, nor fingerprints, nor any other physical evidence of her client having been at the crime scene. Earlier in her brief, Joan had reminded the court that "eyewitness testimony" (such as that of people who claimed seeing Randy Harris in town when he was supposedly a thousand miles away) is infamously unreliable, and she cited both case law as well as secondary legal sources to back up this argument.

If the court was unwilling to set her client free, Joan asked the court in the alternative to grant her client a new trial. Several of the issues she had raised in her brief dealt with errors the trial judge had made in failing to sustain defense objections to certain lines of questioning being developed by the prosecutor. Additionally, the judge had refused to suppress certain mildly incriminating statements that her client had made to the police, which the defense attorney had insisted were improperly obtained. None of these errors, Joan argued, was harmless and therefore the court should grant her client a new trial.

Finally, Joan asked the court if it did not order the release of her client or a new trial, that it reduce her client's death sentence to life in prison. In her brief, she had cited a state statute which provided that if mitigating factors in a murder case outweighed aggravating ones, then someone convicted of murder should not be put to death. She argued that though her client had allegedly killed for money (an aggravating factor), the defense also presented evidence of child sexual abuse which case law held to be a very powerful mitigating factor. She concluded her brief by asking the court to recognize this and other mitigating factors as reasons to reduce her client's sentence from death to life imprisonment.

Oral Arguments

Stuart liked Joan's brief very much. Being the lead attorney of record on the appeal, he took the time to carefully read it and edit it. Aside from a few cosmetic changes, and a couple of additional cases he plugged in as citations, the brief Stuart submitted to the prosecutor and to the appellate court was essentially the one written by Joan. The prosecution submitted its own brief in response to the one submitted by the defense a few weeks later. It attempted to systematically refute each and every argument raised in the appellant's brief. It, too, made heavy use of primary and secondary legal sources, and even threw in some social science research as well with regards to the reliability of eyewitness testimony (citing various psychological studies).

Months passed and the time came for Joan, Stuart, and the prosecutor to make oral arguments. Stuart told Joan that she could come and give him advice but that he felt obliged to be the one to do the actual presentation. Joan understood. After all, this was a capital homicide case and she had never made a single oral argument before a real appellate court in her life.

Oral arguments have been described by a former member of the U.S. Supreme Court as an "absolutely indispensable ingredient of appellate advocacy ... Often my whole notion of what a case is about crystallizes at oral argument. This happens even though I have read the briefs before oral argument ... Oral argument is a Socratic dialogue between Justices and counsel."[9] Oral argu-

---

9. Stern, Robert L. (1981). *Appellate Practice in the United States*. Washington, D.C.: Bureau of National Affairs, at 358.

ment also is believed to give judges a forum to attempt to persuade their colleagues (through the "Socratic dialogue" just referred to) to adopt their views of the merits of a particular issue.[10] Though busy appellate courts often encourage appellants of routine appeals involving clear issues which can be satisfactorily developed in written briefs to forego oral arguments and to **submit on briefs alone**,[11] appellants convicted of serious charges who have non-routine issues to advance would be foolish to give up their right to have their case orally heard.

On the day of the oral arguments, Joan and Stuart made sure to arrive at the court of appeals on time. They were told to be there at 9:30 a.m. but they were there by 9:00 a.m. The prosecutor arguing for the other side was already sitting in one of the benches when they entered the courtroom. To Joan's surprise there were also about eight other attorneys sitting in benches.

"Who are all these people?" Joan asked Stuart.

"They are all lawyers here to make oral arguments," Stuart explained. "The court calls them up one at a time and the rest of us sit and watch until we are called up. Notice that there is nobody here but lawyers. Clients never come to appellate court, be it criminal cases or civil ones. Notice also that there is no jury box or witness stand. Testimony is never given here. The appellate review here is strictly **on the record**—only the trial transcript and original court papers are referred to.[12] This is a place strictly for legal arguments based on facts that were already established in earlier proceedings. Watch and learn, Joan. You'll be back here quite often now that you are a public defender."

Stuart and the other lawyers in the room quietly studied their briefs and the outlines of their oral arguments until 9:30 when the black-robed appellate **tribunal** (panel of three judges who often are randomly assigned to hear a case) entered the room. Most appeals are heard by panels of three judges who are authorized to represent all judges of the particular appellate court, but extremely important and controversial appeals are sometimes heard by all members of the entire appellate court sitting **en banc** (sometimes as many as fifteen or more judges participate in "en banc" arguments depending on the full-size of the court).[13]

The three judges sitting today introduced themselves rather formally to all who were present. They then called for the lawyers involved in some medical

---

10. Smith, Christopher E. (1997). *Courts, Politics, and the Judicial Process.* Chicago: Nelson-Hall, at 267.

11. See, Cecil, Joe S. and Donna Stienstra. (1987). *Deciding Cases without Argument: An Examination of Four Courts of Appeals.* Washington, D.C.: Federal Judicial Center, at 22.

12. See, *Federal Rules of Appellate Procedure* 10.

13. Smith, *supra* note 10, at 238.

malpractice case to come forward to be heard. Joan watched as the lawyer representing the losing party at the malpractice trial begin his argument. It was not long before the judges cut him off with constant questioning. The lawyer never did get back to his presentation. He spent nearly his whole allotted fifteen minutes simply responding to their questions. The second lawyer had the opposite experience. The judges asked a few questions but mostly let the lawyer present her prepared remarks. None of this seemed peculiar to either Joan or Stuart. Both knew that the purpose of oral argument was not primarily to present a prepared speech but rather to respond to judges' questions and concerns. The prepared argument was merely "filler" lawyers used to fill up time between the all-important questions. Every appellant's worst fear is to be asked few or no questions. That is a sure sign that you are going nowhere with your appeal. A lively question-and-answer period is a good sign that one has a real chance of victory.

Most of the cases that Joan and Stuart listened to while waiting involved the appeal of civil rather than criminal cases, though on some days Stuart knew it was the opposite. Stuart knew from personal conversations with appellate court judges that many of them preferred criminal appeals to civil appeals, finding the former usually much more interesting.

Like a business traveler tired of frequent flying, Stuart found the long wait in the benches rather tedious. Joan, being new to appellate court, watched as eagerly as a first-time airline passenger taking in all the sights and sounds of a new adventure.

After a couple of hours, Stuart was happy to hear the judges request the attorneys in the case of Commonwealth vs. Randy Harris to "come forward and be heard." Stuart walked up to the podium while his opponent took a seat in the first bench. Stuart began his prepared remarks, beginning with a very brief recital of the alleged crime and launching into his first legal argument involving issue number one in the brief. After a minute and a half, a judge interrupted him with a question.

"Counsel, I am curious about why you maintain this man should not be put to death," the judge inquired. The other two judges leaned forward expressing keen interest in this issue as well. Given the judges' obvious desire to hear this issue addressed right away out of turn, Stuart sensed correctly that this and this alone was going to be the big issue of the day for these three appellate justices. That was not necessarily a bad thing, Stuart thought. "Harris may not be getting off but maybe we can save him from being executed today," he told himself.

Joan had similar thoughts. She remembered Stuart telling her that whenever their office could prevent a client from being executed in a capital murder case, it was counted as a victory for their office. "In a capital case, you can't just try to get the guy off," she was told. "You have to assume that you might lose the guilt/innocence phase of the trial and so prepare hard to win the sentencing phase if necessary. In a capital case, I personally see life-in-prison as a 'win.'"

Joan watched intently as Stuart fielded question after question regarding the facts of the murder and how they tie in to the law of capital punishment. There were constant questions regarding "aggravating circumstances" and even more regarding "mitigating circumstances." Stuart continued being asked questions until his time completely ran out. The judges were kind enough to permit him to make a closing remark or two.

The prosecutor knew where things were heading. When he stood up to speak, he began his remarks by talking about the appropriateness of the death penalty. He did not want to waste court time arguing that the finding of guilt was legally appropriate despite some errors made by the trial judge. It was obvious that the judges were not going to reverse the verdict. The only question was whether they would affirm the death sentence. Joan was surprised that the judges allowed the prosecutor to speak freely for several minutes before asking a single question. Apparently, the prosecutor was smart enough to anticipate their concerns and could be counted on to address them without much prompting. Eventually, a few questions were posed, followed by more uninterrupted narrative from the prosecutor. The prosecutor summed up his main points on the death penalty and still had a minute to briefly mention his position on a couple of other issues raised in the briefs before time ran out.

Neither attorney had chosen to reserve any of his allotted time for rebuttal (as many lawyers seem to like to do) so after the prosecutor had finished, argument on this case was over. The judges thanked the attorneys for their presentations, and excused them. Joan was surprised when the prosecutor invited Stuart and her to join him for lunch at a local restaurant he heard had high ratings and reasonable prices. The three of them had a fun time discussing local courthouse gossip and personal courtroom horror stories.

The Appellate Court's Opinion

Several months had gone by before Joan had heard the decision of the appellate court in the case of "Commonwealth vs. Harris." By this time she had settled in as a public defender and no longer considered herself a novice to the real world of criminal courts. Public defending may not pay well but one sees a lot of action fast.

Joan was in the chambers of a judge discussing a continuance request when the judge unexpectedly said, "Hey, Joan I hear that you and Stuart got that parent-killer off of death row."

"Really?" Joan asked. "Have you heard something?"

"Oh, yeah, the word is that the appellate court reduced his sentence from death to life. I heard it from Judge Lansing, who, as you know, did the trial."

On hearing this, Joan felt a rush of pride. She and Stuart had saved a human being from being put to death. She did not know how she would have reacted if he had been set free. But as a death penalty opponent, she felt a sense of accomplishment for having helped someone avoid the death penalty.

A week or so later, Joan and Stuart received a copy of the official order of the appellate court instructing the trial court to "re-sentence the defendant to a penalty other than death." This of course meant life in prison but a victory is a victory. Joan especially enjoyed reading the opinion of the court justifying its decision. The ten page published opinion frequently made references to arguments developed in her brief regarding death penalty jurisprudence (it cited the prosecutor's brief heavily when discussing all other issues raised on this appeal).

Stuart allowed Joan to be the one to call the prison to tell their client about the successful outcome. The client seemed satisfied. He did not want to die and he too considered this a victory. After hanging up, Joan turned to Stuart and asked him if he thought the prosecutor would appeal the reduction in sentence to the state supreme court. "Oh, knowing this prosecutor, he'll probably try to appeal," Stuart replied. "But he won't get anywhere. They'll almost for sure 'deny cert.'"

*****

Questions for Class Discussion

1. Why are the vast majority of appeals filed by the defense rather than the prosecution? Is it a good thing that prosecutors cannot file a post-trial appeal no matter how unfair the trial judge's rulings were to their side? When, if ever, are prosecutors permitted to file an appeal without violating double jeopardy?

2. What is the difference between primary and secondary legal sources in terms of doing legal research? What specifically are the primary legal sources in our country?

3. In what ways was the new public defender highlighted in this chapter better prepared by law school to do appellate work than trial work? Should

law schools be teaching future lawyers less legal research and writing and more clinical skills like negotiation techniques and trial advocacy?

4. There is nothing in the Constitution requiring appeals. Would you favor your state abolishing all appeals? Why or why not?

5. What is the difference between an "appeal of right" and a "discretionary appeal?" What is meant by the term "certiorari?"

6. Should poor people be given a free lawyer to do an appeal just as they are given a free lawyer to represent them at trials? Are lay people even more dependent on lawyers for appeals than for trials? As a lay person, would you feel more competent representing yourself at trial or on appeal?

7. Who should get to decide what issues to raise on appeal: the defendant or the lawyer? What if the defendant wants to raise really stupid issues? Should the lawyer be required to argue them in the appeal?

8. How does an appellate lawyer use a transcript of the trial to develop an appeal? What is meant by "spotting issues"? How is a transcript made?

9. How long do trial judges have to rule on objections raised during trial before looking foolish? Why can't judges simply take their time and get it right? If you were a trial judge and had to make a guess as to an objection, would you tend to favor the prosecution or the defense with your guess? Why?

10. What is meant by the "harmless error doctrine"? Why is it necessary? What sort of errors can you think of that would probably be harmless in a trial?

11. What is meant by "preserving an issue for appeal" by making an objection? Why do courts generally not allow errors not objected to during the trial to be raised on appeal? What is meant by "plain error"? Is the "plain error" exception to failing to object and thus preserving an issue for appeal a good thing? What might be an example of plain error?

12. What is the difference between a state trial-level court, a state intermediary appellate court, and a state supreme court? Does your state have an intermediary appellate court? Where is it located? Why is it necessary if there is already a state supreme court? What are the federal versions of these three types of courts called?

13. After reviewing the table on "U.S. Supreme Court Justices and their Philosophical Leanings," which of the current U.S. Supreme Court Justices most reflects what you are like? Which do you admire least? Would you be a liberal or a conservative or a moderate justice?

14. How many people get to appeal all the way to the U.S. Supreme Court? What sort of cases does the Supreme Court agree to hear? What percentage of criminal cases do you think are probably worthy of the High Court's attention and resources?

15. Unlike the highest courts in many countries, the U.S. Supreme Court not only interprets laws but makes laws. Can you give an example of that? Are you comforted or worried that this undemocratic body has more power than any other similar body in the world to make law and impose its will?

16. What is meant by the "Anders Brief"? Why are Anders Briefs often more trouble to write than they are worth?

17. What is meant by "boiler-plate issues" on appeal? What are some of the more common "boiler plate issues" that are all too frequently presented in briefs?

18. How long do attorneys get to speak during oral arguments? Why do appellate court judges constantly interrupt their presentations with questions? Would you resent such interruptions or welcome them if you were arguing an appeal for a defendant who lost at trial?

19. How many judges typically sit on the panel that listens to an appeal? What is meant by an appellate court sitting "en banc"? When do appellate courts sit "en banc"?

20. If you were to go to law school and then be asked to spend most of your professional life either doing appellate work or doing jury trials, which would you prefer? Which requires greater intelligence? Which requires greater creativity? Is a great trial lawyer necessarily a great appellate lawyer and vice versa?

*****

Key Terms: legal briefs, drop dead date, transcript, spot issues, post-trial motions, harmless error doctrine, memorandum of law, appeal of right, boiler-plate issues, Anders Brief, discretionary appeals, intermediate appellate court, state supreme court, certiorari, denies cert, grants cert, interlocutory appeals, error correction, policy review, thirteenth juror, overrules, sustains, object, preserve issue for appeal, plain error, primary legal sources, secondary legal sources, statutes, constitutional provisions, case law, legal treatises, law review articles, Shepardizing, LexisNexis, Westlaw, Findlaw.com, oral arguments, submit on briefs alone, on the record, tribunal, en banc

Additional Concepts: law school preparation for appellate advocacy, clients don't control substance of appeals, law clerk review of petitions to Supreme Court, state and federal appellate systems, members of U.S. Supreme Court and their leanings, trial judges guessing on objections, prosecutors cannot appeal, steps of an appeal, purpose of oral arguments, questioning during oral arguments, allotted time of oral arguments, appellate court's opinion

CHAPTER FIFTEEN

PROBLEM-SOLVING COURTS

Judge Leonard Brothers, president judge of a county court system in the deep South, never regretted having taken the time and expense a few years ago to attend an annual judicial conference in Las Vegas, Nevada. He enjoyed meeting with fellow members of the bench from throughout the country. Most importantly, he discovered something that altered his way of thinking about his own county's courts forever. He learned all about the growing phenomenon of "problem-solving courts." In the years since that conference Judge Brothers "grew" the concept of problem-solving courts in his own jurisdiction. Though initially resistant, fellow-judges and lawyers became increasingly converted to the philosophies behind such courts.

Problem-solving courts are specialized courts that are committed to use innovative ways to concentrate on and tackle a particular societal problem.[1] The courtroom work group (judge, prosecutor and defense lawyer) accepts the challenge of solving the matter rather than just "passing the buck" on to a probation office or jail. There are many different types of problem-solving courts. These include drug courts, domestic violence courts, mental health courts, gun courts, and teen courts. **Community courts**, which deal with neighborhood-wrecking, "quality of life crimes" such as prostitution, shoplifting, and graffiti, also fall under the heading of problem-solving courts.[2]

Beginning with "drug court," Judge Brothers' county expanded the problem-solving court idea to include "domestic violence court" and "mental health court." After just a few short years, all three courts were going strong and judges often seemed to prefer working in them to traditional criminal court.

Nationally, problem-solving courts were borne out of frustration. **Traditional criminal courts** (non-specialized courts that handle all crimes) seemed to be little more than "revolving doors," especially for certain classes of of-

---

1. See, Berman, Greg and John Feinblatt. (2001). "Problem-Solving Courts: A Brief Primer." *Law and Policy,* 23(2):125–140.

2. Center for Court Innovation. (2004). *Problem-Solving Courts.* Web Site at www.problem-solvingcourts.org (Visited March 17, 2004).

Table 1   Common Principles of Problem-Solving Courts

1. Specialize in a particular problem (e.g., drugs, domestic violence, mentally ill defendants, or quality of life crimes like prostitution and graffiti).
2. Focus on Solutions (seek tangible outcomes rather than just case processing and revolving-door punishment).
3. Judicial Monitoring (judge does not pass the buck to probation officers or others to follow-up. Judge personally stays involved in the case until it is completely finished).
4. Improved Information (judges use in-court computers, frequent court appearances by defendants, and in-court treatment staff to closely track the history and progress of defendants as they move through the rehabilitation process).
5. Accountability (defendants are swiftly punished for failing to do what they promise. For example, drug court requires frequent urine testing and defendants testing positive are punished with short jail stays).
6. Collaboration (the court works very closely with treatment providers and community groups).
7. Altered Courtroom Dynamics (traditional roles of dispassionate judges and adversarial lawyers are often replaced with collaboration on everyone's part on how to best solve a problem).

Source: Center For Court Innovation at www.courtinnovation.org (March 17, 2004).

fenders. Judges and lawyers, tired of being assembly-line workers whose main mission in life was to process cases, wanted to rethink judging and lawyering and have a real impact on setting people straight. They no longer wanted to feel like the judge in Minnesota who said, "Judges are frustrated ... You just move 'em, move 'em, move 'em ... I feel like I work for McJustice...."[3]

There are various types of problem-solving courts, but they tend to share common principles. These common principles are found it Table 1.

Judge Brothers felt that his county needed some specialized courts that focused on changing behavior for several reasons. First, he was aware that institutions where he lived like churches and families that used to help more with problems associated with addiction, mentally disturbed people, and domestic violence were no longer as influential as they had once been. Second, his local jail was crowded and was being over-used as an expensive alternative

---

3. Berman, Greg. (2000). "What is a Traditional Judge Anyway?: Problem-Solving in the State Courts." *Judicature,* September–October:78–85.

to treatment. Third, traditional punishment was not working. The same offenders kept getting off probation or getting out of jail and coming back to court over and over again for the same problem that got them in trouble in the first place.[4] Judge Brothers' solution was to bring problem-solving courts to his county. He began first by starting a drug court over which he assigned himself to preside. Later, he persuaded other judges to begin a mental health court and a domestic violence court.

Drug Court

Judge Brothers was excited when he first started drug court in his county shortly after returning from the Las Vegas conference where he first heard a lot about them. Brothers wished that he could have been the first to invent a "drug court" but knew that they have been around ever since 1989 when Dade County, Florida first opened one.[5] Brothers started his own drug court in the Fall of 2000. He was replicating an experiment begun in Florida but copied frequently all over the country. By May 2003 there were 1,042 drug courts in the United States with many more under development.[6] By 2009 the number of drug courts in the country had exploded to 2,108, and not a single state lacked a drug court somewhere within its borders.[7]

Judge Brothers knew that drug courts, though no panacea, were turning up good results. A meta-analysis done by Columbia University's National Center on Addiction and Substance Abuse looked at forty-eight drug courts around the country and found that treatment programs involving people who voluntarily entered treatment had only a ten to thirty percent one-year retention rate, while the one-year retention rate for drug court-mandated programs was sixty percent.[8] Another study done in Illinois looked at three drug courts in Chicago and found that rates of arrest for drug court participants during the first six months of the program was about one-half that of traditional pro-

---

4. See Berman and Feinblatt, *supra* note 1 for a discussion of these and other societal forces that are perceived to have caused the need for the invention of problem-solving courts.

5. Berman, *supra* note 3.

6. Rottman, Casey. (2004). "Problem-Solving Courts: Models and Trends." Williamsburg, VA: National Center for State Courts.

7. U.S. Department of Justice (Office of Justice Programs). (2009). *In the Spotlight: Drug Courts.* Web Site at www. ncjrs.gov. (Visited May 13, 2009).

8. Belenko, Steven. (1998). "Research on Drug Courts: A Critical Review." *National Drug Court Institute Review* 1:1, at 29–30.

bationers.[9] Drug courts also save money. Incarceration costs between $20,000 and $50,000 per year while drug court costs government less than $4,000 per year for each participant.[10]

Judge Brothers started his own drug court by initially limiting it to those charged with simple possession of drugs. As he became convinced of the usefulness of drug court, he allowed those charged with non-violent crimes associated with drug use to participate as well. Judge Brothers did not really know what he was doing at first. Neither did the prosecutor nor the defense attorneys. But as time passed and as they read materials on drug courts, they all got better. Luckily, they all had some guidance. The National Association of Drug Court Professionals has come up with key instructions on how to run a drug court.[11]

Defense lawyers in Judge Brothers' county served as the drug court gatekeepers. They knew who qualified for drug court and who did not. Small users, small dealers, and people who committed petty crimes to get money for drugs qualified (especially if they were repeat offenders). Armed robbers holding people up for drug money did not. When a client seemed to qualify for drug court, the defense attorney would invite him or her to apply to be processed there rather than in traditional criminal court. If the client applied and the prosecutor had no objections, the offender was usually admitted by Judge Brothers into the program.

When first appearing before the court, participants would hear Judge Brothers reiterate the ground rules that were already explained to them by their own attorneys. One of these rules was that a defendant was to agree to undergo drug court supervision for a year, during which time the court would order his or her **charges held in suspension**. If the defendant did all that the court asked and successfully completed any treatment imposed, the charges would be dropped at the end of the court's supervision. The one year could be extended if the defendant was making good progress but still needed some extra time to get his or her life in order. If the defendant failed to make satisfactory progress, he or she would be expelled from the program and processed in traditional criminal court.

Most defendants who applied for drug court did so because they were repeat offenders who were sick of jail and wanted to try something else. Few

---

9. Olson, David E. (2001). "Implementing the Key Components of Specialized Drug Treatment Courts: Practice and Policy Considerations." *Law and Policy*, 23(2):171–196.

10. National Association of Drug Court Professionals. Website at www.nadcp.org (Visited March 17, 2004).

11. National Association of Drug Court Professionals. (1997). *Defining Drug Courts: The Key Components*. Washington, D.C.: Office of National Drug Control Policy.

first time offenders applied since they usually faced only probation in traditional criminal court. They knew that drug court was no picnic.

Traditionally, courts process cases and leave it to jails, probation officers, parole officers, or convicts themselves to see to rehabilitation. Judge Brothers, like all drug court judges, decided to play an active role in offenders' treatment. The prosecutor too was expected to play a big role in the treatment plan of any participant. So was the defense attorney. The three of them reviewed cases together and collaborated in coming up with a way to help the participant break the cycle of drug use.

Judge Brothers made sure that any prosecutor or public defender assigned to his drug court had long terms of service so that he or she knew the ropes. A special probation officer with expertise in community rehabilitation options was permanently assigned to the court and became a member of the courtroom workgroup as well.

Wendy Oaks, the prosecutor assigned by the district attorney to drug court, was an important part of the drug court team. At first she balked at the idea of drug court. She spent her career cracking down on drug law violators and had little tolerance for those who could not or would not obey the law. Methamphetamine was the drug of choice in her county. She had personally sent many a "meth" user to jail and many a meth-lab owner to prison. But by the time she had worked in drug court for a couple of years she had undergone a complete change of heart. "These people aren't really criminals," she came to say. "They are people in need of help, not jail." Wendy even came to believe that those who sold "meth" were really not the evil people she once thought them to be. "These sellers are just as pathetic as the users. They aren't getting rich. They live like dogs in poverty and are addicts themselves," she told others in her office. Wendy was surprised at how completely her attitudes regarding drug offenders had turned around. Drug court tended to have that effect on people.

Wendy's job was not so much one of traditional prosecution but rather of social work mixed with law. The same (mixing social work with law) held true for the judge and for the defense attorney. The trio, assisted by a probation officer, would come up with **treatment plans** for a court participant and then haul the participant regularly into court to see how things were going. The participant would be expected to attend group drug counseling (including narcotics anonymous meetings) and remain drug free. Urine was regularly tested to confirm compliance.

The court used a **graduated sanctions program** in dealing with participants. If a participant had a "hot urine," missed a urine test, missed a court appearance, or missed a counseling session, he or she was given a stinging fine. If it happened a second time, a weekend in jail was required. If it happened a third time, the penalty was thirty days in jail. Any more violations could result in termination from the program.

Dishonesty was not tolerated. Judge Brothers would warn participants that if they ever lied to him in court, any penalty would be severely enhanced. He meant it. Brothers tended to go soft on people who admitted their mistakes (almost every participant messed up at least once or twice in the program) but had little tolerance for liars. Occasionally, Brothers would test a participant's honesty by asking him or her a question to which he already knew the answer.

Compliance with program requirements was rewarded. Judge Brothers joined with the prosecutor and defense attorney in warmly praising all those who made progress during the frequent court appearances.

The favorite part of drug court for the workgroup was **drug court graduation**. This was a formal ceremony in which courtroom workgroup members, family members, and friends all showed up to congratulate those who successfully finished the program. One by one, a participant was called up and publicly recognized for a job well done. Crying was commonplace throughout the courtroom. Participants gave a little speech if they wished to and most used it to thank family and counselors for their support and to thank the judge, prosecutor and defense attorney for patiently working with them even when they messed up. Most of them would announce how many days they had been drug free. What was really strange was the tendency for participants to hug all members in the receiving line, even the prosecutor.

As part of the "graduation," prosecutor Wendy Oaks would make motion after motion that all charges filed against a particular defendant be dismissed. Judge Brothers always responded with a smile and the words, "motion granted."

Wendy Oaks, Judge Brothers, and defense lawyers who participated in drug court sometimes received criticism from members of the legal community who did not understand what was going on in there. Some among the defense bar accused drug court of being "coercive" and "paternalistic." Some prosecutors felt that the "zealous advocacy" role of the prosecutor was compromised. Some judges wondered if judicial "impartiality" was being interfered with. Some state legislators fretted over "separation of powers" concerns (judges infringing on the executive branch and the executive branch infringing on the judicial).[12] But to all these criticisms, Judge Brothers simply would respond,

---

12. Criticisms of drug court such as those listed can be found in Berman and Feinblatt, *supra* note 1.

"traditional court is a worse alternative. I've tried that. When it comes to drugs, traditional criminal court just has not worked."

Mental Health Court

Anne Shoemaker repeatedly found herself in court for shoplifting. She liked to pinch almost anything: clothes, grocery items, makeup, books, candy, cigarettes, gasoline. The strange thing was that she was far from poor. Her husband was a successful plastic surgeon and she lived in a large house with horse stables and a tennis court. On top of this, she had inherited over three hundred thousand dollars when her parents died a couple of years ago. The money just sat in the bank.

Anne's problem was that she was a kleptomaniac. She had a compulsion to steal. She knew it was wrong. She just could not resist. Stealing was more exciting to her than anything she could think of.

Anne was given probation the first several times that she was caught, on condition that she seek psychiatric treatment. But she found the sessions with the therapist boring and would eventually drop out. Then she would steal again and wind up back in court.

The last time she stole, the prosecutor felt compelled to seek jail time. Anne's lawyer brought the case to trial and advanced an insanity defense. The jury of hard-working blue collar workers had little sympathy for wealthy Anne. They promptly convicted her. They agreed with the prosecutor that even though she had a mental illness she still knew right from wrong. The judge gave Anne thirty days in jail.

When Anne was released from jail, she went "straight" for about five months. Then she was caught stealing money from the purse of a school teacher. The teacher had left her purse unattended while having her hair styled at a salon. Anne could not resist lifting the cash while she was waiting for her turn in the chair. The sentencing guidelines called for four months in jail. Anne's defense attorney convinced her to apply to the new "mental health court."

Drug court had become so successful in Judge Brothers' county that he asked his colleague Judge Linda West to start a mental health court. **Mental health court** is a specialized court that tries to help people who repeatedly break the law due to mental problems to get whatever help they need in order to cope with their issues in a law-abiding manner.

Judge West agreed to take on the assignment of starting a mental health court. She was well aware that the local jail was full of mentally ill people convicted of minor crimes who probably did not belong there. She decided to provide an alternative experience to anyone charged with a nonviolent crime who was mentally ill, and who prosecutors and defense attorneys believed could benefit from a different approach.

Judge West decided to pattern her mental health court after the one instituted in King County (Seattle), Washington. King County began its mental health court in 1999 because it realized that in traditional court mentally ill defendants often dealt with a different judge, prosecutor and public defender each time they appeared in court, even on the same case. This lack of cohesion created obstacles in identifying what was wrong with the defendant and what truly needed to be done. Like King County, West wanted to start a mental health court in order to achieve "faster case processing time, improved access to public mental health services, improved well-being, and reduced recidivism."[13]

Soon, Judge West was dealing with Anne the kleptomaniac in addition to the small army of mentally ill people charged repeatedly with vagrancy, disorderly conduct, aggressive begging, public urination, and exhibitionism. Judge West's favorite defendant was "trolley man," a local schizophrenic who liked to disrupt trolley service by lying down in the middle of the tracks. Through some miracle he had not yet been killed.

Judge West knew that she was no expert on mental health, so to help her deal with the likes of "trolley man" and Anne she recruited a psychiatric nurse knowledgeable about available resources to work with her team. West, the nurse, the prosecutor assigned to mental health court, and the defense attorney would all try to come up with plans to get their unique array of criminals the help they needed to live relatively normal lives.

Like drug court, Judge West required every participant in her court to attend court on a regular basis. Judge West had a computer in court which she could use to instantaneously review the criminal and treatment histories of anybody brought before her. She had a little "comment section" on the screen. She would use this area of each defendant's file to write personal notes to herself about the status of a particular case and what she and the courtroom workgroup had attempted to do at the last court appearance. She especially liked to enter promises that participants made to her the last time they appeared in court so that she could hold them accountable.

Unlike drug court, Judge West knew that very little data has yet been collected on the success and failures of criminal mental health courts.[14] But given

---

13. King County District Court. *Mental Health Court Overview.* Website at www.king county.gov/courts/DistrictCourt/MentalHealthCourt.aspx (Visited July 21, 2009).

14. See Berman and Feinblatt, *supra* note 1.

the utter failure of traditional courts to adequately deal with the mentally ill, she thought mental health court was worth a try.

Judge West found Anne Shoemaker, the kleptomaniac, to be a very interesting case study. Unlike most of the participants in her court, Anne was articulate, attractive, and free of strange ticks. Anne dressed even better than the lawyers did. She was a most unusual participant.

Judge West and the courtroom workgroup decided to make Anne attend group counseling. Group counseling seemed to work well for many of the court's participants. Exhibitionists and peeping Toms went to a non-violent sex offenders group. Compulsive gamblers who stole or committed fraud to support their habit had their group as well. But, there was no group for kleptomaniacs like Anne. So, Anne wound up in one of several generic groups that the court had set up.

Anne was told by the court that this was her only chance to avoid jail. She would have the charges against her suspended for one year. If she finished the year successfully, the state would drop the theft charges against her. In addition to attending group therapy and paying restitution, Anne was required to write a letter of apology to the victim. Anne indicated her intention to comply.

Each time Anne appeared for court the judge quizzed her about her attendance at group counseling meetings. To her surprise, Anne actually enjoyed the meetings and felt comfortable sharing her pain with others in trouble. During the first six months she only missed one group session. The prosecutor immediately found out about it and informed the judge, who ordered Anne to pick up trash in the park for six hours one Saturday. Anne found picking up trash humiliating, and made certain never to miss another group session.

The court also required Anne to get individual counseling. Anne did not like psychiatrists so the court allowed her to see a psychiatric social worker instead. The social worker helped Anne to discover things about herself that she had never realized before. Anne still had the urge to shoplift but the social worker taught her how to manage the urge. Once when she was about to steal, she called her social worker who talked her through the temptation.

At the end of the year, Anne "graduated" from mental health court. She was commended by the judge, prosecutor, and defense attorney for having gone straight for so long. They warned her that she would have to keep her guard up the rest of her life. Anne's family members all were there to show their support. They applauded when the prosecutor made a motion that the charges against her be dismissed.

Anne did not steal again for three long years. But then, in a moment of weakness, she stole some golf balls from the shop at her country club without being caught. She immediately returned to counseling to get help all on her own. She did not want to disappoint Jude West, the prosecutor, or her defense attorney by returning to court.

Domestic Violence Court

Will Nash had been beating his wife Patty off and on during the four years of their marriage. The first time Will hit Patty was on a Thanksgiving afternoon just a few weeks after they had married. He had been drinking all day and lost his temper when Patty insisted that he stop watching football and spend some time with her. They argued heatedly with one another over his lack of sensitivity, and when Patty turned off the television in the middle of a field goal attempt, Will smacked her across the face.

Though outraged, Patty at first dismissed Will's aggression as an isolated incident never to be repeated. Will promised as much. But Will's behavior continued to deteriorate over the months and years of their marriage. Things got so bad last year that Patty finally went to the police. The police took one look at her black eye and bloody nose and promptly arrested Will.

Will spent the night in jail but was released the next day on low bail on condition that he obey a newly issued **protection order** (court order that forbids a person from having contact with and/or doing certain things against a victim in the future). The protection order instructed Will to have no contact with Patty until the assault charge was disposed of later in court. Will understood that a violation of the order would be **contempt of court** (for which he could be fined or imprisoned). Will agreed to obey the protection order, and did so for four days at which point he once again began living with Patty (without her permission). Petrified, Patty did not tell the court about Will's contempt of its order. Neither did the court ever check up on Patty to see how things were going. Months later, Will pled guilty to simple assault before a totally different judge and was given a $250 fine and the admonition "to work things out" with his wife. As far as Patty could tell, the protection order just seemed to have vanished on its own. Will made Patty pay the fine since it was "her fault" he was assessed one.

Patty and Will continued to live together with Will occasionally shoving, punching, and kicking her for perceived transgressions. Finally though, Will beat Patty up again so noisily that a neighbor called the police.

This time things were handled quite differently. Upon arresting Will, the arresting officer followed new procedure by immediately calling the prosecutor assigned to the county's new "domestic violence court." **Domestic violence court** is a specialized court with a dedicated judge, prosecutor, and victim's advocate whose goals are two-fold: to improve victim safety and to increase the monitoring of defendants.[15]

Patty was surprised when the prosecutor telephoned Patty and personally invited her to come directly to her office. Upon arrival, the prosecutor introduced Patty to a **victim's advocate**, a person whose job it was to help Patty with advice, information, and emotional support while accompanying Patty through the legal process that was about to take place. The victim's advocate told Patty about community resources (including a local women's shelter) and promised Patty that Will would not be allowed to slip through the system so easily this time.

Before the invention of domestic violence courts, people like Patty had little choice but to seek help through traditional courts. But, traditional courts have not proven very effective in the area of domestic violence, as evidenced by several things.

First, the mere issuance of a protection order with no direct follow-up often provides little real protection. One 1996 study found that sixty percent of protection orders granted by traditional courts were violated within a year.[16] Another study found that seventeen percent of domestic partners killed had a protection order from a court at the time of the homicide.[17]

Second, traditional court handles cases in a very rapid and cursory fashion. Assembly-line justice is bad enough when dealing with standard criminal cases, but can be disastrous when dealing with complex, domestic violence cases needing attention to detail.

Third, many prosecutors and judges who do not specialize in domestic violence cases still falsely believe that domestic violence is a private, family matter and fail to give it the priority it deserves.[18] Though the old **rule of thumb** (a husband could beat his wife as long as the stick was no thicker than a thumb) is obsolete, reluctance to forcefully deal with domestic violence seems to endure in many quarters.

The court Patty was now dealing with was quite different. Borrowing concepts developed in Brooklyn, New York, the domestic violence court in Patty's jurisdiction had several goals. These are illustrated in Table 2.

---

15. Center for Court Innovation. *Brooklyn Domestic Violence Court.* Website at www.courtinnovation.org/demo (Visited March 18, 2004).

16. Tsai, Betsy. (2000). "The Trend Toward Specialized Domestic Violence Courts: Improvements on an Effective Innovation. *Fordham Law Review,* 68:1285–1327, at 1292, citing Buzawa, Eve S. and Carl G. Buzawa (eds.). (1996). *Do Arrests and Restraining Orders Work?* Thousand Oaks, CA: Sage Publications, at 240.

17. Tsai, *supra* note 16, at 1292, citing *The Commission on Domestic Violence, Statistics."* Website at www.courtinnovation.org/demo (Visited Oct. 15, 1999).

18. Tsai, *supra* note 16, at 1293.

Table 2   Goals of Domestic Violence Court

Goal	How Accomplished
Immediacy	No beating around the bush. Punishment is swift and certain.
Safety	Victim's advocate is provided to ensure victim gets resources she needs.
Accountability	Defendant appears frequently in court to be checked up on.
Consistency	Same judge deals with defendant from beginning to end.
Coordination	Court shares info with social service agencies and vice versa.

Source: Center for Court Innovation. "Brooklyn Domestic Violence Court." Website at www.courtinnovation.org/demo. (March 18, 2004).

Unlike other problem-solving courts like drug court or mental health court, domestic violence courts like the one Patty was dealing with remain adversarial. Less patience and sympathy is afforded defendants. Punishment tends to be swift and certain. Courts view domestic assaults as the product of free will rather than conduct rooted mainly in addiction or illness. Nevertheless, domestic violence court still could be considered a problem-solving court due to the use of dedicated judges and prosecutors and the close monitoring by the court itself of a defendant's future conduct.[19]

When Will appeared before the judge in domestic violence court, he was advised that he had two options: go to jail to await trial in traditional court or consent to being intensely supervised for a period of one year by the domestic violence court. Will chose domestic violence court. If he did all that the court required, charges would either be dropped or reduced to a summary offense with no jail time required.

The first thing the domestic court judge did was to enter a new protection order. Will was to have no contact with his wife for six weeks. The victim's advocate would telephone and visit Patty on a frequent basis to ensure that no contact had been attempted. Any violation of this order would result in immediate arrest. This protection order would be revisited in six weeks to see if Will would be permitted to resume living with Patty.

Second, the judge ordered Will to attend and successfully complete a **batterer intervention program** to be determined by the probation office. Most mainstream domestic violence intervention programs involve a group ap-

---

19. See Rottman, *supra* note 6.

proach.[20] In Will's case, the judge assigned a probation officer associated with **DV court** (nickname for domestic violence court) to closely monitor Will's attendance at the weekly group counseling sessions. Any absences would be immediately reported to both Patty (for her protection) and to the court (so that it could mete out appropriate sanctions).

Third, Will was to report to court in person every three weeks so that the court could review his progress and any missteps he might have made. He was given a calendar with the court dates marked.

Fourth, Will was made to understand that any attempted contact with Patty in the next six weeks would result in an automatic 48 hour stay in jail. Any missed court appointments or missed counseling appointments would result in eight hours of immediate community service, probably picking up trash along the highways. Any assault or threats against Patty would get him expelled from the domestic violence court program and he would be sent to jail to await trial in traditional court.

Six months after agreeing to be supervised by domestic violence court, Will seemed to be still behaving himself. He was now back living with Patty with her and the court's consent. Patty's victim's advocate and Will's probation officer felt confident that there had not been any more incidents of violence in the home. Will did miss two appointments during the six months thus far, and spent two days picking up trash on the highway. He was careful not to miss court or counseling again.

Not as much research has been done on the effectiveness of domestic violence courts as has been done on the much more established drug courts. As more data are collected, researchers hope to better know how effective they truly are. For now, the few studies that have been done on the effectiveness of DV courts are inconsistent.[21] Part of the problem is that researchers have been experiencing difficulty in establishing control groups to properly compare domestic violence courts with their traditional counterparts.[22]

Patty and Will were not aware of any studies being done on courts like the one they were now dealing with. Patty only knew that she was finally being paid attention to seriously by those in authority. Will felt that he was being paid close attention to as well, something that he both disliked but knew that he and Patty needed.

*****

---

20. Tsai, *supra* note 16, at 1312.
21. Tsai, *supra* note 16, at 1310.
22. See, Rottman, *supra* note 6.

Questions for Class Discussion

1. What is meant by problem-solving courts? In what ways do they differ from traditional criminal courts?
2. What are some of the weaknesses of traditional criminal courts? How are these weaknesses addressed by problem-solving courts?
3. What types of crimes does the chapter indicate are treated in problem-solving courts? Would you add any other types of crimes to the list? What about repeated drunk driving?
4. Why do first time offenders usually opt for traditional court over problem-solving court? Should first time offenders be forced to be processed through problem-solving courts if they are available?
5. What is meant by having one's charges "held in suspension?" Do you think it is alright that people who successfully finish a problem-solving court typically get to have their charges dismissed at the end of the program?
6. Do you think it is fair that some crimes are treated with special attention in problem-solving court while most are treated using "business as usual" methods in regular courts? Don't most criminals have some sort of problem or another?
7. If you were a judge would you prefer working in a specialized problem-solving court or in a traditional criminal court? What if you were a public defender? A prosecutor?
8. What do you think about mixing law with social work like judges and lawyers in problem-solving courts are asked to do? Does this "trash" the American notion of adversary justice? Or, is it a healthy evolution in American justice?
9. Some critics of problem-solving courts complain that they constitute nothing more than a "soft on crime" approach. What do you think?
10. Drug courts seem to act as though drug crimes are the result of illness rather than free will. Do you believe drug law violators are ill people who need help more than punishment? What about drug dealers?
11. What is meant by a "graduated sanctions program?" What are some examples of "graduated sanctions?" Why are "graduated sanctions" necessary: why not just kick people out of the program the first time they "mess up?"
12. Has anybody in the class ever attended a "drug court graduation?" If so, what was it like? If not, what does the chapter indicate goes on there?
13. In reading the story of the wealthy kleptomaniac who was processed through the mental health court, did you find yourself feeling sorry or

angry at the rich thief? Were you offended that in the end she got to avoid serious jail time despite her repeated offenses?

14. Do you buy the argument that some crime is attributable to mental illness and should be addressed differently than regular crime? Or, are all criminals just bad people? Are all criminals mentally ill?

15. How are domestic violence courts different from most other problem-solving courts? If the focus is more on punishment of the offender and protection of the victim than on rehabilitation, why can't traditional courts be trusted to accomplish these two ordinary goals?

16. Many domestic violence courts use victim advocates to help victims through the judicial process. Why do domestic violence courts arguably need victim advocates more than traditional courts? Are you okay with having your tax dollars used to pay the salaries of victim advocates?

17. What is meant by the old "rule of thumb" in terms of domestic violence? What are some vestiges of this rule today?

18. According to the table in the chapter entitled, "Goals of Domestic Violence Court," what in fact are the specific goals of these types of courts? Which of these goals do you think is the single-most important goal?

19. Suppose your part of town had an enormous problem with prostitution. How might a problem-solving court be used in cleaning up this problem? How would such a court work?

20. Little research has been done on mental health courts and on domestic violence courts. What research that has been done has shown inconsistent results. Given this, would you support the use of mental health or domestic violence courts in your jurisdiction?

*****

Key Terms: problem-solving courts, community courts, traditional criminal courts, charges held in suspension, treatment plans, graduated sanctions program, drug court graduation, mental health court, protection order, contempt of court, domestic violence court, victim's advocate, rule of thumb, batterer intervention program, DV court

Additional Concepts: common principles of problem-solving courts, weaknesses of traditional courts, advantages of drug courts, research on drug courts, criticisms of drug courts, lack of research on mental health courts, group counseling, adversary nature of domestic violence courts, ineffectiveness of traditional protection orders, traditional attitudes toward domestic violence, goals of domestic violence court, lack of research on domestic violence courts

CHAPTER SIXTEEN

PROPOSED REFORMS

In this, the concluding chapter of the textbook, we will be doing something different. Unlike the preceding chapters, which each made use of fictional stories to illuminate real world principles, I will be stepping out as the author of the book to suggest various reforms which I believe should be considered by future, professional court actors and decision-makers (hopefully including some of you).

Whenever I teach a course on America's criminal courts, I like to tell my first-day students why this is my favorite subject to teach in the university. I tell them that it is my favorite subject because, in my sincerely held opinion, the court system is so utterly mangled and broken, that it is a delight to teach. This sometimes gets a smile from the class, but I actually am quite serious when I say it.

I realize that my views of courthouse dysfunction are not shared by all. For example, several years ago I was invited to be the guest speaker at a luncheon of the bar association in the county in which my university is located. In retrospect, I suppose the attorneys, judges, etc. attending the luncheon expected me to deliver a respectful speech about the virtues of our great court system and the fine job each of them were doing in advancing American democracy. Instead, I candidly told them what I thought: that the court system was horribly broken and that reforms were overdue.

As you can imagine, my talk did not sit well with everyone in this group, and the county chief prosecutor seemed particularly annoyed. At the end of my little sermon, he raised his hand and asked, "Professor, are you teaching this sort of thing up there at the university?" When I replied that I was, he told me that I was "teaching students disrespect for our judicial system."

I was rather surprised by his criticism. I had naively just assumed that any professional in the court house simply shared my views of how pathological things were there. But, apparently not all do (and I want you to know this).

I guess I got my dander up with this critic of my speech because all I could think to say in response to his public condemnation was that, "Yes, I teach such ideas up there at the university and I will continue to do so." Well, this attorney (now a judge) was too polite to make anything more of it at the luncheon, but I knew that I had laid an egg with some in this group. Even so,

I wish to use this last opportunity with you, my readers, to lay out some ideas for reforms. You need not agree with all of them or even any of them. But, I still think there is some merit to my sharing them with you.

Legal Education Reforms (Chapter One)

I did not discuss legal education at the above-mentioned luncheon, but I wish to do so now. The one thing that every prosecutor, defense attorney, and non-petty court judge have in common is that all of them went through three long years of law school. There, they were taught (indoctrinated?) to "think like a lawyer."

As was presented in Chapter One of this book, law schools make heavy use of two rather interesting methods in delivering their educational product: the venerable, old "case method" and an aggressive version of the "Socratic method." Though I like both of these pedagogical tools, I do believe there can be too much of a good thing.

When I was a first-year law student, I have to admit that the case method greatly increased my ability to read and analyze difficult materials. However, the trade off was that it was an extremely time-consuming and inefficient way to learn the law. After having read scores of cases, the desired effect (teaching one to read critically and analytically) was achieved but I still had half my law school experience ahead of me. That second half of law school was sheer torture. I was reading so many cases that my vision actually was affected by the end of each semester (I had trouble reading the time on a distant classroom clock, despite (normally) perfect long-range vision). Looking back, I wish we could have spent less time reading yet another case and more time simply doing other things. Think of your undergraduate experience? How would you like to spend it doing *nothing but* reading case studies in nearly every class you ever take? Enough is enough.

As critical as I am about the perceived over-reliance on the case method, I am yet even more critical of the aggressive, "in your face" version of the Socratic method used by so many law professors. Education should be fun, not the academic version of boot camp. What is the point of brow-beating students into submission? This method has been criticized by some as favoring some students over others (e.g., males over females—see Chapter One). I am not sure I agree with the gender concerns, but there is no doubt in my mind that some enjoy and benefit from being grilled more than others. Frankly, I don't see how being intimidated by an educator can be a healthy way to communicate the law.

Another legal education reform I would like to propose is that more practical skills be taught while in law school. Imagine my horror when I was a brand new criminal lawyer and I did not know how to get someone's bail reduced, how (or where) to file a motion of any kind, how to get exhibits admitted into evidence during a trial, or even where to sit in the courtroom. Imagine my embarrassment when a relative or friend asked me to help with a divorce, real estate settlement, or child custody matter. I did not have a clue how to do any of those things. Law school taught me lots of theory but absolutely no practical knowledge. I would have enjoyed some more practical knowledge.

Finally, on the topic of legal education, I have one more suggestion. Why not offer an undergraduate degree in this country in law (not paralegal studies or a few law courses as part of some other major, but law). The in-depth study of law in the United States is reserved exclusively for only those who already have a bachelor's degree. Why? Shouldn't law be offered along with history, chemistry, or physical education as an undergraduate major? Throughout most of the world, one can study law as an undergraduate. Why not here? I think law is too helpful a subject to be left for graduate study only. For example, wouldn't it be great if future police officers, probation officers, government functionaries, military officers, business people, etc. had the option of majoring in law as an undergraduate (not just taking a couple of courses but a full-blown major)? The law schools might object at having their monopoly eroded but so what? They do not own the law. A Juris Doctorate could still be required in order to become an attorney. But, future attorneys are not the only ones who would benefit from a robust exposure to law.

Juvenile Court Reforms (Chapter Two)

I propose two reforms when it comes to our juvenile courts: increase the status of juvenile courts in the eyes of the professional courthouse community and use only dedicated prosecutors, judges, and public defenders in juvenile court.

As Chapter Two revealed, many in the court community look down on juvenile court as somehow inferior to adult court: a sort of "kiddie court." Nothing could be further from the truth. Juvenile court is as important as, if not more important than, adult court. Wouldn't you agree?

We see this bias against juvenile courts even in undergraduate textbooks on the courts. It is often the last or nearly last chapter in such books, as if to say, "We'll cover it if we have time at the end of the semester." As a sort of subtle protest against this indignity, I chose to place my chapter on the juvenile court at the front of the book, rather than at its traditional place at the end. Juvenile court is not kiddie court, and students, judges, prosecutors, and defenders need to be taught to give it the respect it deserves. This will only happen if those who teach juvenile justice and those who work in juvenile court make it happen. It is time we all do.

Chapter Two also suggested that the goals and methods of juvenile court are far different than those of adult criminal court. Because of this, it is foolish to allow generalist judges, prosecutors, or public defenders to work in juvenile court on a sort of ad hoc, "shoot from the hip" basis (as they sometimes do). We do not allow heart doctors to work on someone's ears. Neither should we expect unsophisticated adult court attorneys and judges to "operate" in juvenile court. They simply don't know what they are doing. Vulnerable children's futures are at stake.

Speedy Justice Reforms (Chapter Three)

I can barely approach this next topic with proper detachment. In my view, the Sixth Amendment right to a *speedy* trial is simply an unfilled commitment, an empty I.O.U. that is not being paid. Currently, nobody in American society seems to care about this "right": not state legislatures, nor judges, nor the press, nor ordinary citizens.

When I practiced criminal law in Pennsylvania, cases routinely took six months to process, sometimes much longer. When I spoke to attorneys in one South Carolina county, I was told that judges there do not want to be pestered with "speedy" trial concerns unless at least a year had passed. Could anyone seriously believe that the drafters of the Sixth Amendment would be okay with this situation?

When legislatures ignore the Constitution, the appellate courts are supposed to step in. But instead, even the U.S. Supreme Court has merely given lower courts a list of "squishy" factors to consider in assessing "speediness" (see Chapter Three). These easily manipulated and grossly subjective factors essentially let the system off the hook. The proof? Take a look at how long it is still taking criminal cases to get processed in our country. Apparently, "speedy" does not mean "speedy" but merely, "when we have the time and resources to finally get around to it."

To ease our collective conscience with regards to our slow-motion version of due process, we allow bail bondsmen to help people gain access to pre-trial freedom. This brings us to my next proposal: eliminate private bail bondsmen. They charge huge fees (ten to fifteen percent of the bail amount) for little work. Why should people waiting for their day in court be subjected to such predation? Non-profit, government sponsored bail agencies have been in existence in many areas of the country for decades now. These agencies do the same work as the private bail bondsmen (assessing flight risk that magistrates don't have time to do and granting "bail" when appropriate) but for a tiny fraction of the cost to the client. If the client (accepted into the program) shows up for court as the government bail agent predicts, he or she gets a full refund of the ten to fifteen percent they have posted (minus a fee of just one percent or so to cover the costs of the program). It is time that all areas replace private bail bondsmen with non-profit, government sponsored versions of the same. Let's not force those being deprived of speedy justice to have to pay dearly for their pre-trial liberty.

Defense Attorney Reforms (Chapter Four)

My first job out of law school was as a public defender in suburban Philadelphia. Despite having four years of college plus three years of law school (and the debts to prove it), my salary as a public defender was so small that I could not afford to buy even a broken down row house in the county in which I worked. I made less than starting school teachers (who had less education but the protection of a union). The high school graduate who delivered my mail (also protected with union membership) made far more than I did. This brings me to an obvious reform: pay public defenders a fair wage in keeping with the educational requirements and level of responsibility of their position.

Public defending was the hardest job I have ever done in my life. It was much harder than my later work as a prosecuting attorney (who also are grossly underpaid) and fantastically more difficult than my current job as a college professor. Though I do not regret my three years of hard work as a defender, it would have been nice to have been paid fairly. My colleagues in the public defender's office were mostly Ivy League trained lawyers who took the job out of idealism. But, even idealistic people still need to pay rent.

Speaking of public defenders, we should use them and no other type of "free" criminal defense lawyer. By this I mean that we should do away with "assigned counsel" programs and "contract systems" in providing indigent criminal defense. There is a one in three chance that you live in a county that uses one of these two bad options instead of public defenders. As mentioned in Chapter Four, public defenders do a better job than either of these two other types of indigent defense. If we are going to provide free lawyers, let us go with quality. And, while we are at it, let us require our public defenders to be full-time (no private clients on the side to distract them from their publicly paid duties). We also need to limit their caseloads to manageable levels: lawyers should have time to meet their clients and review the file before the case is about to be called for court.

I also would like to propose a reform regarding private criminal defense attorneys. I believe that there should be some sort of certification process with regards to them. It is very painful to see a tax attorney or a real estate attorney come in to court to "help out" the relative of a client with a criminal matter. This is malpractice. While I do not think that criminal lawyers need to limit their practice exclusively to criminal work, we should not allow civil lawyers to practice in criminal court merely on a "one case basis." Judges need to protect lay people who think all lawyers are familiar with courtrooms. The fact is, the vast majority of lawyers never go to criminal court in their entire professional lifetimes, and many never go to any type of courtroom (criminal or civil). England has lawyers who are barristers (courtroom lawyers) and lawyers who are solicitors (paper-work lawyers). In a practical sense we do as well, but sometimes America's version of solicitors can forget this.

There is also something else that must be raised with regards to private criminal attorneys. Why are they on average no more effective than public defenders in the quality of service rendered clients? We learned in Chapter Four that public defenders do as well as or better than private attorneys in terms of plea bargains negotiated, trials ending in acquittals, and appeals being won. How can this possibly be when public defenders typically have such massive case loads compared to private attorneys? Are public defenders smarter or more talented than private attorneys? Are they more integrated into the dynamics of the court house and hence more on top of things? Or, are private attorney dropping the ball somehow in terms of motivation and preparation (not taking advantage of the extra time they have)? More research in this area definitely should be undertaken so that the root problem, if there is one, can be identified. In the meantime, something indeed seems to be profoundly amiss.

Prosecuting Attorney Reforms (Chapter Five)

I believe that something needs to be done to limit the power of prosecuting attorneys in this country. As we saw in chapter five, they have more power over the lives and futures of people than perhaps any other official in America. What does it mean for our democracy when a young person (many prosecutors are very young—not even out of their 20s yet) gets to decide what charges to bring, how strong the evidence is, and what the sentence should be. In doing thus, the prosecutor obliterates boundaries between self, jury and judge. Most prosecutors are honest and good people, but everyone knows about the potential for abuse in the granting of too much power. The cure for this is plain: eliminate (or at least reduce) plea bargaining which transfers power away from juries (as fact finders) and judges (as sentencers) to prosecuting attorneys (who then become both fact finder and sentencer in addition to the accuser). I'll have more to say on this topic when I discuss plea bargains below. But, clearly, prosecutors simply have too much power in our democracy. It would be prudent to disperse some of this power, as was the original plan.

Judiciary Reforms (Chapter Six)

There are three reforms I think we should consider with regards to our judiciary.

First, states that currently elect judges should switch to a system of appointments based on merit. Unlike most seeking political office, judicial candidates cannot really campaign. They cannot really give any reason why someone should vote for them rather than one of their opponents. For example, judges cannot say, "Vote for me and I'll be tough on crime," or "Vote for me and I'll go soft on marijuana." Such campaigning is forbidden since judges are not allowed to appear to have any agenda. So, if judges cannot truly campaign, what is the point of electing them? Let's switch to appointments, but appointments based on merit rather than politics.

Second, let us require that even our lower-court judges be graduates of law school. Some states require this but many do not. The idea that a right to a "trial de novo" before a law-trained judge fixes the problem of having judges who are not learned in the law is flawed. Many people will give up after losing in lower court. They will simply take their lumps rather than continue the painful process of exercising their right to a "trial de novo."

Third (and perhaps most controversial), let us vastly increase the number of judges in trial courts so that we can have less congestion (and hence more speed and maybe even more trials). This would require two major reforms: creating the judicial specialty of criminal court judge (most judges are generalists) and decreasing the judicial salary for these specialists. If we were to cut judicial salaries in half for these specialists, we could double the number of criminal court judges overnight without spending much more than we do now. We would not have to build more courtrooms, since judges could share courtrooms (most courtrooms sit empty most of the time anyway). Now, you might ask, who would be willing to work as a judge for half the normal judicial salary? I think many public defenders and prosecuting attorneys would be willing, since half a judicial salary would still be more than many of them currently make (not to mention the increase in prestige). Many of these criminal attorneys would be absolutely competent to handle criminal cases as a judge. After all, they become experts after just a few short years of service. I realize that this "reform" would be a hard one to politically effectuate. But, I'd much rather have 100 specialist judges making a respectable wage than 50 generalist judges making a luxury wage. Many (defendants, victims, aspiring judges, the Sixth Amendment) would benefit, though not the current high-priced generalist judges.

Plea Bargain Reforms (Chapter Nine)

I propose that plea bargains be limited to misdemeanor cases only. Nobody charged with a felony will be given a bargain. Accused felons will either plea guilty without a bargain or else go to trial. A clear super-majority of cases in our criminal courts involve misdemeanors only. They can still be processed as usual (via bargain-induced guilty pleas). But the truly serious cases (the felonies) will be processed the way the drafters of the Constitution envisioned, via a straight guilty plea or else a jury trial.

Plea bargaining is the ugly wart on the face of our Constitution. I would like it to be excised entirely, but would settle for its elimination in serious felony cases. Society (as a victim) has the right to expect our system to deny serious criminals any input into what sentence they will get for their bad actions. They can choose to commit a crime, but should not get a choice in the consequences of it. Plea bargaining improperly empowers criminals by asking them, "What punishment are you willing to allow society to give you?" But, as much as I object to plea bargaining from a victim's view point, I am even more concerned with harms done to our Constitution.

As we learned in Chapter Nine, the U.S. Supreme Court not only has ruled that plea bargaining is okay, but "it is to be encouraged." I strongly disagree. I think it should be discouraged. In fact, it should be eliminated.

Thanks to plea bargaining, our criminal courts have become a convicting machine. Over 90 percent of cases are plea bargained, several percent more result in guilty pleas without bargains, several percent more are dropped by the prosecutor for lack of evidence, and whatever is left (maybe 3 percent or so) go to trial. I would expect a 97 percent conviction rate in a totalitarian dictatorship, but such a rate in a democracy seems truly disturbing.

Ultimately, we need to ask ourselves, does a person truly have the right to a jury trial, if the book is thrown at him for exercising that right? Remember, our country incarcerates a greater percentage of its population than any other country on the planet. And, this is so with the vast majority of people "voluntarily" pleading guilty and getting so-called "deals." It seems to me that the government is getting it both ways: convictions without trials and stiff sentences in the name of "bargains." If people getting "bargains" are being incarcerated at world-record rates, what is happening to those who dare to exercise their "right" to a trial and lose?

Plea bargaining is not a fix but a cop out. We need to sit down and truly fix the system. We can do it. Our ancestors did not have plea bargaining (at least not like today). Neither do many of our fellow democrats around the world. If they can do it, so can we.

Trial Reforms (Chapters Ten and Eleven)

I won't belabor minor reforms in this area (e.g., I think eliminating peremptory challenges in jury selection would be a very good idea since they are used to "stack the jury" rather get an unbiased one). Instead, I just want to emphasize the need to get rid of the 800 pound gorilla in the courtroom: the ridiculously long jury trials that often take place there.

Every time someone takes days, weeks or even months to have his or her "day in court," they are effectively denying someone else to have a chance at this limited resource. Judges need to make sure that valuable court time is not squandered by piggish lawyers who examine every scintilla of evidence to a nauseating degree. The 1995 O. J. Simpson's murder "trial of the century" took eight months and 150 witnesses to present (but only four hours for a verdict to be reached by the jury). How many other defendants were denied any trial time at all because of Simpson's gluttonous use of trial time?

As we have learned, studies show that most juries usually decide guilt or innocence during the opening statements and don't change their minds. This is not so surprising. While I don't go so far as to advocate limiting trials to opening statements, I do think that a day is plenty of time for juries to "get it" in most cases (even a "half day" is enough in simple cases). Of course, some cases might require several days or even the occasional couple of weeks (e.g., death penalty cases) for juries to "get it," but trials that go on for many days or weeks are usually time-wasters.

During the "golden age of trials," our American ancestors gave everybody a trial who wanted one, but limited the length of these trials dramatically by today's standards: one jury typically heard eight or so cases a day. While this is probably being too efficient, they at least gave everyone a trial. Today, it seems we would rather give one person a three week trial, even if it means that ten other people get no trial at all. This is not right. Let us convince judges to convince lawyers to put reasonable limits on the length of all jury trials.

Jury Deliberation Reforms (Chapter Twelve)

As we have learned, a great debate exists among legal scholars as to whether or not jury nullification, the ability juries have to find someone not guilty because they disagree with the law, is a right or merely just a power—a virtue or a vice. I side with those people who believe it to be a right. For this reason, I think that juries should be instructed by the judge (upon request of defense counsel) that they can nullify the law if they so choose.

Currently, such an option, though clearly available to every jury, is kept a secret from them by trial judges in almost every state. I like the idea that juries might wish to act as a buffer between someone accused of a crime and the government that accuses them, by judging the law as well as the facts. Let's end the secrecy. Tell juries what the learned insiders already know.

Sentencing Reforms (Chapter Thirteen)

The power to sentence is an awesome one. It is a sad fact that sometimes it matters more what judge will be sentencing you than what crime you committed. Sometimes, two judges in the very same courthouse will have drastically different sentencing philosophies. The problem with this is that it flies in the face of equal justice.

For this reason, I like the idea of sentencing guidelines. Frankly, I do not trust individuals, even judges (especially judges) to always do the right thing. Those jurisdictions that still allow a judge, in his or her near unbridled discretion, to give anywhere from probation to the typically long potential maximum for a crime need to reconsider the desirability of sentencing guidelines.

Jurisdictions also need to dump mandatory minimum sentences where they exist. The problem with them is that they set in motion a chain of events that can produce disastrous results. Minimum mandatory sentences remove any chance for mercy or reason during the sentencing process, however commonsensical. Removing any chance whatsoever for common sense discretion is often worse than the granting of completely unbridled discretion.

The biggest reform though, in the area of sentencing, is that we need to become a less punitive society. As discussed above, we incarcerate a greater percentage of our population than any other nation. I do not want my country to have this dubious distinction. I do not consider myself soft on crime. Bad people deserve to be punished and society needs protection. But, we have gone too far. Our ancestors in times past were less punitive than we are and our foreign, democratic contemporaries are less punitive than we are today. A lot of this has to do with lack of information. The average citizen is not aware of how punitive we are. In fact, most people think we are soft on our criminals. Politicians need to become statesmen and do the right thing. As Winston Churchill said, how we punish our criminals says a lot about how civilized we are. Let's give our criminals, especially the non-violent ones, the punishment that is proportionate to the wrong they have done.

Concluding Thoughts

This brings us to the close of this chapter and to the close of this book. I enjoyed writing this book more than any other article or book I have written. It was in a sense a professional home-coming for me to have told my fictional stories (many of which were somewhat auto-biographical).

I wish we could all be alive in a couple of hundred years to see what changes will have taken place in our courts. Will justice still be so slow? Will plea bargains no longer be the dominant paradigm? Will legal education have been altered dramatically? Will our courts still be locking up a fourth of the world's prison population?

What will our descendants say about our era with regards to the way we ran our country's criminal courts? Do you think they will approve of how we handled things or look upon our stewardship with indignation?

*****

Questions for Class Discussion

What follows is a listing of each proposed "reform" advanced by the author in this chapter. Please consider the following points with regards to each proposed reform:

A. Do you agree or disagree with the proposed reform? Why?
B. Do you think the proposal is realistically possible to accomplish or merely wishful thinking on the part of the author?
C. What would have to be done in order to accomplish the proposed reform? What resisting forces would likely come into play that might thwart the realization of the reform?

The Proposed Reforms

Legal Education Reforms:

1. Reduced reliance on the case study as the nearly sole educational approach.
2. Less use of aggressive "Socratic Method" in classes.
3. Learn more practical legal skills in addition to all the grand theory.
4. Offer undergraduates the opportunity to major in law.

Juvenile Court Reforms:

1. Increase the status of Juvenile Court in the eyes of courthouse professionals.
2. Forbid generalist judges, prosecutors and public defenders from working in juvenile court.

Speedy Justice Reforms:

1. Courts should really enforce the right to a "speedy" resolution of criminal cases.
2. Eliminate private bail bondsmen and their predatory fees.

Defense Attorney Reforms:

1. Pay public defenders more.
2. Use public defenders as the sole type of indigent defense counsel.
3. Certify attorneys as having criminal court expertise before allowing them to represent those charged with crimes.
4. Find out why private criminal lawyers are no better than public defenders when they should be.

Prosecuting Attorney Reforms:

1. Decrease the power prosecutors possess by reducing the prevalence of plea bargaining.

Judiciary Reforms:

1. Don't elect judges. Appoint them based on merit.
2. Require all lower-court judges to have law degrees.
3. Increase the number of trial-court judges by reducing their salaries and hiring qualified public defenders and prosecutors as criminal court specialist judges.

Plea Bargain Reforms:

1. Limit plea bargains to misdemeanor cases only. No plea bargains for felony cases.

Trial Reforms:

1. Shorten the length of jury trials so that more defendants can have one.

Jury Deliberation Reforms:

1. Tell juries about their option to nullify the law.

Sentencing Reforms:

1. Use sentencing guidelines everywhere in order to help achieve more equality in sentences.
2. Eliminate mandatory minimum sentences.
3. Generally, become a less punitive society.

INDEX